WILLIAM SHAKESPE...   ...on-
Avon in April, 1564, and ...   ...ted
on April 23. The facts of his life, known from surviving documents, are sparse. He was one of eight children born to
John Shakespeare, a merchant of some standing in his community. William probably went to the King's New School in
Stratford, but he had no university education. In November
1582, at the age of eighteen, he married Anne Hathaway,
eight years his senior, who was pregnant with their first
child, Susanna. She was born on May 26, 1583. Twins, a boy,
Hamnet (who would die at age eleven), and a girl, Judith,
were born in 1585. By 1592 Shakespeare had gone to London, working as an actor and already known as a playwright. A rival dramatist, Robert Greene, referred to him as
"an upstart crow, beautified with our feathers." Shakespeare became a principal shareholder and playwright of
the successful acting troupe the Lord Chamberlain's men
(later, under James I, called the King's men). In 1599 the
Lord Chamberlain's men built and occupied the Globe Theatre in Southwark near the Thames River. Here many of
Shakespeare's plays were performed by the most famous
actors of his time, including Richard Burbage, Will Kempe,
and Robert Armin. In addition to his 37 plays, Shakespeare
had a hand in others, including *Sir Thomas More* and *The
Two Noble Kinsmen*, and he wrote poems, including *Venus
and Adonis* and *The Rape of Lucrece*. His 154 sonnets were
published, probably without his authorization, in 1609. In
1611 or 1612 he gave up his lodgings in London and devoted
more and more of his time to retirement in Stratford,
though he continued writing such plays as *The Tempest* and
Henry VIII until about 1613. He died on April 23, 1616, and
was buried in Holy Trinity Church, Stratford. No collected
edition of his plays was published during his lifetime,
but in 1623 two members of his acting company, John
Heminges and Henry Condell, published the great collection now called the First Folio.

**Bantam Shakespeare
The Complete Works—29 Volumes
Edited by David Bevington
With forewords by Joseph Papp on the plays**

The Poems: Venus and Adonis, The Rape of Lucrece, The
Phoenix and Turtle, A Lover's Complaint,
the Sonnets

Antony and Cleopatra	*The Merchant of Venice*
As You Like It	*A Midsummer Night's Dream*
The Comedy of Errors	*Much Ado about Nothing*
Hamlet	*Othello*
Henry IV, Part One	*Richard II*
Henry IV, Part Two	*Richard III*
Henry V	*Romeo and Juliet*
Julius Caesar	*The Taming of the Shrew*
King Lear	*The Tempest*
Macbeth	*Twelfth Night*

Together in one volume:

Henry VI, Parts One, Two, and Three
King John and Henry VIII
*Measure for Measure, All's Well that Ends Well, and
Troilus and Cressida*
Three Early Comedies: Love's Labor's Lost, The Two
Gentlemen of Verona, The Merry
Wives of Windsor
Three Classical Tragedies: Titus Andronicus, Timon
of Athens, Coriolanus
The Late Romances: Pericles, Cymbeline, The Winter's
Tale, The Tempest

Two collections:

Four Comedies: The Taming of the Shrew, A Midsummer
Night's Dream, The Merchant of Venice,
Twelfth Night
Four Tragedies: Hamlet, Othello, King Lear, Macbeth

·A BANTAM   IC·A BANTAM CLASSI

William Shakespeare

HENRY VI, PARTS ONE, TWO, and THREE

Edited by
David Bevington

David Scott Kastan,
James Hammersmith,
and Robert Kean Turner,
Associate Editors

With a Foreword by
Joseph Papp

BANTAM BOOKS
TORONTO / NEW YORK / LONDON / SYDNEY / AUCKLAND

HENRY VI, PARTS ONE, TWO, AND THREE
*A Bantam Book / published by arrangement
with Scott, Foresman and Company*

PRINTING HISTORY
*Scott, Foresman edition published / January 1980
Bantam edition, with newly edited text and substantially revised,
edited, and amplified notes, introductions, and other
materials, published / February 1988
Valuable advice on staging matters has been
provided by Richard Hosley.
Collations checked by Eric Rasmussen.
Additional editorial assistance by Claire McEachern.*

Library of Congress Cataloging-in-Publication Data

Shakespeare, William, 1564-1616.
  Henry VI, parts one, two, and three.

  (A Bantam classic)
  "Bantam edition, with newly edited text and
substantially revised, and amplified notes,
introductions, and other materials"—T.p. verso.
  Bibliography: p.
  1. Henry VI, King of England, 1421-1471—Drama.
I. Bevington, David M. II. Title. III. Title:
Henry the Sixth, parts 1, 2, and 3. IV. Title: Henry VI,
parts 1, 2, and 3.
[PR2813.A2B48 1988]   822.3'3   87-19566
ISBN 0-553-21285-0 (pbk.)

Published simultaneously in the United States and Canada

----

*Bantam Books are published by Bantam Books, a division of Bantam
Doubleday Dell Publishing Group, Inc. Its trademark, consisting of the
words "Bantam Books" and the portrayal of a rooster, is Registered in U.S.
Patent and Trademark Office and in other countries. Marca Registrada.
Bantam Books, 1540 Broadway, New York, New York 10036.*

PRINTED   IN   THE   UNITED   STATES   OF   AMERICA

O   0 9 8 7 6 5 4 3 2

Contents

Foreword

It's hard to imagine, but Shakespeare wrote all of his plays with a quill pen, a goose feather whose hard end had to be sharpened frequently. How many times did he scrape the dull end to a point with his knife, dip it into the inkwell, and bring up, dripping wet, those wonderful words and ideas that are known all over the world?

In the age of word processors, typewriters, and ballpoint pens, we have almost forgotten the meaning of the word "blot." Yet when I went to school, in the 1930s, my classmates and I knew all too well what an inkblot from the metal-tipped pens we used would do to a nice clean page of a test paper, and we groaned whenever a splotch fell across the sheet. Most of us finished the school day with ink-stained fingers; those who were less careful also went home with ink-stained shirts, which were almost impossible to get clean.

When I think about how long it took me to write the simplest composition with a metal-tipped pen and ink, I can only marvel at how many plays Shakespeare scratched out with his goose-feather quill pen, year after year. Imagine him walking down one of the narrow cobblestoned streets of London, or perhaps drinking a pint of beer in his local alehouse. Suddenly his mind catches fire with an idea, or a sentence, or a previously elusive phrase. He is burning with impatience to write it down—but because he doesn't have a ballpoint pen or even a pencil in his pocket, he has to keep the idea in his head until he can get to his quill and parchment.

He rushes back to his lodgings on Silver Street, ignoring the vendors hawking brooms, the coaches clattering by, the piteous wails of beggars and prisoners. Bounding up the stairs, he snatches his quill and starts to write furiously, not even bothering to light a candle against the dusk. "To be, or not to be," he scrawls, "that is the—." But the quill point has gone dull, the letters have fattened out illegibly, and in the middle of writing one of the most famous passages in the history of dramatic literature, Shakespeare has to stop to sharpen his pen.

Taking a deep breath, he lights a candle now that it's dark, sits down, and begins again. By the time the candle has burned out and the noisy apprentices of his French Huguenot landlord have quieted down, Shakespeare has finished Act 3 of *Hamlet* with scarcely a blot.

Early the next morning, he hurries through the fog of a London summer morning to the rooms of his colleague Richard Burbage, the actor for whom the role of Hamlet is being written. He finds Burbage asleep and snoring loudly, sprawled across his straw mattress. Not only had the actor performed in *Henry V* the previous afternoon, but he had then gone out carousing all night with some friends who had come to the performance.

Shakespeare shakes his friend awake, until, bleary-eyed, Burbage sits up in his bed. "Dammit, Will," he grumbles, "can't you let an honest man sleep?" But the playwright, his eyes shining and the words tumbling out of his mouth, says, "Shut up and listen—tell me what you think of *this*!"

He begins to read to the still half-asleep Burbage, pacing around the room as he speaks. ". . . Whether 'tis nobler in the mind to suffer the slings and arrows of outrageous fortune—"

Burbage interrupts, suddenly wide awake, "That's excellent, very good, 'the slings and arrows of outrageous fortune,' yes, I think it will work quite well. . . ." He takes the parchment from Shakespeare and murmurs the lines to himself, slowly at first but with growing excitement.

The sun is just coming up, and the words of one of Shakespeare's most famous soliloquies are being uttered for the first time by the first actor ever to bring Hamlet to life. It must have been an exhilarating moment.

Shakespeare wrote most of his plays to be performed live by the actor Richard Burbage and the rest of the Lord Chamberlain's men (later the King's men). Today, however, our first encounter with the plays is usually in the form of the printed word. And there is no question that reading Shakespeare for the first time isn't easy. His plays aren't comic books or magazines or the dime-store detective novels I read when I was young. A lot of his sentences are complex. Many of his words are no longer used in our everyday speech. His profound thoughts are often condensed into poetry, which is not as straightforward as prose.

Yet when you hear the words spoken aloud, a lot of the language may strike you as unexpectedly modern. For Shakespeare's plays, like any dramatic work, weren't really meant to be read; they were meant to be spoken, seen, and performed. It's amazing how lines that are so troublesome in print can flow so naturally and easily when spoken.

I think it was precisely this music that first fascinated me. When I was growing up, Shakespeare was a stranger to me. I had no particular interest in him, for I was from a different cultural tradition. It never occurred to me that his plays might be more than just something to "get through" in school, like science or math or the physical education requirement we had to fulfill. My passions then were movies, radio, and vaudeville—certainly not Elizabethan drama.

I was, however, fascinated by words and language. Because I grew up in a home where Yiddish was spoken, and English was only a second language, I was acutely sensitive to the musical sounds of different languages and had an ear for lilt and cadence and rhythm in the spoken word. And so I loved reciting poems and speeches even as a very young child. In first grade I learned lots of short nature verses— "Who has seen the wind?," one of them began. My first foray into drama was playing the role of Scrooge in Charles Dickens's *A Christmas Carol* when I was eight years old. I liked summoning all the scorn and coldness I possessed and putting them into the words, "Bah, humbug!"

From there I moved on to longer and more famous poems and other works by writers of the 1930s. Then, in junior high school, I made my first acquaintance with Shakespeare through his play *Julius Caesar*. Our teacher, Miss McKay, assigned the class a passage to memorize from the opening scene of the play, the one that begins "Wherefore rejoice? What conquest brings he home?" The passage seemed so wonderfully theatrical and alive to me, and the experience of memorizing and reciting it was so much fun, that I went on to memorize another speech from the play on my own.

I chose Mark Antony's address to the crowd in Act 3,

scene 2, which struck me then as incredibly high drama. Even today, when I speak the words, I feel the same thrill I did that first time. There is the strong and athletic Antony descending from the raised pulpit where he has been speaking, right into the midst of a crowded Roman square. Holding the torn and bloody cloak of the murdered Julius Caesar in his hand, he begins to speak to the people of Rome:

> If you have tears, prepare to shed them now.
> You all do know this mantle. I remember
> The first time ever Caesar put it on;
> 'Twas on a summer's evening in his tent,
> That day he overcame the Nervii.
> Look, in this place ran Cassius' dagger through.
> See what a rent the envious Casca made.
> Through this the well-belovèd Brutus stabbed,
> And as he plucked his cursèd steel away,
> Mark how the blood of Caesar followed it,
> As rushing out of doors to be resolved
> If Brutus so unkindly knocked or no;
> For Brutus, as you know, was Caesar's angel.
> Judge, O you gods, how dearly Caesar loved him!
> This was the most unkindest cut of all . . .

I'm not sure now that I even knew Shakespeare had written a lot of other plays, or that he was considered "timeless," "universal," or "classic"—but I knew a good speech when I heard one, and I found the splendid rhythms of Antony's rhetoric as exciting as anything I'd ever come across.

Fifty years later, I still feel that way. Hearing good actors speak Shakespeare gracefully and naturally is a wonderful experience, unlike any other I know. There's a satisfying fullness to the spoken word that the printed page just can't convey. This is why seeing the plays of Shakespeare performed live in a theater is the best way to appreciate them. If you can't do that, listening to sound recordings or watching film versions of the plays is the next best thing.

But if you do start with the printed word, use the play as a script. Be an actor yourself and say the lines out loud. Don't worry too much at first about words you don't immediately understand. Look them up in the footnotes or a dictionary, but don't spend too much time on this. It is more profitable (and fun) to get the sense of a passage and sing it out. Speak naturally, almost as if you were talking to a friend, but be sure to enunciate the words properly. You'll be surprised at how much you understand simply by speaking the speech "trippingly on the tongue," as Hamlet advises the Players.

You might start, as I once did, with a speech from *Julius Caesar*, in which the tribune (city official) Marullus scolds the commoners for transferring their loyalties so quickly from the defeated and murdered general Pompey to the newly victorious Julius Caesar:

> Wherefore rejoice? What conquest brings he home?
> What tributaries follow him to Rome
> To grace in captive bonds his chariot wheels?
> You blocks, you stones, you worse than senseless
>   things!
> O you hard hearts, you cruel men of Rome,
> Knew you not Pompey? Many a time and oft
> Have you climbed up to walls and battlements,
> To towers and windows, yea, to chimney tops,
> Your infants in your arms, and there have sat
> The livelong day, with patient expectation,
> To see great Pompey pass the streets of Rome.

With the exception of one or two words like "wherefore" (which means "why," not "where"), "tributaries" (which means "captives"), and "patient expectation" (which means patient waiting), the meaning and emotions of this speech can be easily understood.

From here you can go on to dialogues or other more challenging scenes. Although you may stumble over unaccustomed phrases or unfamiliar words at first, and even fall flat when you're crossing some particularly rocky passages, pick yourself up and stay with it. Remember that it takes time to feel at home with anything new. Soon you'll come to recognize Shakespeare's unique sense of humor and way of saying things as easily as you recognize a friend's laughter.

And then it will just be a matter of choosing which one of Shakespeare's plays you want to tackle next. As a true fan of his, you'll find that you're constantly learning from his plays. It's a journey of discovery that you can continue for

the rest of your life. For no matter how many times you read
or see a particular play, there will always be something new
there that you won't have noticed before.

Why do so many thousands of people get hooked on
Shakespeare and develop a habit that lasts a lifetime? What
can he really say to us today, in a world filled with inven-
tions and problems he never could have imagined? And how
do you get past his special language and difficult sentence
structure to understand him?

The best way to answer these questions is to go see a live
production. You might not know much about Shakespeare,
or much about the theater, but when you watch actors performing one of his plays on the stage, it will soon become
clear to you why people get so excited about a playwright
who lived hundreds of years ago.

For the story—what's happening in the play—is the most
accessible part of Shakespeare. In *A Midsummer Night's
Dream*, for example, you can immediately understand the
situation: a girl is chasing a guy who's chasing a girl who's
chasing another guy. No wonder *A Midsummer Night's
Dream* is one of the most popular of Shakespeare's plays:
it's about one of the world's most popular pastimes—
falling in love.

But the course of true love never did run smooth, as the
young suitor Lysander says. Often in Shakespeare's comedies the girl whom the guy loves doesn't love him back, or
she loves him but he loves someone else. In *The Two Gentlemen of Verona*, Julia loves Proteus, Proteus loves Sylvia,
and Sylvia loves Valentine, who is Proteus's best friend. In
the end, of course, true love prevails, but not without lots of
complications along the way.

For in all of his plays—comedies, histories, and tragedies—Shakespeare is showing you human nature. His characters act and react in the most extraordinary ways—and
sometimes in the most incomprehensible ways. People are
always trying to find motivations for what a character does.
They ask, "Why does Iago want to destroy Othello?"

The answer, to me, is very simple—because that's the way
Iago is. That's just his nature. Shakespeare doesn't explain
his characters; he sets them in motion—and away they go.
He doesn't worry about whether they're likable or not. He's

interested in interesting people, and his most fascinating characters are those who are unpredictable. If you lean back in your chair early on in one of his plays, thinking you've figured out what Iago or Shylock (in *The Merchant of Venice*) is up to, don't be too sure—because that great judge of human nature, Shakespeare, will surprise you every time.

He is just as wily in the way he structures a play. In *Macbeth*, a comic scene is suddenly introduced just after the bloodiest and most treacherous slaughter imaginable, of a guest and king by his host and subject, when in comes a drunk porter who has to go to the bathroom. Shakespeare is tickling your emotions by bringing a stand-up comic on-stage right on the heels of a savage murder.

It has taken me thirty years to understand even some of these things, and so I'm not suggesting that Shakespeare is immediately understandable. I've gotten to know him not through theory but through practice, the practice of the *living* Shakespeare—the playwright of the theater.

Of course the plays are a great achievement of dramatic literature, and they should be studied and analyzed in schools and universities. But you must always remember, when reading all the words *about* the playwright and his plays, that *Shakespeare's* words came first and that in the end there is nothing greater than a single actor on the stage speaking the lines of Shakespeare.

Everything important that I know about Shakespeare comes from the practical business of producing and directing his plays in the theater. The task of classifying, criticizing, and editing Shakespeare's printed works I happily leave to others. For me, his plays really do live on the stage, not on the page. That is what he wrote them for and that is how they are best appreciated.

Although Shakespeare lived and wrote hundreds of years ago, his name rolls off my tongue as if he were my brother. As a producer and director, I feel that there is a professional relationship between us that spans the centuries. As a human being, I feel that Shakespeare has enriched my understanding of life immeasurably. I hope you'll let him do the same for you.

❖

The three parts of *Henry VI* are interesting for their history alone; Shakespeare wrote them before he wrote the *Henry IV* plays, which precede them chronologically. And so there's an intriguing contrast between the history *in* the plays and the history *of* the plays. Once you've started reading these plays, it's hard to put them down, because you get caught up in the whole sequence of English history that leads up to Richard III and ends with the beginning of the Tudor dynasty after him.

There's a lot of historical meat in these plays, and I'd be curious to do them all, one after the other, in their proper sequence, just to follow the development of the kings and other characters, the squabblings and usurpations, and the various factions. In what other plays besides Shakespeare's can you find history treated in such an interesting way?

As I think back over these three plays in particular, what I recall are the lovely little touches scattered throughout them—specific scenes, or stage directions, or speeches, or characters. The first scene that comes to mind, one of the most moving in the trilogy, is the death of the noble English hero Talbot in Part One. Throughout the play Shakespeare has portrayed him as brave, valiant, and unstoppable against the French—such a remarkable figure that he wins praise even from his French enemies. In a sense, the whole play builds remorselessly toward his downfall in Act 4, scene 7, where, wounded in battle, he dies with his young son dead in his arms. Knowing he is dying, he bids farewell to the soldiers gathered around him, saying, "Come, come, and lay him in his father's arms. / My spirit can no longer bear these harms. / Soldiers, adieu! I have what I would have, / Now my old arms are young John Talbot's grave." It's an incredibly moving moment.

I've always found Shakespeare's treatment of Joan of Arc, or Joan la Pucelle as he calls her, to be very interesting. He completely abandons fairness in his portrait of her, unabashedly taking the English side. Though history knows her as a shining heroine who was a scourge to the English and later a saint, this play shows her to be a whore, sharp-tongued and ambitious, a shrew who doesn't inspire a jot of sympathy in the audience. Her character tells us more about Shakespeare's interest in catering to English patriotism than it does about who she actually was, but that's precisely what's fascinating about it.

There is another strong-willed Frenchwoman in the *Henry VI* plays—Margaret of Anjou, who enters the story at the end of Part One, when she becomes the wife of King Henry VI. She quickly establishes herself as a force to be reckoned with, and through the rest of the sequence we see her relentlessly building up her role as the power behind the weak-willed Henry, who is totally incapable of dealing with the infighting of the English nobles.

Margaret has a great scene in Part Three, Act 1, scene 4, where she confronts the captured Duke of York, a claimant to the throne, and utterly humiliates him. She sits him on a small mound, puts a paper crown on his head, and waves a handkerchief dipped in the blood of his slaughtered young son in his face. It's a powerful piece of writing and a heart-wrenching scene when played on the stage, as the defeated and sorrowful York suffers Margaret's cruel taunts:

> Look, York, I stained this napkin with the blood
> That valiant Clifford, with his rapier's point,
> Made issue from the bosom of the boy;
> And if thine eyes can water for his death,
> I give thee this to dry thy cheeks withal.
> Alas, poor York, but that I hate thee deadly,
> I should lament thy miserable state.

As usual, Shakespeare doesn't neglect the ordinary people, no matter how many kings and princes are in the play. This leads to a marvelous scene in Part Three (2.5) where the stage directions say *"Enter a Son that hath killed his father, at one door,"* and then *"Enter at another door a Father that hath killed his son."* What's terrible in this scene is that neither the father nor the son knows who it is he's killed—until it's too late. The father says, "But let me see. Is this our foeman's face? / Ah, no, no, no, it is mine only son! / Ah, boy, if any life be left in thee, / Throw up thine eye!" Shakespeare is illustrating the enormous price of civil war, which pits members of the same family against each other. It's an unbearably sad scene, and unforgettable.

And finally, one of the greatest characters in all of Shakespeare—in all of English history, for that matter—

makes his diabolical entrance in Part Three: Richard, Duke of Gloucester, who will take over the stage in the next play as Richard III. Very few people know that he appears at the end of the *Henry VI* sequence, but he's worth looking at. He is depicted at first as a fierce fighter, but Shakespeare also gives a few clues about what this schemer has in store for us.

Though Richard has several good speeches in the play, my favorite is the one he makes at the end of Part Three as he is stabbing King Henry VI to death: "Down, down to hell," he cries, "and say I sent thee thither, / [*Stabs him again*] I, that have neither pity, love, nor fear." He goes on to describe his monstrous birth—feet first, and with teeth—and his hunchback. He reasons, with words that are heavy with omen, "Then, since the heavens have shaped my body so, / Let hell make crook'd my mind to answer it."

And he concludes with a warning to all those who may stand between him and the crown of England, beginning with his brother Clarence, "I am myself alone. / Clarence, beware. Thou keep'st me from the light. . . . Clarence, thy turn is next, and then the rest, / Counting myself but bad till I be best." It's a marvelous speech, and looks straight ahead to the plots and schemings this hunchbacked duke will carry out in the play that bears his name.

JOSEPH PAPP

JOSEPH PAPP GRATEFULLY ACKNOWLEDGES THE HELP OF ELIZABETH KIRKLAND IN PREPARING THIS FOREWORD.

The *Henry VI* Plays

Among Shakespeare's ten plays on English history, the best known are the four plays (c. 1595–1599) from *Richard II* through *1* and *2 Henry IV* to *Henry V*, in which Shakespeare follows the maturation and career of Prince Hal, the future Henry V. This sequence of four plays was actually Shakespeare's second such sequence, for he had begun, in the years from about 1589 to 1594, to write on English history with three plays on the reign of Henry VI and a fourth on the reign of Richard III. Together these four plays told the agonizing and eventually triumphant story of England's civil wars in the fifteenth century, concluding at last in 1485 with the victory of Henry Tudor over Richard III at Bosworth Field. Henry Tudor, thereupon King Henry VII, was to become Henry VIII's father and Queen Elizabeth I's grandfather. These four plays thus dramatized a conflict in which England's very identity as a nation, having been tested in extremity, was restored by the Tudor dynasty that was still in power when Shakespeare wrote. The political relevance of such an account to Elizabethan spectators must have added greatly to their pleasure in the spectacle of sieges, confrontations, and bloodshed. There is good evidence that Shakespeare's first historical plays, though seldom read or seen today, were very popular in his own time.

Together, the three plays about the reign of Henry VI offer a paradigm of civil conflict. (*Richard III*, though last in the series, takes place after the actual civil wars have ceased.) Shakespeare is deeply interested in the causes and evolution of civil war. His villains are, especially at first, not the lower classes but the aristocrats of England bickering among themselves. Because Henry V has died an untimely death in 1422, leaving an infant son on the throne and a disputed claim originating in Henry IV's seizure of the throne from Richard II, a struggle for power is inevitable. Shakespeare depicts Humphrey, Duke of Gloucester, one of young Henry's uncles, as virtuous in his attempts to serve as Protector, but unable to cope with Henry Beaufort, Bishop of Winchester and later Cardinal, a great-uncle of the King. Though barred by his illegitimate birth from claiming the crown for himself, Winchester is ready to foment all the strife he can in an effort to gain political control of the kingdom. The Duke of Somerset joins in a conspiracy to get rid of Gloucester so that the ambitions of the various challengers will be unchecked by the one remaining proponent of honest government. The most dangerous intriguer is Richard Plantagenet, later Duke of York, whose claim to the English throne goes back to Edward III through two grandfathers, Edmund Langley, Duke of York, and Lionel, Duke of Clarence, and is arguably stronger than that of King Henry VI. Richard is the scion of the Yorkist claim, soon to challenge that of the Lancastrian King Henry (so named for his title derived from his grandfather, John of Gaunt, Duke of Lancaster).

Faction of this sort naturally leads to divided authority on the battlefield. The English quickly begin to lose their territories in France, owing in part to the baleful rise of a (as the English see her) witch, Joan of Arc, who dons man's warlike attire and dominates the effete French aristocrats whom she seduces one by one. Still, the main cause of the English failure in France is division at home, and its chief victim is the valiant Lord Talbot, betrayed by lack of English reinforcement at Bordeaux. His death, in company with his son, signals the end of English ascendancy in France. When the Earl of Suffolk cynically negotiates an end to hostilities in terms outrageously favorable to the French and especially to Margaret of Anjou, with whom Suffolk has fallen in love, the capitulation is complete. Margaret is brought back to England, where she will dominate her new husband, King Henry, much as Joan of Arc dominated her French lovers, and where Suffolk can have his adulterous way with her. This yielding to the enervation of erotic passion is symptomatic of the decline into which England continues to plunge.

Once the aristocrats of England have succeeded in betraying their nation by their self-interested grasping, the commoners are not slow to emulate the factionalism of their social betters. *2 Henry VI* gives a significantly increased role to commoners, who turn against one another (1.3), promote themselves through sham miracles (2.1), buzz with restive anger at the suspicious death of their beloved Duke of Gloucester (3.2), and take justice into their own hands by seizing and summarily executing the hated Duke of Suffolk (4.1). These protestations and acts are at least directed against aristocratic villains, but the precedent of popular unrest is an unnerving one, and it soon erupts into a full-scale, if abortive, popular rebellion (4.2–10). Jack Cade and his cohorts ape political ambition in such a way as to render it mordantly amusing, but the Cade rebellion also dismays and threatens those who cling to a hope of public calm. Not the least threatening aspect of this rebellion is that it has been secretly fomented by Richard of York, who sees anarchy as a way to bring down established authority and thereby clear the way for his challenge. He is right, and by the end of this play the country is divided into two warring camps.

Richard of York dies in *3 Henry VI*, in a bloody and revengeful ritual slaughter on the battlefield, but he is succeeded like a many-headed Hydra by his three sons, Edward, Clarence, and Richard of Gloucester. The Yorkist side ultimately achieves victory, after much uncertain shifting back and forth in the fortunes of war, and yet victory is achieved at a terrible cost to England. The struggle has become a feud in which a Yorkist must pay for the blood of a Lancastrian, son for son, brother for brother, until there are few survivors. The conflict is all the more horrible in view of the fact that the two sides are closely bound by the ties of kinship. Emblematically, on the field of battle a father discovers he has killed his own son, while another son discovers he has killed his father. In the family of the new King Edward IV, as well, brother turns against brother: Clarence, offended by his brother's surrender to women (so reminiscent of Henry VI before him), changes sides more than once.

The only person to profit from all this division is Richard of Gloucester, the youngest of the three Yorkist brothers, whose plan is to cut his way to the throne by whatever murder and deception will prove necessary. Richard is the genius of faction and discord, the perfect embodiment and product of the long and enervating wars now drawing to a close. The final scenes of *3 Henry VI*, though offering a seeming hope of peace, are devastated by the contrary perception that Richard is only biding his time until he can seize power. His murder of Henry VI in the Tower of London (5.6) is only a promise of what will follow.

The *Henry VI* Plays
in Performance

Although Shakespeare's *Henry VI* plays are seldom read and seldom staged, they contain individual scenes that have struck the imaginations of theater managers over the centuries: in Part One, Lord Talbot's encounters with the Countess of Auvergne and Joan of Arc, and the deaths of Talbot and his son; in Part Two, the public penance of the Duchess of Gloucester, the murder of Humphrey, Duke of Gloucester, and the instructive end of the Cardinal of Winchester; in Part Three, the killing of the young Rutland, and King Henry's witnessing of a son who has killed his father and of a father who has killed his son. Artists too have found these scenes irresistible, as seen for example in the fifteen paintings of episodes from the plays that appear in John Boydell's nineteenth-century collection of illustrations from Shakespeare. Almost all these scenes are of tragic high emotion.

Prior to the twentieth century especially, on those infrequent occasions when theater managers have deigned to consider the *Henry VI* plays at all, they have been tempted to put together a medley of such scenes, omitting intervening material or indulging in wholesale rewriting. More often than not, the selection of scenes has been politically motivated as well. The earliest known revivals or, more properly, adaptations, John Crowne's two parts of *Henry VI*, acted at the Dorset Garden Theatre in 1680 and in 1681, are a case in point. Crowne's first part, "with the murder of Humphrey, Duke of Gloucester," really centers on the first three acts of Shakespeare's Part Two, including the conspiracy against Duke Humphrey and his Duchess's fatal trafficking in witchcraft. Crowne makes of this material a diatribe against the Catholic Church, with the Cardinal of Winchester as his chief villain, obviously in reference to the then current controversy over the exclusion of the Catholic Duke of York, Charles II's brother, from the English throne. The plotting against the good Duke Humphrey is plainly reminiscent of the infamous Popish Plot of 1678.

At the play's end, the Cardinal dies a horrible, ranting death, visited by the ghost of his noble victim. Like many Englishmen of his time, Crowne tempered his loyalty to Charles II with a strong objection to his brother James's open Catholicism, and said so in this play. It ran into difficulties with the censor and was eventually suppressed.

The title of Crowne's second part, *The Misery of Civil War*, again suggests the kind of didactic analogy to England's current political troubles that Restoration audiences discovered in a number of Shakespeare's plays. Crowne mixes together scenes from Shakespeare's Part Two and Part Three, especially the Cade rebellion, the killing of little Rutland (preceded by a touching scene of farewell between Rutland and his father York), and Edward IV's problems with women. The King's amorous adventures (not unlike those of Charles II) are augmented by the introduction of Lady Elianor Butler, one of Edward's mistresses, and Edward's extensive wooing of Lady Elizabeth Grey. The action and even the scenery magnify the horrors of civil war: in one battle sequence, "the scene is drawn, and there appears houses and towns burning, men and women hanged upon trees, and children on the tops of pikes." King Henry VI, though a weak ruler, is made prophetically wise in his hatred of rebellion and his certain faith that God will eventually punish all those who promote anarchy. Explicit parallels to England's own civil wars of the seventeenth century constitute a warning against mob rule, extremism of the religious left as well as the religious right, and conspiracy.

Throughout the eighteenth century and much of the nineteenth, Shakespeare's *Henry VI* plays continued to be dissected in this manner and employed either as political analogy or as part of some larger theatrical enterprise. Ambrose Philips's *Humfrey, Duke of Gloucester,* acted at the Theatre Royal, Drury Lane, in 1723 and based, like Crowne's first part, on the tragic stories of Duke Humphrey and his Duchess, took even greater liberties than did Crowne. In a text that preserved few of Shakespeare's lines, Philips represented the Duchess as an innocent victim of Queen Margaret, Suffolk, and the Cardinal, thereby eliminating any ambiguity in the didactic contrast between right and wrong—that is, sturdy English national self-interest versus Catholic meddling. Humfrey (or Humphrey, played by Barton Booth) was a saintly martyr, while the Cardinal (played by Colley Cibber) was a melodramatic villain. Theophilus Cibber's adaptation of 1723 included Crowne's touching scene of the Duke of York's farewell to his young son Rutland and went on to provide new love interest, especially that of the young Prince Edward for Warwick's daughter, the Lady Anne.

The one exception to the pattern of redaction was a performance of Shakespeare's *1 Henry VI* with Dennis Delane as Talbot, Anthony Ryan as Henry, and Anne Hallam as Joan, at the Theatre Royal, Covent Garden, in 1738. The play, "not acted these fifty years," according to the playbill, was produced "at the desire of several ladies of quality," members of The Shakespeare Club that some fashionable women of Covent Garden had formed in 1737 to promote the production of Shakespeare's plays. The experiment with the restored Shakespearean text, however, was not soon repeated, and the *Henry VI* plays continued to appear only in cut and adapted form. Edmund Kean's production of *Richard Duke of York* (Drury Lane, 1817, in a version usually attributed to John Herman Merivale) blended material from all three *Henry VI* plays, all heavily cut and interspersed with passages from George Chapman, John Webster, and John Marston. Portions of Shakespeare's Part Three, especially the murder of Henry VI in the Tower by Richard of Gloucester and the coronation of Edward IV, were detached from their original to turn up in Colley Cibber's long-playing *Richard III*.

Not until 1864, at the Surrey Theatre in Lambeth, do we hear of a revival of Shakespeare's Part Two in something like its original form. The *Athenaeum* was delighted with James Anderson's decision to produce it, "particularly as it acts very well, and manifestly excites interest in the audience." Stratford-upon-Avon saw *1 Henry VI* lavishly directed by Osmond Tearle in 1889 (in what was claimed to be the first performance of the play since Shakespeare's time). The year 1899 witnessed Frank Benson's version of *2 Henry VI*. Benson played a tortured Beaufort, his wife, Constance, appeared as Margaret, and Oscar Asche was a truculent Jack Cade. This costly production was revived in 1901 as part of a cycle of six histories, popularly known as

"the Week of Kings." In early May of 1906 Benson produced the three *Henry VI* plays on successive nights. Benson was praised for his boldness in mounting the trilogy,
though the *Athenaeum* complained, "Many may have
wished to see less scenery and more Shakespeare." Benson
revived *2 Henry VI* in 1909. Thereafter the plays did not
again appear at Stratford-upon-Avon until 1963 in Peter
Hall's direction of an adaptation by John Barton. Barton
edited Shakespeare's three plays into two, *Henry VI* and
Edward IV, to form—along with Shakespeare's *Richard III*—a sequence called *The Wars of the Roses*. Set on a
bare stage with massive metallic walls, the plays revealed
with impressive clarity the grim, retributive action of
fifteenth-century England's long agony of civil war.

During the hiatus at Stratford-upon-Avon between Benson's revivals and Barton's adaptation, other theaters continued to show new interest in these forgotten plays. In
London, at the Old Vic in 1923, Robert Atkins used a simple
set and swift pacing to present the plays in a two-part con-
flation. Under the management of Barry Jackson, the Bir-
mingham Repertory Theatre produced *2 Henry VI* in 1951,
and *3 Henry VI* and then *1 Henry VI* in the two subsequent
years. With only minimal cuts in the text, Douglas Seale's
direction revealed how "eminently actable," in Jackson's
phrase, the plays are. All three productions were revived at
the Old Vic in 1953, and four years later Seale was invited
back to that theater to direct the plays in the final year of
the Old Vic's five-year plan to produce all of the plays of the
First Folio. This time Seale made more extensive cuts to re-
duce the material of the three plays to two, the first a con-
flation of *1* and *2 Henry VI* (eliminating both Talbot and
Joan from Part One) and the second a virtually complete
version of *3 Henry VI*. To emphasize the trilogy's links to
Shakespeare's other histories, the epilogue of *Henry V* was
spoken in the funeral scene that opens Part One, and at the
end of Part Three, as all departed after Edward's coronation, a grimly determined Gloucester limped toward the va-
cant throne and began the opening soliloquy of *Richard III*,
his words, however, drowned out by the exuberant celebration offstage.

Productions of the *Henry VI* plays in recent years have
been undertaken almost exclusively by theaters and festi-

vals committed to performing the entire canon, as though they were Shakespearean curiosities unworthy of consideration in their own right, and yet several of those productions have been both successful and artistically rewarding. The Oregon Shakespeare Festival at Ashland, Oregon, has thrice performed the three parts of *Henry VI* in successive years, in the 1950s, 1960s, and 1970s, in intelligent, vigorous productions. In 1970 Stuart Vaughan directed a two-part version of the *Henry VI* plays for the New York Shakespeare Festival that made excellent use of Ming Cho Lee's multilevel platform set. Terry Hands brilliantly directed the trilogy for the Royal Shakespeare Company at Stratford-upon-Avon in 1977. Alan Howard as King Henry grew increasingly aware, even though he was incapable of resisting it, of the sinister political farce playing itself out. Hands's success in presenting the three plays uncut did not, however, discourage renewed tampering with Shakespeare's texts. As directed by Pam Brighton at Stratford, Ontario, in 1980, the three plays were conflated into a single drama focusing on the political machinations of the English court; and even the 1983 BBC television productions, thoughtfully directed by Jane Howell, have suffered the ignominious fate (in parts of the United States at least) of being shown in the late evening over a six-week period, one half a play at a clip, as though they were episodes of *Poldark* or *The Pallisers*.

For all their uneven and often ignoble treatment in stage history, Shakespeare's *Henry VI* plays were among his greatest early successes. *1 Henry VI* was acted fourteen times in 1592 alone, and *2* and *3 Henry VI* were "sundry times acted" by Pembroke's men before 1600. Thomas Nashe, in his *Pierce Penniless* (1592), considers how it would have "joyed brave Talbot, the terror of the French, to think that after he had lain two hundred years in his tomb he should triumph again on the stage, and have his bones new enbalmed with the tears of ten thousand spectators at least, at several times, who in that tragedian that represents his person imagine they behold him fresh bleeding." Nashe's description suggests that the tragic fate of Talbot was the emotional high point of Part One. The titles of the early quarto of Part Two and octavo of Part Three offer similar evidence as to what interested spectators in those plays:

Part Two is called *The First Part of the Contention Betwixt the Two Famous Houses of York and Lancaster, with the Death of the Good Duke Humphrey, and the Banishment and Death of the Duke of Suffolk, and the Tragical End of the Proud Cardinal of Winchester, with the Notable Rebellion of Jack Cade, and the Duke of York's First Claim unto the Crown;* while Part Three is called *The True Tragedy of Richard Duke of York, and the Death of Good King Henry the Sixth, with the Whole Contention Between the Two Houses Lancaster and York.* Actor-managers of the eighteenth and nineteenth centuries were not misguided in their perception that the plays were structured around emotionally powerful scenes, however much they were misled by that perception to dismantle and reassemble them into new plays.

Certainly the actor-managers' mistrust of so much material contained in these plays overlooks the plays' original success and their stageworthiness. Shakespeare designed these plays for the theater. When first produced in the late 1580s and early 1590s, they must have tested to the limit the physical capabilities of the theater building or buildings in which they were staged. *1 Henry VI* makes spectacular vertical demands. Salisbury and others, entering *"on the turrets"* (some upper acting area) in Act 1, scene 4, are blown to bits by French cannon, probably fired offstage. Joan of Arc and her cohorts *"enter the town"* of Orleans in Act 1, scene 5, presumably by breaching the doors onstage leading into the tiring-house, the backstage area of the Elizabethan theater, and then are routed by the English *"with scaling ladders"* set against the back wall of the theater, allowing the English soldiers to climb up to the gallery above the stage. Moments later the French, in undignified retreat, *"leap over the walls in their shirts,"* that is, jump down half-dressed from the gallery onto the main stage. Later, at Rouen (3.2), Joan talks her way through the city gates (i.e., stage doors) disguised as a peasant and appears *"on the top,"* high in the theater, brandishing a signal of attack to her associates at the gate.

In Part Two, similarly, the Duchess of Gloucester watches from aloft, from the gallery (1.4), as the witch Margery Jourdain and two priests summon a spirit by means of a trapdoor to pronounce dire prophecies amid terrible thunder and lightning. Part Three features appearances on the walls of York (4.7) and the Tower of London (5.6), where Henry VI is murdered.

It is as though the young Shakespeare wanted to try out every physical dimension of his theater in order to dramatize the imaginative landscape of civil war on as all-encompassing a pictorial scale as possible. His scenes are full of emblematic effects that lend theatrical power to the emotional high points of the story. Contending noblemen and lawyers choose up sides in *1 Henry VI* by alternately plucking white and red roses in the Temple Garden (2.4). Lord Talbot, entertained by the Countess of Auvergne in Act 2, scene 3, makes the point that he is "but shadow of himself" and that he merely represents in a kind of image or figure the many thousands of troops at his call; he and the Duchess are suggestive of Mars and Venus, the warrior and the fair lady. Talbot's confrontations with Joan of Arc also suggest a pairing of symbolic figures, one a mighty warrior, the other a witch dressed in man's attire. Cade's rebellion in Part Two is an elaborate and profane parody of the struggle for power more somberly visualized in other parts of these plays. In Part Three the sad encounter of a son that has killed his father and a father that has killed his son (2.5) is witnessed by King Henry, sitting on a symbolic molehill while he ponders the vanity of human striving and his own longing for rustic solitude. These are potent theatrical moments, highly visual in their impact, and it may be that the plays' eclipse over the centuries owes something to the fact that so many theater managers (until recently, at least) lost touch with the theatrical conventions in which these plays were conceived.

The Playhouse

This early copy of a drawing by Johannes de Witt of the Swan Theatre in London (c. 1596), made by his friend Arend van Buchell, is the only surviving contemporary sketch of the interior of a public theater in the 1590s.

From other contemporary evidence, including the stage directions and dialogue of Elizabethan plays, we can surmise that the various public theaters where Shakespeare's plays were produced (the Theatre, the Curtain, the Globe) resembled the Swan in many important particulars, though there must have been some variations as well. The public playhouses were essentially round, or polygonal, and open to the sky, forming an acting arena approximately 70 feet in diameter; they did not have a large curtain with which to open and close a scene, such as we see today in opera and some traditional theater. A platform measuring approximately 43 feet across and 27 feet deep, referred to in the de Witt drawing as the *proscaenium*, projected into the yard, *planities sive arena*. The roof, *tectum*, above the stage and supported by two pillars, could contain machinery for ascents and descents, as were required in several of Shakespeare's late plays. Above this roof was a hut, shown in the drawing with a flag flying atop it and a trumpeter at its door announcing the performance of a play. The underside of the stage roof, called the heavens, was usually richly decorated with symbolic figures of the sun, the moon, and the constellations. The platform stage stood at a height of 5½ feet or so above the yard, providing room under the stage for underworldly effects. A trapdoor, which is not visible in this drawing, gave access to the space below.

The structure at the back of the platform (labeled *mimorum aedes*), known as the tiring-house because it was the actors' attiring (dressing) space, featured at least two doors, as shown here. Some theaters seem to have also had a discovery space, or curtained recessed alcove, perhaps between the two doors—in which Falstaff could have hidden from the sheriff (*1 Henry IV*, 2.4) or Polonius could have eavesdropped on Hamlet and his mother (*Hamlet*, 3.4). This discovery space probably gave the actors a means of access to and from the tiring-house. Curtains may also have been hung in front of the stage doors on occasion. The de Witt drawing shows a gallery above the doors that extends across the back and evidently contains spectators. On occasions when action "above" demanded the use of this space, as when Juliet appears at her "window" (*Romeo and Juliet*, 2.2 and 3.5), the gallery seems to have been used by the actors, but large scenes there were impractical.

The three-tiered auditorium is perhaps best described by Thomas Platter, a visitor to London in 1599 who saw on that occasion Shakespeare's *Julius Caesar* performed at the Globe:

> The playhouses are so constructed that they play on a raised platform, so that everyone has a good view. There are different galleries and places [*orchestra, sedilia, porticus*], however, where the seating is better and more comfortable and therefore more expensive. For whoever cares to stand below only pays one English penny, but if he wishes to sit, he enters by another door [*ingressus*] and pays another penny, while if he desires to sit in the most comfortable seats, which are cushioned, where he not only sees everything well but can also be seen, then he pays yet another English penny at another door. And during the performance food and drink are carried round the audience, so that for what one cares to pay one may also have refreshment.

Scenery was not used, though the theater building itself was handsome enough to invoke a feeling of order and hierarchy that lent itself to the splendor and pageantry onstage. Portable properties, such as thrones, stools, tables, and beds, could be carried or thrust on as needed. In the scene pictured here by de Witt, a lady on a bench, attended perhaps by her waiting-gentlewoman, receives the address of a male figure. If Shakespeare had written *Twelfth Night* by 1596 for performance at the Swan, we could imagine Malvolio appearing like this as he bows before the Countess Olivia and her gentlewoman, Maria.

HENRY VI,
PART ONE

Introduction

Throughout much of the fifteenth century, England had suffered the ravages of civil war. From the long struggles between the Lancastrians and the Yorkists, the so-called Wars of the Roses, the country had emerged in 1485 shaken but united at last under the strong rule of the Tudors. To Elizabethans, this period of civil war was a still-recent event that had tested and almost destroyed England's nationhood. They were, moreover, still troubled by political and dynastic uncertainties of their own. Queen Elizabeth, granddaughter of the first Tudor king, Henry VII, was unmarried and aging, her successor unchosen. Her Catholic enemies at home and abroad plotted a return to the ancient faith renounced by Henry VIII in his reformation of the church. Spain had attempted an invasion of England with the great Armada in 1588, perhaps one year before Shakespeare began writing his *Henry VI* plays. It was in such an era of crisis and patriotic excitement that the *Henry VI* plays first appeared. Indeed, they helped to establish the vogue of the English history play, which was to flourish throughout the 1590s. England's civil wars could be studied and analyzed now, from a perspective of over one hundred years later, and perhaps could provide a key to the present time. At hand was a new edition of Raphael Holinshed's *Chronicles*, 1587, along with the earlier chronicle writings of Robert Fabyan, John Stow, and Richard Grafton, as well as Edward Hall's *Union of the Two Noble and Illustre Families of Lancaster and York*, John Foxe's *Acts and Monuments of Martyrs*, and *A Mirror for Magistrates*.

How had these wars begun? Elizabethan Englishmen searched for an answer not in economic or social terms, but in religious and moral ones. According to a traditional and government-sponsored explanation, reflected to a large extent (though with many contradictions) in the chronicles of Edward Hall and familiar to Shakespeare whether he accepted it fully or not, the Wars of the Roses were a manifestation of God's wrath, a divine punishment inflicted on the English people for their wayward behavior. The people and their rulers had brought civil war on themselves by

self-serving ambition, arrogance, and disloyalty. King
Henry VI's grandfather, Henry IV, had come to the throne
in 1399 by deposing and then executing his own cousin
Richard II (a momentous event to be portrayed by Shakespeare in a later history play). Henry VI was himself an infant when he succeeded to the throne in 1422, owing to the
untimely death of his father Henry V. Too young at first to
rule, and never blessed with his father's ability to act decisively, Henry VI was utterly unable to halt the struggle for
power that developed among members of his large but dis-
cordant family. Ultimately, his very title to the throne was
challenged by his kinsman Richard Plantagenet, Duke of
York, who claimed to be rightful king by virtue of his descent from Henry IV's uncle Lionel, Duke of Clarence. The
Yorkist faction marched to battle against Henry VI's Lancastrian faction (so named because for generations the family had been possessors of the dukedom of Lancaster), and
the war was on.

This official view was never wholly endorsed by the
chroniclers, and certainly not by Shakespeare. Edward
Hall's overall scheme is undeniably providential, and yet as
a historian he presents a multiplicity of detail that cumula-
tively raises difficult issues of interpretation. At the same
time, the providential view served the purposes of the
Tudor state, and as such it gave widespread currency to the
theory of God's anger toward a rebellious people. The outcome of the war seemed to confirm this pattern: universal
devastation and the deaths of those most responsible for
the conflict led eventually, according to the theory, to appeasement of God's anger and a restoration of order. Richard Plantagenet died in the struggle, as did Henry VI,
Henry's son Edward, and much of the English nobility.
Richard's son Edward survived to become Edward IV; but
his manner of obtaining the throne was so manifestly offen-
sive to Providence that (according to the theory) he suffered
a retributive death at the hands of an angry God and was
succeeded by his younger brother, Richard III. This last
Yorkist ruler governed only two years, 1483–1485, and it
was through Richard's insane vengeance that God finally
settled all his scores against the wayward English people.
Having completed this purgation, God chose as his instrument of a new order Henry Tudor, Earl of Richmond,

Henry VII. Although Henry's return to England and defeat of Richard at the battle of Bosworth Field might outwardly resemble Henry IV's seizure of power from Richard II, the difference was crucial to Tudor apologists. Richard III had to be seen, from the Tudor point of view, not as a flawed legitimate monarch but as a mad usurper and tyrant; his defeat was not the disobedient act of one man but a rising up of the entire English nation at the prompting of divine command. Henry VII's accession to power was officially viewed not as a precedent for further rebellion but as a manifestation of divine will without parallel in human history.

The essence of this providential view of events was that divine retribution and eventual reconciliation revealed themselves in the history of the war. The theory of course served the interests of the Tudor state and was in part a propaganda weapon calculatedly employed by the ruling class. Shakespeare's commitment to it should not be taken for granted, and indeed a number of recent studies have expressed a profound skepticism toward the theory as the basis of Shakespeare's dramaturgy. Especially in his later tetralogy, or four-play series, from *Richard II* to *Henry V*, Shakespeare reveals considerably more interest in the clash of personalities than in patterns of divine retribution. Shakespeare does not endorse the orthodox view that Bolingbroke's seizure of the throne is a violation of divine purpose for which he and England must be humbled; instead, Shakespeare portrays the issues as many-sided and subject to varying interpretations.

Throughout his history plays, indeed, Shakespeare avoids expressing the Tudor providential view of recent history through didactic narrators or chorus figures who might seem to represent the point of view of the entire plays; instead, he puts this providential interpretation into the mouths of avowedly biased and self-interested characters whose motives and testimony the audience can then evaluate as it sees fit. In *1 Henry VI*, for example, the most detailed exposition of the providential historical view is given to Mortimer (2.5), whose interpretation, though strengthened by a dying man's last speech, is self-interestedly consistent with his own frustrated claim to the English throne. His nephew, Richard Plantagenet, who of course endorses the providential logic of Mortimer's speech, is portrayed as consumed with ambition for the crown. In Shakespeare's depiction of the Lancastrian-Yorkist conflict, neither side maintains a consistent ideological position, but instead shifts argument as required by the expediency of the moment. Although in his earlier tetralogy from *1 Henry VI* to *Richard III* Shakespeare does sometimes allow his contending characters to hearken back to the deposition of Richard II in order to explain the misfortunes of England's civil wars, those characters speak from self-interest and interpret history to their own advantage.

The individual plays of this earlier tetralogy, if seen or read separately, do not consistently comfort the spectator or reader with an assurance that all is working out according to God's plan. At the end of *1 Henry VI*, King Henry has surrendered to a disastrous marriage and has lost most of France; at the end of *2 Henry VI* the good Duke Humphrey of Gloucester is dead and his opportunistic political enemies are about to turn King Henry out of his throne. The hostilities of Lancaster and York end at the conclusion of *3 Henry VI*, to be sure, but prospects for a stable peace are doubtful in view of Richard of Gloucester's baleful presence. The reciprocity of slaughter visited on both sides appears to stem as much from humanity's insane desire for vengeance as from God's evening of the score. Only in *Richard III* do we retroactively see a pattern of divine anger, retribution, and eventual appeasement that can then be applied to the tetralogy as a continuous narrative. E.M.W. Tillyard's argument for a providential reading of these plays (in his *Shakespeare's History Plays*, 1944) is based not coincidentally on a view of the tetralogy as a cohesive whole. What about the playgoers who saw the plays one at a time? The plays, so far as we know, were written and produced singly and were never staged in a continuous series. Even though the tetralogy as a whole may harmonize in part with the chronicles of Edward Hall and others, written to glorify the Tudor state and to give thanks for its having ended the prolonged anarchy of the fifteenth century, we can see that Shakespeare is no apologist for the Tudor state. He gives expression to a widely felt distrust of political chaos. A pattern of divine wrath and appeasement, seen ret-

rospectively in *Richard III*, provides at last a causal explanation of England's darkest hour. More immediately, in
each individual play, the overriding cosmic irony stressing
the gulf between foolish humanity and the inscrutable intentions of Providence offers a potentially stirring conflict
of which Shakespeare makes rich use.

Shakespeare wrote his first tetralogy some time between
1589 and 1594. Just how much of this first tetralogy may
have been planned out when Shakespeare began work is
hard to say. In fact the very order of composition has long
been in dispute. Despite the commonsense pleading of Dr.
Johnson that Part Two follows from Part One as a logical
consequence, some scholars argue that Part One was composed last. One piece of evidence is that a corrupt version
of Part Two was published in quarto version in 1594 as *The
First Part of the Contention Betwixt the Two Famous Houses
of York and Lancaster*, and a corrupt version of Part Three in
octavo in 1595 as *The True Tragedy of Richard Duke of York*.
Part One had to await publication in the First Folio of 1623
and was registered for publication at that time as "The
third part of Henry the sixth." It seems odd, moreover, that
Parts Two and Three make no mention of Lord Talbot, so
prominent in Part One. If, however, as seems likely, the
early printed versions of Parts Two and Three were memorial reconstructions without the authority of the official
promptbook, the claim of Part Two to have been written
first may be unsubstantial. The very fact of prior publication of Parts Two and Three could explain why Part One
was called "The third part" in 1623. Although Talbot is not
mentioned in Parts Two and Three, these texts do recall important aspects of Part One. It is certainly possible that
Shakespeare wrote all three parts in normal order.

Equally vexing is the question of authorship. Many Elizabethan plays were written by teams of authors, and Shakespeare might have collaborated, especially at the beginning
of his career. Perhaps he rewrote older works by such writers as Thomas Nashe, Robert Greene, and Christopher
Marlowe. Yet the theories of multiple authorship, once a
commonplace of scholarship, are now generally in disfavor.
Greene's famous resentment toward Shakespeare as the
"upstart crow beautified with our feathers" seems more
the envy of a lesser talent than the righteous indignation of

one who has been plagiarized. The chief criteria used to "disintegrate" the plays into the hands of various supposed contributors are those of taste and style: for example, the low comic scenes of Joan of Arc were long held to be too coarse for Shakespeare's genius. Today most critics see a consistency of view throughout the *Henry VI* plays despite minor inconsistencies of fact that might be the result of simple error or of using multiple sources, and find nothing in these plays inimical to Shakespeare's budding genius. This belief confirms the judgment of Heminges and Condell, Shakespeare's fellow actors and editors of the 1623 Folio, who placed all the *Henry VI* plays among Shakespeare's collected works in their historical order.

If Shakespeare was at least chiefly responsible for the *Henry VI* series, he may also have been an important innovator in the new genre of the history play. Only the anonymous *Famous Victories of Henry V* is certainly earlier in dealing with recent English history. There were, to be sure, plays about legendary British history such as *Gorboduc* or *The Misfortunes of Arthur,* or about far-off lands such as *Cambises* or Marlowe's *Tamburlaine.* All these plays had explored by analogue political questions fascinating to Elizabethan England, and *Tamburlaine*'s immense success had certainly established a vogue for grand scenes of military conquest. Still, the English history play as a recognizable form came into being with *Henry VI.* The success was evidently tremendous and established Shakespeare as a major playwright.

1 Henry VI, like all the plays in Shakespeare's first tetralogy, comprises a large number of episodes, a sizable cast of characters, and a wide geographical range. The subject is England's loss of French territories because of political division at home. The structure of the play is one of sequential action displayed in great variety and in alternating scenes that are thematically juxtaposed and contrasted with one another. In the rapid shifting back and forth between the English and French court, for example, Shakespeare establishes a paradoxical theme: France triumphs in England's weakness, not in her own strength. The French court is merely one of debased sexual frivolity. The English are naturally superior but are torn apart by internal dissension, by a "jarring discord of nobility" and a "shouldering of each other in the court" (4.1.188–189) among those attempting to take advantage of Henry VI's weak minority rule and his vulnerable genealogical claim. Two of young Henry's kinsmen jockeying for position are Humphrey, Duke of Gloucester, and the Bishop of Winchester. Humphrey's intentions are virtuous, but he is unable to prevent the opportunistic scheming of his rival. Winchester, despite his ecclesiastical calling, is a man of evil ambition and corrupt life, wholly intent on destroying the right-minded Gloucester. Shakespeare employs derisive anticlerical humor against Winchester, and enlists the Protestant sympathies of his Elizabethan audience against the meddling Catholic church attempting to exploit England's weak kingship for its own ulterior purposes.

Even so, the menace threatening England is not seen as a Catholic conspiracy throughout; Winchester is only one opportunist seeking to exploit the political vacillation and faction at court. Of greater danger in the long term is Richard Plantagenet, scion of the Yorkist claim. From the start, Shakespeare portrays him as cunning, able to ingratiate himself and bide his time, ultimately ruthless. In these qualities he ominously foreshadows his youngest son and namesake, Richard III. In this play, Plantagenet's strategy is to allow England to wear herself down by the various conflicts at court and military losses abroad; once the situation is reduced to anarchy, Plantagenet will be able to move in. The strategy works only too well.

Chief defender of England's military might in France, and eventual victim of the bickering among the English nobility, is Lord Talbot. He is the heroic figure of this play with whom Elizabethan audiences identified. He pleads for political and military unity against the French and demonstrates that with such unity England would be invincible. Talbot is "the terror of the French" (1.4.42), able to hold off a troop of French soldiers with his bare fists, reputed to twist bars of steel. As the embodiment of chivalry, he delivers a richly deserved rebuke to Sir John Falstaff (historically "Fastolfe," but called "Falstaff" in the Folio text of this play), the cowardly soldier who foreshadows the fat knight of *1 Henry IV*. In *1 Henry VI*, cowardice and honor are rendered in black and white extremes. Talbot is a model general, illustrating all the qualities of great leadership ad-

vocated by the textbooks of the age: he is a stirring orator,
fearless, witty, and concerned with a proper lasting fame.
In the touching scenes with his son, Talbot rises triumphantly above death to become the immortal embodiment
of brave soldiership. Yet even if *1 Henry VI* offers this one
important model of rhetoric and arts of leadership put to
right use, Talbot's presence nonetheless lends itself more to
a profound anxiety about historical event than to a reassur-
ing confidence in divine assistance. Talbot's unnecessary
death offers a devastating critique of the weak leadership
that has allowed authority in France to be divided among
political rivals.

The relations between men and women in this play are
also used to create thematic contrasts. Talbot's chief military rival in France is Joan of Arc; and, although many
earlier scholars have wanted to deny Shakespeare's authorship of the Joan of Arc scenes, their thematic function is
central. As a woman in armor, Joan is the embodiment of
the domineering Amazonian woman to whom the effete and
self-indulgent dauphin, Charles, weakly capitulates. The
sexual roles have been reversed; Venus triumphs over Mars.
Joan's role as virgin-warrior, her trafficking in demonol-
ogy, and her obscenely parodic resemblance to the Virgin
Mary all suggest a profound male-oriented ambivalence
toward women in positions of authority—including, by implication, Queen Elizabeth. Joan's sexuality is not only de-
monic but obsessive in its promiscuity and seeming
insatiability. The name by which she is known in France, *la
Pucelle*, can mean both "virgin" and "slut." She even attempts to practice her witchcraft (with sexual overtones) on
Talbot and his son, but in vain. Talbot's sense of duty never
succumbs to Circean voluptuousness. In his encounter with
the Countess of Auvergne, Talbot resourcefully outwits another woman who, like Joan, seeks to entrap him. The
Countess finally submits to Talbot's courteous but firm authority, thereby reestablishing the traditional relationship
of male and female. Talbot stands for every kind of decency
and order that ought to prevail but is senselessly destroyed
through England's political division.

The last woman introduced in the play, Margaret of Anjou, is another domineering female. Her adulterous relationship with the fleshly Suffolk, and her ascendancy over

the weak Henry VI, are to be of fateful consequence in the
ensuing plays. Her scenes, although once dismissed as an
afterthought linking *1 Henry VI* with the following plays, in
fact recapitulate the motifs of female dominance with great
dramatic effect. Young Henry VI is no Talbot; inexperienced in love and highly impressionable, he surrenders to
the mere description of a woman he has not even seen and
refuses a politically advantageous match arranged by Duke
Humphrey in order that he may marry a conniving Frenchwoman without dowry. The marriage also anticipates that
of Edward IV (in *3 Henry VI*) to a penniless widow who has
caught his roving eye, when Edward could have obtained a
handsome dowry and a favorable alliance by marrying the
French King's sister-in-law. Such dismal triumphs of passion over reason are emblematic of the general decay
among the English aristocracy. Despite Henry's weakness,
he is the central character of this play after all, and his enervating surrender in love is a fitting anticlimax with which to
end the first installment of England's decline. It is events
such as these that seriously challenge any providential view
of history.

HENRY VI,
PART ONE

GENERAL *of the French forces at Bordeaux*
COUNTESS *of Auvergne*
PORTER *to the Countess*
MASTER GUNNER *of Orleans*
A BOY, *his son*
JOAN LA PUCELLE, *Joan of Arc*
SHEPHERD, *her father*
SERGEANT *of a French detachment*
SENTINEL *of a French detachment*
SOLDIER *with Pucelle at Rouen*
A SCOUT *in the Dauphin's army at Angiers*

English and French Heralds, Soldiers, Officers, Sentinels, Servingmen, Keepers or Jailers, Attendants, the Governor of Paris, Ambassadors, Fiends attending on La Pucelle

SCENE: *Partly in England, and partly in France*]

1.1 *Dead march. Enter the funeral of King Henry*
the Fifth, attended on by the Duke of Bedford,
Regent of France; the Duke of Gloucester,
Protector; the Duke of Exeter, [the Earl of]
Warwick, the Bishop of Winchester, and the
Duke of Somerset, [heralds, etc.].

BEDFORD
Hung be the heavens with black, yield day to night!   1
Comets, importing change of times and states,   2
Brandish your crystal tresses in the sky,   3
And with them scourge the bad revolting stars   4
That have consented unto Henry's death—   5
King Henry the Fifth, too famous to live long!
England ne'er lost a king of so much worth.

GLOUCESTER
England ne'er had a king until his time.
Virtue he had, deserving to command.   9
His brandished sword did blind men with his beams;   10
His arms spread wider than a dragon's wings;
His sparkling eyes, replete with wrathful fire,
More dazzled and drove back his enemies
Than midday sun fierce bent against their faces.
What should I say? His deeds exceed all speech.
He ne'er lift up his hand but conquerèd.   16

EXETER
We mourn in black. Why mourn we not in blood?
Henry is dead and never shall revive.
Upon a wooden coffin we attend,
And death's dishonorable victory
We with our stately presence glorify,
Like captives bound to a triumphant car.   22
What? Shall we curse the planets of mishap   23

1.1. Location: Westminster Abbey.
1 Hung . . . black (A metaphor from the theatrical practice of draping
the "heavens" or roof projecting over the stage in black when a tragedy
was to be performed.)   2 importing foretelling, portending   3 crystal
bright, shining.   tresses hair, i.e., the trail of the comet   4 scourge (as
if the tresses were whips).   revolting rebelling   5 consented unto
conspired to bring about   9 Virtue excellence, authority   10 his beams
its beams   16 lift lifted.   but conquerèd without conquering   22 car
chariot   23 planets of mishap misfortune-causing planets

That plotted thus our glory's overthrow?
Or shall we think the subtle-witted French
Conjurers and sorcerers, that, afraid of him,
By magic verses have contrived his end?   27

WINCHESTER
He was a king blest of the King of kings.
Unto the French the dreadful Judgment Day
So dreadful will not be as was his sight.   30
The battles of the Lord of hosts he fought;
The Church's prayers made him so prosperous.   32

GLOUCESTER
The Church? Where is it? Had not churchmen prayed,   33
His thread of life had not so soon decayed.   34
None do you like but an effeminate prince,
Whom like a schoolboy you may overawe.

WINCHESTER
Gloucester, whate'er we like, thou art Protector,   37
And lookest to command the Prince and realm.
Thy wife is proud. She holdeth thee in awe   39
More than God or religious churchmen may.

GLOUCESTER
Name not religion, for thou lov'st the flesh,
And ne'er throughout the year to church thou go'st
Except it be to pray against thy foes.

BEDFORD
Cease, cease these jars and rest your minds in peace!   44
Let's to the altar. Heralds, wait on us.   45
                              [*They prepare to leave.*]
Instead of gold we'll offer up our arms,
Since arms avail not now that Henry's dead.
Posterity, await for wretched years,   48

---

27 verses spells   **30 his sight** the sight of him   **32 prosperous** successful
33 prayed (with pun on *preyed;* also in l. 43)   **34 decayed** been destroyed
37 Protector head of state during the king's minority   **39 Thy wife is
proud** (A reference to Gloucester's ambitious wife, Eleanor, whose inordi-
nate desire for greatness is depicted in *2 Henry VI.*)   **holdeth . . . awe**
overawes you   **44 jars** discords   **45 wait on us** i.e., lead the procession
s.d. They prepare to leave (Here or later in the scene, the various members of the funeral procession not specifically mentioned in the exits at ll.
166–177, including Warwick, Somerset, and the heralds, must leave the
stage.)   **48 await for** expect

When at their mothers' moistened eyes babes shall
   suck,   49
Our isle be made a nourish of salt tears,   50
And none but women left to wail the dead.
Henry the Fifth, thy ghost I invocate: 52
Prosper this realm, keep it from civil broils;   53
Combat with adverse planets in the heavens!
A far more glorious star thy soul will make
Than Julius Caesar or bright——

    Enter a Messenger.

FIRST MESSENGER
My honorable lords, health to you all!
Sad tidings bring I to you out of France,
Of loss, of slaughter, and discomfiture.
Guyenne, Champagne, Rouen, Rheims, Orleans,   60
Paris, Gisors, Poitiers, are all quite lost.

BEDFORD
What sayst thou, man, before dead Henry's corpse?
Speak softly, or the loss of those great towns
Will make him burst his lead and rise from death.   64

GLOUCESTER
Is Paris lost? Is Rouen yielded up?
If Henry were recalled to life again,
These news would cause him once more yield the ghost.

EXETER
How were they lost? What treachery was used?

FIRST MESSENGER
No treachery, but want of men and money.
Amongst the soldiers this is muttered,
That here you maintain several factions,   71
And whilst a field should be dispatched and fought,   72
You are disputing of your generals.   73
One would have lingering wars with little cost;

---

49 When . . . suck i.e., when mothers will feed their children with tears
only **50 nourish . . . tears** i.e., a nurse feeding with tears only **52 invocate** invoke, as one would call on a saint **53 Prosper** make prosperous **60 Champagne** the city of Compiègne **64 lead** leaden inner coffin
or wrapping, inside the wooden coffin (l. 19) **71 several** separate (and
divisive) **72 field** (1) battle (2) combat force **73 of** about

Another would fly swift, but wanteth wings;   75
A third thinks, without expense at all,
By guileful fair words peace may be obtained.
Awake, awake, English nobility!
Let not sloth dim your honors new-begot.
Cropped are the flower-de-luces in your arms;   80
Of England's coat one half is cut away.   *[Exit.]*

EXETER
Were our tears wanting to this funeral,   82
These tidings would call forth her flowing tides.

BEDFORD
Me they concern; Regent I am of France.   84
Give me my steelèd coat. I'll fight for France.
Away with these disgraceful wailing robes!
Wounds will I lend the French instead of eyes,   87
To weep their intermissive miseries.   88

Enter to them another Messenger, [with letters].

SECOND MESSENGER
Lords, view these letters, full of bad mischance.
France is revolted from the English quite,
Except some petty towns of no import.
The Dauphin Charles is crownèd king in Rheims;
The Bastard of Orleans with him is joined;
Reignier, Duke of Anjou, doth take his part;   94
The Duke of Alençon flieth to his side.   *Exit.*

EXETER
The Dauphin crownèd king? All fly to him?   96
O, whither shall we fly from this reproach?   97

---

75 wanteth lacks **80 Cropped** plucked. **flower-de-luces** the *fleur-de-lis*, or iris, national emblem of France. (According to the Treaty of Troyes, 1420, the crown of France was ceded to England but was nominally to belong to the French king, Charles VI, as long as he lived. Henry V's title was designated "King of England and Heir of France." At his death this title passed to Henry VI; but within two months after this took place, Charles VI died and his son Charles VII was proclaimed king. The loss of the French crown would deprive the English king of the right to display the *fleur-de-lis* in his coat of arms.) **82 wanting** lacking **84 Regent** ruler in the king's absence **87–88 Wounds . . . weep** i.e., I'll make the French shed blood instead of weep tears **88 intermissive** intermittent but now to be resumed **94 Reignier** René **96–97 fly . . . fly** flock . . . flee

GLOUCESTER
We will not fly but to our enemies' throats!   98
Bedford, if thou be slack, I'll fight it out.

BEDFORD
Gloucester, why doubt'st thou of my forwardness?
An army have I mustered in my thoughts,
Wherewith already France is overrun.

Enter another Messenger.

THIRD MESSENGER
My gracious lords, to add to your laments,
Wherewith you now bedew King Henry's hearse,
I must inform you of a dismal fight   105
Betwixt the stout Lord Talbot and the French.   ● 106

WINCHESTER
What? Wherein Talbot overcame, is 't so?

THIRD MESSENGER
O, no! Wherein Lord Talbot was o'erthrown.
The circumstance I'll tell you more at large.   109
The tenth of August last this dreadful lord,   110
Retiring from the siege of Orleans,
Having full scarce six thousand in his troop,   112
By three-and-twenty thousand of the French
Was round encompassèd and set upon.   114
No leisure had he to enrank his men.   115
He wanted pikes to set before his archers,   116
Instead whereof sharp stakes plucked out of hedges
They pitchèd in the ground confusedly,
To keep the horsemen off from breaking in.
More than three hours the fight continuèd,
Where valiant Talbot above human thought   121
Enacted wonders with his sword and lance.
Hundreds he sent to hell, and none durst stand him;   123

98 fly (Gloucester turns the word to mean "fly at their throats.")
105 dismal savage, terrible   **106 stout** brave   **109 circumstance** particulars.   **at large** in full detail   **110 dreadful** to be dreaded   **112 full
scarce** scarce full, barely   **114 round encompassèd** surrounded
115 enrank draw up in battle array   **116 wanted pikes** lacked iron-
bound stakes, sharpened at the ends and set in the ground in front of
archers as protection against cavalry   **121 above human thought** beyond imagining   **123 stand him** stand up against him

Here, there, and everywhere, enraged he slew.
The French exclaimed the devil was in arms;
All the whole army stood agazed on him.   126
His soldiers, spying his undaunted spirit,
"A Talbot, a Talbot!" crièd out amain   128
And rushed into the bowels of the battle.
Here had the conquest fully been sealed up   130
If Sir John Falstaff had not played the coward.   131
He, being in the vaward, placed behind   132
With purpose to relieve and follow them,
Cowardly fled, not having struck one stroke.
Hence grew the general wrack and massacre.   135
Enclosèd were they with their enemies.   136
A base Walloon, to win the Dauphin's grace,   137
Thrust Talbot with a spear into the back,
Whom all France with their chief assembled strength
Durst not presume to look once in the face.

BEDFORD
Is Talbot slain? Then I will slay myself
For living idly here in pomp and ease
Whilst such a worthy leader, wanting aid,
Unto his dastard foemen is betrayed.

THIRD MESSENGER
O no, he lives, but is took prisoner,
And Lord Scales with him, and Lord Hungerford;
Most of the rest slaughtered or took likewise.

BEDFORD
His ransom there is none but I shall pay.   148
I'll hale the Dauphin headlong from his throne;
His crown shall be the ransom of my friend.
Four of their lords I'll change for one of ours.   151
Farewell, my masters; to my task will I.
Bonfires in France forthwith I am to make,   153

---

126 agazed on astounded at   **128 A Talbot** rally to Talbot.   **amain** with full
force   **130 sealed up** completed   **131 Falstaff** ("Fastolfe" in the chronicles;
but the Shakespearean spelling used here shows us the origin of the name
used in the *Henry IV* plays.)   **132 vaward** vanguard   **135 wrack** wreckage,
destruction   **136 with** by   **137 Walloon** an inhabitant of that province,
now a part of southern Belgium and the adjoining part of France
148 His . . . pay i.e., I'll pay all the ransom there's going to be, by retaliat-
ing   **151 change** i.e., kill in exchange   **153 am** intend

To keep our great Saint George's feast withal.   154
Ten thousand soldiers with me I will take,
Whose bloody deeds shall make all Europe quake.

THIRD MESSENGER
So you had need, for Orleans is besieged;   157
The English army is grown weak and faint;
The Earl of Salisbury craveth supply   159
And hardly keeps his men from mutiny,
Since they, so few, watch such a multitude.   [*Exit.*]

EXETER
Remember, lords, your oaths to Henry sworn,
Either to quell the Dauphin utterly
Or bring him in obedience to your yoke.

BEDFORD
I do remember it, and here take my leave
To go about my preparation.   *Exit Bedford.*

GLOUCESTER
I'll to the Tower with all the haste I can   167
To view th' artillery and munition,
And then I will proclaim young Henry king.
                              Exit Gloucester.

EXETER
To Eltham will I, where the young King is,   170
Being ordained his special governor,
And for his safety there I'll best devise.   *Exit.*

WINCHESTER
Each hath his place and function to attend.
I am left out; for me nothing remains.
But long I will not be jack-out-of-office.   175
The King from Eltham I intend to steal
And sit at chiefest stern of public weal.   *Exit.* 177

154 Saint George's feast the twenty-third of April. (Saint George was the
patron saint of England. To celebrate his day in France would be to assert
England's claim to that territory.)   **157 Orleans is besieged** (At l. 60 a
messenger says that Orleans has fallen; at 1.2.8 ff. an English siege to
recover Orleans is under way. The messenger here may mean that the
besieging English army needs help.)   **159 supply** reinforcements
167 Tower Tower of London, ancient palace-fortress, later a prison for
persons of eminence   **170 Eltham** a royal residence southeast of London
175 jack-out-of-office i.e., a dismissed fellow with nothing to do   **177 at
chiefest stern** in the steersman's seat; i.e., in a position of supreme control

1.2   *Sound a flourish. Enter Charles, Alençon, and*
          Reignier, marching with drum and soldiers.

CHARLES
  Mars his true moving, even as in the heavens   1
  So in the earth, to this day is not known.
  Late did he shine upon the English side;   3
  Now we are victors, upon us he smiles.
  What towns of any moment but we have?   5
  At pleasure here we lie near Orleans;   6
  Otherwhiles the famished English, like pale ghosts,   7
  Faintly besiege us one hour in a month.

ALENÇON
  They want their porridge and their fat bull-beeves.
  Either they must be dieted like mules   10
  And have their provender tied to their mouths,
  Or piteous they will look, like drownèd mice.

REIGNIER
  Let's raise the siege. Why live we idly here?   13
  Talbot is taken, whom we wont to fear.   14
  Remaineth none but mad-brained Salisbury,
  And he may well in fretting spend his gall—   16
  Nor men nor money hath he to make war.   17

CHARLES
  Sound, sound alarum! We will rush on them.   18
  Now for the honor of the forlorn French!   19
  Him I forgive my death that killeth me
  When he sees me go back one foot or fly.   *Exeunt.*

    Here alarum. They are beaten back by the
    English with great loss. Enter Charles, Alençon,
    and Reignier.

1.2. Location: France. Before Orleans.
s.d. flourish trumpet fanfare.   **drum** drummer   **1 Mars . . . moving** Mars's
precise orbit. (The planet's seemingly eccentric orbit was a source of
perplexity in Shakespeare's day; here, its influence on earth in human
affairs is likewise mysterious. Mars is also the god of war.)   **3 Late** lately,
recently   **5 What . . . have** what towns of any consequence do we not
possess   **6 lie** are encamped   **7 Otherwhiles** at times   **10 dieted** fed. (The
eating of beef, l. 9, was believed to confer courage.)   **13 raise the siege** i.e.,
drive off the English from their siege   **14 wont** were accustomed
16 spend expend, waste.   **gall** i.e., bitterness of spirit   **17 Nor** neither
18 alarum call to arms   **19 forlorn** in extreme risk

CHARLES
Who ever saw the like? What men have I!
Dogs, cowards, dastards! I would ne'er have fled
But that they left me 'midst my enemies.

REIGNIER
Salisbury is a desperate homicide;
He fighteth as one weary of his life.   26
The other lords, like lions wanting food,
Do rush upon us as their hungry prey.   28

ALENÇON
Froissart, a countryman of ours, records   29
England all Olivers and Rolands bred   30
During the time Edward the Third did reign.
More truly now may this be verified,
For none but Samsons and Goliases   33
It sendeth forth to skirmish. One to ten!
Lean raw-boned rascals! Who would e'er suppose   35
They had such courage and audacity?

CHARLES
Let's leave this town; for they are harebrained slaves,
And hunger will enforce them to be more eager.   38
Of old I know them. Rather with their teeth
The walls they'll tear down than forsake the siege.

REIGNIER
I think by some odd gimmers or device   41
Their arms are set, like clocks, still to strike on;   42
Else ne'er could they hold out so as they do.
By my consent, we'll even let them alone.   44
ALENÇON   Be it so.

  Enter the Bastard of Orleans.

BASTARD
Where's the Prince Dauphin? I have news for him.

26 **as one** like one who is   28 **hungry prey** prey of their hunger
29 **Froissart** a fourteenth-century French chronicler who wrote of
contemporary events in Flanders, France, Spain, and England
30 **Olivers and Rolands** paladins in the Charlemagne legends, the most
famous of the twelve for their daring exploits   33 **Samsons, Goliases**
(i.e., Goliaths), biblical characters typifying great physical strength
35 **rascals** young, lean, or inferior deer of a herd   38 **eager** (1) fierce
(2) hungry   41 **gimmers** gimmals, joints or connecting parts for trans-
mitting motion   42 **still** continually   44 **consent** advice.   **even** i.e., do
nothing but

CHARLES
  Bastard of Orleans, thrice welcome to us.
BASTARD
  Methinks your looks are sad, your cheer appalled.   48
  Hath the late overthrow wrought this offense?   49
  Be not dismayed, for succor is at hand.
  A holy maid hither with me I bring,
  Which, by a vision sent to her from heaven,
  Ordainèd is to raise this tedious siege
  And drive the English forth the bounds of France.   54
  The spirit of deep prophecy she hath,
  Exceeding the nine sibyls of old Rome.   56
  What's past and what's to come she can descry.
  Speak, shall I call her in? Believe my words,
  For they are certain and unfallible.
CHARLES
  Go, call her in. [*Bastard goes to the door.*] But first, to try
    her skill,
  Reignier, stand thou as Dauphin in my place.
  Question her proudly; let thy looks be stern.
  By this means shall we sound what skill she hath.   63
                              [*They exchange places.*]

    *Enter Joan [la] Pucelle, [the Bastard escorting
    her].*

REIGNIER
  Fair maid, is 't thou wilt do these wondrous feats?
PUCELLE
  Reignier, is 't thou that thinkest to beguile me?
  Where is the Dauphin?—Come, come from behind;
  I know thee well, though never seen before.
  Be not amazed. There's nothing hid from me.
  In private will I talk with thee apart.
  Stand back, you lords, and give us leave awhile.
                              [*The lords stand aside.*]

---

48 cheer appalled countenances made pale   **49 late . . . offense** recent
defeat brought about this harm   **54 forth** out of   **56 nine . . . Rome**
inspired women of the ancient world. (Not only of Rome, however; the
phrase here is probably owing to a confusion with the Cumaean sibyl
who came to Tarquin with nine prophetic books.)   **63 sound** test, determine   **s.d. Pucelle** virgin

REIGNIER
  She takes upon her bravely at first dash.   71
PUCELLE
  Dauphin, I am by birth a shepherd's daughter,
  My wit untrained in any kind of art.   73
  Heaven and our Lady gracious hath it pleased
  To shine on my contemptible estate.
  Lo, whilst I waited on my tender lambs
  And to sun's parching heat displayed my cheeks,
  God's mother deignèd to appear to me,
  And in a vision full of majesty
  Willed me to leave my base vocation
  And free my country from calamity.
  Her aid she promised, and assured success.
  In complete glory she revealed herself;
  And, whereas I was black and swart before,   84
  With those clear rays which she infused on me   85
  That beauty am I blest with which you may see.
  Ask me what question thou canst possible,
  And I will answer unpremeditated.
  My courage try by combat, if thou dar'st,
  And thou shalt find that I exceed my sex.
  Resolve on this: thou shalt be fortunate   91
  If thou receive me for thy warlike mate.   92
CHARLES
  Thou hast astonished me with thy high terms.   93
  Only this proof I'll of thy valor make: 94
  In single combat thou shalt buckle with me,   95
  And if thou vanquishest, thy words are true.
  Otherwise I renounce all confidence.   97
PUCELLE
  I am prepared. Here is my keen-edged sword,
  Decked with five flower-de-luces on each side,   99
  The which at Touraine, in Saint Katharine's churchyard,
  Out of a great deal of old iron I chose forth.

---

71 **takes . . . bravely** plays her part well   73 **wit** mind, intelligence.   **art**
learning   84 **black and swart** i.e., heavily tanned   85 **infused** poured
91 **Resolve on** be sure of   92 **warlike mate** (with sexual suggestion, as in
the military terms throughout this interview)   93 **high** lofty   94 **proof**
trial, test   95 **buckle** join in close combat (with bawdy suggestion)
97 **confidence** (1) trust in your speech (2) intimacy   99 **Decked** adorned

CHARLES
Then come, i' God's name! I fear no woman.

PUCELLE
And while I live, I'll ne'er fly from a man.   103
    Here they fight, and Joan la Pucelle overcomes.

CHARLES
Stay, stay thy hands! Thou art an Amazon,   104
And fightest with the sword of Deborah.   105

PUCELLE
Christ's mother helps me, else I were too weak.

CHARLES
Whoe'er helps thee, 'tis thou that must help me!
Impatiently I burn with thy desire;   108
My heart and hands thou hast at once subdued.
Excellent Pucelle, if thy name be so,
Let me thy servant and not sovereign be.   111
'Tis the French Dauphin sueth to thee thus.

PUCELLE
I must not yield to any rites of love,
For my profession's sacred from above.
When I have chasèd all thy foes from hence,
Then will I think upon a recompense.

CHARLES
Meantime, look gracious on thy prostrate thrall.

REIGNIER [*To the other lords apart*]
My lord, methinks, is very long in talk.

ALENÇON
Doubtless he shrives this woman to her smock;   119
Else ne'er could he so long protract his speech.

REIGNIER
Shall we disturb him, since he keeps no mean?   121

---

103 ne'er . . . man (with bawdy suggestion)   **104 Amazon** race of warrior women   **105 Deborah** Hebrew prophetess who "judged" Israel in
the fourteenth century B.C. (She led an army against the Canaanite
oppressors, whom she overcame; Judges 4, 5.)   **108 thy desire** desire for
you   **111 servant** (with suggestion of a lover who will fulfill his mistress's commands)   **119 shrives** hears confession, i.e., examines.   **to her
smock** to her undergarment, i.e., completely (with bawdy suggestion)
121 keeps no mean observes no middle position, is immoderate

ALENÇON
He may mean more than we poor men do know.
These women are shrewd tempters with their tongues. 123

REIGNIER [*To Charles*]
My lord, where are you? What devise you on? 124
Shall we give o'er Orleans, or no?

PUCELLE
Why, no, I say. Distrustful recreants, 126
Fight till the last gasp. I'll be your guard.

CHARLES
What she says I'll confirm. We'll fight it out.

PUCELLE
Assigned am I to be the English scourge.
This night the siege assuredly I'll raise.
Expect Saint Martin's summer, halcyon days, 131
Since I have enterèd into these wars.
Glory is like a circle in the water,
Which never ceaseth to enlarge itself
Till by broad spreading it disperse to naught.
With Henry's death the English circle ends;
Dispersèd are the glories it included.
Now am I like that proud insulting ship 138
Which Caesar and his fortune bare at once. 139

CHARLES
Was Mahomet inspirèd with a dove? 140
Thou with an eagle art inspirèd then.
Helen, the mother of great Constantine, 142
Nor yet Saint Philip's daughters, were like thee. 143

---

123 shrewd cunning, mischievous **124 where are you** i.e., what are you
up to. **devise** decide **126 Distrustful recreants** faithless cowards
131 Saint Martin's summer i.e., Indian summer; Saint Martin's Day is
November 11. **halcyon days** i.e., unseasonable calm. (The halcyon is
the kingfisher, which, according to fable, nested at midwinter on the
seas, which became calm for that purpose.) **138–139 Now . . . once**
(North's translation of Plutarch relates how Caesar, encountering a
storm, said to the mariners, "Fear not, for thou hast Caesar and his
fortune with thee.") **140 Was . . . dove** (Mohammed supposedly
claimed that he received divine inspiration from a dove whispering in
his ear.) **142 Helen** mother of the emperor Constantine and supposed
discoverer of the holy cross and sepulcher of the Lord **143 Saint
Philip's daughters** the four daughters of Philip the Evangelist, said in
Acts 21:9 to have the power of prophecy

Bright star of Venus, fall'n down on the earth,
How may I reverently worship thee enough?

ALENÇON
Leave off delays, and let us raise the siege.

REIGNIER
Woman, do what thou canst to save our honors.
Drive them from Orleans and be immortalized.

CHARLES
Presently we'll try. Come, let's away about it.   149
No prophet will I trust, if she prove false.   *Exeunt.*

❖

1.3   *Enter [the Duke of] Gloucester, with his
          Servingmen [in blue coats].*

GLOUCESTER
I am come to survey the Tower this day.   1
Since Henry's death, I fear, there is conveyance.   2
Where be these warders, that they wait not here?
Open the gates! 'Tis Gloucester that calls.
                    [*They knock.*]

FIRST WARDER [*Within*]
Who's there that knocks so imperiously?

FIRST SERVINGMAN
It is the noble Duke of Gloucester.

SECOND WARDER [*Within*]
Whoe'er he be, you may not be let in.

FIRST SERVINGMAN
Villains, answer you so the Lord Protector?

FIRST WARDER [*Within*]
The Lord protect him! So we answer him.
We do no otherwise than we are willed.   10

GLOUCESTER
Who willèd you? Or whose will stands but mine?   11

---

149 Presently immediately

1.3. Location: Before the Tower of London.
s.d. blue coats (Customarily worn by servingmen.) **1 survey** inspect
2 conveyance trickery **10 willed** commanded **11 stands** has authority

There's none Protector of the realm but I.—
Break up the gates. I'll be your warrantize.   13
Shall I be flouted thus by dunghill grooms?   14

Gloucester's men rush at the Tower gates, and
Woodville the Lieutenant speaks within.

WOODVILLE [*Within*]
What noise is this? What traitors have we here?
GLOUCESTER
Lieutenant, is it you whose voice I hear?
Open the gates. Here's Gloucester that would enter.
WOODVILLE [*Within*]
Have patience, noble Duke. I may not open;
The Cardinal of Winchester forbids.   19
From him I have express commandement   20
That thou nor none of thine shall be let in.
GLOUCESTER
Fainthearted Woodville, prizest him 'fore me?
Arrogant Winchester, that haughty prelate,
Whom Henry, our late sovereign, ne'er could brook?   24
Thou art no friend to God or to the King.
Open the gates, or I'll shut thee out shortly.   26
SERVINGMEN
Open the gates unto the Lord Protector,
Or we'll burst them open, if that you come not quickly.   28

Enter to the Protector at the Tower gates
Winchester and his men in tawny coats.

WINCHESTER
How now, ambitious Humphrey, what means this?
GLOUCESTER
Peeled priest, dost thou command me to be shut out?   30

---

13 warrantize guarantee   **14 dunghill grooms** i.e., base fellows   **s.d. rush
. . . gates** (Gloucester's men assault the facade of the tiring-house wall
backstage, which represents the Tower gates; Woodville and the warders
are "within," or behind that wall, invisible to the audience.)   **19 Cardinal** (An inconsistency with 5.1.28 ff., where Winchester has just been
installed as cardinal.)   **20 commandement** commandment (pronounced
in four syllables)   **24 brook** endure   **26 I'll . . . shortly** i.e., I'll take
possession and shut you out   **28 if that** if   **s.d. tawny coats** (Customarily worn by attendants of a mighty churchman.)   **30 Peeled** shaven,
tonsured

WINCHESTER
  I do, thou most usurping proditor,   31
  And not Protector, of the King or realm.

GLOUCESTER
  Stand back, thou manifest conspirator,
  Thou that contrivedst to murder our dead lord,   34
  Thou that giv'st whores indulgences to sin.   35
  I'll canvass thee in thy broad cardinal's hat   36
  If thou proceed in this thy insolence.

WINCHESTER
  Nay, stand thou back. I will not budge a foot.
  This be Damascus, be thou cursèd Cain,   39
  To slay thy brother Abel, if thou wilt.   40

GLOUCESTER
  I will not slay thee, but I'll drive thee back.
  Thy scarlet robes as a child's bearing cloth   42
  I'll use to carry thee out of this place.

WINCHESTER
  Do what thou dar'st! I beard thee to thy face.   44

GLOUCESTER
  What, am I dared and bearded to my face?
  Draw, men, for all this privilegèd place—   46
  Blue coats to tawny coats. Priest, beware your beard.
  I mean to tug it and to cuff you soundly.
  Under my feet I stamp thy cardinal's hat.
  In spite of Pope or dignities of Church,   50
  Here by the cheeks I'll drag thee up and down.

WINCHESTER
  Gloucester, thou wilt answer this before the Pope.   52

---

31 proditor traitor   **34–35 Thou . . . sin** (Gloucester, in his bill of particulars against Winchester, charged that the cleric had suborned someone
to attempt the murder of Henry V. Here he refers also to the fact that
Winchester collected revenues from houses of prostitution on the south
bank of the Thames.)   **indulgences** forgiveness of sins. (One could buy
indulgences from the Church.)   **36 canvass** i.e., deal with severely. (The
metaphor is that of tossing someone in a canvas or blanket as sport or
punishment.)   **39 This be** let this be.   **Damascus** a city reputed to have
been built on the site of Cain's slaying of Abel.   **40 thy brother** (Winchester is Gloucester's half uncle.)   **42 bearing cloth** christening
robe   **44 beard** openly defy   **46 for all this** in spite of this being a.
privilegèd place (The Tower, as a royal residence, was one of the precincts where drawing of weapons was forbidden by the law of arms; cf.
2.4.86, note.)   **50 dignities** dignitaries   **52 answer** render an account of,
pay for

GLOUCESTER
Winchester goose! I cry, a rope, a rope!   53
[*To his Servingmen.*] Now beat them hence. Why do you
 let them stay?—
Thee I'll chase hence, thou wolf in sheep's array.
Out, tawny coats! Out, scarlet hypocrite!

*Here Gloucester's men beat out the Cardinal's
men, and enter in the hurly-burly the Mayor of
London and his Officers.*

MAYOR
Fie, lords, that you, being supreme magistrates,   57
Thus contumeliously should break the peace!   58

GLOUCESTER
Peace, Mayor! Thou know'st little of my wrongs.
Here's Beaufort, that regards nor God nor king,   60
Hath here distrained the Tower to his use.   61

WINCHESTER
Here's Gloucester, a foe to citizens,
One that still motions war and never peace,   63
O'ercharging your free purses with large fines,   64
That seeks to overthrow religion
Because he is Protector of the realm,
And would have armor here out of the Tower
To crown himself king and suppress the Prince.   68

GLOUCESTER
I will not answer thee with words, but blows.
                              Here they skirmish again.

MAYOR
Naught rests for me in this tumultuous strife   70
But to make open proclamation.
Come, officer, as loud as e'er thou canst,
Cry.

OFFICER   All manner of men assembled here in arms
 this day against God's peace and the King's, we charge

---

53 Winchester goose (Slang for a symptom of venereal disease.) **a rope**
i.e., a halter for hanging **57 magistrates** rulers **58 contumeliously**
arrogantly, contemptuously **60 regards nor** has a proper respect for
neither **61 distrained** confiscated **63 still motions** incessantly advo-
cates **64 O'ercharging . . . fines** overburdening you with excessive taxation **68 Prince** i.e., Henry VI **70 rests for me** remains for me to do

and command you, in His Highness' name, to repair
to your several dwelling places, and not to wear, han- 77
dle, or use any sword, weapon, or dagger henceforward, upon pain of death.   79

GLOUCESTER
Cardinal, I'll be no breaker of the law;
But we shall meet and break our minds at large.   81

WINCHESTER
Gloucester, we'll meet to thy cost, be sure.
Thy heart-blood I will have for this day's work.

MAYOR
I'll call for clubs, if you will not away.   84
This cardinal's more haughty than the devil.

GLOUCESTER
Mayor, farewell. Thou dost but what thou mayst.

WINCHESTER
Abominable Gloucester, guard thy head,
For I intend to have it ere long.
                    Exeunt, [separately, Gloucester and
                              Winchester with their
                                    Servingmen].

MAYOR
See the coast cleared, and then we will depart.
Good God, these nobles should such stomachs bear!   90
I myself fight not once in forty year.   *Exeunt.*

♣

1.4   *Enter the Master Gunner of Orleans and his*
          Boy.

MASTER GUNNER
Sirrah, thou know'st how Orleans is besieged   1
And how the English have the suburbs won.

---

77 several individual   **79 pain** punishment   **81 break our minds**
(1) reveal our purposes (2) crack our heads.   **at large** at length   **84 call
for clubs** i.e., sound the rallying cry for London apprentices armed with
clubs   **90 these** that these.   **stomachs** i.e., angry tempers

1.4. Location: France. Orleans.
1 Sirrah (Customary form of address to an inferior.)

BOY
   Father, I know, and oft have shot at them,
   Howe'er unfortunate I missed my aim.   4

MASTER GUNNER
   But now thou shalt not. Be thou ruled by me.
   Chief master gunner am I of this town;
   Something I must do to procure me grace.   7
   The Prince's espials have informèd me   8
   How the English, in the suburbs close entrenched,
   Wont through a secret grate of iron bars   10
   In yonder tower to overpeer the city
   And thence discover how with most advantage
   They may vex us with shot or with assault.
   To intercept this inconvenience,   14
   A piece of ordnance 'gainst it I have placed,   15
   And even these three days have I watched,
   If I could see them. Now do thou watch,
   For I can stay no longer.
   If thou spy'st any, run and bring me word,
   And thou shalt find me at the governor's.   *Exit.*

BOY
   Father, I warrant you; take you no care.   21
   I'll never trouble you, if I may spy them.   *Exit.* 22

         Enter Salisbury and Talbot on the turrets, with
         [Sir William Glansdale, Sir Thomas Gargrave,
         and] others.

SALISBURY
   Talbot, my life, my joy, again returned?
   How wert thou handled, being prisoner?
   Or by what means gott'st thou to be released?
   Discourse, I prithee, on this turret's top.

TALBOT
   The Duke of Bedford had a prisoner
   Called the brave Lord Ponton de Santrailles;
   For him was I exchanged and ransomèd.
   But with a baser man-of-arms by far   30

4 **Howe'er unfortunate** although unfortunately   7 **grace** honor, credit
8 **espials** spies   10 **Wont** are accustomed   14 **inconvenience** mischief
15 **'gainst** directed toward   21 **take you no care** don't you worry
22 **s.d. turrets** i.e., some high point of vantage in the theater, above the
main stage   30 **baser** of lower rank

Once in contempt they would have bartered me;
Which I disdaining scorned, and cravèd death
Rather than I would be so pilled esteemed.   33
In fine, redeemed I was as I desired.   34
But O, the treacherous Falstaff wounds my heart,
Whom with my bare fists I would execute
If I now had him brought into my power.

SALISBURY
Yet tell'st thou not how thou wert entertained.   38

TALBOT
With scoffs and scorns and contumelious taunts.
In open marketplace produced they me
To be a public spectacle to all.
"Here," said they, "is the terror of the French,
The scarecrow that affrights our children so."
Then broke I from the officers that led me
And with my nails digged stones out of the ground
To hurl at the beholders of my shame.
My grisly countenance made others fly;
None durst come near for fear of sudden death.
In iron walls they deemed me not secure;
So great fear of my name 'mongst them were spread
That they supposed I could rend bars of steel
And spurn in pieces posts of adamant.   52
Wherefore a guard of chosen shot I had   53
That walked about me every minute while;   54
And if I did but stir out of my bed,
Ready they were to shoot me to the heart.   56

Enter the Boy with a linstock.

SALISBURY
I grieve to hear what torments you endured.
But we will be revenged sufficiently.
Now it is suppertime in Orleans.
Here, through this grate, I count each one

---

33 pilled peeled, i.e., despoiled of honor   **34 In fine** finally.   **redeemed**
ransomed   **38 entertained** treated   **52 spurn** kick.   **adamant** a legendary substance supposedly of incredible hardness, like diamond, or like a
magnet   **53 chosen shot** carefully selected marksmen   **54 every minute
while** i.e., constantly, at minute intervals   **56 s.d. linstock** forked stick
used to hold a lighted match for firing cannon

And view the Frenchmen how they fortify.
Let us look in; the sight will much delight thee.
Sir Thomas Gargrave and Sir William Glansdale,
Let me have your express opinions   64
Where is best place to make our battery next.   65

GARGRAVE
I think at the north gate, for there stands lords.

GLANSDALE
And I here, at the bulwark of the bridge.   67

TALBOT
For aught I see, this city must be famished   68
Or with light skirmishes enfeeblèd.   69

> Here they shoot, and Salisbury falls down
> [together with Gargrave].

SALISBURY
O Lord, have mercy on us, wretched sinners!

GARGRAVE
O Lord, have mercy on me, woeful man!

TALBOT
What chance is this that suddenly hath crossed us?   72
Speak, Salisbury—at least, if thou canst, speak.
How far'st thou, mirror of all martial men?   74
One of thy eyes and thy cheek's side struck off?
Accursèd tower! Accursèd fatal hand
That hath contrived this woeful tragedy!
In thirteen battles Salisbury o'ercame;
Henry the Fifth he first trained to the wars.
Whilst any trump did sound or drum struck up,
His sword did ne'er leave striking in the field.   81
Yet liv'st thou, Salisbury? Though thy speech doth fail,
One eye thou hast to look to heaven for grace.
The sun with one eye vieweth all the world.
Heaven, be thou gracious to none alive
If Salisbury wants mercy at thy hands!   86
Sir Thomas Gargrave, hast thou any life?

64 express precise **65 battery** attack **67 bulwark** fortification (protect-
ing the bridge) **68 must be famished** will have to be reduced to famine **69 s.d. Here they shoot** i.e., the French. (Probably offstage, though
the Boy's appearance with the linstock at l. 56 visually symbolizes the
action of preparing to fire.) **72 chance** misfortune. **crossed** afflicted
74 mirror of example to **81 leave** leave off **86 wants** lacks

Speak unto Talbot. Nay, look up to him.—
Bear hence his body; I will help to bury it.
                         [*Gargrave's body is borne off.*]
Salisbury, cheer thy spirit with this comfort;
Thou shalt not die whiles—
He beckons with his hand and smiles on me,
As who should say "When I am dead and gone,   93
Remember to avenge me on the French."
Plantagenet, I will; and Nero-like   95
Play on the lute, beholding the towns burn.
Wretched shall France be only in my name.   97
          Here an alarum, and it thunders and lightens.
What stir is this? What tumult's in the heavens?
Whence cometh this alarum and the noise?

          Enter a Messenger.

MESSENGER
My lord, my lord, the French have gathered head!   100
The Dauphin, with one Joan la Pucelle joined,
A holy prophetess new risen up,
Is come with a great power to raise the siege.   103
          Here Salisbury lifteth himself up and groans.
TALBOT
Hear, hear how dying Salisbury doth groan!
It irks his heart he cannot be revenged.
Frenchmen, I'll be a Salisbury to you.
Pucelle or pussel, Dauphin or dogfish,   107
Your hearts I'll stamp out with my horse's heels
And make a quagmire of your mingled brains.
Convey me Salisbury into his tent,   110
And then we'll try what these dastard Frenchmen dare.
          Alarum. Exeunt, [bearing out Salisbury].

---

93 As who as one who   **95 Plantagenet** (The Earl of Salisbury was
Thomas Montacute; he was descended from the Plantagenet Edward I.)   **Nero-like** (Talbot is being compared to Nero, who played
music while Rome burned.)   **97 only in** at the mere sound of
100 gathered head drawn their forces together   **103 power** army
107 pussel drab, slut. (A punning spelling variant of *pucelle*, maid.)
Dauphin (The normal Folio Elizabethan spelling of Dauphin is *Dolphin*.
The sea mammal by that name is included in the meaning and is contrasted with *dogfish*, a very low form of sealife.)   **110 me** for my benefit. (*Me* is used colloquially.)

1.5 *Here an alarum again, and Talbot pursueth the*
Dauphin and driveth him. Then enter Joan la
Pucelle, driving Englishmen before her [and
exit after them]. Then enter [again] Talbot.

TALBOT
  Where is my strength, my valor, and my force?
  Our English troops retire; I cannot stay them;   2
  A woman clad in armor chaseth them.

        Enter [Joan la] Pucelle.

  Here, here she comes.—I'll have a bout with thee;   4
  Devil or devil's dam, I'll conjure thee.   5
  Blood will I draw on thee—thou art a witch—   6
  And straightway give thy soul to him thou serv'st.   7
PUCELLE
  Come, come, 'tis only I that must disgrace thee.
                              Here they fight.

TALBOT
  Heavens, can you suffer hell so to prevail?
  My breast I'll burst with straining of my courage
  And from my shoulders crack my arms asunder,
  But I will chastise this high-minded strumpet.   12
                              They fight again.

PUCELLE
  Talbot, farewell. Thy hour is not yet come.
  I must go victual Orleans forthwith.   14
                    A short alarum. Then enter the
                              town with soldiers.
  O'ertake me if thou canst! I scorn thy strength.
  Go, go, cheer up thy hungry starvèd men;
  Help Salisbury to make his testament.
  This day is ours, as many more shall be.   *Exit.*
TALBOT
  My thoughts are whirlèd like a potter's wheel;

1.5. Location: Scene continues at Orleans.
2 stay halt   **4 bout** encounter in the fighting (but with sexual overtones)
5 dam dame, mother   **6 Blood . . . witch** (Anyone who succeeded in
drawing blood from a witch was thought to be invulnerable to her
magic.)   **7 him** i.e., the devil   **12 But I will** if I do not.   **high-minded**
arrogant   **14 victual** supply with provisions   **s.d. enter** i.e., they, the
French, enter Orleans; Joan follows four lines later

I know not where I am nor what I do.
A witch by fear, not force, like Hannibal   21
Drives back our troops and conquers as she lists.   22
So bees with smoke and doves with noisome stench   23
Are from their hives and houses driven away.
They called us, for our fierceness, English dogs;
Now, like to whelps, we crying run away.
                                    A short alarum.
Hark, countrymen! Either renew the fight
Or tear the lions out of England's coat!   28
Renounce your soil; give sheep in lions' stead.   29
Sheep run not half so treacherous from the wolf,   30
Or horse or oxen from the leopard,
As you fly from your oft-subduèd slaves.
                          Alarum. Here another skirmish.
It will not be. Retire into your trenches.   33
You all consented unto Salisbury's death,
For none would strike a stroke in his revenge.   35
Pucelle is entered into Orleans
In spite of us or aught that we could do.
O, would I were to die with Salisbury!
The shame hereof will make me hide my head.   39
                          Exit Talbot. Alarum. Retreat.

1.6   *Flourish. Enter, on the walls, Pucelle, Dauphin*
           [Charles], Reignier, Alençon, and soldiers.

PUCELLE
Advance our waving colors on the walls;   1

---

21 Hannibal Carthaginian general who once repulsed a Roman army by
tying firebrands to the horns of a herd of oxen and driving the animals
toward the Romans   **22 lists** pleases   **23 noisome** noxious   **28 lions . . .
coat** i.e., the three lions passant displayed in the English coat of arms
29 soil country (?) disgrace (?)   **give** display (on coat of arms)
30 treacherous i.e., cowardly   **33 It will not be** i.e., it's hopeless   **35 his
revenge** revenge of him   **39 s.d. Retreat** trumpet call to signal a withdrawal from the attack

1.6. Location: Scene continues at Orleans.
s.d. on the walls i.e., in the gallery backstage, above the main doors of
the tiring-house facade. (When Joan enters Orleans in 1.5, she enters the
tiring-house through one of its doors, and that tiring-house facade
remains the visual equivalent of the walls of Orleans through 2.1.)
1 Advance lift up

Rescued is Orleans from the English!
Thus Joan la Pucelle hath performed her word.

CHARLES
Divinest creature, Astraea's daughter,   4
How shall I honor thee for this success?
Thy promises are like Adonis' garden,   6
That one day bloomed and fruitful were the next.
France, triumph in thy glorious prophetess!
Recovered is the town of Orleans.
More blessèd hap did ne'er befall our state.   10

REIGNIER
Why ring not out the bells aloud throughout the town?
Dauphin, command the citizens make bonfires
And feast and banquet in the open streets
To celebrate the joy that God hath given us.

ALENÇON
All France will be replete with mirth and joy
When they shall hear how we have played the men.

CHARLES
'Tis Joan, not we, by whom the day is won;
For which I will divide my crown with her,
And all the priests and friars in my realm
Shall in procession sing her endless praise.
A statelier pyramid to her I'll rear
Than Rhodope's of Memphis ever was.   22
In memory of her when she is dead,
Her ashes, in an urn more precious
Than the rich-jeweled coffer of Darius,   25
Transported shall be at high festivals
Before the kings and queens of France.
No longer on Saint Denis will we cry,   28
But Joan la Pucelle shall be France's saint.
Come in, and let us banquet royally
After this golden day of victory.   *Flourish. Exeunt.*

✦

4 Astraea goddess of Justice **6 Adonis' garden** mythical garden of
eternal fecundity **10 hap** event **22 Rhodope** a Greek courtesan who
became the wife of the King of Egypt. (A legend was current that she
built the third pyramid.) **Memphis** an ancient city of Egypt near which
stand the pyramids of Ramses II **25 Darius** King of Persia conquered
by Alexander the Great. Alexander, according to legend, used Darius'
rich-jeweled coffer to carry about the poems of Homer. **28 on** in the
name of. **Saint Denis** patron saint of France

2.1   *Enter [on the walls] a [French] Sergeant of a band, with two Sentinels.*

SERGEANT
  Sirs, take your places and be vigilant.
  If any noise or soldier you perceive
  Near to the walls, by some apparent sign   3
  Let us have knowledge at the court of guard.   4
FIRST SENTINEL
  Sergeant, you shall. [*Exit Sergeant.*] Thus are poor
    servitors,   5
  When others sleep upon their quiet beds,   6
  Constrained to watch in darkness, rain, and cold.   7

    Enter Talbot, Bedford, and Burgundy, [and forces,] with scaling ladders.

TALBOT
  Lord Regent, and redoubted Burgundy,
  By whose approach the regions of Artois,   9
  Walloon, and Picardy are friends to us,
  This happy night the Frenchmen are secure,   11
  Having all day caroused and banqueted.
  Embrace we then this opportunity
  As fitting best to quittance their deceit,   14
  Contrived by art and baleful sorcery.   15
BEDFORD
  Coward of France, how much he wrongs his fame,   16
  Despairing of his own arm's fortitude,
  To join with witches and the help of hell!
BURGUNDY
  Traitors have never other company.
  But what's that Pucelle whom they term so pure?

2.1. **Location:** Before Orleans, as in the previous scenes; the time is later that night.
s.d. band detachment of soldiers   **3 apparent** plain   **4 court of guard** guardhouse   **5 servitors** soldiers   **6 upon their quiet beds** quietly in their beds   **7 s.d. Burgundy** the Duke of Burgundy, allied to the English by the Treaty of Troyes, 1420. (His support brought with it the cooperation of territories near to Burgundy, in the Low Countries, such as Walloon and Picardy.)   **9 By whose approach** by means of whose joining our alliance   **11 secure** overconfident   **14 quittance** requite   **15 art** i.e., black magic   **16 Coward of France** i.e., the Dauphin.   **fame** reputation

TALBOT
　A maid, they say.
BEDFORD　　　　　　　A maid, and be so martial?
BURGUNDY
　Pray God she prove not masculine ere long,　　　　22
　If underneath the standard of the French
　She carry armor as she hath begun.
TALBOT
　Well, let them practice and converse with spirits.
　God is our fortress, in whose conquering name
　Let us resolve to scale their flinty bulwarks.
BEDFORD
　Ascend, brave Talbot. We will follow thee.
TALBOT
　Not all together. Better far, I guess,
　That we do make our entrance several ways,　　　　30
　That, if it chance the one of us do fail,　　　　31
　The other yet may rise against their force.
BEDFORD
　Agreed. I'll to yond corner.
BURGUNDY　　　　　　　　And I to this.
TALBOT
　And here will Talbot mount, or make his grave.
　Now, Salisbury, for thee, and for the right
　Of English Henry, shall this night appear　　　　36
　How much in duty I am bound to both.
FIRST SENTINEL
　Arm, arm! The enemy doth make assault!　　　　38
　　　　　[The English scale the walls, Talbot in the
　　　　　　　center, and exeunt above into the city.]
　　　　　　　　　Cry: "Saint George! A Talbot!"

---

22 prove not masculine i.e., (1) proves not to be so manly after all
(2) proves herself feminine by becoming pregnant. (The bawdy punning
continues in *standard*, "that which stands up," *carry armor*, "bear the
weight of a man," *practice and converse*, "engage in sexual contact,"
etc.)　**30 several ways** i.e., on ladders at different points. (The three
leaders place their ladders against the tiring-house facade, one in the
middle for Talbot and one on each wing, and actually ascend to the
gallery or top of the "walls" where they surprise the French. Some of
the French, thus surprised, leap from the gallery down onto the main
stage, where the Bastard, Alençon, and others consult in a state of
disorder about their situation.)　**31 That** so that　**36 shall** it shall

The French leap o'er the walls in their shirts.
Enter, several ways, [the] Bastard [of Orleans],
Alençon, [and] Reignier, half ready, and half
unready.

ALENÇON
How now, my lords? What, all unready so?

BASTARD
Unready? Ay, and glad we scaped so well.

REIGNIER
'Twas time, I trow, to wake and leave our beds,   41
Hearing alarums at our chamber doors.

ALENÇON
Of all exploits since first I followed arms,
Ne'er heard I of a warlike enterprise
More venturous or desperate than this.

BASTARD
I think this Talbot be a fiend of hell.

REIGNIER
If not of hell, the heavens sure favor him.

ALENÇON
Here cometh Charles. I marvel how he sped.   48

Enter Charles and Joan [la Pucelle].

BASTARD
Tut, holy Joan was his defensive guard.

CHARLES
Is this thy cunning, thou deceitful dame?   50
Didst thou at first, to flatter us withal,   51
Make us partakers of a little gain
That now our loss might be ten times so much?

PUCELLE
Wherefore is Charles impatient with his friend?
At all times will you have my power alike?
Sleeping or waking must I still prevail,   56
Or will you blame and lay the fault on me?

---

38 s.d. unready not fully clothed. (This scene is based on an incident
occurring at Le Mans, a year prior to the siege of Orleans.)   **41 trow**
believe   **48 marvel** wonder.   **sped** fared   **50 cunning** skill   **51 flatter**
lead on with false hopes.   **withal** with it   **56 still prevail** always
succeed

Improvident soldiers! Had your watch been good,
This sudden mischief never could have fallen.

CHARLES
Duke of Alençon, this was your default,   60
That, being captain of the watch tonight,   61
Did look no better to that weighty charge.   62

ALENÇON
Had all your quarters been as safely kept
As that whereof I had the government,
We had not been thus shamefully surprised.

BASTARD
Mine was secure.

REIGNIER   And so was mine, my lord.

CHARLES
And, for myself, most part of all this night
Within her quarter and mine own precinct   68
I was employed in passing to and fro
About relieving of the sentinels.
Then how or which way should they first break in?

PUCELLE
Question, my lords, no further of the case,
How or which way. 'Tis sure they found some place
But weakly guarded, where the breach was made.
And now there rests no other shift but this: 75
To gather our soldiers, scattered and dispersed,
And lay new platforms to endamage them.   77

*Alarum. Enter a[n English] Soldier, crying "A
Talbot! A Talbot!" They fly, leaving their clothes
behind.*

SOLDIER
I'll be so bold to take what they have left.
The cry of "Talbot" serves me for a sword,
For I have loaden me with many spoils,   80
Using no other weapon but his name.
                              Exit, [bearing spoils].

✣

60 default failure   61 tonight i.e., this previous night   62 charge responsibility   68 her i.e., Joan's (with a bawdy suggestion, continued in
passing to and fro, l. 69)   75 rests remains.   shift strategy   77 platforms plans   80 loaden me laden myself

2.2 *Enter Talbot, Bedford, Burgundy, [a Captain,*
       and others].

BEDFORD
  The day begins to break, and night is fled,
  Whose pitchy mantle overveiled the earth.   2
  Here sound retreat and cease our hot pursuit.
                              Retreat [sounded].

TALBOT
  Bring forth the body of old Salisbury
  And here advance it in the marketplace,   5
  The middle center of this cursèd town.

      [*Enter a funeral procession with Salisbury's*
      body,] *their drums beating a dead march.*

  Now have I paid my vow unto his soul;
  For every drop of blood was drawn from him   8
  There hath at least five Frenchmen died tonight.
  And that hereafter ages may behold
  What ruin happened in revenge of him,
  Within their chiefest temple I'll erect
  A tomb, wherein his corpse shall be interred;
  Upon the which, that everyone may read,
  Shall be engraved the sack of Orleans,
  The treacherous manner of his mournful death,
  And what a terror he had been to France.
                         [*Exit funeral procession.*]
  But, lords, in all our bloody massacre,
  I muse we met not with the Dauphin's grace,   19
  His new-come champion, virtuous Joan of Arc,   20
  Nor any of his false confederates.

BEDFORD
  'Tis thought, Lord Talbot, when the fight began,
  Roused on the sudden from their drowsy beds,
  They did amongst the troops of armèd men
  Leap o'er the walls for refuge in the field.

2.2. **Location: Orleans. Within the town.**
2 pitchy i.e., pitch black   **5 advance** raise aloft (on a bier)   **8 was** that
was   **19 muse** wonder.   **the Dauphin's grace** His Grace the Dauphin
20 virtuous (Said ironically.)

BURGUNDY
Myself, as far as I could well discern
For smoke and dusky vapors of the night,
Am sure I scared the Dauphin and his trull,   28
When arm in arm they both came swiftly running,
Like to a pair of loving turtledoves
That could not live asunder day or night.
After that things are set in order here,
We'll follow them with all the power we have.

Enter a Messenger.

MESSENGER
All hail, my lords! Which of this princely train
Call ye the warlike Talbot, for his acts
So much applauded through the realm of France?

TALBOT
Here is the Talbot. Who would speak with him?

MESSENGER
The virtuous lady, Countess of Auvergne,
With modesty admiring thy renown,
By me entreats, great lord, thou wouldst vouchsafe
To visit her poor castle where she lies,   41
That she may boast she hath beheld the man
Whose glory fills the world with loud report.   43

BURGUNDY
Is it even so? Nay, then, I see our wars
Will turn unto a peaceful comic sport,
When ladies crave to be encountered with.   46
You may not, my lord, despise her gentle suit.   47

TALBOT
Ne'er trust me, then; for when a world of men
Could not prevail with all their oratory,
Yet hath a woman's kindness overruled.   50
And therefore tell her I return great thanks,
And in submission will attend on her.
Will not your honors bear me company?

---

28 trull strumpet (i.e., Joan)   **41 lies** dwells   **43 report** (1) acclaim
(2) noise of battle   **46 encountered with** i.e., encountered socially, as an
adversary in the battle of the sexes, and as the object of wooing
47 gentle gracious, courteous   **50 overruled** prevailed

BEDFORD

  No, truly, 'tis more than manners will;   54
  And I have heard it said unbidden guests
  Are often welcomest when they are gone.

TALBOT

  Well then, alone, since there's no remedy,
  I mean to prove this lady's courtesy.   58
  Come hither, Captain. (*Whispers.*) You perceive my
    mind?

CAPTAIN

  I do, my lord, and mean accordingly.   *Exeunt.* 60

❧

2.3   *Enter [the] Countess [and her Porter].*

COUNTESS

  Porter, remember what I gave in charge,   1
  And when you have done so, bring the keys to me.

PORTER Madam, I will.   *Exit.*

COUNTESS

  The plot is laid. If all things fall out right,
  I shall as famous be by this exploit
  As Scythian Tomyris by Cyrus' death.   6
  Great is the rumor of this dreadful knight,   7
  And his achievements of no less account.
  Fain would mine eyes be witness with mine ears,
  To give their censure of these rare reports.   10

    Enter Messenger and Talbot.

MESSENGER Madam,
  According as your ladyship desired,
  By message craved, so is Lord Talbot come.

COUNTESS

  And he is welcome. What? Is this the man?

---

54 will require, allow **58 prove** test **60 mean** i.e., intend to act

2.3. Location: Auvergne. The Countess's castle.
1 gave in charge commanded **6 Scythian Tomyris** tribal queen of the
Massagetae, who slew Cyrus the Great when he invaded her territory
and, in revenge for her son's death, had the head of Cyrus placed in a
wineskin filled with blood **7 rumor** reputation. **dreadful** inspiring
dread **10 censure** judgment. **rare** remarkable

MESSENGER
  Madam, it is.
COUNTESS   Is this the scourge of France?
  Is this the Talbot, so much feared abroad   16
  That with his name the mothers still their babes?   17
  I see report is fabulous and false.
  I thought I should have seen some Hercules,   19
  A second Hector, for his grim aspect   20
  And large proportion of his strong-knit limbs.   21
  Alas, this is a child, a silly dwarf!   22
  It cannot be this weak and writhled shrimp   23
  Should strike such terror to his enemies.

TALBOT
  Madam, I have been bold to trouble you;
  But since your ladyship is not at leisure,
  I'll sort some other time to visit you.   [*Going.*] 27
COUNTESS
  What means he now? Go ask him whither he goes.

MESSENGER
  Stay, my Lord Talbot, for my lady craves
  To know the cause of your abrupt departure.

TALBOT
  Marry, for that she's in a wrong belief,   31
  I go to certify her Talbot's here.   32

        Enter Porter with keys.

COUNTESS
  If thou be he, then art thou prisoner.

TALBOT
  Prisoner? To whom?
COUNTESS   To me, bloodthirsty lord;
  And for that cause I trained thee to my house.   35
  Long time thy shadow hath been thrall to me,   36
  For in my gallery thy picture hangs;

---

16 abroad everywhere   **17 still** quiet   **19–20 Hercules, Hector** (Types of
great physical strength.)   **21 proportion** size   **22 silly** i.e., frail, mere
23 writhled wrinkled   **27 sort** choose   **31 Marry** (A mild interjection;
originally an oath, "by the Virgin Mary.")   **for that** because   **32 I
go . . . here** i.e., I leave as a way of informing her that I am the real
Talbot, not the legendary figure of popular report   **35 trained** lured,
enticed   **36 shadow** image, likeness.   **thrall** enslaved

But now the substance shall endure the like,
And I will chain these legs and arms of thine
That hast by tyranny these many years   40
Wasted our country, slain our citizens,
And sent our sons and husbands captivate.   42

TALBOT   Ha, ha, ha!

COUNTESS
Laughest thou, wretch? Thy mirth shall turn to moan.

TALBOT
I laugh to see your ladyship so fond   45
To think that you have aught but Talbot's shadow
Whereon to practice your severity.

COUNTESS   Why, art not thou the man?

TALBOT   I am indeed.

COUNTESS   Then have I substance too.

TALBOT
No, no, I am but shadow of myself.
You are deceived. My substance is not here;
For what you see is but the smallest part
And least proportion of humanity.   54
I tell you, madam, were the whole frame here,   55
It is of such a spacious lofty pitch   56
Your roof were not sufficient to contain 't.

COUNTESS
This is a riddling merchant for the nonce!   58
He will be here, and yet he is not here.
How can these contrarieties agree?

TALBOT
That will I show you presently.   61

   *Winds his horn. Drums strike up. A peal of
   ordnance. Enter soldiers.*

How say you, madam? Are you now persuaded
That Talbot is but shadow of himself?
These are his substance, sinews, arms, and strength,
With which he yoketh your rebellious necks,

---

40 tyranny cruelty   **42 captivate** taken captive   **45 fond** foolish
54 proportion of humanity (1) part of the whole man (2) portion of my
army   **55 frame** structure, construct, i.e., of man and of the army
56 pitch height   **58 riddling merchant** dealer in riddles.   **nonce** occasion   **61 presently** immediately   **s.d. Winds** sounds

Razeth your cities, and subverts your towns,   66
And in a moment makes them desolate.

COUNTESS
Victorious Talbot, pardon my abuse.   68
I find thou art no less than fame hath bruited,   69
And more than may be gathered by thy shape.
Let my presumption not provoke thy wrath,
For I am sorry that with reverence
I did not entertain thee as thou art.   73

TALBOT
Be not dismayed, fair lady, nor misconster   74
The mind of Talbot, as you did mistake
The outward composition of his body.
What you have done hath not offended me;
Nor other satisfaction do I crave
But only, with your patience, that we may   79
Taste of your wine and see what cates you have;   80
For soldiers' stomachs always serve them well.   81

COUNTESS
With all my heart, and think me honorèd
To feast so great a warrior in my house.   *Exeunt.*

✦

2.4   *Enter Richard Plantagenet, Warwick, Somerset,*
          [William de la] Pole, [Earl of Suffolk, Vernon],
          and others [including a Lawyer].

PLANTAGENET
Great lords and gentlemen, what means this silence?
Dare no man answer in a case of truth?

---

66 subverts overthrows   **68 abuse** (1) error (2) deception   **69 fame**
report.   **bruited** reported, rumored   **73 entertain** receive   **74 misconster** misconstrue   **79 patience** permission   **80 cates** delicacies, dainty
confections   **81 stomachs** (1) appetites (2) bravery

**2.4. Location: London. The Temple Garden, with rosebushes. (The
Temple was a district of London taking its name from the Knights
Templars, who owned it during the twelfth and thirteenth centuries. Its
buildings were converted into Inns of Court, housing the legal societies
of London, including the Inner Temple and the Middle Temple, in the
fourteenth century.)**

SUFFOLK
 Within the Temple hall we were too loud.   3
 The garden here is more convenient.

PLANTAGENET
 Then say at once if I maintained the truth;
 Or else was wrangling Somerset in th' error?   6

SUFFOLK
 Faith, I have been a truant in the law   7
 And never yet could frame my will to it,   8
 And therefore frame the law unto my will.

SOMERSET
 Judge you, my lord of Warwick, then, between us.

WARWICK
 Between two hawks, which flies the higher pitch,   11
 Between two dogs, which hath the deeper mouth,   12
 Between two blades, which bears the better temper,
 Between two horses, which doth bear him best,   14
 Between two girls, which hath the merriest eye,
 I have perhaps some shallow spirit of judgment;
 But in these nice sharp quillets of the law,   17
 Good faith, I am no wiser than a daw.   18

PLANTAGENET
 Tut, tut, here is a mannerly forbearance.   19
 The truth appears so naked on my side
 That any purblind eye may find it out.   21

SOMERSET
 And on my side it is so well appareled,
 So clear, so shining, and so evident,
 That it will glimmer through a blind man's eye.

PLANTAGENET
 Since you are tongue-tied and so loath to speak,
 In dumb significants proclaim your thoughts.   26
 Let him that is a trueborn gentleman
 And stands upon the honor of his birth,

3 **were** would have been   6 **Or else** i.e., in other words (?) (Or Plantagenet may be saying, ll. 5–6, with intended humor, Am I right or is Somerset wrong?)   7 **a truant** a neglectful student   8 **frame** adapt   11 **pitch** elevation in flight   12 **mouth** voice   14 **bear him** carry himself   17 **nice** subtle, precise.   **quillets** subtle distinctions   18 **daw** jackdaw. (A type of foolishness.)   19 **here . . . forbearance** (Plantagenet sardonically deplores this offering of polite excuses.)   21 **purblind** dimsighted   26 **dumb significants** silent tokens, signs

If he suppose that I have pleaded truth,   29
From off this brier pluck a white rose with me.   30
                    [*He plucks a white rose.*]

SOMERSET
  Let him that is no coward nor no flatterer,
  But dare maintain the party of the truth,   32
  Pluck a red rose from off this thorn with me.   33
        [*He plucks a red rose. The others similarly
                      pluck roses as they speak.*]

WARWICK
  I love no colors, and without all color   34
  Of base insinuating flattery
  I pluck this white rose with Plantagenet.   36

SUFFOLK
  I pluck this red rose with young Somerset
  And say withal I think he held the right.   38

VERNON
  Stay, lords and gentlemen, and pluck no more
  Till you conclude that he upon whose side
  The fewest roses are cropped from the tree
  Shall yield the other in the right opinion.   42

SOMERSET
  Good Master Vernon, it is well objected.   43
  If I have fewest, I subscribe in silence.   44

PLANTAGENET And I.

VERNON
  Then, for the truth and plainness of the case,
  I pluck this pale and maiden blossom here,
  Giving my verdict on the white rose side.

SOMERSET
  Prick not your finger as you pluck it off,

---

29 pleaded argued. (One of many legal terms occurring throughout this
scene.)   **30 white rose** badge of the Mortimers and subsequently of the
house of York   **32 party** side (in law)   **33 red rose** badge of the house of
Lancaster   **34 colors** pretexts   **36 Plantagenet** (The nickname of Geoffrey of Anjou, founder of the Angevin dynasty, which ruled England
from the reign of Geoffrey's son, Henry II, to that of Richard III. None
of Geoffrey's descendants assumed the name until Richard, Duke of
York, adopted it in order to proclaim his superior right to the crown.)
38 withal besides   **42 yield** concede. (Another legal term, like *objected*
and *subscribe* in the following two lines and *verdict* in l. 48.)
43 objected urged   **44 subscribe** submit

Lest, bleeding, you do paint the white rose red,
And fall on my side so against your will.

VERNON
If I, my lord, for my opinion bleed,
Opinion shall be surgeon to my hurt   53
And keep me on the side where still I am.

SOMERSET   Well, well, come on, who else?

LAWYER [*To Somerset*]
Unless my study and my books be false,
The argument you held was wrong in law;
In sign whereof I pluck a white rose too.

PLANTAGENET
Now, Somerset, where is your argument?

SOMERSET
Here in my scabbard, meditating that   60
Shall dye your white rose in a bloody red.

PLANTAGENET
Meantime your cheeks do counterfeit our roses;   62
For pale they look with fear, as witnessing
The truth on our side.

SOMERSET   No, Plantagenet,
'Tis not for fear, but anger, that thy cheeks
Blush for pure shame to counterfeit our roses,
And yet thy tongue will not confess thy error.

PLANTAGENET
Hath not thy rose a canker, Somerset?   68

SOMERSET
Hath not thy rose a thorn, Plantagenet?

PLANTAGENET
Ay, sharp and piercing, to maintain his truth,   70
Whiles thy consuming canker eats his falsehood.

SOMERSET
Well, I'll find friends to wear my bleeding roses
That shall maintain what I have said is true,
Where false Plantagenet dare not be seen.

---

53 Opinion public opinion, i.e., my reputation (punning on *opinion* in
the sense of "conviction" in the previous line)   **60 that** that which
62 counterfeit imitate   **68 canker** cankerworm (that feeds on buds)
70 his its (also in l. 71)

PLANTAGENET
Now, by this maiden blossom in my hand,
I scorn thee and thy fashion, peevish boy.   76
SUFFOLK
Turn not thy scorns this way, Plantagenet.
PLANTAGENET
Proud Pole, I will, and scorn both him and thee.   78
SUFFOLK
I'll turn my part thereof into thy throat.   79
SOMERSET
Away, away, good William de la Pole!
We grace the yeoman by conversing with him.   81
WARWICK
Now, by God's will, thou wrong'st him, Somerset.
His grandfather was Lionel, Duke of Clarence,   83
Third son to the third Edward, King of England.
Spring crestless yeomen from so deep a root?   85
PLANTAGENET
He bears him on the place's privilege,   86
Or durst not, for his craven heart, say thus.
SOMERSET
By him that made me, I'll maintain my words
On any plot of ground in Christendom.
Was not thy father, Richard, Earl of Cambridge,
For treason executed in our late king's days?   91

---

76 fashion sort, or, the fashion of wearing red roses. **peevish** silly
78 Pole family name of the Duke of Suffolk. (See also l. 80.) **79 I'll . . .
throat** I'll throw the lies or slanders back into the throat from which
they proceeded **81 grace** do honor to. **yeoman** a small freeholder,
below the rank of landed gentleman. (A jibe at Plantagenet for having
lost his lands and titles when his father, Richard, Earl of Cambridge,
was executed in 1415 by Henry V for treason.) **83 His . . . Clarence**
(Lionel was actually Richard's maternal great-great-grandfather; but
Edmund, Duke of York, fifth son of Edward III, was his paternal grandfather. Richard thus could trace his descent from Edward III through
both Lionel and Edmund.) **85 crestless** lacking heraldic titles (with a
suggestion also of cowardice) **86 He . . . privilege** i.e., Somerset presumes upon the safety of a privileged place (since engaging in quarrels
with drawn weapons was prohibited in certain precincts including the
official residences of the sovereign; in fact, however, the Inns of Court
were not thus privileged) **91 late king's** i.e., Henry V's

And by his treason stand'st not thou attainted,   92
Corrupted, and exempt from ancient gentry?   93
His trespass yet lives guilty in thy blood,
And till thou be restored, thou art a yeoman.

PLANTAGENET
My father was attachèd, not attainted,   96
Condemned to die for treason, but no traitor;
And that I'll prove on better men than Somerset,
Were growing time once ripened to my will.   99
For your partaker Pole, and you yourself,   100
I'll note you in my book of memory
To scourge you for this apprehension.   102
Look to it well, and say you are well warned.

SOMERSET
Ah, thou shalt find us ready for thee still,   104
And know us by these colors for thy foes,   105
For these my friends in spite of thee shall wear.

PLANTAGENET
And, by my soul, this pale and angry rose,
As cognizance of my blood-drinking hate,   108
Will I forever, and my faction, wear
Until it wither with me to my grave
Or flourish to the height of my degree.   111

SUFFOLK
Go forward, and be choked with thy ambition!
And so farewell until I meet thee next.   *Exit.*

SOMERSET
Have with thee, Pole. Farewell, ambitious Richard.   114
                                                Exit.

PLANTAGENET
How I am braved and must perforce endure it!   115

---

92 attainted convicted and condemned. (According to law, the heirs of a
person so attainted were deprived of all the rights and titles of their
forebears; their blood was pronounced *corrupted*.)   **93 exempt** excluded.   **ancient gentry** hereditary rank   **96 attachèd, not attainted**
(Historically, as Plantagenet insists, his father was *attached*, i.e., arrested, and summarily executed for treason without a bill of attain-
der.)   **99 Were . . . will** i.e., if the unfolding of time provides
me opportunity   **100 For your partaker** as for your supporter
102 apprehension conception   **104 still** always   **105 know . . . foes** i.e.,
recognize us by these red badges as your enemies   **108 cognizance**
badge   **111 degree** noble rank   **114 Have with thee** let us go
115 braved defied.   **perforce** necessarily

WARWICK
  This blot that they object against your house   116
  Shall be wiped out in the next parliament,
  Called for the truce of Winchester and Gloucester;   118
  And if thou be not then created York,
  I will not live to be accounted Warwick.
  Meantime, in signal of my love to thee,   121
  Against proud Somerset and William Pole,
  Will I upon thy party wear this rose.
  And here I prophesy: this brawl today,
  Grown to this faction in the Temple Garden,
  Shall send, between the red rose and the white,
  A thousand souls to death and deadly night.
PLANTAGENET
  Good Master Vernon, I am bound to you
  That you on my behalf would pluck a flower.
VERNON
  In your behalf still will I wear the same.
LAWYER   And so will I.
PLANTAGENET   Thanks, gentlemen.
  Come, let us four to dinner. I dare say
  This quarrel will drink blood another day.   *Exeunt.*

✚

2.5   *Enter Mortimer, brought in a chair, and Jailers.*

MORTIMER
  Kind keepers of my weak decaying age,
  Let dying Mortimer here rest himself.
  Even like a man new-halèd from the rack,
  So fare my limbs with long imprisonment;
  And these gray locks, the pursuivants of death,   5
  Nestor-like agèd in an age of care,   6
  Argue the end of Edmund Mortimer.   7

---

116 object urge, allege   **118 Called . . . of** assembled to make peace
between   **121 signal** token

2.5. Location: The Tower of London.
5 pursuivants heralds   **6 Nestor-like** i.e., extremely old. (Nestor, the
oldest of the Greek chieftains at the siege of Troy, came to represent a
type of old age.)   **7 Argue** portend

These eyes, like lamps whose wasting oil is spent,
Wax dim, as drawing to their exigent;   9
Weak shoulders, overborne with burdening grief,
And pithless arms, like to a withered vine   11
That droops his sapless branches to the ground.
Yet are these feet, whose strengthless stay is numb,   13
Unable to support this lump of clay,
Swift-wingèd with desire to get a grave,
As witting I no other comfort have.   16
But tell me, keeper, will my nephew come?   17

FIRST KEEPER
Richard Plantagenet, my lord, will come.
We sent unto the Temple, unto his chamber,
And answer was returned that he will come.

MORTIMER
Enough. My soul shall then be satisfied.
Poor gentleman, his wrong doth equal mine.   22
Since Henry Monmouth first began to reign,   23
Before whose glory I was great in arms,
This loathsome sequestration have I had;   25
And even since then hath Richard been obscured,
Deprived of honor and inheritance.
But now the arbitrator of despairs,   28
Just Death, kind umpire of men's miseries,
With sweet enlargement doth dismiss me hence.   30
I would his troubles likewise were expired,   31
That so he might recover what was lost.

Enter Richard [Plantagenet].

9 **exigent** end   11 **pithless** marrowless, weak   13 **stay** support   16 **As
witting** as if knowing   17 **nephew** (Richard was son of the fifth Earl of
March's sister, Anne Mortimer, who married Richard, Earl of Cambridge.)   22 **his wrong** i.e., the wrong done him   23 **Henry Monmouth**
i.e., Henry V   25 **sequestration** imprisonment. (Shakespeare, following
the chroniclers, confuses Edmund Mortimer, fifth Earl of March and
great-grandson of Lionel, Duke of Clarence, hence potential heir to the
throne, with his uncle Sir Edmund Mortimer, who was imprisoned by
Glendower, and also with the Earl of March's cousin Sir John Mortimer,
who was imprisoned and finally executed for agitating in behalf of
Edmund's royal claim. The Earl of March remained loyal to Henry V.)
28 **arbitrator** bringer about of a definite issue   30 **enlargement** release
from confinement   31 **his** i.e., Richard's

FIRST KEEPER
My lord, your loving nephew now is come.

MORTIMER
Richard Plantagenet, my friend, is he come?

PLANTAGENET
Ay, noble uncle, thus ignobly used,
Your nephew, late despisèd Richard, comes.   36

MORTIMER
Direct mine arms I may embrace his neck   37
And in his bosom spend my latter gasp.   38
O, tell me when my lips do touch his cheeks,
That I may kindly give one fainting kiss.
                         [*He embraces Richard.*]
And now declare, sweet stem from York's great stock,
Why didst thou say of late thou wert despised?

PLANTAGENET
First, lean thine agèd back against mine arm,
And, in that ease, I'll tell thee my disease.   44
This day, in argument upon a case,
Some words there grew twixt Somerset and me;
Among which terms he used his lavish tongue
And did upbraid me with my father's death;
Which obloquy set bars before my tongue,
Else with the like I had requited him.
Therefore, good uncle, for my father's sake,
In honor of a true Plantagenet,
And for alliance' sake, declare the cause   53
My father, Earl of Cambridge, lost his head.

MORTIMER
That cause, fair nephew, that imprisoned me
And hath detained me all my flowering youth
Within a loathsome dungeon, there to pine,
Was cursèd instrument of his decease.

PLANTAGENET
Discover more at large what cause that was,   59
For I am ignorant and cannot guess.

36 late lately   **37 I may** so that I may   **38 latter** last   **44 disease** unease, trouble, grievance   **53 alliance'** kinship's   **59 Discover** make known.   **at large** at length

MORTIMER
   I will, if that my fading breath permit
   And death approach not ere my tale be done.
   Henry the Fourth, grandfather to this king,
   Deposed his nephew Richard, Edward's son,   64
   The first-begotten and the lawful heir
   Of Edward king, the third of that descent;
   During whose reign the Percys of the north,   67
   Finding his usurpation most unjust,
   Endeavored my advancement to the throne.
   The reason moved these warlike lords to this   70
   Was for that—young King Richard thus removed,   71
   Leaving no heir begotten of his body—
   I was the next by birth and parentage;
   For by my mother I derivèd am   74
   From Lionel, Duke of Clarence, third son
   To King Edward the Third; whereas he   76
   From John of Gaunt doth bring his pedigree,
   Being but fourth of that heroic line.
   But mark. As in this haughty great attempt   79
   They laborèd to plant the rightful heir,
   I lost my liberty and they their lives.
   Long after this, when Henry the Fifth,
   Succeeding his father Bolingbroke, did reign,
   Thy father, Earl of Cambridge, then derived
   From famous Edmund Langley, Duke of York,
   Marrying my sister that thy mother was,
   Again, in pity of my hard distress,
   Levied an army, weening to redeem   88
   And have installed me in the diadem.   89
   But, as the rest, so fell that noble earl
   And was beheaded. Thus the Mortimers,
   In whom the title rested, were suppressed.
PLANTAGENET
   Of which, my lord, your honor is the last.

---

64 nephew kinsman. (Here, cousin.)　**67 whose** i.e., Henry IV's
70 moved i.e., that moved　**71 for that** that　**74 mother** (Shakespeare
appears to confuse this Edmund with his uncle, Edmund Mortimer,
second son of Lionel's daughter Philippa.)　**76 he** i.e., Henry VI, or
perhaps Henry IV. (See l. 63.)　**79 haughty** proud　**88 weening** thinking　**89 installed . . . diadem** crowned me king

MORTIMER

True, and thou seest that I no issue have,
And that my fainting words do warrant death.   95
Thou art my heir. The rest I wish thee gather;   96
But yet be wary in thy studious care.   97

PLANTAGENET

Thy grave admonishments prevail with me.
But yet methinks my father's execution
Was nothing less than bloody tyranny.

MORTIMER

With silence, nephew, be thou politic.
Strong-fixèd is the house of Lancaster
And like a mountain, not to be removed.
But now thy uncle is removing hence,   104
As princes do their courts, when they are cloyed
With long continuance in a settled place.

PLANTAGENET

O uncle, would some part of my young years
Might but redeem the passage of your age!   108

MORTIMER

Thou dost then wrong me, as that slaughterer doth
Which giveth many wounds when one will kill.
Mourn not, except thou sorrow for my good;   111
Only give order for my funeral.   112
And so farewell, and fair be all thy hopes,
And prosperous be thy life in peace and war!   *Dies.*

PLANTAGENET

And peace, no war, befall thy parting soul!
In prison hast thou spent a pilgrimage
And like a hermit overpassed thy days.   117
Well, I will lock his counsel in my breast,
And what I do imagine, let that rest.   119
Keepers, convey him hence, and I myself
Will see his burial better than his life.

                      Exeunt [Keepers, bearing out
                          the body of Mortimer].

95 warrant promise, assure   **96 gather** infer   **97 studious** diligent
104 removing hence departing from here, i.e., dying   **108 redeem the
passage** buy back the passing   **111 except** unless   **112 give order** make
arrangements   **117 overpassed** passed   **119 let that rest** leave it alone,
i.e., let that be my business

Here dies the dusky torch of Mortimer,
Choked with ambition of the meaner sort.   123
And for those wrongs, those bitter injuries,
Which Somerset hath offered to my house,
I doubt not but with honor to redress;
And therefore haste I to the parliament,
Either to be restorèd to my blood   128
Or make mine ill th' advantage of my good.   *Exit.* 129

✙

123 with by.   **meaner sort** those whose claim to the throne was inferior
to his, i.e., the Lancastrians   **128 blood** hereditary rights   **129 Or . . .**
good or make my wrongs the means of achieving my ambition

3.1 *Flourish. Enter King, Exeter, Gloucester,*
Winchester, Warwick, Somerset, Suffolk,
Richard Plantagenet, [and others]. Gloucester
offers to put up a bill; Winchester snatches it,
[and] tears it.

WINCHESTER
Com'st thou with deep premeditated lines,
With written pamphlets studiously devised?
Humphrey of Gloucester, if thou canst accuse,
Or aught intend'st to lay unto my charge,   4
Do it without invention, suddenly,   5
As I with sudden and extemporal speech
Purpose to answer what thou canst object.   7
GLOUCESTER
Presumptuous priest, this place commands my
    patience,   8
Or thou shouldst find thou hast dishonored me.
Think not, although in writing I preferred   10
The manner of thy vile outrageous crimes,
That therefore I have forged, or am not able
Verbatim to rehearse the method of my pen.   13
No, prelate, such is thy audacious wickedness,
Thy lewd, pestiferous, and dissentious pranks,   15
As very infants prattle of thy pride.   16
Thou art a most pernicious usurer,
Froward by nature, enemy to peace,   18
Lascivious, wanton, more than well beseems
A man of thy profession and degree.
And for thy treachery, what's more manifest?   21
In that thou laidst a trap to take my life,

3.1. Location: London. The Parliament House.
s.d. offers tries, starts.   **bill** (Here, a written accusation.)   **4 lay unto**
my charge charge me with   **5 invention** premeditated design.   **sud-**
denly extempore   **7 object** urge, present   **8 this place** i.e., Parliament,
with the King presiding   **10 preferred** put forward. (See 1.3.34–35 and
note.)   **13 Verbatim . . . pen** orally to recount what I have written
15 lewd wicked.   **pestiferous** deadly   **16 As** that   **18 Froward** perverse   **21 for** as for (also in l. 33)

As well at London Bridge as at the Tower.   23
Besides, I fear me, if thy thoughts were sifted,
The King, thy sovereign, is not quite exempt
From envious malice of thy swelling heart.

WINCHESTER
Gloucester, I do defy thee. Lords, vouchsafe
To give me hearing what I shall reply.
If I were covetous, ambitious, or perverse,
As he will have me, how am I so poor?
Or how haps it I seek not to advance   31
Or raise myself, but keep my wonted calling?   32
And for dissension, who preferreth peace
More than I do, except I be provoked?   34
No, my good lords, it is not that offends;   35
It is not that that hath incensed the Duke.
It is because no one should sway but he,   37
No one but he should be about the King;   38
And that engenders thunder in his breast
And makes him roar these accusations forth.
But he shall know I am as good—

GLOUCESTER   As good?
Thou bastard of my grandfather!   42

WINCHESTER
Ay, lordly sir! For what are you, I pray,
But one imperious in another's throne?   44

GLOUCESTER
Am I not Protector, saucy priest?

WINCHESTER
And am not I a prelate of the Church?

GLOUCESTER
Yes, as an outlaw in a castle keeps   47
And useth it to patronage his theft.   48

---

23 at London Bridge (Gloucester's articles of accusation against Winchester presented to the Parliament stated that the latter had "set men-
of-arms and archers at the end of London Bridge next Southwark," to
prevent Gloucester's going to Eltham to interfere with the Bishop's
plans regarding the young King.)   **31 haps** happens   **32 wonted calling**
customary profession   **34 except** unless   **35 that** that that   **37 sway**
govern   **38 about** near to   **42 Thou bastard** (Winchester—son of John
of Gaunt and Katharine Swynford before their marriage—was, with his
two brothers and one sister, legitimatized by act of Parliament in Richard II's reign.)   **44 imperious** (1) exercising rule (2) domineering
47 keeps dwells   **48 patronage** maintain

WINCHESTER
  Unreverent Gloucester!
GLOUCESTER   Thou art reverend   49
  Touching thy spiritual function, not thy life.   50
WINCHESTER
  Rome shall remedy this.
WARWICK   Roam thither, then.
SOMERSET [*To Warwick*]
  My lord, it were your duty to forbear.   52
WARWICK
  Ay, see the Bishop be not overborne.   53
SOMERSET
  Methinks my lord should be religious   54
  And know the office that belongs to such.   55
WARWICK
  Methinks his lordship should be humbler.
  It fitteth not a prelate so to plead.
SOMERSET
  Yes, when his holy state is touched so near.   58
WARWICK
  State holy or unhallowed, what of that?
  Is not His Grace Protector to the King?   60
PLANTAGENET [*Aside*]
  Plantagenet, I see, must hold his tongue,
  Lest it be said, "Speak, sirrah, when you should;
  Must your bold verdict enter talk with lords?"   63
  Else would I have a fling at Winchester.
KING
  Uncles of Gloucester and of Winchester,
  The special watchmen of our English weal,   66
  I would prevail, if prayers might prevail,
  To join your hearts in love and amity.
  O, what a scandal is it to our crown
  That two such noble peers as ye should jar!   70

49 Unreverent . . . reverend irreverent, hostile to spiritual authority . . .
respected, revered. (The Folio spellings, *Vnreuerent* and *reuerent*, accen-
tuate the wordplay.) **50 Touching . . . function** i.e., in ecclesiastical title
only **52 were** should be **53 overborne** prevailed over **54 my lord** i.e.,
Winchester. **should be** i.e., should be regarded as. (But Warwick, two
lines below, uses the phrase in the sense "ought to be.") **55 office**
duty **58 state** degree, rank. **touched so near** so closely concerned
60 His Grace i.e., Gloucester **63 bold verdict** audacious opinion. **enter
talk** hold conversation **66 weal** common good **70 jar** quarrel

Believe me, lords, my tender years can tell   71
Civil dissension is a viperous worm
That gnaws the bowels of the commonwealth.
        A noise within, "Down with the tawny coats!"
What tumult's this?
WARWICK   An uproar, I dare warrant,
    Begun through malice of the Bishop's men.
                        A noise again, "Stones! Stones!"

        Enter Mayor.

MAYOR
    O my good lords, and virtuous Henry,
    Pity the city of London, pity us!
    The Bishop and the Duke of Gloucester's men,   80
    Forbidden late to carry any weapon,   81
    Have filled their pockets full of pebblestones
    And, banding themselves in contrary parts,   83
    Do pelt so fast at one another's pate
    That many have their giddy brains knocked out.
    Our windows are broke down in every street,
    And we for fear compelled to shut our shops.

        *Enter [Servingmen of both parties], in skirmish,
        with bloody pates.*

KING
    We charge you, on allegiance to ourself,
    To hold your slaughtering hands and keep the peace.
    Pray, uncle Gloucester, mitigate this strife.
FIRST SERVINGMAN   Nay, if we be forbidden stones,
    we'll fall to it with our teeth.
SECOND SERVINGMAN
    Do what ye dare, we are as resolute.   *Skirmish again.*
GLOUCESTER
    You of my household, leave this peevish broil   94
    And set this unaccustomed fight aside.   95
THIRD SERVINGMAN
    My lord, we know Your Grace to be a man

71 **my tender years** (The King was actually five years old at the time of
this episode.) 80 **Bishop** i.e., Bishop's 81 **late** lately 83 **contrary
parts** contending factions 94 **peevish** petty, senseless
95 **unaccustomed** contrary to custom and normality

Just and upright, and for your royal birth
Inferior to none but to His Majesty;
And ere that we will suffer such a prince,   99
So kind a father of the commonweal,
To be disgracèd by an inkhorn mate,   101
We and our wives and children all will fight
And have our bodies slaughtered by thy foes.

FIRST SERVINGMAN
Ay, and the very parings of our nails
Shall pitch a field when we are dead.   *Begin again.*
GLOUCESTER   Stay, stay, I say!   105
An if you love me, as you say you do,
Let me persuade you to forbear awhile.

KING
O, how this discord doth afflict my soul!
Can you, my lord of Winchester, behold
My sighs and tears and will not once relent?
Who should be pitiful, if you be not?
Or who should study to prefer a peace   112
If holy churchmen take delight in broils?

WARWICK
Yield, my Lord Protector, yield, Winchester,
Except you mean with obstinate repulse   115
To slay your sovereign and destroy the realm.
You see what mischief, and what murder too,
Hath been enacted through your enmity.
Then be at peace, except ye thirst for blood.

WINCHESTER
He shall submit, or I will never yield.

GLOUCESTER
Compassion on the King commands me stoop,
Or I would see his heart out ere the priest
Should ever get that privilege of me.   123

WARWICK
Behold, my lord of Winchester, the Duke
Hath banished moody discontented fury,   125

99 ere that before   **101 inkhorn mate** scribbler. (Alludes scornfully to
Winchester as a cleric or clerk.)   **105 pitch a field** fight a battle, set in
array for fighting   **112 prefer** propose, assist in arranging   **115 Except**
unless.   **repulse** refusal   **123 privilege of** advantage over   **125 moody**
haughty

As by his smoothèd brows it doth appear.
Why look you still so stern and tragical?

GLOUCESTER
Here, Winchester, I offer thee my hand.
                [*He offers his hand, which Winchester refuses.*]

KING
Fie, uncle Beaufort! I have heard you preach
That malice was a great and grievous sin;
And will not you maintain the thing you teach,
But prove a chief offender in the same?

WARWICK
Sweet King! The Bishop hath a kindly gird.   133
For shame, my lord of Winchester, relent!
What, shall a child instruct you what to do?

WINCHESTER
Well, Duke of Gloucester, I will yield to thee;
Love for thy love and hand for hand I give.
                            [*They clasp hands.*]

GLOUCESTER [*Aside*]
Ay, but, I fear me, with a hollow heart.—   138
See here, my friends and loving countrymen,
This token serveth for a flag of truce   140
Betwixt ourselves and all our followers.
So help me God, as I dissemble not!

WINCHESTER [*Aside*]
So help me God, as I intend it not!

KING
O loving uncle, kind Duke of Gloucester,
How joyful am I made by this contract!
[*To Servingmen.*] Away, my masters. Trouble us no more,   146
But join in friendship, as your lords have done.

FIRST SERVINGMAN
Content. I'll to the surgeon's.

SECOND SERVINGMAN   And so will I.

THIRD SERVINGMAN
And I will see what physic the tavern affords.   149
                    Exeunt [*Servingmen and Mayor*].

---

133 kindly gird appropriate rebuke   **138 hollow** treacherous   **140 This
token** i.e., the handshake   **146 masters** (Condescending term of address
to social inferiors.)   **149 physic** remedy

WARWICK [*Proffering scroll*]
  Accept this scroll, most gracious sovereign,
  Which in the right of Richard Plantagenet
  We do exhibit to Your Majesty.   152

GLOUCESTER
  Well urged, my lord of Warwick. For, sweet prince,
  An if Your Grace mark every circumstance,   154
  You have great reason to do Richard right,
  Especially for those occasions   156
  At Eltham Place I told Your Majesty.

KING
  And those occasions, uncle, were of force.   158
  Therefore, my loving lords, our pleasure is
  That Richard be restorèd to his blood.   160

WARWICK
  Let Richard be restorèd to his blood;
  So shall his father's wrongs be recompensed.

WINCHESTER
  As will the rest, so willeth Winchester.

KING
  If Richard will be true, not that alone
  But all the whole inheritance I give
  That doth belong unto the house of York,
  From whence you spring by lineal descent.

PLANTAGENET
  Thy humble servant vows obedience
  And humble service till the point of death.

KING
  Stoop then and set your knee against my foot.
                              [*Richard kneels.*]
  And in reguerdon of that duty done,   171
  I gird thee with the valiant sword of York.
  Rise, Richard, like a true Plantagenet,
  And rise created princely Duke of York.

PLANTAGENET [*Rising*]
  And so thrive Richard as thy foes may fall!
  And as my duty springs, so perish they

---

152 exhibit present for official consideration   **154 An if** if   **156 occasions** reasons   **158 of force** compelling   **160 blood** hereditary right, inherited from his father   **171 reguerdon** reward

That grudge one thought against Your Majesty!   177

ALL
Welcome, high prince, the mighty Duke of York!

SOMERSET [*Aside*]
Perish, base prince, ignoble Duke of York!

GLOUCESTER
Now will it best avail Your Majesty
To cross the seas and to be crowned in France.
The presence of a king engenders love
Amongst his subjects and his loyal friends,
As it disanimates his enemies.   184

KING
When Gloucester says the word, King Henry goes,
For friendly counsel cuts off many foes.

GLOUCESTER
Your ships already are in readiness.   187
          Sennet. Flourish. Exeunt. Manet Exeter.

EXETER
Ay, we may march in England or in France,
Not seeing what is likely to ensue.
This late dissension grown betwixt the peers   190
Burns under feignèd ashes of forged love   191
And will at last break out into a flame.
As festered members rot but by degree
Till bones and flesh and sinews fall away,
So will this base and envious discord breed.
And now I fear that fatal prophecy
Which in the time of Henry named the Fifth
Was in the mouth of every sucking babe:
That Henry born at Monmouth should win all   199
And Henry born at Windsor lose all;   200
Which is so plain that Exeter doth wish
His days may finish ere that hapless time.   *Exit.*

❖

---

177 **grudge one thought** harbor one grudging thought   184 **disanimates**
discourages   187 **s.d. Sennet** set of notes played on a trumpet as a
signal for the approach or departure of processions.   **Manet** he remains
onstage   190 **late** recent   191 **forged** feigned   199 **Henry born at
Monmouth** i.e., Henry V   200 **Henry born at Windsor** i.e., Henry VI

3.2   *Enter [Joan la] Pucelle disguised, with four Soldiers with sacks upon their backs.*

PUCELLE
These are the city gates, the gates of Rouen,   1
Through which our policy must make a breach.   2
Take heed, be wary how you place your words;
Talk like the vulgar sort of marketmen   4
That come to gather money for their corn.   5
If we have entrance, as I hope we shall,
And that we find the slothful watch but weak,   7
I'll by a sign give notice to our friends,
That Charles the Dauphin may encounter them.

FIRST SOLDIER
Our sacks shall be a mean to sack the city,   10
And we be lords and rulers over Rouen.
Therefore we'll knock.   *Knock.*

WATCH [*Within*]   *Qui là?*   13

PUCELLE
Paysans, la pauvre gens de France,
Poor market folks that come to sell their corn.

WATCH [*Opening the gates*]
Enter, go in. The market bell is rung.

PUCELLE
Now, Rouen, I'll shake thy bulwarks to the ground.
                 Exeunt [to the town].

   Enter Charles, [the] Bastard [of Orleans],
   Alençon, [Reignier, and forces].

CHARLES
Saint Denis bless this happy stratagem!
And once again we'll sleep secure in Rouen.

BASTARD
Here entered Pucelle and her practisants.   20

3.2. Location: France. Before Rouen.
1 Rouen (As at Orleans in 1.5 through 2.1, the city gates here are represented by doors in the tiring-house facade, the "walls" of Rouen. Appearances "on the walls," as at l. 40 s.d., take place on the gallery
backstage.)   **2 policy** stratagem   **4 vulgar** common   **5 corn** grain
7 that if   **10 mean** means   **13 Qui là** qui est là, who is there. (Rustic
French.)   **20 practisants** conspirators

Now she is there, how will she specify
Here is the best and safest passage in?   22

REIGNIER
By thrusting out a torch from yonder tower,
Which, once discerned, shows that her meaning is,
No way to that, for weakness, which she entered.   25

    Enter Pucelle on the top, thrusting out a torch
    burning.

PUCELLE
Behold, this is the happy wedding torch
That joineth Rouen unto her countrymen,
But burning fatal to the Talbonites!   28

BASTARD
See, noble Charles, the beacon of our friend!
The burning torch in yonder turret stands.

CHARLES
Now shine it like a comet of revenge,   31
A prophet to the fall of all our foes!

REIGNIER
Defer no time! Delays have dangerous ends.
Enter, and cry "The Dauphin!" presently,   34
And then do execution on the watch.   35
           Alarum. [*They storm the gates.*]

    An alarum. [*Enter*] *Talbot in an excursion* [*from*
    within].

TALBOT
France, thou shalt rue this treason with thy tears,
If Talbot but survive thy treachery.
Pucelle, that witch, that damnèd sorceress,
Hath wrought this hellish mischief unawares,   39

---

22 Here . . . in i.e., that here (the same spot she entered) is the best and
safest place for us to enter as well   **25 No . . . entered** i.e., no other
place can be compared to the one where she entered for weakness; it is
the most weakly defended   **s.d. on the top** i.e., at some upper vantage
point in the theater   **28 Talbonites** followers of Talbot   **31 shine it** may
it shine   **34 presently** immediately   **35 do . . . watch** kill all the
guards   **s.d. excursion** skirmish, sortie   **39 unawares** unexpectedly

That hardly we escaped the pride of France.   *Exit.* 40

An alarum. Excursions. Bedford, brought in sick
in a chair. Enter Talbot and Burgundy without;
within, Pucelle, Charles, Bastard, [Alençon,] and
Reignier, on the walls.

PUCELLE
Good morrow, gallants, want ye corn for bread?
I think the Duke of Burgundy will fast
Before he'll buy again at such a rate.
'Twas full of darnel. Do you like the taste?   44

BURGUNDY
Scoff on, vile fiend and shameless courtesan!
I trust ere long to choke thee with thine own   46
And make thee curse the harvest of that corn.

CHARLES
Your Grace may starve, perhaps, before that time.

BEDFORD
O, let no words, but deeds, revenge this treason!

PUCELLE
What will you do, good graybeard, break a lance
And run atilt at Death within a chair?   51

TALBOT
Foul fiend of France and hag of all despite,   52
Encompassed with thy lustful paramours!
Becomes it thee to taunt his valiant age
And twit with cowardice a man half dead?
Damsel, I'll have a bout with you again,   56
Or else let Talbot perish with this shame.

PUCELLE
Are ye so hot, sir? Yet, Pucelle, hold thy peace.   58

---

40 pride princely power   **s.d. Bedford . . . sick** (Actually, Bedford out-
lived Joan of Arc by four years. The entire episode of the capture of
Rouen, as presented here, is unhistorical; the English did not relinquish
the city until 1449, some eighteen years after Joan's death.)   **without**
i.e., on the main stage.   **within** i.e., in the gallery backstage   **44 darnel**
injurious weed   **46 thine own** i.e., your own bread   **51 run atilt at** joust
with.   **within** i.e., sitting in   **52 of all despite** thoroughly despicable
56 bout encounter with weapons (with sexual overtones, as earlier at
1.5.4)   **58 hot** (1) hot-tempered (2) lustful

If Talbot do but thunder, rain will follow.   59
          They [the English] whisper together in council.
God speed the parliament! Who shall be the speaker?   60
TALBOT
Dare ye come forth and meet us in the field?
PUCELLE
Belike your lordship takes us then for fools,
To try if that our own be ours or no.
TALBOT
I speak not to that railing Hecate,   64
But unto thee, Alençon, and the rest.
Will ye, like soldiers, come and fight it out?
ALENÇON   Seigneur, no.
TALBOT
Seigneur, hang! Base muleteers of France!   68
Like peasant footboys do they keep the walls   69
And dare not take up arms like gentlemen.
PUCELLE
Away, captains. Let's get us from the walls,
For Talbot means no goodness by his looks.
Good-bye, my lord. We came but to tell you
That we are here.   *Exeunt from the walls.*
TALBOT
And there will we be too, ere it be long,
Or else reproach be Talbot's greatest fame!   76
Vow, Burgundy, by honor of thy house,
Pricked on by public wrongs sustained in France,   78
Either to get the town again or die.
And I, as sure as English Henry lives
And as his father here was conqueror,   81
As sure as in this late-betrayèd town   82

59 If . . . follow (A proverb, suggesting that ranting is usually followed
by grief; Talbot will soon have reason to be sorry.)   **60 speaker** spokes-
man (playing on the sense of "parliamentary leader")   **64 Hecate**
goddess of night and of black magic   **68 muleteers** mule drivers
69 keep keep safely within   **76 fame** reputation   **78 Pricked on**
goaded   **81 father . . . conqueror** (Henry V captured Rouen in 1419.)
82 late-betrayèd recently lost to the enemy through treachery

Great Coeur de Lion's heart was buried,   83
So sure I swear to get the town or die.

BURGUNDY
My vows are equal partners with thy vows.

TALBOT
But ere we go, regard this dying prince,   86
The valiant Duke of Bedford.—Come, my lord,
We will bestow you in some better place,
Fitter for sickness and for crazy age.   89

BEDFORD
Lord Talbot, do not so dishonor me.
Here will I sit before the walls of Rouen
And will be partner of your weal or woe.   92

BURGUNDY
Courageous Bedford, let us now persuade you.

BEDFORD
Not to be gone from hence; for once I read
That stout Pendragon in his litter sick   95
Came to the field and vanquishèd his foes.
Methinks I should revive the soldiers' hearts,
Because I ever found them as myself.

TALBOT
Undaunted spirit in a dying breast!
Then be it so. Heavens keep old Bedford safe!
And now no more ado, brave Burgundy,
But gather we our forces out of hand   102
And set upon our boasting enemy.
                    Exeunt [*all but Bedford and attendants*].

*An alarum. Excursions. Enter Sir John Falstaff
and a Captain.*

---

83 Great . . . heart (According to Holinshed, Richard Coeur de Lion, "the
lion-hearted," King of England 1189–1199, had willed that "his heart be
conveyed unto Rouen and there buried, in testimony of the love which he
had ever borne unto that city.")   **86 regard** attend to   **89 crazy** decrepit
92 weal welfare   **95 Pendragon** (According to Holinshed, it was the brother
of Uther Pendragon who, "even sick as he was, caused himself to be
carried forth in a litter; with whose presence his people were so encouraged that, encountering with the Saxons, they won the victory." Geoffrey of
Monmouth, on the other hand, credits this feat to Uther himself. Uther was
father of King Arthur.)   **102 out of hand** at once

CAPTAIN
　Whither away, Sir John Falstaff, in such haste?
FALSTAFF
　Whither away? To save myself by flight.
　We are like to have the overthrow again.   106
CAPTAIN
　What? Will you fly, and leave Lord Talbot?
FALSTAFF   Ay,
　All the Talbots in the world, to save my life.   *Exit.*
CAPTAIN
　Cowardly knight, ill fortune follow thee!   *Exit.*

　　　Retreat. Excursions. Pucelle, Alençon, and
　　　Charles fly.

BEDFORD
　Now, quiet soul, depart when heaven please,   110
　For I have seen our enemies' overthrow.   111
　What is the trust or strength of foolish man?
　They that of late were daring with their scoffs
　Are glad and fain by flight to save themselves.   114
　　　Bedford dies, and is carried in by two in his chair.

　　　An alarum. Enter Talbot, Burgundy, and the rest
　　　[of the English soldiers].

TALBOT
　Lost and recovered in a day again!
　This is a double honor, Burgundy.
　Yet heavens have glory for this victory!
BURGUNDY
　Warlike and martial Talbot, Burgundy
　Enshrines thee in his heart and there erects
　Thy noble deeds as valor's monuments.
TALBOT
　Thanks, gentle Duke. But where is Pucelle now?   121
　I think her old familiar is asleep.   122

---

106 like to . . . overthrow likely to be overthrown　**110–111 Now . . .
overthrow** (A secular version of Luke 2:29–30, "Lord, now lettest thou
thy servant depart in peace," etc., sung as the *Nunc dimittis* in evensong
in the Book of Common Prayer.)　**114 fain** eager　**s.d. carried in** carried
offstage　**121 gentle** noble　**122 old familiar** customary attendant
demon

Now where's the Bastard's braves, and Charles his
   gleeks?   123
What, all amort? Rouen hangs her head for grief   124
That such a valiant company are fled.
Now will we take some order in the town,   126
Placing therein some expert officers,
And then depart to Paris to the King,
For there young Henry with his nobles lie.

BURGUNDY
What wills Lord Talbot pleaseth Burgundy.

TALBOT
But yet, before we go, let's not forget
The noble Duke of Bedford late deceased,
But see his exequies fulfilled in Rouen.   133
A braver soldier never couchèd lance;   134
A gentler heart did never sway in court.   135
But kings and mightiest potentates must die,
For that's the end of human misery.   *Exeunt.*

❖

3.3   *Enter Charles, [the] Bastard [of Orleans],*
          Alençon, Pucelle, [and French soldiers].

PUCELLE
Dismay not, princes, at this accident,   1
Nor grieve that Rouen is so recoverèd.
Care is no cure, but rather corrosive,   3
For things that are not to be remedied.
Let frantic Talbot triumph for a while
And like a peacock sweep along his tail;
We'll pull his plumes and take away his train,   7
If Dauphin and the rest will be but ruled.

---

123 braves boasts.   **Charles his gleeks** Charles's gibes, jests   **124 amort**
sick to death, dispirited   **126 take some order** establish order and
government   **133 exequies** funeral rites   **134 couchèd lance** carried his
lance lowered, in the position of attack   **135 gentler** more noble.   **sway**
exercise influence

3.3. Location: Near Rouen.
1 Dismay not be not dismayed, disheartened.   **accident** bad luck,
untoward event   **3 Care** sorrow   **7 train** (1) peacock's tail (2) army

CHARLES
We have been guided by thee hitherto,
And of thy cunning had no diffidence.   10
One sudden foil shall never breed distrust.   11

BASTARD
Search out thy wit for secret policies,   12
And we will make thee famous through the world.

ALENÇON
We'll set thy statue in some holy place
And have thee reverenced like a blessèd saint.
Employ thee, then, sweet virgin, for our good.

PUCELLE
Then thus it must be; this doth Joan devise:
By fair persuasions, mixed with sugared words,
We will entice the Duke of Burgundy
To leave the Talbot and to follow us.

CHARLES
Ay, marry, sweeting, if we could do that,
France were no place for Henry's warriors,
Nor should that nation boast it so with us,
But be extirpèd from our provinces.   24

ALENÇON
Forever should they be expulsed from France
And not have title of an earldom here.

PUCELLE
Your honors shall perceive how I will work
To bring this matter to the wishèd end.
                              Drum sounds afar off.
Hark, by the sound of drum you may perceive
Their powers are marching unto Paris-ward.   30
                         Here sound an English march.
There goes the Talbot, with his colors spread,
And all the troops of English after him.
                              French march.
Now in the rearward comes the Duke and his.
Fortune in favor makes him lag behind.   34

---

10 diffidence distrust   **11 foil** repulse, defeat   **12 policies** stratagems
24 extirpèd rooted out   **30 s.d. Here . . . march** (Probably the English
are heard from offstage, and the French at l. 32, but conceivably soldiers could pass over the stage.)   **34 in favor** benevolently, i.e., in our
favor

Summon a parley. We will talk with him.   35
            Trumpets sound a parley.

[*Enter the Duke of Burgundy.*]

CHARLES
A parley with the Duke of Burgundy!
BURGUNDY
Who craves a parley with the Burgundy?
PUCELLE
The princely Charles of France, thy countryman.
BURGUNDY
What sayst thou, Charles? For I am marching hence.
CHARLES
Speak, Pucelle, and enchant him with thy words.   40
PUCELLE
Brave Burgundy, undoubted hope of France,   41
Stay. Let thy humble handmaid speak to thee.
BURGUNDY
Speak on, but be not overtedious.
PUCELLE
Look on thy country, look on fertile France,
And see the cities and the towns defaced
By wasting ruin of the cruel foe.
As looks the mother on her lowly babe   47
When death doth close his tender-dying eyes,   48
See, see the pining malady of France!   49
Behold the wounds, the most unnatural wounds,   50
Which thou thyself hast given her woeful breast.
O, turn thy edgèd sword another way!
Strike those that hurt, and hurt not those that help!
One drop of blood drawn from thy country's bosom
Should grieve thee more than streams of foreign gore.
Return thee therefore with a flood of tears
And wash away thy country's stainèd spots.   57

35 Summon a parley sound a trumpet signal requesting negotiations
40 enchant put spells on   **41 undoubted** i.e., whose bravery and
strength are sure bulwarks   **47 lowly** little, or humbled by misfortune,
lying low   **48 tender-dying** dying at a tender age   **49 malady of France**
(With comic double meaning; the phrase normally refers to venereal
disease.)   **50 unnatural** i.e., turned against the doer's own country
57 thy . . . spots blemishes to your country's reputation

BURGUNDY [*Aside*]
  Either she hath bewitched me with her words,
  Or nature makes me suddenly relent.

PUCELLE
  Besides, all French and France exclaims on thee,   60
  Doubting thy birth and lawful progeny.   61
  Who join'st thou with but with a lordly nation
  That will not trust thee but for profit's sake?
  When Talbot hath set footing once in France
  And fashioned thee that instrument of ill,   65
  Who then but English Henry will be lord,
  And thou be thrust out like a fugitive?   67
  Call we to mind, and mark but this for proof: 68
  Was not the Duke of Orleans thy foe?
  And was he not in England prisoner?
  But when they heard he was thine enemy,
  They set him free without his ransom paid,
  In spite of Burgundy and all his friends.
  See, then, thou fight'st against thy countrymen
  And join'st with them will be thy slaughtermen.   75
  Come, come, return. Return, thou wandering lord!
  Charles and the rest will take thee in their arms.

BURGUNDY [*Aside*]
  I am vanquished. These haughty words of hers   78
  Have battered me like roaring cannon-shot
  And made me almost yield upon my knees.—
  Forgive me, country, and sweet countrymen!
  And, lords, accept this hearty kind embrace.
  My forces and my power of men are yours.
  So farewell, Talbot. I'll no longer trust thee.

PUCELLE
  Done like a Frenchman—[*Aside*] turn and turn again!

CHARLES
  Welcome, brave Duke! Thy friendship makes us fresh.

---

60 exclaims on denounces, accuses **61 progeny** ancestry **65 fashioned
thee** turned you into **67 fugitive** renegade, deserter of your own nation **68 Call we to mind** let us remember **75 them** those who **78 I
am vanquished** (Historically, Burgundy did not desert the English
alliance until four years after Joan's death. This desertion occurred five
years before the Duke of Orleans was released by the English; see
ll. 69–73.) **haughty** lofty

BASTARD
And doth beget new courage in our breasts.

ALENÇON
Pucelle hath bravely played her part in this   88
And doth deserve a coronet of gold.

CHARLES
Now let us on, my lords, and join our powers,   90
And seek how we may prejudice the foe.   *Exeunt.* 91

✣

3.4   *Enter the King, Gloucester, Winchester,*
[Richard, Duke of] York, Suffolk, Somerset,
Warwick, Exeter, [Vernon, wearing a white
rose, Basset, wearing a red rose, and others]. To
them, with his soldiers, Talbot.

TALBOT
My gracious prince, and honorable peers,
Hearing of your arrival in this realm,
I have awhile given truce unto my wars
To do my duty to my sovereign;   4
In sign whereof, this arm, that hath reclaimed
To your obedience fifty fortresses,
Twelve cities, and seven walled towns of strength,
Besides five hundred prisoners of esteem,
Lets fall his sword before Your Highness' feet,
And with submissive loyalty of heart
Ascribes the glory of his conquest got
First to my God and next unto Your Grace. [*He kneels.*]

KING
Is this the Lord Talbot, uncle Gloucester,
That hath so long been resident in France?

GLOUCESTER
Yes, if it please Your Majesty, my liege.

KING
Welcome, brave captain and victorious lord!

88 bravely courageously and excellently   **90 powers** armed forces
91 prejudice harm

3.4. Location: Paris. The royal court.
4 duty homage

When I was young—as yet I am not old—
I do remember how my father said   18
A stouter champion never handled sword.   19
Long since we were resolvèd of your truth,   20
Your faithful service, and your toil in war;
Yet never have you tasted our reward
Or been reguerdoned with so much as thanks,   23
Because till now we never saw your face.
Therefore, stand up. [*Talbot rises.*] And for these good
    deserts   25
We here create you Earl of Shrewsbury;
And in our coronation take your place.   27
    Sennet. Flourish. Exeunt. Manent Vernon and
                                              Basset.

VERNON
Now, sir, to you, that were so hot at sea,   28
Disgracing of these colors that I wear   29
In honor of my noble lord of York:
Dar'st thou maintain the former words thou spak'st?
BASSET
Yes, sir, as well as you dare patronage   32
The envious barking of your saucy tongue
Against my lord the Duke of Somerset.
VERNON
Sirrah, thy lord I honor as he is.   35
BASSET
Why, what is he? As good a man as York.
VERNON
Hark ye, not so. In witness, take ye that.
                                              Strikes him.
BASSET
Villain, thou knowest the law of arms is such   38

18 I . . . said (Historically, Henry VI was an infant of nine months at his
father's death.)   19 stouter more intrepid   20 we i.e., I. (The royal
"we.")   resolvèd convinced.   truth loyalty   23 reguerdoned rewarded
25 deserts deservings   27 s.d. Manent they remain onstage   28 so hot
at sea (The details of this quarrel are given below, 4.1.87–97.)
29 Disgracing of insulting.   these colors i.e., the white rose of York
32 patronage defend   35 as he is i.e., for what he is—a person of no
worth   38 law of arms (This law forbade the drawing of weapons near
a royal residence; see 1.3.46 and note, and 2.4.86 and note.)

That whoso draws a sword, 'tis present death,   39
Or else this blow should broach thy dearest blood.   40
But I'll unto His Majesty and crave
I may have liberty to venge this wrong,   42
When thou shalt see I'll meet thee to thy cost.

VERNON
Well, miscreant, I'll be there as soon as you,
And after meet you, sooner than you would.   *Exeunt.* 45

4.1   *Enter King, Gloucester, Winchester, [Richard,*
          Duke of] York, Suffolk, Somerset, Warwick,
          Talbot, Exeter, Governor [of Paris, and others].

GLOUCESTER
Lord Bishop, set the crown upon his head.

WINCHESTER
God save King Henry, of that name the sixth!
                    [*The King is crowned.*]

GLOUCESTER
Now, Governor of Paris, take your oath,
                    [*The Governor kneels*]
That you elect no other king but him,   4
Esteem none friends but such as are his friends,
And none your foes but such as shall pretend   6
Malicious practices against his state.   7
This shall ye do, so help you righteous God!
                    [*The Governor retires.*]

          Enter [Sir John] Falstaff.

FALSTAFF
My gracious sovereign, as I rode from Calais

39 present instant   **40 broach** tap, draw.   **dearest blood** i.e., lifeblood
42 wrong insult   **45 after** i.e., once the royal permission to fight a duel
has been obtained

**4.1. Location: Paris. Scene continues. (The action appears to go on
immediately after the events of 3.4.)**
s.d. York i.e., Richard Plantagenet, created Duke of York in 3.1 and
hereafter identified by the speech prefix YORK   **4 elect** acknowledge
6 pretend purpose, intend   **7 practices** stratagems

To haste unto your coronation,
A letter was delivered to my hands,
Writ to Your Grace from th' Duke of Burgundy.

                    [He presents a letter.]

TALBOT
Shame to the Duke of Burgundy and thee!
I vowed, base knight, when I did meet thee next,
To tear the Garter from thy craven's leg,   15

                    [Plucking it off]

Which I have done, because unworthily
Thou wast installèd in that high degree.
Pardon me, princely Henry, and the rest.
This dastard, at the battle of Poitiers,   19
When but in all I was six thousand strong   20
And that the French were almost ten to one,   21
Before we met or that a stroke was given,
Like to a trusty squire did run away;   23
In which assault we lost twelve hundred men.
Myself and divers gentlemen besides
Were there surprised and taken prisoners.
Then judge, great lords, if I have done amiss,
Or whether that such cowards ought to wear
This ornament of knighthood, yea or no?

GLOUCESTER
To say the truth, this fact was infamous   30
And ill beseeming any common man,
Much more a knight, a captain, and a leader.

TALBOT
When first this order was ordained, my lords,
Knights of the Garter were of noble birth,
Valiant and virtuous, full of haughty courage,   35
Such as were grown to credit by the wars—   36
Not fearing death, nor shrinking for distress,

---

15 Garter badge of the Knights of the Garter, a ribbon of blue velvet
edged and buckled with gold, worn below the left knee. (Historically,
the Garter was apparently taken from Fastolfe by the Duke of Bedford;
Talbot, who was a captive of the French at the time of Henry VI's
coronation in Paris, was opposed to the restoration of the Garter to
Fastolfe.) **19 Poitiers** (Seemingly confused with Patay.) **20 but in all** all
told   **21 And that** and   **23 trusty squire** (Said contemptuously.)   **30 fact**
deed   **35 haughty** exalted   **36 were grown to credit** had achieved
renown

But always resolute in most extremes.   38
He then that is not furnished in this sort   39
Doth but usurp the sacred name of knight,
Profaning this most honorable order,
And should, if I were worthy to be judge,
Be quite degraded, like a hedge-born swain   43
That doth presume to boast of gentle blood.   44

KING
Stain to thy countrymen, thou hear'st thy doom.   45
Be packing, therefore, thou that wast a knight.   46
Henceforth we banish thee, on pain of death.
                                    [*Exit Falstaff.*]
And now, my Lord Protector, view the letter
Sent from our uncle, Duke of Burgundy.   49

GLOUCESTER [*Taking the letter*]
What means His Grace, that he hath changed his style?   50
No more but, plain and bluntly, "To the King"?
Hath he forgot he is his sovereign?
Or doth this churlish superscription   53
Pretend some alteration in good will?   54
What's here? [*He reads.*] "I have, upon especial cause,
Moved with compassion of my country's wrack,   56
Together with the pitiful complaints
Of such as your oppression feeds upon,
Forsaken your pernicious faction
And joined with Charles, the rightful King of France."
O monstrous treachery! Can this be so,
That in alliance, amity, and oaths
There should be found such false dissembling guile?

KING
What? Doth my uncle Burgundy revolt?   64

GLOUCESTER
He doth, my lord, and is become your foe.

---

38 most greatest   **39 furnished . . . sort** endowed thus   **43 degraded**
lowered in rank.   **hedge-born swain** lowly-born rustic   **44 gentle** noble   **45 doom** sentence   **46 Be packing** be off   **49 uncle** (The Lancastrian and Burgundian houses were allied by the marriage of the Duke
of Bedford, the King's uncle, to Anne, sister of the Duke of Burgundy.)
50 style form of address   **53 churlish superscription** insolent form of
address on the outside of the letter   **54 Pretend** portend, import
56 wrack ruin   **64 revolt** fall away to the other side

KING
  Is that the worst this letter doth contain?
GLOUCESTER
  It is the worst, and all, my lord, he writes.
KING
  Why, then, Lord Talbot there shall talk with him
  And give him chastisement for this abuse.   69
  [*To Talbot*.] How say you, my lord? Are you not content?
TALBOT
  Content, my liege? Yes. But that I am prevented,   71
  I should have begged I might have been employed.
KING
  Then gather strength and march unto him straight.   73
  Let him perceive how ill we brook his treason,   74
  And what offense it is to flout his friends.
TALBOT
  I go, my lord, in heart desiring still   76
  You may behold confusion of your foes.   [*Exit*.] 77

  *Enter Vernon and Basset, [wearing a white and a
  red rose respectively, as before].*

VERNON
  Grant me the combat, gracious sovereign.   78
BASSET
  And me, my lord, grant me the combat too.
YORK
  This is my servant. Hear him, noble prince.   80
SOMERSET
  And this is mine. Sweet Henry, favor him.
KING
  Be patient, lords, and give them leave to speak.
  Say, gentlemen, what makes you thus exclaim?
  And wherefore crave you combat, or with whom?
VERNON
  With him, my lord, for he hath done me wrong.
BASSET
  And I with him, for he hath done me wrong.

---

69 abuse deception **71 prevented** anticipated **73 straight** immediately **74 brook** endure **76 still** always **77 confusion** destruction **78 the combat** permission to fight a trial by duel **80 servant** i.e., follower

KING
What is that wrong whereof you both complain?
First let me know, and then I'll answer you.

BASSET
Crossing the sea from England into France,
This fellow here, with envious carping tongue,   90
Upbraided me about the rose I wear,
Saying the sanguine color of the leaves   92
Did represent my master's blushing cheeks,
When stubbornly he did repugn the truth   94
About a certain question in the law
Argued betwixt the Duke of York and him;
With other vile and ignominious terms.
In confutation of which rude reproach,
And in defense of my lord's worthiness,
I crave the benefit of law of arms.   100

VERNON
And that is my petition, noble lord.
For though he seem with forgèd quaint conceit   102
To set a gloss upon his bold intent,   103
Yet know, my lord, I was provoked by him,
And he first took exceptions at this badge,
Pronouncing that the paleness of this flower
Bewrayed the faintness of my master's heart.   107

YORK
Will not this malice, Somerset, be left?   108

SOMERSET
Your private grudge, my lord of York, will out,   109
Though ne'er so cunningly you smother it.

KING
Good Lord, what madness rules in brainsick men,
When for so slight and frivolous a cause
Such factious emulations shall arise!   113
Good cousins both, of York and Somerset,   114
Quiet yourselves, I pray, and be at peace.

---

90 envious malicious   **92 sanguine** bloodred.   **leaves** petals   **94 repugn**
oppose, resist   **100 benefit . . . arms** right to protect my honor in a
duel   **102 forgèd quaint conceit** false ingenious rhetoric   **103 gloss**
speciously fair appearance   **107 Bewrayed** revealed   **108 left** i.e.,
forgotten   **109 out** appear, be revealed   **113 emulations** contentions
between rivals   **114 cousins** kinsmen

YORK
  Let this dissension first be tried by fight,
  And then Your Highness shall command a peace.
SOMERSET
  The quarrel toucheth none but us alone;   118
  Betwixt ourselves let us decide it, then.
YORK
  There is my pledge. Accept it, Somerset.   120
                              [*He throws down a gage.*]
VERNON [*To Somerset*]
  Nay, let it rest where it began at first.   121
BASSET [*To Somerset*]
  Confirm it so, mine honorable lord.   122
GLOUCESTER
  Confirm it so? Confounded be your strife!
  And perish ye, with your audacious prate!
  Presumptuous vassals, are you not ashamed
  With this immodest clamorous outrage   126
  To trouble and disturb the King and us?
  And you, my lords, methinks you do not well   128
  To bear with their perverse objections,   129
  Much less to take occasion from their mouths
  To raise a mutiny betwixt yourselves.   131
  Let me persuade you take a better course.
EXETER
  It grieves His Highness. Good my lords, be friends.
KING
  Come hither, you that would be combatants:
  Henceforth I charge you, as you love our favor,
  Quite to forget this quarrel and the cause.
  And you, my lords: remember where we are—
  In France, amongst a fickle wavering nation.
  If they perceive dissension in our looks

---

118 toucheth concerns   **120 pledge** i.e., a glove or gauntlet flung down
as a gage in a duel   **121 let . . . first** i.e., let the quarrel remain with me
and Basset, who began it. Don't answer York's challenge by throwing
down your gage.   **122 Confirm . . . lord** (Basset, contradicting Vernon,
asks his lord, Somerset, to confirm York's challenge by throwing down
his glove, or perhaps asks Somerset to confirm the suggestion that
Vernon and Basset fight it out themselves.)   **126 immodest** arrogant,
impudent   **128 my lords** i.e., York and Somerset (also in l. 137)
129 objections charges, accusations   **131 mutiny** quarrel, strife

And that within ourselves we disagree,   140
How will their grudging stomachs be provoked   141
To willful disobedience, and rebel!
Besides, what infamy will there arise
When foreign princes shall be certified   144
That for a toy, a thing of no regard,   145
King Henry's peers and chief nobility
Destroyed themselves and lost the realm of France!
O, think upon the conquest of my father,
My tender years, and let us not forgo
That for a trifle that was bought with blood!   150
Let me be umpire in this doubtful strife.   151
I see no reason, if I wear this rose,
                    [*Putting on a red rose*]
That anyone should therefore be suspicious
I more incline to Somerset than York.
Both are my kinsmen, and I love them both.
As well they may upbraid me with my crown
Because, forsooth, the King of Scots is crowned.
But your discretions better can persuade
Than I am able to instruct or teach;
And therefore, as we hither came in peace,
So let us still continue peace and love.   161
Cousin of York, we institute Your Grace
To be our regent in these parts of France.
And, good my lord of Somerset, unite
Your troops of horsemen with his bands of foot;   165
And like true subjects, sons of your progenitors,
Go cheerfully together and digest   167
Your angry choler on your enemies.
Ourself, my Lord Protector, and the rest,
After some respite, will return to Calais;
From thence to England, where I hope ere long
To be presented by your victories
With Charles, Alençon, and that traitorous rout.   173
            Flourish. Exeunt. Manent York, Warwick,
                        Exeter, [and] Vernon.

140 within among   **141 grudging stomachs** resentful tempers
144 certified informed   **145 toy** trifle   **150 That . . . that** for a trifle that
which   **151 doubtful** causing apprehension   **161 still** ever   **165 bands
of foot** troops of infantry   **167 digest** disperse, dissipate   **173 rout**
rabble   **s.d. Manent** they remain onstage

WARWICK
My lord of York, I promise you, the King   174
Prettily, methought, did play the orator.

YORK
And so he did; but yet I like it not
In that he wears the badge of Somerset.

WARWICK
Tush, that was but his fancy. Blame him not.
I dare presume, sweet prince, he thought no harm.

YORK
An if I wist he did—But let it rest.   180
Other affairs must now be managèd.
                    Exeunt. Manet Exeter.

EXETER
Well didst thou, Richard, to suppress thy voice;
For, had the passions of thy heart burst out,
I fear we should have seen deciphered there   184
More rancorous spite, more furious raging broils,
Than yet can be imagined or supposed.
But howsoe'er, no simple man that sees   187
This jarring discord of nobility,
This shouldering of each other in the court,
This factious bandying of their favorites,   190
But that it doth presage some ill event.   191
'Tis much when scepters are in children's hands,
But more when envy breeds unkind division.   193
There comes the ruin, there begins confusion.   *Exit.*

4.2   *Enter Talbot, with trump and drum [and
          forces], before Bordeaux.*

174 **promise** assure   180 **An . . . wist** if I knew for certain
184 **deciphered** detected, expressed   187 **simple** common
190 **bandying** contending.   **favorites** followers   191 **But that** i.e., but
sees that.   **event** outcome   193 **envy** malice.   **unkind** unnatural

4.2. **Location:** France. Before Bordeaux.
s.d. **trump and drum** trumpeter and drummer

TALBOT
  Go to the gates of Bordeaux, trumpeter.   1
  Summon their general unto the wall.

    [Trumpet] sounds. Enter General, aloft.

  English John Talbot, captains, calls you forth,
  Servant in arms to Harry King of England,
  And thus he would: Open your city gates,   5
  Be humble to us, call my sovereign yours,
  And do him homage as obedient subjects,
  And I'll withdraw me and my bloody power.   8
  But if you frown upon this proffered peace,
  You tempt the fury of my three attendants,
  Lean famine, quartering steel, and climbing fire,   11
  Who in a moment even with the earth   12
  Shall lay your stately and air-braving towers,   13
  If you forsake the offer of their love.   14
GENERAL
  Thou ominous and fearful owl of death,   15
  Our nation's terror and their bloody scourge,
  The period of thy tyranny approacheth.   17
  On us thou canst not enter but by death;
  For I protest we are well fortified
  And strong enough to issue out and fight.
  If thou retire, the Dauphin, well appointed,   21
  Stands with the snares of war to tangle thee.
  On either hand thee there are squadrons pitched   23
  To wall thee from the liberty of flight;
  And no way canst thou turn thee for redress
  But death doth front thee with apparent spoil   26

---

1 gates (As before at Orleans and Rouen, these city gates are represented
by a door in the tiring-house facade, which is imagined to be the walls
of Bordeaux. Occupants of Bordeaux appearing *aloft* or on the walls are
seen in the gallery backstage.) **5 would** wishes **8 bloody power** bloodthirsty army **11 quartering** dismembering **12 even** level **13 air-
braving** defying the heavens (by their height) **14 forsake** refuse. **their**
i.e., *famine, steel,* and *fire* **15 owl** i.e., portent **17 period** termination. **tyranny** cruelty **21 appointed** equipped **23 thee** i.e., of you.
pitched set in battle array **26 front** face. **apparent spoil** obvious
destruction

And pale destruction meets thee in the face.   27
Ten thousand French have ta'en the Sacrament   28
To rive their dangerous artillery   29
Upon no Christian soul but English Talbot.
Lo, there thou stand'st, a breathing valiant man
Of an invincible unconquered spirit.
This is the latest glory of thy praise   33
That I, thy enemy, due thee withal;   34
For ere the glass that now begins to run   35
Finish the process of his sandy hour,   36
These eyes, that see thee now well colorèd,   37
Shall see thee withered, bloody, pale, and dead.
                                        Drum afar off.
Hark, hark! The Dauphin's drum, a warning bell,
Sings heavy music to thy timorous soul,
And mine shall ring thy dire departure out.   41
                                        Exit [with his men].

TALBOT
He fables not. I hear the enemy.
Out, some light horsemen, and peruse their wings.   43
                                        [Exeunt some.]

O, negligent and heedless discipline!   44
How are we parked and bounded in a pale—   45
A little herd of England's timorous deer,
Mazed with a yelping kennel of French curs!   47
If we be English deer, be then in blood: 48
Not rascal-like to fall down with a pinch,   49
But rather, moody-mad and desperate stags,   50
Turn on the bloody hounds with heads of steel   51
And make the cowards stand aloof at bay.
Sell every man his life as dear as mine
And they shall find dear deer of us, my friends.

27 **pale** (because Death is portrayed as pale)   28 **ta'en the Sacrament**
i.e., confirmed their solemn oaths by taking the Sacrament   29 **rive**
burst, fire   33 **latest** final   34 **due** endue, invest   35 **glass** hourglass
36 **sandy hour** hour as measured by the running of the sand   37 **well
colorèd** i.e., in health   41 **departure** i.e., death   43 **peruse** survey,
reconnoiter.   **wings** flanks   44 **discipline** military tactics   45 **parked**
enclosed.   **pale** fenced-in space   47 **Mazed with** (1) bewildered, amazed
by (2) enclosed by, as in a labyrinth (?)   48 **in blood** in prime condition   49 **rascal-like** (1) like young or inferior deer (2) like rascals.   **pinch**
nip   50 **moody-mad** high-spirited and mad with rage   51 **heads of steel**
(1) swordlike antlers (2) helmeted heads

God and Saint George, Talbot and England's right,
Prosper our colors in this dangerous fight!   [*Exeunt.*]

✣

4.3   *Enter a Messenger that meets York. Enter York*
with trumpet and many soldiers.

YORK
   Are not the speedy scouts returned again
   That dogged the mighty army of the Dauphin?

MESSENGER
   They are returned, my lord, and give it out   3
   That he is marched to Bordeaux with his power
   To fight with Talbot. As he marched along,
   By your espials were discoverèd   6
   Two mightier troops than that the Dauphin led,
   Which joined with him and made their march for
     Bordeaux.

YORK
   A plague upon that villain Somerset,
   That thus delays my promisèd supply   10
   Of horsemen that were levied for this siege!
   Renownèd Talbot doth expect my aid,
   And I am louted by a traitor villain   13
   And cannot help the noble chevalier.
   God comfort him in this necessity!
   If he miscarry, farewell wars in France.   16

     Enter another Messenger, [Sir William Lucy].

LUCY
   Thou princely leader of our English strength,
   Never so needful on the earth of France,
   Spur to the rescue of the noble Talbot,
   Who now is girdled with a waist of iron
   And hemmed about with grim destruction.
   To Bordeaux, warlike Duke! To Bordeaux, York!
   Else, farewell Talbot, France, and England's honor.

4.3. Location: France. Plains in Gascony.
3 **give it out** report   6 **espials** spies   10 **supply** reinforcements
13 **louted** made a fool of, mocked   16 **miscarry** come to grief

YORK
  O God, that Somerset, who in proud heart
  Doth stop my cornets, were in Talbot's place!   25
  So should we save a valiant gentleman
  By forfeiting a traitor and a coward.
  Mad ire and wrathful fury makes me weep
  That thus we die while remiss traitors sleep.

LUCY
  O, send some succor to the distressed lord!   30

YORK
  He dies, we lose; I break my warlike word;
  We mourn, France smiles; we lose, they daily get;
  All 'long of this vile traitor Somerset.   33

LUCY
  Then God take mercy on brave Talbot's soul,
  And on his son young John, who two hours since
  I met in travel toward his warlike father.
  This seven years did not Talbot see his son,
  And now they meet where both their lives are done.

YORK
  Alas, what joy shall noble Talbot have
  To bid his young son welcome to his grave?
  Away! Vexation almost stops my breath,   41
  That sundered friends greet in the hour of death.
  Lucy, farewell. No more my fortune can   43
  But curse the cause I cannot aid the man.
  Maine, Blois, Poitiers, and Tours are won away,
  'Long all of Somerset and his delay.
                          Exit [with his soldiers].

LUCY
  Thus, while the vulture of sedition
  Feeds in the bosom of such great commanders,
  Sleeping neglection doth betray to loss
  The conquest of our scarce-cold conqueror,
  That ever-living man of memory,   51
  Henry the Fifth. Whiles they each other cross,
  Lives, honors, lands, and all hurry to loss.

---

25 stop hold back.   **cornets** cavalry units   **30 distressed** in difficulties   **33 'long of** on account of   **41 Vexation** anguish   **43 can** is able to do   **51 ever-living . . . memory** man of ever-living memory

4.4 *Enter Somerset, with his army; [a Captain of Talbot's with him].*

SOMERSET
  It is too late. I cannot send them now.
  This expedition was by York and Talbot
  Too rashly plotted. All our general force   3
  Might with a sally of the very town   4
  Be buckled with. The overdaring Talbot   5
  Hath sullied all his gloss of former honor
  By this unheedful, desperate, wild adventure.
  York set him on to fight and die in shame,
  That, Talbot dead, great York might bear the name.   9
CAPTAIN
  Here is Sir William Lucy, who with me
  Set from our o'ermatched forces forth for aid.

  [Sir William Lucy comes forward.]

SOMERSET
  How now, Sir William, whither were you sent?
LUCY
  Whither, my lord? From bought and sold Lord Talbot,
  Who, ringed about with bold adversity,
  Cries out for noble York and Somerset
  To beat assailing death from his weak legions;
  And whiles the honorable captain there
  Drops bloody sweat from his war-wearied limbs,
  And, in advantage lingering, looks for rescue,   19
  You, his false hopes, the trust of England's honor,   20
  Keep off aloof with worthless emulation.   21
  Let not your private discord keep away
  The levied succors that should lend him aid,   23
  While he, renownèd noble gentleman,

4.4. **Location:** France. Scene continues. Lucy does not leave the stage.
3–5 All . . . with i.e., our entire army might be successfully encountered
by a sortie of the mere French garrison in Bordeaux, unsupported by
the other French armies coming to the relief of Bordeaux   **9 That** so
that.   **bear the name** i.e., receive all honor as supreme commander in
France   **19 in advantage lingering** making the best he can out of delay-
ing tactics, or finding every way he can to delay matters   **20 trust**
guardian   **21 worthless emulation** ignoble rivalry   **23 levied succors**
raised reinforcements

Yield up his life unto a world of odds.   25
Orleans the Bastard, Charles, Burgundy,
Alençon, Reignier, compass him about,
And Talbot perisheth by your default.   28

SOMERSET
York set him on. York should have sent him aid.

LUCY
And York as fast upon Your Grace exclaims,   30
Swearing that you withhold his levied horse,
Collected for this expedition.

SOMERSET
York lies. He might have sent and had the horse.   33
I owe him little duty, and less love,
And take foul scorn to fawn on him by sending.   35

LUCY
The fraud of England, not the force of France,
Hath now entrapped the noble-minded Talbot.
Never to England shall he bear his life,
But dies betrayed to fortune by your strife.

SOMERSET
Come, go. I will dispatch the horsemen straight.
Within six hours they will be at his aid.

LUCY
Too late comes rescue. He is ta'en or slain;
For fly he could not, if he would have fled;
And fly would Talbot never, though he might.

SOMERSET
If he be dead, brave Talbot, then adieu!

LUCY
His fame lives in the world, his shame in you.
                                        Exeunt [separately].

❧

4.5   *Enter Talbot and his son [John].*

TALBOT
O young John Talbot, I did send for thee

25 a world of huge **28 default** failure **30 upon . . . exclaims** accuses
Your Grace **33 might . . . had** i.e., had and could have sent **35 take
foul scorn** consider it humiliating

4.5. Location: France. A field of battle near Bordeaux.

To tutor thee in stratagems of war,
That Talbot's name might be in thee revived
When sapless age and weak unable limbs
Should bring thy father to his drooping chair.   5
But, O malignant and ill-boding stars!
Now thou art come unto a feast of death,
A terrible and unavoided danger.   8
Therefore, dear boy, mount on my swiftest horse,
And I'll direct thee how thou shalt escape
By sudden flight. Come, dally not, begone.

JOHN
Is my name Talbot, and am I your son,
And shall I fly? O, if you love my mother,
Dishonor not her honorable name
To make a bastard and a slave of me!   15
The world will say he is not Talbot's blood
That basely fled when noble Talbot stood.

TALBOT
Fly to revenge my death if I be slain.

JOHN
He that flies so will ne'er return again.

TALBOT
If we both stay, we both are sure to die.

JOHN
Then let me stay, and, Father, do you fly.
Your loss is great; so your regard should be.   22
My worth unknown, no loss is known in me.   23
Upon my death the French can little boast;
In yours they will, in you all hopes are lost.
Flight cannot stain the honor you have won;
But mine it will, that no exploit have done.   27
You fled for vantage, everyone will swear,   28
But if I bow they'll say it was for fear.
There is no hope that ever I will stay,
If the first hour I shrink and run away.

---

5 drooping invalid   **8 unavoided** unavoidable   **15 To . . . me** by prompting me to act the part of a bastard and contemptible low person
22 Your loss is great the loss of you would be a severe setback.   **regard**
heed for yourself   **23 no loss . . . me** the loss of me would scarcely be
noticed   **27 that** I who   **28 vantage** military advantage

Here on my knee I beg mortality,   32
Rather than life preserved with infamy.

TALBOT
Shall all thy mother's hopes lie in one tomb?

JOHN
Ay, rather than I'll shame my mother's womb.

TALBOT
Upon my blessing I command thee go.

JOHN
To fight I will, but not to fly the foe.

TALBOT
Part of thy father may be saved in thee.

JOHN
No part of him but will be shame in me.

TALBOT
Thou never hadst renown, nor canst not lose it.

JOHN
Yes, your renownèd name. Shall flight abuse it?   41

TALBOT
Thy father's charge shall clear thee from that stain.   42

JOHN
You cannot witness for me, being slain.   43
If death be so apparent, then both fly.

TALBOT
And leave my followers here to fight and die?
My age was never tainted with such shame.   46

JOHN
And shall my youth be guilty of such blame?
No more can I be severed from your side
Than can yourself yourself in twain divide.
Stay, go, do what you will—the like do I;
For live I will not, if my father die.

TALBOT
Then here I take my leave of thee, fair son,
Born to eclipse thy life this afternoon.   53
Come, side by side together live and die,
And soul with soul from France to heaven fly.

                                                              Exeunt.

32 **mortality** death 41 **abuse** dishonor 42 **charge** giving you an order 43 **being slain** i.e., you having been slain 46 **age** lifetime
53 **eclipse** (suggesting a pun on *son, sun* in the previous line)

4.6   *Alarum. Excursions, wherein Talbot's son is hemmed about, and Talbot rescues him.*

TALBOT
Saint George and victory! Fight, soldiers, fight!
The Regent hath with Talbot broke his word   2
And left us to the rage of France his sword.   3
Where is John Talbot?—Pause, and take thy breath.
I gave thee life and rescued thee from death.

JOHN
O, twice my father, twice am I thy son!
The life thou gav'st me first was lost and done
Till with thy warlike sword, despite of fate,   8
To my determined time thou gav'st new date.   9

TALBOT
When from the Dauphin's crest thy sword struck fire,   10
It warmed thy father's heart with proud desire
Of boldfaced victory. Then leaden age,
Quickened with youthful spleen and warlike rage,   13
Beat down Alençon, Orleans, Burgundy,
And from the pride of Gallia rescued thee.   15
The ireful bastard Orleans, that drew blood
From thee, my boy, and had the maidenhood
Of thy first fight, I soon encounterèd,
And interchanging blows, I quickly shed
Some of his bastard blood; and in disgrace   20
Bespoke him thus: "Contaminated, base,
And misbegotten blood I spill of thine,
Mean and right poor, for that pure blood of mine   23
Which thou didst force from Talbot, my brave boy."
Here, purposing the Bastard to destroy,   25
Came in strong rescue. Speak, thy father's care.
Art thou not weary, John? How dost thou fare?

4.6. Location: The battlefield still, moments later; the scene is continuous.
2 The Regent i.e., the Duke of York. (Cf. 4.1.162–163.)   **3 France his**
France's   **8 despite of fate** defying what fate had seemingly decreed
9 determined having been determined to end.   **date** limit, termination
10 crest i.e., helmet   **13 Quickened** revived.   **spleen** i.e., courage,
ardor   **15 Gallia** France   **20 in disgrace** by way of insult   **23 Mean**
base, inferior   **25 purposing** as I purposed

Wilt thou yet leave the battle, boy, and fly,
Now thou art sealed the son of chivalry?   29
Fly, to revenge my death when I am dead.
The help of one stands me in little stead.
O, too much folly is it, well I wot,   32
To hazard all our lives in one small boat!
If I today die not with Frenchmen's rage,
Tomorrow I shall die with mickle age.   35
By me they nothing gain an if I stay;
'Tis but the shortening of my life one day.
In thee thy mother dies, our household's name,
My death's revenge, thy youth, and England's fame.
All these and more we hazard by thy stay;
All these are saved if thou wilt fly away.

JOHN
The sword of Orleans hath not made me smart;   42
These words of yours draw lifeblood from my heart.
On that advantage, bought with such a shame,   44
To save a paltry life and slay bright fame,
Before young Talbot from old Talbot fly,
The coward horse that bears me fall and die!   47
And like me to the peasant boys of France,   48
To be shame's scorn and subject of mischance!
Surely, by all the glory you have won,
An if I fly, I am not Talbot's son.
Then talk no more of flight. It is no boot.   52
If son to Talbot, die at Talbot's foot.

TALBOT
Then follow thou thy desperate sire of Crete,
Thou Icarus. Thy life to me is sweet.   55
If thou wilt fight, fight by thy father's side;
And, commendable proved, let's die in pride.

                                        Exeunt.

---

29 sealed certified   **32 wot** know   **35 mickle** great   **42 smart** feel
pain   **44 On that advantage** i.e., to gain that advantage of safety
47 fall i.e., may it fall   **48 like** liken   **52 boot** profit, advantage
55 Thou Icarus (Daedalus of Crete and his son Icarus escaped from the
labyrinth by means of wings that the father's ingenuity had devised. As
they flew across the sea, Icarus mounted too high, the sun's heat melted
the wax by which his wings were attached, and he fell into the sea,
hence called the Icarian Sea, and was lost.)

4.7   *Alarum. Excursions. Enter old Talbot*
          led [by a Servant].

TALBOT
   Where is my other life? Mine own is gone.
   O, where's young Talbot? Where is valiant John?
   Triumphant Death, smeared with captivity,   3
   Young Talbot's valor makes me smile at thee.
   When he perceived me shrink and on my knee,   5
   His bloody sword he brandished over me,
   And like a hungry lion did commence
   Rough deeds of rage and stern impatience.
   But when my angry guardant stood alone,   9
   Tend'ring my ruin and assailed of none,   10
   Dizzy-eyed fury and great rage of heart
   Suddenly made him from my side to start
   Into the clustering battle of the French;   13
   And in that sea of blood my boy did drench   14
   His overmounting spirit; and there died
   My Icarus, my blossom, in his pride.   16

     Enter [soldiers], with John Talbot, borne.

SERVANT
   O my dear lord, lo, where your son is borne!
TALBOT
   Thou antic Death, which laugh'st us here to scorn,   18
   Anon, from thy insulting tyranny,
   Coupled in bonds of perpetuity,
   Two Talbots, wingèd through the lither sky,   21
   In thy despite shall scape mortality.   22
   O thou, whose wounds become hard-favored Death,   23

4.7. Location: The battlefield still; the scene is continuous.
3 smeared with captivity i.e., stained with the blood of your captives.
(The image is of a triumphal procession.)   **5 shrink** retire in battle
9 guardant guardian   **10 Tend'ring** being concerned for.   **of** by
13 battle army   **14 drench** drown   **16 pride** glory   **18 antic** i.e., grin-
ning. (A personification probably suggested by grotesque pictorial
representations in the Middle Ages and early Renaissance such as the
Dance of Death.)   **here** here on earth   **21 lither** yielding   **22 In thy
despite** in spite of you.   **scape mortality** escape the bonds of death
(through immortality)   **23 thou** i.e., John.   **become . . . Death** make
Death, otherwise hideous, beautiful

Speak to thy father ere thou yield thy breath!
Brave Death by speaking, whether he will or no;   25
Imagine him a Frenchman and thy foe.
Poor boy! He smiles, methinks, as who should say,   27
"Had Death been French, then Death had died today."
Come, come, and lay him in his father's arms.
                    [*John is laid in his father's arms.*]
My spirit can no longer bear these harms.
Soldiers, adieu! I have what I would have,
Now my old arms are young John Talbot's grave.   32
                    Dies. [*Exeunt soldiers.*]

Enter Charles, Alençon, Burgundy, Bastard,
and Pucelle.

CHARLES
Had York and Somerset brought rescue in,
We should have found a bloody day of this.
BASTARD
How the young whelp of Talbot's, raging wood,   35
Did flesh his puny sword in Frenchmen's blood!   36
PUCELLE
Once I encountered him, and thus I said:
"Thou maiden youth, be vanquished by a maid."   38
But with a proud, majestical high scorn
He answered thus: "Young Talbot was not born
To be the pillage of a giglot wench."   41
So, rushing in the bowels of the French,
He left me proudly, as unworthy fight.   43
BURGUNDY
Doubtless he would have made a noble knight.
See where he lies inhearsèd in the arms   45
Of the most bloody nurser of his harms!   46

---

25 Brave defy   **27 as who** as if one   **32 s.d. Dies** (Historically, Talbot did
not die until some twenty-two years after Henry VI's coronation in Paris.
Talbot's campaign in the Bordeaux region was successful, and included the
taking of the city.)   **35 whelp of Talbot's** (Talbot is the name of a species of
hound.)   **wood** mad   **36 flesh** use for the first time in battle.   **puny**
inexperienced (in bloodshed)   **38 maiden** i.e., not yet initiated in warfare
41 giglot wanton   **43 unworthy** unworthy of   **45 inhearsèd** as in a coffin
46 nurser . . . harms i.e., sire of his capacity for doing harm to his enemy

BASTARD

 Hew them to pieces, hack their bones asunder,
 Whose life was England's glory, Gallia's wonder.

CHARLES

 O, no, forbear! For that which we have fled
 During the life, let us not wrong it dead.

 Enter [Sir William] Lucy [attended; Herald of the
 French preceding].

LUCY

 Herald, conduct me to the Dauphin's tent,
 To know who hath obtained the glory of the day.

CHARLES

 On what submissive message art thou sent?

LUCY

 Submission, Dauphin? 'Tis a mere French word.
 We English warriors wot not what it means.
 I come to know what prisoners thou hast ta'en
 And to survey the bodies of the dead.

CHARLES

 For prisoners ask'st thou? Hell our prison is.   58
 But tell me whom thou seek'st.

LUCY

 But where's the great Alcides of the field,   60
 Valiant Lord Talbot, Earl of Shrewsbury,
 Created for his rare success in arms
 Great Earl of Wexford, Waterford, and Valence,
 Lord Talbot of Goodrich and Urchinfield,
 Lord Strange of Blackmere, Lord Verdun of Alton,
 Lord Cromwell of Wingfield, Lord Furnival of Sheffield,
 The thrice-victorious Lord of Falconbridge,
 Knight of the noble order of Saint George,
 Worthy Saint Michael, and the Golden Fleece,
 Great Marshal to Henry the Sixth
 Of all his wars within the realm of France?

PUCELLE

 Here's a silly stately style indeed!   72

---

58 Hell . . . is i.e., we have slain and thus sent our enemies to hell rather
than taking any prisoners   **60 Alcides** Hercules. (Literally, descendant
of Alcaeus, who was the father of Hercules' stepfather.)   **72 style** list of
titles, manner of address

The Turk, that two-and-fifty kingdoms hath,   73
Writes not so tedious a style as this.
Him that thou magnifi'st with all these titles
Stinking and flyblown lies here at our feet.

LUCY
Is Talbot slain, the Frenchmen's only scourge,   77
Your kingdom's terror and black nemesis?   78
O, were mine eyeballs into bullets turned,
That I in rage might shoot them at your faces!
O, that I could but call these dead to life!
It were enough to fright the realm of France.
Were but his picture left amongst you here,
It would amaze the proudest of you all.   84
Give me their bodies, that I may bear them hence
And give them burial as beseems their worth.   86

PUCELLE
I think this upstart is old Talbot's ghost,
He speaks with such a proud commanding spirit.
For God's sake, let him have them! To keep them here,
They would but stink and putrefy the air.

CHARLES   Go, take their bodies hence.

LUCY
I'll bear them hence; but from their ashes shall be reared
A phoenix that shall make all France afeard.   93
                    [Exeunt Lucy, Herald, and attendants
                              with the bodies.]

CHARLES
So we be rid of them, do with them what thou wilt.   94
And now to Paris in this conquering vein.
All will be ours, now bloody Talbot's slain.   Exeunt.

❖

73 **The Turk** i.e., the Sultan of Turkey   77 **only** supreme   78 **nemesis**
agent for retribution or punishment   84 **amaze** stun, throw into confusion   86 **beseems their worth** befits their rank   93 **phoenix** fabulous
bird, the only one of its kind, which every five hundred years built itself
a funeral pile and died upon it; from the ashes a new phoenix arose
94 **So** as long as

5.1 *Sennet. Enter King, Gloucester, and Exeter.*

KING
Have you perused the letters from the Pope,   1
The Emperor, and the Earl of Armagnac?   2
GLOUCESTER
I have, my lord, and their intent is this:
They humbly sue unto your excellence
To have a godly peace concluded of
Between the realms of England and of France.
KING
How doth Your Grace affect their motion?   7
GLOUCESTER
Well, my good lord, and as the only means
To stop effusion of our Christian blood
And stablish quietness on every side.
KING
Ay, marry, uncle; for I always thought
It was both impious and unnatural
That such immanity and bloody strife   13
Should reign among professors of one faith.
GLOUCESTER
Besides, my lord, the sooner to effect
And surer bind this knot of amity,
The Earl of Armagnac, near knit to Charles,   17
A man of great authority in France,
Proffers his only daughter to Your Grace
In marriage, with a large and sumptuous dowry.
KING
Marriage, uncle! Alas, my years are young,
And fitter is my study and my books
Than wanton dalliance with a paramour.
Yet call th' ambassadors. [*Exit one or more.*] And, as
    you please,

5.1. Location: London. The royal court.
1–2 Pope . . . Armagnac (During the year 1434–1435 efforts were made
by the Emperor Sigismund and other potentates to effect a peace. The
marriage proposal of the King to the Earl of Armagnac's daughter,
however, was made eight or nine years later.) **7 affect their motion**
incline toward their proposal **13 immanity** atrocious savagery **17 knit**
i.e., by ties of kinship

So let them have their answers every one.
I shall be well content with any choice
Tends to God's glory and my country's weal.   27

> *Enter Winchester [in cardinal's habit], and three*
> *Ambassadors, [one a Papal Legate].*

EXETER [*Aside*]
What? Is my lord of Winchester installed
And called unto a cardinal's degree?   29
Then I perceive that will be verified
Henry the Fifth did sometime prophesy: 31
"If once he come to be a cardinal,
He'll make his cap coequal with the crown."   33

KING
My Lords Ambassadors, your several suits   34
Have been considered and debated on.
Your purpose is both good and reasonable,
And therefore are we certainly resolved
To draw conditions of a friendly peace,   38
Which by my lord of Winchester we mean
Shall be transported presently to France.   40

GLOUCESTER [*To the Ambassadors from Armagnac*]
And for the proffer of my lord your master,   41
I have informed His Highness so at large   42
As, liking of the lady's virtuous gifts,
Her beauty, and the value of her dower,
He doth intend she shall be England's queen.

KING
In argument and proof of which contract,
Bear her this jewel, pledge of my affection.
> [*A jewel is presented to the Ambassadors.*]
And so, my Lord Protector, see them guarded
And safely brought to Dover, wherein shipped,   49
Commit them to the fortune of the sea.
> *Exeunt [all but Winchester and Legate].*

---

27 Tends that tends   **29 called . . . degree** (Winchester's newly being
made a cardinal is inconsistent with l.3.19 and 36.)   **31 sometime** at one
time   **33 cap** i.e., cardinal's skullcap   **34 several** various   **38 draw**
draw up   **40 presently** immediately   **41 for** as for, regarding   **42 at
large** in full   **49 shipped** embarked

WINCHESTER
   Stay, my Lord Legate. You shall first receive
   The sum of money which I promisèd
   Should be delivered to His Holiness
   For clothing me in these grave ornaments.   54

LEGATE
   I will attend upon your lordship's leisure.
                                        [*He steps aside.*]

WINCHESTER [*Aside*]
   Now Winchester will not submit, I trow,
   Or be inferior to the proudest peer.
   Humphrey of Gloucester, thou shalt well perceive
   That neither in birth or for authority
   The Bishop will be overborne by thee.
   I'll either make thee stoop and bend thy knee,
   Or sack this country with a mutiny.   *Exeunt.* 62

❖

5.2   *Enter Charles, Burgundy, Alençon, Bastard,*
        Reignier, and Joan [*la Pucelle*].

CHARLES
   These news, my lords, may cheer our drooping spirits:
   'Tis said the stout Parisians do revolt   2
   And turn again unto the warlike French.

ALENÇON
   Then march to Paris, royal Charles of France,
   And keep not back your powers in dalliance.   5

PUCELLE
   Peace be amongst them, if they turn to us;
   Else, ruin combat with their palaces!   7

    Enter Scout.

---

54 grave ornaments i.e., solemn robes of ecclesiastical office
62 mutiny rebellion

5.2. Location: France. Fields before Angiers.
2 stout courageous   **5 powers** forces   **7 Else . . . palaces** otherwise, let
ruin destroy their palaces

SCOUT
Success unto our valiant general,
And happiness to his accomplices!   9

CHARLES
What tidings send our scouts? I prithee, speak.

SCOUT
The English army, that divided was
Into two parties, is now conjoined in one
And means to give you battle presently.

CHARLES
Somewhat too sudden, sirs, the warning is,
But we will presently provide for them.

BURGUNDY
I trust the ghost of Talbot is not there.
Now he is gone, my lord, you need not fear.

PUCELLE
Of all base passions, fear is most accurst.
Command the conquest, Charles, it shall be thine,
Let Henry fret and all the world repine.

CHARLES
Then on, my lords, and France be fortunate!
                                           Exeunt.

5.3   *Alarum. Excursions. Enter Joan la Pucelle.*

PUCELLE
The Regent conquers and the Frenchmen fly.   1
Now help, ye charming spells and periapts,   2
And ye choice spirits that admonish me   3
And give me signs of future accidents.   *Thunder.*   4
You speedy helpers, that are substitutes   5
Under the lordly monarch of the north,   6
Appear and aid me in this enterprise!

     Enter Fiends.

This speedy and quick appearance argues proof   8

---

9 **accomplices** allies

5.3. **Location: Before Angiers still. The scene is continuous.**
1 **The Regent** i.e., the Duke of York   2 **charming** working by charms.
periapts amulets   3 **admonish** forewarn   4 **accidents** occurrences
5 **substitutes** deputies, agents   6 **north** (Evil spirits were frequently
associated with the north.)   8 **argues proof** gives evidence

Of your accustomed diligence to me.
Now, ye familiar spirits, that are culled
Out of the powerful regions under earth,
Help me this once, that France may get the field.   12
                    They walk, and speak not.
O, hold me not with silence overlong!
Where I was wont to feed you with my blood,   14
I'll lop a member off and give it you
In earnest of a further benefit,   16
So you do condescend to help me now.   17
                    They hang their heads.
No hope to have redress? My body shall
Pay recompense, if you will grant my suit.
                    They shake their heads.
Cannot my body nor blood sacrifice
Entreat you to your wonted furtherance?   21
Then take my soul—my body, soul, and all—
Before that England give the French the foil.   23
                    They depart.
See, they forsake me! Now the time is come
That France must vail her lofty-plumèd crest   25
And let her head fall into England's lap.
My ancient incantations are too weak,   27
And hell too strong for me to buckle with.   28
Now, France, thy glory droopeth to the dust.   *Exit.*

*Excursions. Burgundy and York fight hand to
hand. French fly. [Joan la Pucelle is taken.]*

YORK
Damsel of France, I think I have you fast.
Unchain your spirits now with spelling charms,   31
And try if they can gain your liberty.
A goodly prize, fit for the devil's grace!   33

12 get the field win the battle   **14 Where** (1) whereas (2) where
16 earnest advance payment.   **further benefit** (with sexual suggestion,
as in *member*, l. 15, and *Pay recompense*, l. 19)   **17 So** provided
21 wonted furtherance customary aid   **23 Before that** before.   **foil**
defeat   **25 vail** lower.   **lofty-plumèd crest** plume proudly waving at the
top of the helmet (in token of arrogant pride)   **27 ancient** former
28 buckle with do combat with (continuing the sexual suggestion of
ll. 15–19)   **31 spirits** i.e., the demons—"familiars"—attending on Joan.
(Cf. l. 10.)   **spelling charms** charms that cast a spell   **33 the devil's
grace** His Grace the devil. (Said sardonically.)

See how the ugly witch doth bend her brows
As if, with Circe, she would change my shape!   35
PUCELLE
Changed to a worser shape thou canst not be.
YORK
O, Charles the Dauphin is a proper man!   37
No shape but his can please your dainty eye.   38
PUCELLE
A plaguing mischief light on Charles and thee!   39
And may ye both be suddenly surprised   40
By bloody hands in sleeping on your beds!
YORK
Fell banning hag! Enchantress, hold thy tongue!   42
PUCELLE
I prithee, give me leave to curse awhile.
YORK
Curse, miscreant, when thou com'st to the stake.   44
                                        Exeunt.

Alarum. Enter Suffolk, with Margaret in his hand.

SUFFOLK
Be what thou wilt, thou art my prisoner.
                                        Gazes on her.

O fairest beauty, do not fear nor fly!
For I will touch thee but with reverent hands.
I kiss these fingers for eternal peace   48
And lay them gently on thy tender side.   49
Who art thou? Say, that I may honor thee.
MARGARET
Margaret my name, and daughter to a king,
The King of Naples, whosoe'er thou art.
SUFFOLK
An earl I am, and Suffolk am I called.

---

35 with like. **Circe** sorceress celebrated for her power to change men
into swine   **37 proper** handsome. (Said sardonically.)   **38 dainty** fastidi-
ous   **39 mischief** misfortune   **40 surprised** assailed, taken   **42 Fell**
fierce, cruel.   **banning** cursing   **44 s.d. in his hand** by the hand
48–49 I kiss . . . side i.e., I kiss your hand (which I am holding) in token
of eternal peace between us, and then I release your hand to hang by
your side in token of giving you your freedom. (See l. 61, where Suffolk
speaks of freeing her hand, even though his heart tells him to keep her.)

Be not offended, nature's miracle,
Thou art allotted to be ta'en by me.   55
So doth the swan her downy cygnets save,
Keeping them prisoner underneath her wings.
Yet if this servile usage once offend,   58
Go and be free again as Suffolk's friend.   59
                                        She is going.
O, stay! [*Aside.*] I have no power to let her pass;
My hand would free her, but my heart says no.
As plays the sun upon the glassy streams,   62
Twinkling another counterfeited beam,   63
So seems this gorgeous beauty to mine eyes.
Fain would I woo her, yet I dare not speak.
I'll call for pen and ink and write my mind.
Fie, de la Pole, disable not thyself!   67
Hast not a tongue? Is she not here?   68
Wilt thou be daunted at a woman's sight?   69
Ay, beauty's princely majesty is such
Confounds the tongue and makes the senses rough.   71

MARGARET
Say, Earl of Suffolk—if thy name be so—
What ransom must I pay before I pass?
For I perceive I am thy prisoner.

SUFFOLK [*Aside*]
How canst thou tell she will deny thy suit
Before thou make a trial of her love?

MARGARET
Why speak'st thou not? What ransom must I pay?

SUFFOLK [*Aside*]
She's beautiful, and therefore to be wooed;
She is a woman, therefore to be won.

MARGARET
Wilt thou accept of ransom, yea or no?

SUFFOLK [*Aside*]
Fond man, remember that thou hast a wife.   81
Then how can Margaret be thy paramour?

55 allotted destined   **58 servile usage** being treated as a captive
59 friend (with suggestion of "lover")   **62 As . . . streams** just as the sun
plays upon the glassy surface of a stream   **63 Twinkling** causing to
twinkle.   **counterfeited** i.e., reflected   **67 disable** disparage   **68 here**
i.e., here with me, ready to be wooed   **69 a woman's sight** the sight of a
woman   **71 Confounds** that it confounds   **81 Fond** foolish

MARGARET
  I were best to leave him, for he will not hear.
SUFFOLK [*Aside*]
  There all is marred; there lies a cooling card.   84
MARGARET
  He talks at random. Sure the man is mad.
SUFFOLK [*Aside*]
  And yet a dispensation may be had.   86
MARGARET
  And yet I would that you would answer me.
SUFFOLK [*Aside*]
  I'll win this Lady Margaret. For whom?
  Why, for my king. Tush, that's a wooden thing!   89
MARGARET
  He talks of wood. It is some carpenter.
SUFFOLK [*Aside*]
  Yet so my fancy may be satisfied,   91
  And peace establishèd between these realms.
  But there remains a scruple in that too;
  For though her father be the King of Naples,
  Duke of Anjou and Maine, yet is he poor,
  And our nobility will scorn the match.
MARGARET
  Hear ye, Captain, are you not at leisure?
SUFFOLK [*Aside*]
  It shall be so, disdain they ne'er so much.
  Henry is youthful and will quickly yield.—
  Madam, I have a secret to reveal.
MARGARET [*Aside*]
  What though I be enthralled? He seems a knight,   101
  And will not any way dishonor me.
SUFFOLK
  Lady, vouchsafe to listen what I say.
MARGARET [*Aside*]
  Perhaps I shall be rescued by the French,
  And then I need not crave his courtesy.

---

84 cooling card something that cools one's ardor or dashes one's hopes.
(A metaphor from card playing.)   **86 dispensation** papal permission (to
divorce a wife)   **89 wooden** stupid (i.e., either King Henry, or Suffolk's
plan)   **91 fancy** desire in love   **101 enthralled** captured

SUFFOLK
  Sweet madam, give me hearing in a cause—
MARGARET [*Aside*]
  Tush, women have been captivate ere now.   107
SUFFOLK
  Lady, wherefore talk you so?
MARGARET
  I cry you mercy, 'tis but quid for quo.   109
SUFFOLK
  Say, gentle Princess, would you not suppose
  Your bondage happy, to be made a queen?   111
MARGARET
  To be a queen in bondage is more vile
  Than is a slave in base servility,
  For princes should be free.
SUFFOLK   And so shall you,   114
  If happy England's royal king be free.   115
MARGARET
  Why, what concerns his freedom unto me?
SUFFOLK
  I'll undertake to make thee Henry's queen,
  To put a golden scepter in thy hand,
  And set a precious crown upon thy head,
  If thou wilt condescend to be my—
MARGARET   What?   120
SUFFOLK His love.
MARGARET
  I am unworthy to be Henry's wife.
SUFFOLK
  No, gentle madam. I unworthy am
  To woo so fair a dame to be his wife
  And have no portion in the choice myself.   125
  How say you, madam, are ye so content?

---

107 captive taken captive **109 cry you mercy** beg your pardon. **quid
for quo** tit for tat **111 to be** i.e., if you were to be **114 princes** i.e.,
men or women of royal birth **115 happy** fortunate **120 condescend**
consent **125 And have . . . myself** (Suffolk seems to say to Margaret
that he is only the unworthy agent, not deserving to have any other role,
but his double meaning points to his having a "piece" out of this for
himself.) **choice** (1) choosing (2) person chosen

MARGARET
An if my father please, I am content.   127
SUFFOLK
Then call our captains and our colors forth.   128
And, madam, at your father's castle walls
We'll crave a parley, to confer with him.   130

    Sound [a parley]. Enter Reignier on the walls.

See, Reignier, see thy daughter prisoner!
REIGNIER
To whom?
SUFFOLK   To me.
REIGNIER   Suffolk, what remedy?
I am a soldier, and unapt to weep
Or to exclaim on fortune's fickleness.   134
SUFFOLK
Yes, there is remedy enough, my lord.
Consent, and for thy honor give consent,   136
Thy daughter shall be wedded to my king,
Whom I with pain have wooed and won thereto;   138
And this her easy-held imprisonment   139
Hath gained thy daughter princely liberty.
REIGNIER
Speaks Suffolk as he thinks?
SUFFOLK   Fair Margaret knows
That Suffolk doth not flatter, face, or feign.   142
REIGNIER
Upon thy princely warrant, I descend
To give thee answer of thy just demand.
                        [Exit from the walls.]
SUFFOLK
And here I will expect thy coming.   145

    Trumpets sound. Enter Reignier [below].

127 An if if   **128 Then . . . forth** (Suffolk probably calls offstage to
attendants.)   **130 s.d. on the walls** (As in previous sieges, the "walls" of
Angiers are here represented by the tiring-house facade, with Reignier
appearing above, in the gallery backstage.)   **134 exclaim on** complain
against   **136 Consent . . . consent** consent, and do so for the sake of
your honor   **138 Whom** i.e., Margaret   **139 easy-held** easily endured
142 face show a false face, deceive   **145 expect** await

REIGNIER
Welcome, brave earl, into our territories.
Command in Anjou what your honor pleases.

SUFFOLK
Thanks, Reignier, happy for so sweet a child,   148
Fit to be made companion with a king.
What answer makes Your Grace unto my suit?

REIGNIER
Since thou dost deign to woo her little worth   151
To be the princely bride of such a lord,
Upon condition I may quietly
Enjoy mine own, the country Maine and Anjou,   154
Free from oppression or the stroke of war,
My daughter shall be Henry's, if he please.

SUFFOLK
That is her ransom. I deliver her,   157
And those two counties I will undertake
Your Grace shall well and quietly enjoy.

REIGNIER
And I again, in Henry's royal name,   160
As deputy unto that gracious king,   161
Give thee her hand for sign of plighted faith.

SUFFOLK
Reignier of France, I give thee kingly thanks,
Because this is in traffic of a king.   164
[*Aside.*] And yet methinks I could be well content
To be mine own attorney in this case.—
I'll over then to England with this news
And make this marriage to be solemnized.
So farewell, Reignier. Set this diamond safe
In golden palaces, as it becomes.   170

REIGNIER
I do embrace thee, as I would embrace
The Christian prince, King Henry, were he here.
                    [*He embraces Suffolk.*]

---

148 happy for fortunate in having   **151 her little worth** her, little worthy as
she is   **154 country** i.e., district or region including   **157 deliver** free. (*Her
ransom* having been agreed upon, Suffolk releases her.)   **160 again** in
return. (In return for promises made in the name of King Henry, Reignier
gives back his daughter into the hands of Suffolk, who released her to her
father three lines earlier.)   **161 As deputy** i.e., to you, Suffolk, as deputy
164 traffic business   **170 as it becomes** as befits such a jewel

MARGARET
  Farewell, my lord. Good wishes, praise, and prayers
  Shall Suffolk ever have of Margaret.   *She is going.*
SUFFOLK
  Farewell, sweet madam. But hark you, Margaret—
  No princely commendations to my king?
MARGARET
  Such commendations as becomes a maid,
  A virgin, and his servant, say to him.
SUFFOLK
  Words sweetly placed and modestly directed.   179
  But, madam, I must trouble you again—
  No loving token to His Majesty?
MARGARET
  Yes, my good lord: a pure unspotted heart,
  Never yet taint with love, I send the King.   183
SUFFOLK   And this withal.   *Kiss her.* 184
MARGARET
  That for thyself. I will not so presume
  To send such peevish tokens to a king.   186
                    [*Exeunt Reignier and Margaret.*]
SUFFOLK
  O, wert thou for myself! But, Suffolk, stay.
  Thou mayest not wander in that labyrinth;   188
  There Minotaurs and ugly treasons lurk.
  Solicit Henry with her wondrous praise;   190
  Bethink thee on her virtues that surmount
  And natural graces that extinguish art;   192
  Repeat their semblance often on the seas,   193
  That, when thou com'st to kneel at Henry's feet,
  Thou mayest bereave him of his wits with wonder.
                              Exit.

❖

179 **placed** arranged   183 **taint** tainted   184 **withal** in addition
186 **peevish** trivial   188 **labyrinth** a structure built by Daedalus consisting of intricate passageways where the Minotaur—a monster born from
the union of the Cretan king's wife with a bull—was confined   190 **her
wondrous praise** praise of her wondrous beauty   192 **extinguish** eclipse
193 **Repeat their semblance** rehearse mentally the image of her virtues

5.4   *Enter York, Warwick, Shepherd, [and] Pucelle [guarded].*

YORK
  Bring forth that sorceress condemned to burn.
SHEPHERD
  Ah, Joan, this kills thy father's heart outright!
  Have I sought every country far and near,   3
  And, now it is my chance to find thee out,   4
  Must I behold thy timeless cruel death?   5
  Ah, Joan, sweet daughter Joan, I'll die with thee!
PUCELLE
  Decrepit miser, base ignoble wretch!   7
  I am descended of a gentler blood.   8
  Thou art no father nor no friend of mine.   9
SHEPHERD
  Out, out! My lords, an please you, 'tis not so.
  I did beget her, all the parish knows.
  Her mother liveth yet, can testify
  She was the first fruit of my bach'lorship.   13
WARWICK
  Graceless, wilt thou deny thy parentage?
YORK
  This argues what her kind of life hath been,
  Wicked and vile; and so her death concludes.   16
SHEPHERD
  Fie, Joan, that thou wilt be so obstacle!   17
  God knows thou art a collop of my flesh,   18
  And for thy sake have I shed many a tear.
  Deny me not, I prithee, gentle Joan.
PUCELLE
  Peasant, avaunt!—You have suborned this man   21
  Of purpose to obscure my noble birth.   22

5.4. Location: France. Camp of the Duke of York in Anjou.
3 country district **4 chance** fortune. **find thee out** discover you
5 timeless premature **7 miser** wretch **8 gentler** more noble **9 friend**
kinsman **13 was . . . bach'lorship** i.e., was conceived out of wedlock,
was the first product of my endeavor as a young man **16 concludes**
(1) confirms (2) ends **17 obstacle** (For *obstinate*.) **18 collop** slice
21 suborned induced to commit perjury **22 Of** on

SHEPHERD
    'Tis true, I gave a noble to the priest   23
    The morn that I was wedded to her mother.
    Kneel down and take my blessing, good my girl.
    Wilt thou not stoop? Now cursèd be the time
    Of thy nativity! I would the milk
    Thy mother gave thee when thou suckedst her breast
    Had been a little ratsbane for thy sake!   29
    Or else, when thou didst keep my lambs afield,   30
    I wish some ravenous wolf had eaten thee!
    Dost thou deny thy father, cursèd drab?   32
    O, burn her, burn her! Hanging is too good.   *Exit.*
YORK [*To guards*]
    Take her away, for she hath lived too long,
    To fill the world with vicious qualities.
PUCELLE
    First, let me tell you whom you have condemned:
    Not me begotten of a shepherd swain,
    But issued from the progeny of kings,
    Virtuous and holy, chosen from above
    By inspiration of celestial grace
    To work exceeding miracles on earth.   41
    I never had to do with wicked spirits.
    But you, that are polluted with your lusts,
    Stained with the guiltless blood of innocents,
    Corrupt and tainted with a thousand vices—
    Because you want the grace that others have,   46
    You judge it straight a thing impossible   47
    To compass wonders but by help of devils.   48
    No, misconceivèd! Joan of Arc hath been   49
    A virgin from her tender infancy,
    Chaste and immaculate in very thought,
    Whose maiden blood, thus rigorously effused,   52
    Will cry for vengeance at the gates of heaven.
YORK
    Ay, ay. Away with her to execution.

---

23 noble coin worth 6 shillings 8 pence   **29 ratsbane** rat poison
30 keep tend   **32 drab** whore   **41 exceeding** exceptional   **46 want**
lack   **47 straight** straightway, at once   **48 compass** encompass, bring
about   **49 misconceivèd** you who have a wrong idea. (The word has an
ironic application to Joan.)   **52 rigorously effused** mercilessly shed

WARWICK
And hark ye, sirs: because she is a maid,
Spare for no faggots. Let there be enough.
Place barrels of pitch upon the fatal stake,   57
That so her torture may be shortenèd.

PUCELLE
Will nothing turn your unrelenting hearts?
Then, Joan, discover thine infirmity,   60
That warranteth by law to be thy privilege: 61
I am with child, ye bloody homicides.
Murder not then the fruit within my womb,
Although ye hale me to a violent death.

YORK
Now heaven forfend! The holy maid with child?   65

WARWICK
The greatest miracle that e'er ye wrought.
Is all your strict preciseness come to this?   67

YORK
She and the Dauphin have been juggling.   68
I did imagine what would be her refuge.

WARWICK
Well, go to. We'll have no bastards live,
Especially since Charles must father it.   71

PUCELLE
You are deceived. My child is none of his.
It was Alençon that enjoyed my love.

YORK
Alençon, that notorious Machiavel?   74
It dies an if it had a thousand lives.

PUCELLE
O, give me leave, I have deluded you.

---

57 pitch (Pitch would produce heavy smoke, asphyxiating the person
being burned and thereby shortening the suffering. Warwick may be
speaking sardonically, however: we're going to give you a nice quick
death.)   **60 discover** reveal   **61 warranteth** guarantees.   **privilege** i.e., to
be spared until the birth of her supposed child   **65 forfend** forbid. (Said
sardonically.)   **67 preciseness** propriety, modesty   **68 juggling** playing
conjuring tricks (with sexual suggestion)   **71 must father it** is evidently
the father   **74 Machiavel** (In the popular Elizabethan conception,
Niccolò Machiavelli, Italian political philosopher, symbolized political
immorality and ruthless ambition.)

'Twas neither Charles nor yet the Duke I named,
But Reignier, King of Naples, that prevailed.

WARWICK
A married man! That's most intolerable.

YORK
Why, here's a girl! I think she knows not well,
There were so many, whom she may accuse.

WARWICK
It's sign she hath been liberal and free.   82

YORK
And yet, forsooth, she is a virgin pure!
Strumpet, thy words condemn thy brat and thee.
Use no entreaty, for it is in vain.

PUCELLE
Then lead me hence; with whom I leave my curse.
May never glorious sun reflex his beams   87
Upon the country where you make abode,
But darkness and the gloomy shade of death
Environ you, till mischief and despair   90
Drive you to break your necks or hang yourselves!
                                        Exit [guarded].

*Enter [Winchester, now] Cardinal [Beaufort, with
letters, attended].*

YORK [*To Joan as she exits*]
Break thou in pieces and consume to ashes,   92
Thou foul accursèd minister of hell!   93

CARDINAL
Lord Regent, I do greet your excellence
With letters of commission from the King.
For know, my lords, the states of Christendom,
Moved with remorse of these outrageous broils,   97
Have earnestly implored a general peace
Betwixt our nation and the aspiring French;
And here at hand the Dauphin and his train   100
Approacheth, to confer about some matter.

---

82 liberal unrestrained, licentious (with a mocking glance at a more innocent meaning, "generous")   **87 reflex** reflect, shed   **90 mischief** misfortune   **92–93 Break . . . hell** (Winchester's entrance in time to hear these
lines seemingly directed at Joan provides added irony, since Winchester is
also a villain.)   **97 remorse of** pity for   **100 train** entourage

YORK
  Is all our travail turned to this effect?   102
  After the slaughter of so many peers,
  So many captains, gentlemen, and soldiers,
  That in this quarrel have been overthrown
  And sold their bodies for their country's benefit,
  Shall we at last conclude effeminate peace?
  Have we not lost most part of all the towns,
  By treason, falsehood, and by treachery,
  Our great progenitors had conquerèd?
  O Warwick, Warwick! I foresee with grief
  The utter loss of all the realm of France.

WARWICK
  Be patient, York. If we conclude a peace,
  It shall be with such strict and severe covenants   114
  As little shall the Frenchmen gain thereby.

    Enter Charles, Alençon, Bastard, Reignier.

CHARLES
  Since, lords of England, it is thus agreed
  That peaceful truce shall be proclaimed in France,
  We come to be informèd by yourselves
  What the conditions of that league must be.

YORK
  Speak, Winchester, for boiling choler chokes   120
  The hollow passage of my poisoned voice
  By sight of these our baleful enemies.   122

CARDINAL
  Charles, and the rest, it is enacted thus:
  That, in regard King Henry gives consent,   124
  Of mere compassion and of lenity,   125
  To ease your country of distressful war
  And suffer you to breathe in fruitful peace,
  You shall become true liegemen to his crown.   128
  And, Charles, upon condition thou wilt swear
  To pay him tribute and submit thyself,
  Thou shalt be placed as viceroy under him,
  And still enjoy thy regal dignity.

102 travail labor   **114 covenants** articles of agreement   **120 choler** i.e.,
anger   **122 By** at the   **124 in regard** inasmuch as   **125 Of mere** out of
pure   **128 true liegemen** loyal subjects

ALENÇON
  Must he be then as shadow of himself?
  Adorn his temples with a coronet,
  And yet in substance and authority   135
  Retain but privilege of a private man?
  This proffer is absurd and reasonless.

CHARLES
  'Tis known already that I am possessed
  With more than half the Gallian territories   139
  And therein reverenced for their lawful king.
  Shall I, for lucre of the rest unvanquished,   141
  Detract so much from that prerogative   142
  As to be called but viceroy of the whole?   143
  No, Lord Ambassador, I'll rather keep
  That which I have than, coveting for more,
  Be cast from possibility of all.   146

YORK
  Insulting Charles, hast thou by secret means
  Used intercession to obtain a league,
  And, now the matter grows to compromise,   149
  Stand'st thou aloof upon comparison?   150
  Either accept the title thou usurp'st,
  Of benefit proceeding from our king   152
  And not of any challenge of desert,   153
  Or we will plague thee with incessant wars.

REIGNIER [*Aside to Charles*]
  My lord, you do not well in obstinacy
  To cavil in the course of this contract.   156
  If once it be neglected, ten to one
  We shall not find like opportunity.

ALENÇON [*Aside to Charles*]
  To say the truth, it is your policy   159
  To save your subjects from such massacre
  And ruthless slaughters as are daily seen

---

135 **in . . . authority** in actual power   139 **Gallian** French   141 **for lucre of** in order to gain   142 **Detract . . . prerogative** i.e., yield up my right to be called king in the territories I already possess   143 **As** so as, in order to   146 **cast** excluded   149 **grows to compromise** moves toward a peaceful settlement   150 **upon comparison** i.e., quibbling about the proposed articles   152 **Of benefit** as a feudal bestowal   153 **challenge of desert** claim of inherent right   156 **cavil** raise frivolous or fault-finding objections   159 **policy** politic course

By our proceeding in hostility;
And therefore take this compact of a truce,
Although you break it when your pleasure serves.

WARWICK
How sayst thou, Charles? Shall our condition stand?   165
CHARLES   It shall;
Only reserved, you claim no interest   167
In any of our towns of garrison.   168

YORK
Then swear allegiance to His Majesty,
As thou art knight, never to disobey
Nor be rebellious to the crown of England,
Thou nor thy nobles, to the crown of England.
        [*Charles and his nobles give tokens of fealty.*]
So, now dismiss your army when ye please.
Hang up your ensigns, let your drums be still,
For here we entertain a solemn peace.   *Exeunt.*   175

✤

5.5   *Enter Suffolk in conference with the King,
Gloucester, and Exeter.*

KING
Your wondrous rare description, noble earl,
Of beauteous Margaret hath astonished me.
Her virtues, gracèd with external gifts,
Do breed love's settled passions in my heart;   4
And like as rigor of tempestuous gusts   5
Provokes the mightiest hulk against the tide,   6
So am I driven by breath of her renown   7
Either to suffer shipwreck or arrive
Where I may have fruition of her love.

SUFFOLK
Tush, my good lord, this superficial tale

---

165 condition treaty, contract   **167 Only reserved** with this single
proviso, that   **168 towns of garrison** fortified towns   **175 entertain**
accept

5.5. Location: London. The royal court.
4 settled fixed, rooted   **5 like as rigor** just as the severity   **6 Provokes**
drives.   **hulk** vessel   **7 breath** (1) report (2) wind in the sails

Is but a preface of her worthy praise.   11
The chief perfections of that lovely dame,
Had I sufficient skill to utter them,
Would make a volume of enticing lines
Able to ravish any dull conceit;   15
And, which is more, she is not so divine,
So full replete with choice of all delights,   17
But with as humble lowliness of mind
She is content to be at your command—
Command, I mean, of virtuous chaste intents,
To love and honor Henry as her lord.

KING
And otherwise will Henry ne'er presume.
Therefore, my Lord Protector, give consent
That Margaret may be England's royal queen.

GLOUCESTER
So should I give consent to flatter sin.   25
You know, my lord, Your Highness is betrothed
Unto another lady of esteem.   27
How shall we then dispense with that contract
And not deface your honor with reproach?

SUFFOLK
As doth a ruler with unlawful oaths;
Or one that, at a triumph having vowed   31
To try his strength, forsaketh yet the lists   32
By reason of his adversary's odds.
A poor earl's daughter is unequal odds,
And therefore may be broke without offense.   35

GLOUCESTER
Why, what, I pray, is Margaret more than that?
Her father is no better than an earl,
Although in glorious titles he excel.

SUFFOLK
Yes, my lord, her father is a king,
The King of Naples and Jerusalem,
And of such great authority in France

---

11 **her worthy praise** the praise she is truly worth   15 **conceit** imagination   17 **full** fully   25 **flatter** countenance, excuse   27 **another lady** i.e.,
the Earl of Armagnac's daughter. (See 5.1.17ff.)   31 **triumph** tournament   32 **lists** place of combat in a tournament   35 **may be broke** i.e.,
the contract with her may be broken

As his alliance will confirm our peace   42
And keep the Frenchmen in allegiance.

GLOUCESTER
And so the Earl of Armagnac may do,
Because he is near kinsman unto Charles.

EXETER
Besides, his wealth doth warrant a liberal dower,   46
Where Reignier sooner will receive than give.   47

SUFFOLK
A dower, my lords? Disgrace not so your king
That he should be so abject, base, and poor
To choose for wealth and not for perfect love.
Henry is able to enrich his queen,
And not to seek a queen to make him rich.
So worthless peasants bargain for their wives,   53
As marketmen for oxen, sheep, or horse.
Marriage is a matter of more worth
Than to be dealt in by attorneyship.   56
Not whom we will, but whom His Grace affects,   57
Must be companion of his nuptial bed.
And therefore, lords, since he affects her most,
That most of all these reasons bindeth us
In our opinions she should be preferred.
For what is wedlock forcèd but a hell,
An age of discord and continual strife?   63
Whereas the contrary bringeth bliss,
And is a pattern of celestial peace.   65
Whom should we match with Henry, being a king,
But Margaret, that is daughter to a king?
Her peerless feature, joinèd with her birth,   68
Approves her fit for none but for a king.
Her valiant courage and undaunted spirit,
More than in women commonly is seen,
Will answer our hope in issue of a king;   72
For Henry, son unto a conqueror,
Is likely to beget more conquerors,

---

42 As that. **confirm** strengthen   **46 warrant** guarantee   **47 Where**
whereas   **53 So** thus do   **56 attorneyship** haggling proxies   **57 affects**
desires   **63 age** lifetime   **65 pattern** image.   **peace** harmony
68 feature figure   **72 Will . . . king** i.e., will fulfill our hopes of royal
progeny

If with a lady of so high resolve
As is fair Margaret he be linked in love.
Then yield, my lords, and here conclude with me
That Margaret shall be queen, and none but she.

KING
Whether it be through force of your report,
My noble lord of Suffolk, or for that   80
My tender youth was never yet attaint   81
With any passion of inflaming love,
I cannot tell; but this I am assured,
I feel such sharp dissension in my breast,
Such fierce alarums both of hope and fear,
As I am sick with working of my thoughts.
Take therefore shipping; post, my lord, to France.   87
Agree to any covenants, and procure   88
That Lady Margaret do vouchsafe to come
To cross the seas to England and be crowned
King Henry's faithful and anointed queen.
For your expenses and sufficient charge,   92
Among the people gather up a tenth.   93
Begone, I say, for till you do return
I rest perplexèd with a thousand cares.   95
And you, good uncle, banish all offense.   96
If you do censure me by what you were,   97
Not what you are, I know it will excuse   98
This sudden execution of my will.
And so, conduct me where, from company.   100
I may revolve and ruminate my grief.   *Exit.* 101

GLOUCESTER
Ay, grief, I fear me, both at first and last.   102
                        Exit Gloucester [with Exeter].

SUFFOLK
Thus Suffolk hath prevailed; and thus he goes,
As did the youthful Paris once to Greece,   104

---

80 for that because   **81 attaint** infected   **87 post** hasten   **88 procure**
bring it about   **92 charge** money   **93 gather up a tenth** levy a tax of ten
percent of the produce of lands and industry   **95 rest** remain
96 offense feeling of resentment and disapproval   **97–98 censure . . . are**
i.e., judge me (in my lovesickness) in comparison to your own youthful
ways, not to your present wisdom   **100 from company** i.e., alone
101–102 grief . . . grief love melancholy . . . remorse   **104 Paris** Trojan
prince whose abduction of Helen of Sparta instigated the Trojan war

With hope to find the like event in love,   105
But prosper better than the Trojan did.
Margaret shall now be Queen and rule the King;
But I will rule both her, the King, and realm.   *Exit.*

105 the like event a similar outcome

Date and Text

The date and textual situation for *1 Henry VI* needs to be discussed in the context of all three *Henry VI* plays. *1 Henry VI* was not the first to be published. Shortened versions of *2* and *3 Henry VI* appeared in 1594 and 1595. One was titled as follows:

> THE First part of the Contention betwixt the two famous Houses of Yorke and Lancaster, with the death of the good Duke Humphrey: And the banishment and death of the Duke of *Suffolke,* and the Tragicall end of the proud Cardinall of *VVinchester, vvith* the notable Rebellion of *Iacke Cade: And the Duke of Yorkes first claime vnto the Crowne.* LONDON Printed by Thomas Creed, for Thomas Millington, and are to be sold at his shop vnder Saint Peters Church in Cornwall. 1594.

Its sequel was titled as follows:

> The true Tragedie of Richard *Duke of Yorke, and the death of* good King Henrie the Sixt, *with the whole contention betweene* the two Houses Lancaster and Yorke, as it was sundrie times acted by the Right Honourable the Earle of Pembrooke his seruants. Printed at London by P. S. [Peter Short] for Thomas Milling*ton, and are to be sold at his shoppe vnder Saint Peters Church in Cornwal.* 1595.

Once thought to be source plays for Shakespeare's *2* and *3 Henry VI,* these texts, the first a quarto and the second an octavo, have been independently demonstrated by Peter Alexander and Madeleine Doran to be "bad quartos" or memorial reconstructions of Shakespeare's texts, put together by actors for sale to a printer or for acting in the provinces. As such, they have little textual authority but may be of significance in those occasional passages where the Folio compositors seem to have had recourse to a later reprint (the third quarto) of these texts. In 1619 they were combined in a reprint by the printer William Jaggard called *The Whole Contention betweene the two Famous Houses, Lancaster and Yorke.* These texts are considerably shorter than the Folio versions of 1623, which appeared there under the titles "The second Part of Henry the Sixt, with the death of the Good Duke HVMFREY," and "The third Part of Henry the Sixt, with the death of the Duke of YORKE." Since, as memorially reconstructed texts, they are ultimately derived from the promptbook, these texts may contain some materials that were revised as the plays were put into performance, but the likelihood of contamination through reporting, actors' interpolations, and transmission are so great that the textual authority here must be regarded with great caution. The Folio texts seem to have been based on authorial manuscripts, although there is evidence too that both plays or portions thereof were printed from pages of the third quartos of each play or at least with some consultation of the respective third quartos by the Folio compositors. The third quarto of *2 Henry VI* may embody some independent authority, although not necessarily the author's; the third quarto of *3 Henry VI* seems to have no such independent authority.

The text of *1 Henry VI*, based seemingly on an authorial manuscript that had been annotated in the theater and possibly recopied, was first published in the Folio of 1623. It alone of the three parts was registered for publication at this time. The Stationers' Register entry refers to this play as "The thirde parte of Henry the sixt." These circumstances once led to the assumption that *1 Henry VI* was written after the other two plays, especially since those two plays do not often recall events of *1 Henry VI*—for example, they make no mention of its hero, Lord Talbot. The seeming fact that the 1594 and 1595 quartos were pirated editions would, however, explain their publication before *1 Henry VI* and the necessity of registering Part One later. In other ways, *1 Henry VI* has shown itself to be no hasty afterthought, but a play with thematic unity throughout and a sense of direction anticipating the remainder of the series. Hence, scholars now tend to support Dr. Johnson's commonsense hunch that the three plays in this historical tetralogy were written in order.

With the notable exception of the editors of the recent Oxford Shakespeare, scholars also generally agree now that the entire series is Shakespeare's own work, or at the very least dominated by his artistic conception of the whole. The once-prevailing and recently reasserted hypotheses of multiple authorship rest on questionable internal evidence such as vocabulary or versification. What sounds like Robert Greene or George Peele in these very early plays may simply be the result of those men's undoubted influence on Shakespeare during his apprenticeship. Greene's famous outburst at Shakespeare (see below) suggests that he was keenly aware of Shakespeare's facility for learning quickly from his contemporaries. The inconsistencies in these early plays, especially in Part One—mislineation, defective verse, inaccuracy in speech prefixes, confusion about time, discrepancy in facts—may be the result not of multiple authorship but of reliance on various sources, hasty composition, and problems of transcription.

Several contemporary allusions to the *Henry VI* plays help considerably with dating the series. Thomas Nashe wrote in his *Pierce Penniless* (registered August 1592) that it would "have joyed brave Talbot (the terror of the French) to think that after he had lain two hundred years in his tomb, he should triumph again on the stage." Probably he was referring to Shakespeare's play. The reference in Henslowe's diary to a "ne" (new?) performance of *Harey the vi* in March of 1592 may or may not refer to Shakespeare's work, however, for this performance was by Lord Strange's men whereas Shakespeare's *Henry VI* series is associated elsewhere with Pembroke's men. In any event, *3 Henry VI* must have been completed by the time of Robert Greene's death in September of 1592, when Greene (or his literary executor, Chettle) alludes plainly to it (1.4.137) in his angry remark about "an upstart crow, beautified with our feathers, that with his *tiger's heart wrapped in a player's hide* supposes he is as well able to bombast out a blank verse as the best of you." These contemporary references are confirmed by allusions in the texts themselves, for all the *Henry VI* plays seem to contain echoes of Books 1–3 of Edmund Spenser's *Faerie Queene* (printed 1590), whereas *3 Henry VI* seems to have influenced parts of *The Troublesome Reign of King John* (printed 1591). An inclusive date of 1589–1591 or 1592 ought to account for the entire series.

Textual Notes

These textual notes are not a historical collation, either of the early folios or of more recent editions; they are simply a record of departures in this edition from the copy text. The reading adopted in this edition appears in boldface, followed by the rejected reading from the copy text, i.e., the First Folio. Only major alterations in punctuation are noted. Changes in lineation are not indicated, nor are some minor and obvious typographical errors.

Abbreviations used:
F the First Folio
s.d. stage direction
s.p. speech prefix

Copy text: the First Folio.

1.1. 57 s.p. First Messenger Mess [also at l. 69] **60 Rouen** [not in F] **65 [and elsewhere] Rouen** Roan **89 s.p. Second Messenger** Mess **94 Reignier** Reynold **103 s.p. Third Messenger** Mes **176 steal** send

1.2. 30 bred breed **47 s.p. [and elsewhere] Charles** Dolph **63 s.d. [and elsewhere] Pucelle** Puzel **76 whilst** whilest **99 five** fine **103 s.d. [and elsewhere] la** de **113 rites** rights **131 halcyon** Halcyons

1.3. 6 s.p. First Servingman Glost. 1. Man [at l. 8, 1. Man] **29 Humphrey** Vmpheir **30 Peeled** Piel'd **74 s.p. Officer** [not in F]

1.4. 10 Wont Went **25 gott'st** got's **27 Duke** Earle **69 s.d. shoot** shot **89 Bear . . . bury it** [before l. 87 in F] **95 Nero-like** like thee **107 [and elsewhere] Dauphin** Dolphin

1.5. 16 hungry starvèd hungry-starued

1.6. 21 pyramid Pyramis **22 of** or

2.1. 5 s.p. First Sentinel Sent [also at l. 38] **7 s.d. ladders** [F adds "Their Drummes beating a Dead March"; see textual note at 2.2.s.d.] **54 s.p. Pucelle** Ioane [also at l. 72] **77 s.d.** [F has Exeunt preceding this s.d.]

2.2. 6 s.d. their . . . march [appears at 2.1.7 in F] **20 Arc** Acre **38 Auvergne** Ouergne

2.4. 1 s.p. Plantagenet Yorke [and thus through Act 3] **57 law** you **117 wiped** whipt **132 gentlemen** gentle

2.5. 18 s.p. First Keeper Keeper [and at l. 33] **35 s.p. [and elsewhere] Plantagenet** Rich **71 King Richard** Richard **121 s.d. Exeunt** Exit **129 mine ill** my will

3.1. 52 s.p. Somerset [not in F] **53 s.p. Warwick** Som **54 s.p. Somerset** [not in F] **74** [F provides an s.p. here, "King"] **164 that** that all

3.2. 10 s.p. First Soldier Souldier **13 Qui là** Che la **21–22 specify . . . in?** specifie? . . . in. **40 s.d. Burgundy** Burgonie [also at l. 42] **41 Good** God **103 s.d. Exeunt** Exit

3.4. 27 s.d. Manent Manet

4.1. s.d. Exeter, Governor and Gouernor Exeter   **14 thee** the   **48 my Lord**
Lord   **151 umpire** Vmper   **173 s.d. Flourish** [at l. 181 in F]   **Manent**
Manet   **180 wist** wish

4.2. 3 calls call   **15 s.p. General** Cap

4.3. 5 Talbot . . . along, Talbot as he march'd along.   **17 s.p. [and throughout**
scene] Lucy 2 Mes [or *Mes*]   **20 waist** waste   **36 travel** trauaile   **53 lands**
Lauds

4.4. 13 Whither Whether   **16 legions** Regions   **27 Reignier** Reignard
31 horse hoast

4.5. 55 s.d. Exeunt Exit

4.6. 57 s.d. Exeunt Exit

4.7. 18 antic antique   **25 whether** whither   **63 Wexford** Washford
64 Goodrich Goodrig   **89 have them** haue him   **94 with them** with him
96 s.d. Exeunt Exit

5.1. 0 [F here reads "Scena secunda"]

5.2. 0 [F here reads "Scoena Tertia"]

5.3. 57 her his   **65 [and elsewhere in scene] woo** woe   **85 random** randon
179 modestly modestie   **192 And** Mad

5.4. 28 suckedst suck'st   **49 Arc** Aire   **74 Machiavel** Macheuile   **102 travail**
trauell   **123 s.p. Cardinal** Win   **127 breathe** breath   **149 compromise**
compremize

5.5. 0 [F here reads "Actus Quintus"]   **60 That most** Most   **82 love** Ioue

HENRY VI,
PART TWO

Introduction

Henry VI, Part Two is at once a continuation of the historical narrative begun in *1 Henry VI* (based indeed on the same
chronicle sources) and an independent play that must have
been staged on a separate occasion in Shakespeare's theater. As a middle play of a four-play series it is open-ended,
commencing in a state of political flux and concluding as
the civil war is in its early phase. Providential consolation
seems far away, even if there are signs of divine wrath at
work in human affairs. At the same time, this play has its
own integrity of theme and dramatic form.

2 Henry VI picks up where the first play ends (in the year
1445) and continues down to the start of actual civil war
at the Battle of St. Albans (1455). The major events portrayed are the downfall of Humphrey, Duke of Gloucester,
and the angry stirrings of the commoners leading finally to
Jack Cade's rebellion. Popular agitation brings about the
death of the Duke of Suffolk, thereby claiming the life of
one of those most cynically responsible for England's troubles. The villainous Cardinal of Winchester also dies a horrible and edifying death, suggesting that divine retribution
is beginning to reveal its inexorable force. Yet throughout
this declining action we witness in countermovement the
ominous rise of Richard Plantagenet, Duke of York.

Richard's strategy, like that of his namesake in *Richard III*, is to exploit antagonisms at the English court, turning feuding nobles against one another until his potential
rivals for power have destroyed themselves. In particular,
he takes advantage of the animosity between the new Queen
Margaret and Duke Humphrey. Margaret, daughter of a foreign prince, is a consort in the autocratic European style.
She haughtily insists on the privileges of her exalted rank
and spurns those who govern in the name of justice. "Is this
the guise, / Is this the fashions in the court of England?"
she incredulously inquires of Suffolk, her lover and political
ally (1.3.42–43). Suffolk is an apt mate for Margaret, since
he too oppresses the commoners. A petition "against the
Duke of Suffolk, for enclosing the commons of Melford"
(ll. 23–24) is one of many heartfelt grievances brought to the

attention of the throne by the common people. Margaret naturally resents the moderate and fair-minded counsel of Duke Humphrey, who urges King Henry to remedy the distress of the commoners.

Richard of York has no inherent admiration for Suffolk and Margaret but cynically backs them as a way of destroying the good Duke of Gloucester. He advises his partners Salisbury and Warwick, "Wink at the Duke of Suffolk's insolence, / At Beaufort's pride, at Somerset's ambition, / At Buckingham, and all the crew of them, / Till they have snared the shepherd of the flock, / That virtuous prince, the good Duke Humphrey" (2.2.70–74). And Humphrey has in fact a fatal weakness through which he can be pulled down: the ambition of his wife, Eleanor. Intent on being first lady of the land, Eleanor comes into inevitable conflict with the remorseless Queen Margaret. Winchester and Suffolk, knowing Eleanor's self-blinding pride, find it pathetically easy to plant spies in her household who will encourage her penchant for witchcraft. Humphrey is never contaminated personally by his wife's pride but is doomed nonetheless. King Henry knows of Humphrey's goodness but cannot save him. This fall of a courageous moderate, highlighted in the title of the 1594 quarto text ("with the death of the good Duke Humphrey"), singles Humphrey out as the most prominent victim of the second play, like Talbot in Part One. He is cut down by an insincere and temporary alliance of extremists from both sides: those such as Margaret and Suffolk who cling to despotic privilege, and those such as York who wish to stir up the commoners for their own ulterior purposes. In times of confrontation the middle position is inherently vulnerable, and its destruction leads to escalating polarization.

As York both foresees and desires, the commoners are indeed unruly when deprived of Humphrey's moderating leadership. Shakespeare has already shown that they tend to ape the quarrels of their elders (as in the ludicrous duels between Horner the Armorer and his man Peter Thump), and are superstitiously gullible (as in the episode of Simpcox the fraudulent blind man). Now, no longer able to petition through channels, their voice becomes importunate. "The commons, like an angry hive of bees / That want their leader, scatter up and down / And care not who they sting in his revenge" (3.2.125–127). At first their grievances are plausible and their wrath directed at guilty objects. They suspect rightly that their hero, Humphrey, has been destroyed by Suffolk and the Cardinal, and they demand Suffolk's banishment. The request is laudable, but the peremptory tone suggests that the people are beginning to feel their own political power. Unless Suffolk is banished, they warn, they will take him by force from the palace. Poor King Henry, lamenting the lost conciliatory authority of Humphrey, aptly points up the central issue of royal prerogative: "And had I not been cited so by them, / Yet did I purpose as they do entreat" (3.2.281–282). In the perspective of this play, Henry's yielding to popular force is regrettable, but he has no alternative. Equally lamentable is the execution of Suffolk by private citizens taking justice into their own hands. However much this despot deserved to be condemned, his murder is an affront to justice. Servant has turned against master; the commoners have begun to feel their own power.

The popular rebellion itself, Cade's uprising, is a travesty of popular longings for social justice, and suggests that any movement of this sort is bound to end in absurdity. Shakespeare, for all his appreciative depiction of individual commoners, never credits them with collective political sagacity once they are demonstrating for their rights. In fact Shakespeare unhistorically brings together the worst excesses of the Cade rebellion itself (1450) and the famous Peasants' Revolt of 1381 in order to exaggerate the dangers of popular agitation. The Cade scenes abound in degrading comedy in the shape of lower-class self-assertion. We laugh at the contrast between Cade's professed utopian notions of abundance for all and his petty ambition to be king. He kills those who refer to him as Jack Cade rather than by his pretended title of Lord Mortimer. His movement is fiercely anti-intellectual. Yet the sour joke does not indict the commoners alone. Cade's insolent pretentions and his claptrap genealogical claims are an exaggerated but recognizable parody of aristocratic behavior. More important, we remember that Cade was whetted on to his rebellion by the demagogic York. That schemer has "seduced" Cade to make commotion while York himself raises a huge personal army and advances his fortunes in Ireland. "This devil

here shall be my substitute" (3.1.371). The commoners can
indeed prove irresponsible when goaded, but throughout
2 Henry VI feuding aristocrats must bear the chief blame
for causing popular discontent.

   In view of the need for some kind of coherence amid this
universal decline into anarchy and strife, prophecy as-
sumes a structural importance in *2 Henry VI* that is to be
accentuated in later plays of the tetralogy. As in ancient
Greek drama, prophecies are always eventually fulfilled.
They reveal divine necessity, but in such ambiguous and
riddling language that the persons affected by the prophecy
do not comprehend the true nature of the utterance until
the event itself is upon them. In this play, for example, the
spirit conjured to appear before the Duchess of Gloucester
(1.4) predicts that Suffolk will die "by water" and that Somerset should "shun castles." What sorts of warnings are
these? When his time comes, Suffolk dies at the hands of a
man named Walter (pronounced "water," though Suffolk
tries desperately to insist on the French "Gualtier"), whereas
Somerset dies at the Castle Inn near St. Albans, at the
play's end. Through such paltry quibbles, as in *Macbeth*,
great men are misled into a false security. No less riddling
is the prophecy about King Henry and his political antago-
nist: "The duke yet lives that Henry shall depose, / But him
outlive, and die a violent death" (1.4.31–32). The first
phrase of this oracle is perfectly ambiguous: it can mean
that a still-living duke will depose Henry, or that Henry will
depose this duke. Both interpretations turn out to be valid;
during the wars of Lancaster and York shown in *3 Henry VI*,
King Henry and his Yorkist opponent will by turns take the
throne from one another. Eventually, too, in *3 Henry VI* and
Richard III, Edward of York will outlive Henry only to die a
retributive death. In such prophecy there is already the con-
cept of an eye for an eye, a Lancastrian for a Yorkist,
through which Providence will finally impose its penalty on
a rebellious people. Prophecy then serves not to allow human beings to escape their destiny, which is unavoidable,
but to give them the opportunity to perceive at last the pattern of divine justice. The audience realizes that prophecy
is a divine warning too often unheeded by foolish human
beings, and acknowledges the necessity of a fulfillment that

is tragic and dispiriting but also comforting to the extent
that it shows the heavens to be just.

The role of prophecy is thus central in *2 Henry VI*, in that
it gives to the play a dominant pattern of prediction and
eventual fulfillment. Yet the experience of *2 Henry VI* is
one of turbulence. Events increasingly take on their own
unstoppable momentum. Ceremonies and institutions attempt to control the flux without success. Abstract ideas
conflict with stern realities; the idea of kingship is ap-
pealed to as a rallying cry for authority and stability, but
the fact of King Henry's inept leadership and the self-
serving ambitions of his antagonists invite continual dis-
array. As a work of art, *2 Henry VI* thus grapples with the
problem of making something artistically coherent out of
chaos. It does so, as does *3 Henry VI*, by containing the instability within the recurring pattern of an eye for an eye.

Any sense of comfort is slow to arrive in this play. England's political and moral decline remains unchecked. The
commoner's rebellion, cynically fomented by Richard,
Duke of York, has established the precedent for further rebellion. Knowing his enemies to be weak and divided, Richard no longer conceals the ambition that has led him to
accept an assignment in Ireland and thereby raise an army.
His excuse for returning to England in arms, to rid King
Henry of the hated adviser Somerset, is similarly shown to
be no more than a pretext for declaring open civil war. His
final justification for challenging King Henry, despite all
the fine talk about genealogies, is that Richard has the ambition and the raw power to carry out his plan. Henry's as-
sertions of right are no less governed by expediency, for he
privately confesses the weakness of his claim. The admirable example, shown late in this play, of a Kentish gentleman
named Iden who is content to live peaceably on his estate,
serves as a contrast to the dismaying ambitions that have
seized not only Richard of York and his allies but also the
remorseless Queen Margaret and those loyal to her. If, as
A. P. Rossiter has cogently argued, *2 Henry VI* is a "morality
of state" in which forces of good and evil struggle for the
soul of that beleaguered heroine, Respublica, the commonwealth, then the play must ultimately be viewed as one in
which the forces of good do not fare well. To be sure, the

haughty Suffolk meets his dire fate, though by a means that
encourages further private revenge; Somerset falls as pre-
dicted at St. Albans; and Winchester suffers a death of edifying horror. Still, Richard of York and Queen Margaret,
having profited from the victimization of the virtuous Duke
Humphrey, are more powerful than ever, and Richard's son
and namesake is only beginning to make his presence felt.
Many scores remain to be settled at the close of *2 Henry VI*.

HENRY VI,
PART TWO

A TOWNSMAN *of St. Albans*
SIMPCOX *or Simon, supposedly restored to sight*
His WIFE
MAYOR *of St. Albans*
A BEADLE *of St. Albans*

LIEUTENANT *or Captain of a ship*
MASTER *of the ship*
WALTER WHITMORE
Two GENTLEMEN *prisoners*

JACK CADE, *rebel leader from Kent*
GEORGE BEVIS,
JOHN HOLLAND,
DICK, *the butcher,* } *followers of Cade*
SMITH, *the weaver,*
MICHAEL,

MESSENGERS
Two SERVINGMEN, *of Gloucester and York*
A HERALD
POST *or Messenger to Parliament*
Two MURDERERS *of Gloucester*
VAUX, *a messenger*
A CLERK *of Chartham*
ALEXANDER IDEN, *a gentleman of Kent*

*Falconers, Townsmen and Aldermen, Commons, Rebels, a
Sawyer, Soldiers, Servingmen, Attendants, Guards, Officers,
Matthew Gough*

SCENE: *England*]

1.1 *Flourish of trumpets, then hautboys. Enter*
[the] King, Duke Humphrey [of Gloucester],
Salisbury, Warwick, and [Cardinal] Beaufort,
on the one side; the Queen, Suffolk, York,
Somerset, and Buckingham, on the other.

SUFFOLK
As by Your High Imperial Majesty
I had in charge at my depart for France,   2
As procurator to Your Excellence,   3
To marry Princess Margaret for Your Grace,
So, in the famous ancient city Tours,
In presence of the Kings of France and Sicil,   6
The Dukes of Orleans, Calaber, Brittaine, and Alençon,   7
Seven earls, twelve barons, and twenty reverend
    bishops,
I have performed my task and was espoused;
And humbly now upon my bended knee, [*Kneeling*]
In sight of England and her lordly peers,
Deliver up my title in the Queen
To your most gracious hands, that are the substance
Of that great shadow I did represent: 14
The happiest gift that ever marquess gave,   15
The fairest queen that ever king received.

KING
Suffolk, arise. Welcome, Queen Margaret.
                                    [*Suffolk rises.*]
I can express no kinder sign of love   18
Than this kind kiss. [*He kisses her.*] O Lord, that lends
    me life,   19
Lend me a heart replete with thankfulness!
For thou hast given me in this beauteous face
A world of earthly blessings to my soul,
If sympathy of love unite our thoughts.

1.1. Location: London. The royal court.
s.d. **Flourish** fanfare.   **hautboys** oboelike instruments   **2 had in charge**
was commissioned.   **depart** departure   **3 procurator** agent, proxy
6 Sicil Sicily. (Titularly ruled by Margaret's father, the Duke of Anjou.)   **7 Calaber** Calabria, in southern Italy   **14 shadow** image, i.e., of
royalty   **15 happiest** most fortunate   **18 kinder** more natural   **19 kind**
loving

QUEEN
  Great King of England and my gracious lord,
  The mutual conference that my mind hath had   25
  By day, by night, waking and in my dreams,
  In courtly company or at my beads,   27
  With you, mine alderliefest sovereign,   28
  Makes me the bolder to salute my king
  With ruder terms, such as my wit affords   30
  And overjoy of heart doth minister.   31
KING
  Her sight did ravish, but her grace in speech,   32
  Her words yclad with wisdom's majesty,   33
  Makes me from wondering fall to weeping joys,   34
  Such is the fullness of my heart's content.
  Lords, with one cheerful voice welcome my love.
ALL (*Kneeling*)
  Long live Queen Margaret, England's happiness!
QUEEN   We thank you all.   *Flourish. [They all rise.]*
SUFFOLK
  My Lord Protector, so it please Your Grace,
  Here are the articles of contracted peace
  Between our sovereign and the French king Charles,
  For eighteen months concluded by consent.
GLOUCESTER (*Reads*) "Imprimis, it is agreed between   43
  the French king Charles and William de la Pole, Mar-   44
  quess of Suffolk, ambassador for Henry, King of En-   45
  gland, that the said Henry shall espouse the Lady Margaret, daughter unto Reignier, King of Naples, Sicilia,
  and Jerusalem, and crown her Queen of England ere
  the thirtieth of May next ensuing. Item, that the duchy   49
  of Anjou and the county of Maine shall be released and
  delivered to the King her father—"

                                        [He lets the paper fall.]

---

25 mutual conference intimate communication (of the mind with itself)   **27 In . . . beads** in courtly society or at my prayers (with the
rosary)   **28 alderliefest** most loved   **30 ruder** less polished.   **wit** intelligence   **31 minister** supply   **32 Her sight** the sight of her   **33 yclad**
clad, clothed   **34 wondering** admiring   **43 Imprimis** in the first place
44–45 Marquess (William de la Pole was fourth Earl and then first Duke
of Suffolk. Edward Hall writes that he was elevated from earl to marquess "when the marriage contract was agreed.")   **49 Item** also

KING
  Uncle, how now?
GLOUCESTER   Pardon me, gracious lord.
  Some sudden qualm hath struck me at the heart
  And dimmed mine eyes, that I can read no further.   54
KING
  Uncle of Winchester, I pray, read on.   55
CARDINAL [*Reads*] "Item, it is further agreed between
  them that the duchies of Anjou and Maine shall be   57
  released and delivered over to the King her father, and
  she sent over of the King of England's own proper cost   59
  and charges, without having any dowry."
KING
  They please us well. Lord Marquess, kneel down.
                              [*Suffolk kneels.*]
  We here create thee the first Duke of Suffolk,
  And gird thee with the sword. [*Suffolk rises.*] Cousin
    of York,   63
  We here discharge Your Grace from being regent
  I' the parts of France, till term of eighteen months   65
  Be full expired. Thanks, uncle Winchester,
  Gloucester, York, Buckingham, Somerset,
  Salisbury, and Warwick;
  We thank you all for this great favor done
  In entertainment to my princely queen.   70
  Come, let us in, and with all speed provide
  To see her coronation be performed.   72
                    Exeunt King, Queen, and Suffolk.
                    Manent the rest.

GLOUCESTER
  Brave peers of England, pillars of the state,
  To you Duke Humphrey must unload his grief,
  Your grief, the common grief of all the land.
  What? Did my brother Henry spend his youth,   76

54 that so that   **55 Uncle** (Actually, great-uncle.)   **57 duchies . . . Maine**
i.e., the duchy of Anjou and the county of Maine, as in ll. 49–50 above.
(Perhaps the text is in error.)   **59 of** at.   **proper** personal   **63 Cousin**
(An appropriate title for the King to use toward any peer, but York is
also his distant cousin.)   **65 parts** territories.   **term . . . months** i.e., the
period of the truce between England and France   **70 entertainment to**
gracious reception of   **72 s.d. Manent** they remain onstage   **76 Henry**
i.e., Henry V

His valor, coin, and people in the wars?
Did he so often lodge in open field,
In winter's cold and summer's parching heat,
To conquer France, his true inheritance?
And did my brother Bedford toil his wits   81
To keep by policy what Henry got?   82
Have you yourselves, Somerset, Buckingham,
Brave York, Salisbury, and victorious Warwick,
Received deep scars in France and Normandy?
Or hath mine uncle Beaufort and myself,
With all the learnèd Council of the realm,
Studied so long, sat in the Council House
Early and late, debating to and fro
How France and Frenchmen might be kept in awe,   90
And had His Highness in his infancy
Crowned in Paris in despite of foes?
And shall these labors and these honors die?
Shall Henry's conquest, Bedford's vigilance,
Your deeds of war, and all our counsel die?
O peers of England, shameful is this league!
Fatal this marriage, canceling your fame,
Blotting your names from books of memory,   98
Rasing the characters of your renown,   99
Defacing monuments of conquered France,
Undoing all, as all had never been!   101

CARDINAL
Nephew, what means this passionate discourse,
This peroration with such circumstance?   103
For France, 'tis ours; and we will keep it still.   104

GLOUCESTER
Ay, uncle, we will keep it if we can,
But now it is impossible we should.
Suffolk, the new-made duke that rules the roast,   107
Hath given the duchy of Anjou, and Maine,

---

81 **Bedford** (as portrayed in *1 Henry VI*)   82 **policy** prudent management   90 **awe** subjection   98 **books of memory** i.e., chronicles   99 **Rasing the characters** erasing the records, or *razing,* scraping away   101 **as**
as if   103 **circumstance** detail   104 **For** as for.   **still** always   107 **rules
the roast** i.e., domineers. (The Folio spelling, "rost," may also suggest
"roost," but the etymology is uncertain.)

Unto the poor King Reignier, whose large style   109
Agrees not with the leanness of his purse.

SALISBURY
Now, by the death of Him that died for all,
These counties were the keys of Normandy.
But wherefore weeps Warwick, my valiant son?

WARWICK
For grief that they are past recovery;
For, were there hope to conquer them again,
My sword should shed hot blood, mine eyes no tears.
Anjou and Maine? Myself did win them both!
Those provinces these arms of mine did conquer.
And are the cities that I got with wounds
Delivered up again with peaceful words?
Mort Dieu!   121

YORK
For Suffolk's duke, may he be suffocate,   122
That dims the honor of this warlike isle!
France should have torn and rent my very heart
Before I would have yielded to this league.   125
I never read but England's kings have had
Large sums of gold and dowries with their wives;
And our King Henry gives away his own
To match with her that brings no vantages.   129

GLOUCESTER
A proper jest, and never heard before,
That Suffolk should demand a whole fifteenth   131
For costs and charges in transporting her!
She should have stayed in France and starved in France
Before—

CARDINAL
My lord of Gloucester, now ye grow too hot.
It was the pleasure of my lord the King.

GLOUCESTER
My lord of Winchester, I know your mind.

109 large style lavish title   **121 Mort Dieu** by God's (Christ's) death
122 For as for.   **suffocate** (punning on *Suffolk*)   **125 yielded** consented   **129 vantages** benefits, profits   **131 whole fifteenth** i.e., tax levy
consisting of one-fifteenth of the produce of lands and industry.
(Cf. *1 Henry VI*, 5.5.92–93, where the figure is put at one tenth.)

'Tis not my speeches that you do mislike,
But 'tis my presence that doth trouble ye.
Rancor will out. Proud prelate, in thy face
I see thy fury. If I longer stay,
We shall begin our ancient bickerings.
Lordings, farewell; and say, when I am gone,   143
I prophesied France will be lost ere long.

                                        Exit Humphrey.

CARDINAL
So, there goes our Protector in a rage.
'Tis known to you he is mine enemy,
Nay, more, an enemy unto you all,
And no great friend, I fear me, to the King.
Consider, lords, he is the next of blood   149
And heir apparent to the English crown.
Had Henry got an empire by his marriage,
And all the wealthy kingdoms of the west,   152
There's reason he should be displeased at it.   153
Look to it, lords; let not his smoothing words   154
Bewitch your hearts. Be wise and circumspect.
What though the common people favor him,
Calling him "Humphrey, the good Duke of Gloucester,"
Clapping their hands and crying with loud voice,
"Jesu maintain Your Royal Excellence!"
With "God preserve the good Duke Humphrey!"
I fear me, lords, for all this flattering gloss,   161
He will be found a dangerous Protector.

BUCKINGHAM
Why should he, then, protect our sovereign,
He being of age to govern of himself?   164
Cousin of Somerset, join you with me,   165
And all together, with the Duke of Suffolk,
We'll quickly hoist Duke Humphrey from his seat.

CARDINAL
This weighty business will not brook delay.   168

---

143 Lordings my lords, gentlemen   **149 next of blood** i.e., in line to
succeed to the throne, as Henry's eldest uncle. (Henry was as yet child-
less.)   **152 the wealthy . . . west** (Seemingly an anachronistic reference
to New World possessions.)   **153 he** i.e., Gloucester   **154 smoothing**
flattering   **161 flattering gloss** i.e., attractive appearance   **164 He** i.e.,
King Henry   **165 join you** if you join   **168 brook** endure, permit

I'll to the Duke of Suffolk presently.   *Exit Cardinal.* 169

SOMERSET
Cousin of Buckingham, though Humphrey's pride   170
And greatness of his place be grief to us,   171
Yet let us watch the haughty Cardinal.
His insolence is more intolerable
Than all the princes in the land besides.   174
If Gloucester be displaced, he'll be Protector.

BUCKINGHAM
Or thou or I, Somerset, will be Protector,   176
Despite Duke Humphrey or the Cardinal.
        Exeunt Buckingham and Somerset.

SALISBURY
Pride went before, Ambition follows him.   178
While these do labor for their own preferment,   179
Behooves it us to labor for the realm.
I never saw but Humphrey, Duke of Gloucester,
Did bear him like a noble gentleman.   182
Oft have I seen the haughty Cardinal,
More like a soldier than a man o' the Church,
As stout and proud as he were lord of all,   185
Swear like a ruffian and demean himself   186
Unlike the ruler of a commonweal.
Warwick, my son, the comfort of my age,
Thy deeds, thy plainness, and thy housekeeping   189
Hath won the greatest favor of the commons,
Excepting none but good Duke Humphrey.   191
And, brother York, thy acts in Ireland,   192
In bringing them to civil discipline,
Thy late exploits done in the heart of France,
When thou wert regent for our sovereign,
Have made thee feared and honored of the people.
Join we together for the public good,
In what we can, to bridle and suppress
The pride of Suffolk and the Cardinal,

---

169 presently immediately   **170 Cousin** kinsman, fellow peer   **171 grief**
grievance   **174 Than** i.e., than that of.   **princes** peers   **176 Or** either
178 Pride i.e., Winchester.   **Ambition** i.e., Buckingham and Somerset
179 preferment advancement   **182 him** himself   **185 stout** haughty.   **as**
as if   **186 demean** conduct   **189 housekeeping** hospitality   **191 Excepting none but** second only to   **192 brother** i.e., brother-in-law; see note to
l. 238 below

With Somerset's and Buckingham's ambition;
And, as we may, cherish Duke Humphrey's deeds,   201
While they do tend the profit of the land.   202

WARWICK
So God help Warwick, as he loves the land
And common profit of his country!

YORK
And so says York—[*Aside*] for he hath greatest cause.   205

SALISBURY
Then let's away and look unto the main.   206

WARWICK
Unto the main? O Father, Maine is lost!
That Maine which by main force Warwick did win,
And would have kept so long as breath did last!
Main chance, Father, you meant; but I meant Maine,
Which I will win from France, or else be slain.   211

         Exeunt Warwick and Salisbury.
         Manet York.

YORK
Anjou and Maine are given to the French;
Paris is lost; the state of Normandy
Stands on a tickle point now they are gone.   214
Suffolk concluded on the articles,   215
The peers agreed, and Henry was well pleased
To change two dukedoms for a duke's fair daughter.
I cannot blame them all. What is 't to them?
'Tis thine they give away, and not their own.   219
Pirates may make cheap pennyworths of their pillage,   220
And purchase friends, and give to courtesans,   221
Still reveling like lords till all be gone;   222
Whileas the silly owner of the goods   223

---

201 cherish support **202 tend** tend to, serve **205 greatest cause** i.e., as hopeful claimant to the throne **206 unto the main** to the most important business (with several puns in the following lines: [1] *Maine*, a French province lost in the treaty [2] *main force*, brute force [3] *Main chance*, a gambling term from the dice game called hazard) **211 s.d. Manet** he remains onstage **214 tickle** unstable, insecure **215 concluded on the articles** negotiated the exact terms (of the marriage agreement) **219 thine** (York speaks to himself.) **220 make cheap pennyworths of** i.e., practically give away **221 purchase friends** i.e., win friends through reckless generosity **222 Still** continually **223 Whileas** while. **silly** wretched, helpless

Weeps over them, and wrings his hapless hands,
And shakes his head, and trembling stands aloof,   225
While all is shared and all is borne away,
Ready to starve and dare not touch his own.   227
So York must sit and fret and bite his tongue,
While his own lands are bargained for and sold.
Methinks the realms of England, France, and Ireland
Bear that proportion to my flesh and blood   231
As did the fatal brand Althaea burnt   232
Unto the Prince's heart of Calydon.   233
Anjou and Maine both given unto the French!
Cold news for me, for I had hope of France,
Even as I have of fertile England's soil.
A day will come when York shall claim his own;
And therefore I will take the Nevilles' parts   238
And make a show of love to proud Duke Humphrey,
And, when I spy advantage, claim the crown,   240
For that's the golden mark I seek to hit.   241
Nor shall proud Lancaster usurp my right,   242
Nor hold the scepter in his childish fist,
Nor wear the diadem upon his head,
Whose churchlike humors fits not for a crown.   245
Then, York, be still awhile, till time do serve.
Watch thou and wake when others be asleep,
To pry into the secrets of the state,
Till Henry, surfeiting in joys of love
With his new bride and England's dear-bought queen,
And Humphrey with the peers be fall'n at jars.   251
Then will I raise aloft the milk-white rose,   252

---

225 stands aloof stands to one side (unable to intervene)   **227 Ready . . . and** he being on the point of starvation and yet   **231 proportion** relationship   **232 Althaea** mother of Meleager, prince of Calydon. (At his birth she was told that her son would live only as long as a brand of wood remained unconsumed. She snatched the brand from the fire; but years later, when Meleager quarreled with Althaea's brothers and slew them, she resentfully threw the fatal brand into the fire, thus causing his death.)   **233 Unto . . . Calydon** unto the heart of the Prince of Calydon   **238 the Nevilles'** i.e., Salisbury's and his son Warwick's (to whom Richard of York was allied by marriage, having married Cecille or Cicely Neville, Salisbury's sister)   **240 advantage** opportunity   **241 mark** archery target   **242 Lancaster** i.e., Henry VI, here demoted to his title of duke   **245 humors** temperament   **251 at jars** in discords, quarreling   **252 milk-white rose** (Emblem of the Yorkist dynasty.)

With whose sweet smell the air shall be perfumed,
And in my standard bear the arms of York,   254
To grapple with the house of Lancaster;
And force perforce I'll make him yield the crown,   256
Whose bookish rule hath pulled fair England down.   257

                                          Exit York.

                              ❖

1.2   *Enter Duke Humphrey and his wife Eleanor.*

DUCHESS
   Why droops my lord, like overripened corn,   1
   Hanging the head at Ceres' plenteous load?   2
   Why doth the great Duke Humphrey knit his brows,
   As frowning at the favors of the world?   4
   Why are thine eyes fixed to the sullen earth,
   Gazing on that which seems to dim thy sight?
   What seest thou there? King Henry's diadem,
   Enchased with all the honors of the world?   8
   If so, gaze on, and grovel on thy face,
   Until thy head be circled with the same.
   Put forth thy hand; reach at the glorious gold.
   What, is 't too short? I'll lengthen it with mine;   12
   And having both together heaved it up,   13
   We'll both together lift our heads to heaven
   And nevermore abase our sight so low
   As to vouchsafe one glance unto the ground.
GLOUCESTER
   O Nell, sweet Nell, if thou dost love thy lord,
   Banish the canker of ambitious thoughts!   18
   And may that hour when I imagine ill
   Against my king and nephew, virtuous Henry,

---

254 standard battle standard, ensign.   **arms** coat of arms   **256 force
perforce** by violent compulsion   **257 bookish** scholarly and ineffectual

1.2. Location: The Duke of Gloucester's house.
1 corn grain   **2 Ceres** goddess of the harvest and agriculture   **4 As**
as if   **8 Enchased** adorned as with gems   **12 is 't** i.e., is your arm
13 heaved it i.e., lifted the crown   **18 canker** ulcer

Be my last breathing in this mortal world!
My troublous dream this night doth make me sad.   22

DUCHESS
What dreamed my lord? Tell me, and I'll requite it
With sweet rehearsal of my morning's dream.   24

GLOUCESTER
Methought this staff, mine office badge in court,   25
Was broke in twain—by whom, I have forgot,
But, as I think, it was by the Cardinal—
And on the pieces of the broken wand
Were placed the heads of Edmund, Duke of Somerset,
And William de la Pole, first Duke of Suffolk.
This was my dream. What it doth bode, God knows.

DUCHESS
Tut, this was nothing but an argument   32
That he that breaks a stick of Gloucester's grove
Shall lose his head for his presumption.
But list to me, my Humphrey, my sweet duke: 35
Methought I sat in seat of majesty
In the cathedral church of Westminster,
And in that chair where kings and queens are crowned,
Where Henry and Dame Margaret kneeled to me
And on my head did set the diadem.

GLOUCESTER
Nay, Eleanor, then must I chide outright.
Presumptuous dame, ill-nurtured Eleanor,   42
Art thou not second woman in the realm,
And the Protector's wife, beloved of him?
Hast thou not worldly pleasure at command
Above the reach or compass of thy thought?   46
And wilt thou still be hammering treachery,   47
To tumble down thy husband and thyself
From top of honor to disgrace's feet?
Away from me, and let me hear no more!

---

22 this night this past night   **24 rehearsal** recounting. **morning's dream** (Morning dreams were, in folklore, regarded as foretelling true things.)   **25 mine office badge** the symbol of my office of Protector   **32 argument** proof, evidence   **35 list** listen   **42 ill-nurtured** ill-bred   **46 compass** encompassing   **47 hammering** i.e., devising

DUCHESS
What, what, my lord? Are you so choleric
With Eleanor for telling but her dream?
Next time I'll keep my dreams unto myself,
And not be checked.   54
GLOUCESTER
Nay, be not angry. I am pleased again.

Enter Messenger.

MESSENGER
My Lord Protector, 'tis His Highness' pleasure
You do prepare to ride unto Saint Albans,
Whereas the King and Queen do mean to hawk.   58
GLOUCESTER
I go. Come, Nell, thou wilt ride with us?
DUCHESS
Yes, my good lord, I'll follow presently.   60
                        Exit Humphrey [with Messenger].
Follow I must; I cannot go before   61
While Gloucester bears this base and humble mind.
Were I a man, a duke, and next of blood,
I would remove these tedious stumbling blocks
And smooth my way upon their headless necks;
And, being a woman, I will not be slack
To play my part in Fortune's pageant.—   67
Where are you there? Sir John! Nay, fear not, man,   68
We are alone; here's none but thee and I.

Enter Hume.

HUME
Jesus preserve Your Royal Majesty!
DUCHESS
What sayst thou? "Majesty"? I am but "Grace."   71
HUME
But by the grace of God and Hume's advice
Your Grace's title shall be multiplied.

54 **checked** rebuked   58 **Whereas** where.   **hawk** hunt with hawks
60 **presently** at once   61 **go before** i.e., advance my own ambitions to be
second to none   67 **pageant** spectacular entertainment   68 **Sir John**
(Conventional form of addressing a priest.)   71 **Grace** (Appropriate
address to a duchess.)

DUCHESS
What sayst thou, man? Hast thou as yet conferred
With Margery Jourdain, the cunning witch,
With Roger Bolingbroke, the conjurer?
And will they undertake to do me good?

HUME
This they have promisèd: to show Your Highness
A spirit raised from depth of underground
That shall make answer to such questions
As by Your Grace shall be propounded him.

DUCHESS
It is enough. I'll think upon the questions.
When from Saint Albans we do make return,
We'll see these things effected to the full.
Here, Hume, take this reward. [*She gives money.*]
   Make merry, man,
With thy confederates in this weighty cause.
                          Exit Eleanor.

HUME
Hume must make merry with the Duchess' gold.
Marry, and shall! But, how now, Sir John Hume?   88
Seal up your lips, and give no words but mum;
The business asketh silent secrecy.
Dame Eleanor gives gold to bring the witch;
Gold cannot come amiss, were she a devil.
Yet have I gold flies from another coast—   93
I dare not say, from the rich Cardinal
And from the great and new-made Duke of Suffolk,
Yet I do find it so; for, to be plain,
They, knowing Dame Eleanor's aspiring humor,   97
Have hirèd me to undermine the Duchess
And buzz these conjurations in her brain.
They say "A crafty knave does need no broker,"   100
Yet am I Suffolk and the Cardinal's broker.
Hume, if you take not heed, you shall go near   102
To call them both a pair of crafty knaves.   103
Well, so it stands; and thus, I fear, at last

---

88 Marry, and shall i.e., indeed he will. (*Marry* was originally an oath,
"by the Virgin Mary.")   **93 flies** i.e., that flies, approaches.   **coast**
quarter, source   **97 humor** temperament, fancy   **100 They say** people
say.   **broker** agent   **102-103 go near To call** come close to calling

Hume's knavery will be the Duchess' wrack, 105
And her attainture will be Humphrey's fall. 106
Sort how it will, I shall have gold for all. *Exit.* 107

✤

1.3   *Enter three or four Petitioners, [Peter,] the Armorer's man, being one.*

FIRST PETITIONER   My masters, let's stand close. My 1
Lord Protector will come this way by and by, and then
we may deliver our supplications in the quill. 3

SECOND PETITIONER   Marry, the Lord protect him, for
he's a good man! Jesu bless him!

Enter Suffolk and Queen.

FIRST PETITIONER   Here 'a comes, methinks, and the Queen 6
with him. I'll be the first, sure.   [*He starts forward.*]

SECOND PETITIONER   Come back, fool. This is the Duke
of Suffolk, and not my Lord Protector.

SUFFOLK   How now, fellow? Wouldst anything with
me?

FIRST PETITIONER   I pray, my lord, pardon me. I took ye
for my Lord Protector.

QUEEN [*Reads*]   "To my Lord Protector"? Are your sup- 14
plications to his lordship? Let me see them. What is
thine? [*She takes the petition.*]

FIRST PETITIONER   Mine is, an 't please Your Grace, 17
against John Goodman, my Lord Cardinal's man, for
keeping my house, and lands, and wife and all,
from me.

SUFFOLK   Thy wife too? That's some wrong, indeed.—
What's yours? What's here? [*He takes the petition.*]

---

105 **wrack** destruction, ruin   106 **attainture** conviction and disgrace
107 **Sort . . . will** turn out which way it will.   **for all** i.e., in any case

1.3. Location: London. The royal court.
1 **close** near together   3 **in the quill** i.e., simultaneously, in a body   6 **'a**
he   14 **s.d. Reads** (The Queen evidently reads the superscription while
the First Petitioner is holding his petition.)   17 **an 't** if it

"Against the Duke of Suffolk, for enclosing the 23
commons of Melford." How now, sir knave?   24
SECOND PETITIONER   Alas, sir, I am but a poor petitioner
of our whole township.   26
PETER [*Giving his petition*]   Against my master, Thomas
Horner, for saying that the Duke of York was rightful
heir to the crown.
QUEEN   What sayst thou? Did the Duke of York say he
was rightful heir to the crown?
PETER   That my master was? No, forsooth; my master
said that he was, and that the King was an usurper.
SUFFOLK   Who is there? (*Enter Servant.*) Take this fellow
in, and send for his master with a pursuivant pres-   35
ently.—We'll hear more of your matter before the King. 36
                              Exit [*Servant with Peter*].
QUEEN [*To the Petitioners*]
And as for you, that love to be protected
Under the wings of our Protector's grace,
Begin your suits anew and sue to him.
                              Tear the supplication.
Away, base cullions! Suffolk, let them go.   40
ALL   Come, let's be gone.   *Exeunt* [*Petitioners*].
QUEEN
My lord of Suffolk, say, is this the guise,   42
Is this the fashions in the court of England?
Is this the government of Britain's isle,
And this the royalty of Albion's king?   45
What, shall King Henry be a pupil still
Under the surly Gloucester's governance?
Am I a queen in title and in style,
And must be made a subject to a duke?
I tell thee, Pole, when in the city Tours   50
Thou rann'st atilt in honor of my love   51

23–24 enclosing the commons the action of a lord of a manor in enclosing or converting into private property lands formerly undivided and
used by the community as a whole   **26 of** on behalf of   **35 pursuivant**
minor messenger or officer with authority to execute warrants
35–36 presently at once   **40 cullions** base fellows. (Originally, *cullion*
meant "testicle.")   **42 guise** custom, manner   **45 Albion's** England's
50 Pole i.e., Suffolk   **51 rann'st atilt** jousted in a tournament

And stol'st away the ladies' hearts of France,
I thought King Henry had resembled thee
In courage, courtship, and proportion.   54
But all his mind is bent to holiness,
To number Ave Marys on his beads.
His champions are the prophets and apostles,
His weapons holy saws of sacred writ,   58
His study is his tiltyard, and his loves   59
Are brazen images of canonized saints.   60
I would the College of the Cardinals
Would choose him Pope and carry him to Rome
And set the triple crown upon his head;   63
That were a state fit for his holiness.   64

SUFFOLK
Madam, be patient. As I was cause
Your Highness came to England, so will I
In England work Your Grace's full content.

QUEEN
Besides the haughty Protector, have we Beaufort
The imperious churchman, Somerset, Buckingham,
And grumbling York; and not the least of these
But can do more in England than the King.

SUFFOLK
And he of these that can do most of all
Cannot do more in England than the Nevilles.
Salisbury and Warwick are no simple peers.

QUEEN
Not all these lords do vex me half so much
As that proud dame, the Lord Protector's wife.
She sweeps it through the court with troops of ladies, 77
More like an empress than Duke Humphrey's wife.
Strangers in court do take her for the Queen.   79

---

54 courtship courtly manners. **proportion** carriage, build **58 saws**
sayings **59 tiltyard** enclosed space for tilts or tournaments **60 brazen
images** bronze statues **63 the triple crown** i.e., the diadem of the
papacy—a large hat enriched by three gold crowns symbolizing perhaps
the Church militant, suffering, and triumphant **64 state** status. **his
holiness** Henry's piety (but playing on the Pope's title, "His Holiness") **77 sweeps it** moves majestically, with trailing garments
79 Strangers visiting foreigners

She bears a duke's revenues on her back,   80
And in her heart she scorns our poverty.
Shall I not live to be avenged on her?
Contemptuous baseborn callet as she is,   83
She vaunted 'mongst her minions t' other day   84
The very train of her worst wearing gown   85
Was better worth than all my father's lands,   86
Till Suffolk gave two dukedoms for his daughter.   87

SUFFOLK
Madam, myself have limed a bush for her,   88
And placed a choir of such enticing birds   89
That she will light to listen to the lays   90
And never mount to trouble you again.   91
So let her rest. And, madam, list to me,   92
For I am bold to counsel you in this:
Although we fancy not the Cardinal,   94
Yet must we join with him and with the lords
Till we have brought Duke Humphrey in disgrace.
As for the Duke of York, this late complaint   97
Will make but little for his benefit.
So one by one we'll weed them all at last,
And you yourself shall steer the happy helm.   100

*Sound a sennet. Enter the King, Duke Humphrey
[of Gloucester], Cardinal [Beaufort], Buckingham,
York, [Somerset,] Salisbury, Warwick, and the
Duchess [of Gloucester].*

80 on her back i.e., in her garments **83 Contemptuous** (1) contemptible
(2) full of contempt. **callet** lewd woman **84 vaunted** boasted. **minions** followers, attendants (with overtones of "saucy women")
85–87 The very . . . daughter i.e., (Eleanor boasted that) the mere trailing part of her least expensive gown was worth more than all the lands
possessed by the Duke of Anjou until Suffolk arranged a dowry whereby
the Duke received two rich dukedoms (Anjou and Maine) in return for
the marriage of me, his daughter, to King Henry **88 limed a bush** set a
trap. (A metaphor from the practice of catching birds by putting sticky
birdlime on twigs of trees.) **89 enticing birds** i.e., decoys **90 light**
alight. **lays** songs **91 mount** (1) fly off, fly aloft (2) aspire **92 let her
rest** i.e., forget about her **94 fancy not** do not like **97 late complaint**
i.e., recent allegation made by Peter that his master, the armorer, had
spoken of York as the proper King of England **100 s.d. sennet** trumpet
signal for the approach or departure of processions

KING
  For my part, noble lords, I care not which;   101
  Or Somerset or York, all's one to me.   102

YORK
  If York have ill demeaned himself in France,   103
  Then let him be denied the regentship.

SOMERSET
  If Somerset be unworthy of the place,
  Let York be regent. I will yield to him.

WARWICK
  Whether Your Grace be worthy, yea or no,
  Dispute not that. York is the worthier.

CARDINAL
  Ambitious Warwick, let thy betters speak.

WARWICK
  The Cardinal's not my better in the field.   110

BUCKINGHAM
  All in this presence are thy betters, Warwick.

WARWICK
  Warwick may live to be the best of all.

SALISBURY
  Peace, son!—And show some reason, Buckingham,
  Why Somerset should be preferred in this.

QUEEN
  Because the King, forsooth, will have it so.

GLOUCESTER
  Madam, the King is old enough himself
  To give his censure. These are no women's matters.   117

QUEEN
  If he be old enough, what needs Your Grace
  To be Protector of His Excellence?

GLOUCESTER
  Madam, I am Protector of the realm,
  And at his pleasure will resign my place.

SUFFOLK
  Resign it then, and leave thine insolence.
  Since thou wert king—as who is king but thou?—

101 For my part (The quarto stage direction makes it clear that York
and Somerset enter "on both sides of the King, whispering with him."
The King is thus answering their requests.)   **102 Or** either   **103 have
. . . himself** has conducted himself badly   **110 field** field of combat
117 censure opinion

The commonwealth hath daily run to wrack,
The Dauphin hath prevailed beyond the seas, 125
And all the peers and nobles of the realm
Have been as bondmen to thy sovereignty. 127

CARDINAL
The commons hast thou racked; the clergy's bags 128
Are lank and lean with thy extortions.

SOMERSET
Thy sumptuous buildings and thy wife's attire
Have cost a mass of public treasury.

BUCKINGHAM
Thy cruelty in execution
Upon offenders hath exceeded law,
And left thee to the mercy of the law.

QUEEN
Thy sale of offices and towns in France—
If they were known, as the suspect is great— 136
Would make thee quickly hop without thy head.
        Exit Humphrey. [The Queen drops her fan.]
Give me my fan. What, minion, can ye not?
            She gives the Duchess a box on the ear.
I cry you mercy, madam. Was it you? 139

DUCHESS
Was 't I? Yea, I it was, proud Frenchwoman.
Could I come near your beauty with my nails,
I'd set my ten commandments in your face. 142

KING
Sweet aunt, be quiet. 'Twas against her will. 143

DUCHESS
Against her will, good King? Look to 't in time.
She'll hamper thee and dandle thee like a baby. 145

125 **Dauphin** (Suffolk here uses the title of the heir apparent of France
to refer to King Charles VII because Suffolk, like all Englishmen,
considers Henry the rightful King of France.)   127 **bondmen** slaves
128 **racked** (Literally, tortured; here, strained beyond endurance in
matters of taxation.)   **bags** moneybags   136 **suspect** suspicion   139 **cry
you mercy** beg your pardon. (The Queen pretends that she thought she
was merely slapping one of her ladies in attendance for being slow to
obey.)   142 **ten commandments** i.e., ten fingernails (like the fingernails
Moses is proverbially thought to have used in inscribing the ten commandments)   143 **against her will** unintentional   145 **hamper** (1) fetter
(2) cradle

Though in this place most master wear no breeches,   146
She shall not strike Dame Eleanor unrevenged.
                              Exit Eleanor.

BUCKINGHAM [*Aside to Cardinal*]
Lord Cardinal, I will follow Eleanor,
And listen after Humphrey, how he proceeds.   149
She's tickled now; her fume needs no spurs.   150
She'll gallop far enough to her destruction.
                              Exit Buckingham.

  Enter Humphrey.

GLOUCESTER
Now, lords, my choler being overblown   152
With walking once about the quadrangle,
I come to talk of commonwealth affairs.
As for your spiteful false objections,
Prove them, and I lie open to the law;
But God in mercy so deal with my soul
As I in duty love my king and country!
But, to the matter that we have in hand:
I say, my sovereign, York is meetest man   160
To be your regent in the realm of France.

SUFFOLK
Before we make election, give me leave   162
To show some reason, of no little force,
That York is most unmeet of any man.

YORK
I'll tell thee, Suffolk, why I am unmeet:
First, for I cannot flatter thee in pride;   166
Next, if I be appointed for the place,
My lord of Somerset will keep me here
Without discharge, money, or furniture   169
Till France be won into the Dauphin's hands.
Last time I danced attendance on his will   171
Till Paris was besieged, famished, and lost.

---

146 most master the one most in command (i.e., the Queen)   **149 listen**
inquire   **150 tickled** (1) vexed, irritated (2) like a fish about to be caught
by tickling.   **fume** smoke, i.e., rage   **152 choler . . . overblown** anger
being dissipated   **160 meetest** fittest   **162 election** choice   **166 for**
because   **169 discharge** payment of what is owed.   **furniture** military
equipment   **171 Last time** (See *1 Henry VI*, 4.3.)

WARWICK
    That can I witness, and a fouler fact   173
    Did never traitor in the land commit.
SUFFOLK Peace, headstrong Warwick!
WARWICK
    Image of pride, why should I hold my peace?   176

     Enter [Horner, the] Armorer, and his man
     [Peter, guarded].

SUFFOLK
    Because here is a man accused of treason.
    Pray God the Duke of York excuse himself!
YORK
    Doth anyone accuse York for a traitor?   179
KING
    What mean'st thou, Suffolk? Tell me, what are these? 180
SUFFOLK
    Please it Your Majesty, this is the man
    That doth accuse his master of high treason.
    His words were these: that Richard, Duke of York,
    Was rightful heir unto the English crown,
    And that Your Majesty was an usurper.
KING Say, man, were these thy words?
HORNER An 't shall please Your Majesty, I never said   187
    nor thought any such matter. God is my witness, I am
    falsely accused by the villain.
PETER By these ten bones, my lords, he did speak them 190
    to me in the garret one night as we were scouring my
    lord of York's armor.
YORK
    Base dunghill villain and mechanical,   193
    I'll have thy head for this thy traitor's speech!
    [To the King.] I do beseech Your Royal Majesty,
    Let him have all the rigor of the law.
HORNER Alas, my lord, hang me if ever I spake the
    words. My accuser is my prentice; and when I did
    correct him for his fault the other day, he did vow   199
    upon his knees he would be even with me. I have

---

173 fact deed   **176 Image** i.e., symbol   **179 for** of being   **180 what**
who   **187 An 't** if it   **190 bones** i.e., fingers   **193 mechanical** common
workman   **199 correct** punish. **fault** mistake

good witness of this. Therefore I beseech Your Majesty,
do not cast away an honest man for a villain's accusa- 202
tion.

KING [*To Gloucester*]

Uncle, what shall we say to this in law?

GLOUCESTER

This doom, my lord, if I may judge: 205
Let Somerset be regent o'er the French,
Because in York this breeds suspicion;   207
And let these have a day appointed them   208
For single combat in convenient place,   209
For he hath witness of his servant's malice.
This is the law, and this Duke Humphrey's doom.

KING

Then be it so. My lord of Somerset,
We make Your Grace regent over the French.

SOMERSET

I humbly thank Your Royal Majesty.

HORNER   And I accept the combat willingly.

PETER   Alas, my lord, I cannot fight. For God's sake, pity
my case. The spite of man prevaileth against me. O
Lord, have mercy upon me! I shall never be able to
fight a blow. O Lord, my heart!

GLOUCESTER

Sirrah, or you must fight or else be hanged.   220

KING   Away with them to prison; and the day of combat
shall be the last of the next month. Come, Somerset,
we'll see thee sent away.   *Flourish. Exeunt.*

✤

202 for because of   **205 doom** judgment   **207 in York . . . breeds** i.e.,
this arouses suspicions about York's loyalty   **208 these** i.e., Peter and
Horner   **209 single combat** combat one-on-one   **220 Sirrah** (Customary
form of address to servants.)

1.4   *Enter [Margery Jourdain] the Witch,*
the two priests [Hume and Southwell],
and Bolingbroke.

HUME   Come, my masters. The Duchess, I tell you, ex- 1
pects performance of your promises.

BOLINGBROKE   Master Hume, we are therefore pro- 3
vided. Will her ladyship behold and hear our exor- 4
cisms? 5

HUME   Ay, what else? Fear you not her courage. 6

BOLINGBROKE   I have heard her reported to be a woman
of an invincible spirit. But it shall be convenient, Master Hume, that you be by her aloft, while we be busy
below; and so, I pray you, go in God's name and
leave us. (*Exit Hume.*) Mother Jourdain, be you prostrate and grovel on the earth. John Southwell, read 12
you; and let us to our work. 13

        [*Margery Jourdain lies face downward.*]

    Enter [Duchess] Eleanor aloft, [Hume following].

DUCHESS   Well said, my masters, and welcome all. To 14
this gear, the sooner the better. 15

BOLINGBROKE
Patience, good lady. Wizards know their times.
Deep night, dark night, the silent of the night,
The time of night when Troy was set on fire, 18
The time when screech owls cry and bandogs howl, 19
And spirits walk, and ghosts break up their graves—
That time best fits the work we have in hand.

1.4. Location: Gloucester's house.
1 my masters sirs   **3 therefore** for that very purpose   **4–5 exorcisms**
conjurations   **6 Fear** doubt   **12–13 read you** (In the stage direction at
l. 23, Southwell or Bolingbroke *reads* or recites a black magic spell.)
13 s.d. aloft (The quarto specifies that the Duchess "goes up to the
tower," i.e., some elevated place in the theater.)   **14 Well said** well done
14–15 To this gear get on with this business   **18 set on fire** (i.e., by the
Greeks concealed in the Trojan horse; described in Virgil, *Aeneid*,
Book 2)   **19 bandogs** leashed watchdogs

Madam, sit you and fear not. Whom we raise
We will make fast within a hallowed verge.   23

> *Here [they] do the ceremonies belonging, and*
> *make the circle. Bolingbroke or Southwell reads*
> *Conjuro te, etc. It thunders and lightens terribly;*
> *then the Spirit riseth.*

SPIRIT   *Adsum.*   24
MARGERY JOURDAIN   Asnath,   25
By the eternal God, whose name and power
Thou tremblest at, answer that I shall ask,   27
For till thou speak thou shalt not pass from hence.
SPIRIT
Ask what thou wilt. That I had said and done!   29
BOLINGBROKE [*Reading out of a paper*]
"First, of the King: what shall of him become?"
SPIRIT
The duke yet lives that Henry shall depose,   31
But him outlive, and die a violent death.   32
        [*As the Spirit speaks, Southwell writes the answer.*]
BOLINGBROKE
"What fates await the Duke of Suffolk?"
SPIRIT
By water shall he die and take his end.
BOLINGBROKE
"What shall befall the Duke of Somerset?"
SPIRIT   Let him shun castles;   36
Safer shall he be upon the sandy plains
Than where castles mounted stand.   38
Have done, for more I hardly can endure.   39

---

23 hallowed verge magic circle   **s.d. the ceremonies belonging** i.e., the
"hocus-pocus" necessary to conjure spirits, such as drawing a magic
circle and reciting a formula.   **Conjuro te** I conjure you.   **riseth** (Presumably a trapdoor is used on the main stage.)   **24 Adsum** I am here
25 Asnath (An anagram for *Sathan*.)   **27 that** that which   **29 That** would
that. (The Spirit is reluctant to answer questions.)   **31–32 The duke . . .
death** (The first line of the prophecy, as is characteristic of such utter-
ances, is capable of a double construction: "whom Henry will depose,"
or "who will depose Henry." The second line is fulfilled in *3 Henry VI*
in the deaths of Henry VI and Edward IV.)   **36 Let him shun castles**
(The warning is fulfilled in 5.2.65 ff.)   **38 mounted** on a mount
39 Have done finish up

BOLINGBROKE

Descend to darkness and the burning lake!
False fiend, avoid!   41

Thunder and lightning. Exit Spirit,
[sinking down again].

Enter the Duke of York and the Duke of
Buckingham with their guard and break in.
[They seize Jourdain and her cohorts, with their
papers.]

YORK

Lay hands upon these traitors and their trash.
[*To Jourdain.*] Beldam, I think we watched you at an
  inch.   43
[*To the Duchess.*] What, madam, are you there? The King
  and commonweal
Are deeply indebted for this piece of pains.   45
My Lord Protector will, I doubt it not,
See you well guerdoned for these good deserts.   47

DUCHESS

Not half so bad as thine to England's king,
Injurious Duke, that threatest where's no cause.   49

BUCKINGHAM

True, madam, none at all. What call you this?
[He shows her the papers he has seized.]
Away with them! Let them be clapped up close   51
And kept asunder. You, madam, shall with us.
Stafford, take her to thee.   53
[Exeunt above Duchess and Hume, guarded.]
We'll see your trinkets here all forthcoming.   54
All away!   *Exit [guard with Jourdain, Southwell,*
and Bolingbroke].

YORK

Lord Buckingham, methinks you watched her well.   56

---

41 False treacherous. **avoid** begone   **43 Beldam** witch, hag.   **at an
inch** i.e., closely   **45 piece of pains** trouble undergone. (Said ironically.)   **47 guerdoned** rewarded.   **deserts** deserving acts. (Said ironically.)   **49 Injurious** insulting   **51 clapped up close** imprisoned
securely   **53 Stafford** (Presumably one of Buckingham's kinsmen,
perhaps Sir Humphrey Stafford, acting as an officer of the arresting
guard.)   **54 trinkets** trifles, rubbish (used in performing magical acts,
and now confiscated to be *forthcoming,* used as legal evidence)
56 watched kept surveillance over

A pretty plot, well chosen to build upon!   57
Now, pray, my lord, let's see the devil's writ.
What have we here?   *Reads.*
"The duke yet lives that Henry shall depose;
But him outlive, and die a violent death."
Why, this is just *"Aio te, Aeacida,*   62
Romanos vincere posse." Well, to the rest: 63
"Tell me what fate awaits the Duke of Suffolk?"
"By water shall he die and take his end."
"What shall betide the Duke of Somerset?"
"Let him shun castles;
Safer shall he be upon the sandy plains
Than where castles mounted stand."
Come, come, my lords, these oracles
Are hardly attained and hardly understood.   71
The King is now in progress towards Saint Albans;   72
With him the husband of this lovely lady.
Thither goes these news, as fast as horse can carry
      them—
A sorry breakfast for my Lord Protector.

BUCKINGHAM

Your Grace shall give me leave, my lord of York,
To be the post, in hope of his reward.   77

YORK

At your pleasure, my good lord.   [*Exit Buckingham.*]
Who's within there, ho!

        Enter a Servingman.

Invite my lords of Salisbury and Warwick
To sup with me tomorrow night. Away!   *Exeunt.*

✤

57 plot clever plan (with pun on the sense of "plot of ground").   **build
upon** erect a scheme on (continuing the architectural pun)   **62 just**
precisely   **62–63 Aio . . . posse** I say that you, Aeacides, the Romans can
conquer. (This prophecy, given by the Delphic oracle to Pyrrhus, descendant of Aeacus, is grammatically ambiguous in just the same fashion as
the English oracle about Henry and the Yorkists, ll. 31–32.)   **71 hardly
attained** with difficulty obtained, or comprehended   **72 in progress** on
a state journey   **77 post** messenger

2.1   *Enter the King, Queen [with her hawk on her fist], Protector [Gloucester], Cardinal, and Suffolk, with falconers halloing.*

QUEEN
Believe me, lords, for flying at the brook   1
I saw not better sport these seven years' day.   2
Yet, by your leave, the wind was very high,
And ten to one old Joan had not gone out.   4

KING [*To Gloucester*]
But what a point, my lord, your falcon made,   5
And what a pitch she flew above the rest!   6
To see how God in all his creatures works!
Yea, man and birds are fain of climbing high.   8

SUFFOLK
No marvel, an it like Your Majesty,   9
My Lord Protector's hawks do tower so well;   10
They know their master loves to be aloft
And bears his thoughts above his falcon's pitch.

GLOUCESTER
My lord, 'tis but a base ignoble mind
That mounts no higher than a bird can soar.

CARDINAL
I thought as much. He would be above the clouds.

GLOUCESTER
Ay, my Lord Cardinal, how think you by that?
Were it not good Your Grace could fly to heaven?

KING
The treasury of everlasting joy.

CARDINAL [*To Gloucester*]
Thy heaven is on earth; thine eyes and thoughts

2.1. Location: St. Albans.
1 flying . . . brook i.e., hawking for waterfowl   **2 these . . . day** in seven years' time   **4 old . . . out** i.e., the hawk named old Joan would not have flown in such a high wind   **5 point** advantageous position from which the hawk attacks the bird   **6 pitch** height to which a hawk soars before descending on its prey   **8 fain** fond   **9 an it like** if it please (also in ll. 30 and 78)   **10 hawks** (Refers not only to the hawks flown by Gloucester in this hunt, but also to the falcon with a maiden's head portrayed on his heraldic badge.)   **tower** rise wheeling up to the *point* from which the hawk swoops down

Beat on a crown, the treasure of thy heart.   20
Pernicious Protector, dangerous peer,
That smooth'st it so with King and commonweal!   22

GLOUCESTER
What, Cardinal, is your priesthood grown peremptory?
Tantaene animis caelestibus irae?   24
Churchmen so hot? Good uncle, hide such malice.
With such holiness, can you do it?

SUFFOLK
No malice, sir, no more than well becomes
So good a quarrel and so bad a peer.

GLOUCESTER
As who, my lord?

SUFFOLK   Why, as you, my lord,
An 't like your lordly Lord-Protectorship.

GLOUCESTER
Why, Suffolk, England knows thine insolence.

QUEEN
And thy ambition, Gloucester.

KING   I prithee, peace,
Good Queen, and whet not on these furious peers;   33
For blessèd are the peacemakers on earth.   34

CARDINAL
Let me be blessèd for the peace I make
Against this proud Protector with my sword!

GLOUCESTER [*Aside to Cardinal*]
Faith, holy uncle, would 'twere come to that!

CARDINAL [*Aside to Gloucester*]   Marry, when thou dar'st.

GLOUCESTER [*Aside to Cardinal*]
Make up no factious numbers for the matter;   39
In thine own person answer thy abuse.   40

CARDINAL [*Aside to Gloucester*]
Ay, where thou dar'st not peep. An if thou dar'st,   41
This evening, on the east side of the grove.

---

20 Beat on dwell on, think about constantly   **22 smooth'st it** flatters
24 Tantaene . . . irae can there be such resentment in heavenly minds.
(Virgil, *Aeneid*, 1.11.)   **33 whet not on** do not encourage   **34 blessèd . . .
earth** (King Henry cites the Sermon on the Mount, Matthew 5:9.)
39 Make . . . numbers i.e., do not bring a party of your quarrelsome
supporters into the quarrel   **40 abuse** offense, insult   **41 peep** i.e., show
your face.   **An if** if

KING
  How now, my lords?
CARDINAL [*Aloud*]   Believe me, cousin Gloucester,
  Had not your man put up the fowl so suddenly,   44
  We had had more sport. [*Aside to Gloucester.*] Come
  . with thy two-hand sword.
GLOUCESTER [*Aloud*]   True, uncle.
  [*Aside to Cardinal.*] Are ye advised? The east side of
    the grove.   47
CARDINAL [*Aside to Gloucester*]
  I am with you.
KING   Why, how now, uncle Gloucester?
GLOUCESTER
  Talking of hawking; nothing else, my lord.
  [*Aside to Cardinal.*] Now by God's mother, priest,
    I'll shave your crown for this,   50
  Or all my fence shall fail.
CARDINAL [*Aside to Gloucester*]   *Medice, teipsum*—   51
  Protector, see to 't well. Protect yourself.   52
KING
  The winds grow high; so do your stomachs, lords.   53
  How irksome is this music to my heart!
  When such strings jar, what hope of harmony?
  I pray, my lords, let me compound this strife.   56

        Enter one [a Townsman of Saint Albans] crying
        "A miracle!"

GLOUCESTER   What means this noise?
  Fellow, what miracle dost thou proclaim?
TOWNSMAN   A miracle! A miracle!
SUFFOLK
  Come to the King and tell him what miracle.

44 man i.e., falconer. **put . . . fowl** startled the game into flight
47 advised agreed   **50 I'll shave your crown** (Since a priest is already
tonsured, this would be to give him a close shave indeed.)   **51 fence**
skill in fighting with a sword.   **Medice, teipsum** physician, [heal] thyself. (Luke 4:23.)   **52 Protect** (with a pun on *Protector*)   **53 stomachs**
tempers   **56 compound** settle   **s.d. Saint Albans** a shrine and a town
named for Saint Alban, supposedly the first Christian martyr in Britain,
executed under the edicts of Diocletian in 304 B.C. for sheltering a
Christian priest

TOWNSMAN
　Forsooth, a blind man at Saint Alban's shrine
　Within this half hour hath received his sight—
　A man that ne'er saw in his life before.
KING
　Now, God be praised, that to believing souls
　Gives light in darkness, comfort in despair!　　　　65

　　Enter the Mayor of Saint Albans and his
　　brethren, bearing the man [Simpcox]
　　between two in a chair, [Simpcox's Wife
　　and others following].

CARDINAL
　Here comes the townsmen on procession,　　　　66
　To present Your Highness with the man.
KING
　Great is his comfort in this earthly vale,
　Although by his sight his sin be multiplied.　　　　69
GLOUCESTER
　Stand by, my masters. Bring him near the King;
　His Highness' pleasure is to talk with him.
KING
　Good fellow, tell us here the circumstance,
　That we for thee may glorify the Lord.
　What, hast thou been long blind and now restored?
SIMPCOX　Born blind, an 't please Your Grace.
WIFE　Ay, indeed, was he.
SUFFOLK　What woman is this?
WIFE　His wife, an 't like your worship.
GLOUCESTER　Hadst thou been his mother, thou couldst
　have better told.
KING　Where wert thou born?
SIMPCOX
　At Berwick in the north, an 't like Your Grace.
KING
　Poor soul, God's goodness hath been great to thee.
　Let never day nor night unhallowed pass,　　　　84
　But still remember what the Lord hath done.　　　　85

65 s.d. brethren aldermen, fellow members of the corporation or guild
66 on in　　**69 by his sight . . . multiplied** i.e., he may now be subject to
more temptations, being able to see　　**84 unhallowed** unblessed　　**85 still**
continually

QUEEN

Tell me, good fellow, cam'st thou here by chance,
Or of devotion, to this holy shrine?

SIMPCOX

God knows, of pure devotion, being called
A hundred times and oftener in my sleep
By good Saint Alban, who said, "Simon, come,   90
Come offer at my shrine and I will help thee."   91

WIFE

Most true, forsooth; and many time and oft
Myself have heard a voice to call him so.

CARDINAL   What, art thou lame?

SIMPCOX   Ay, God Almighty help me!

SUFFOLK   How cam'st thou so?

SIMPCOX   A fall off of a tree.

WIFE   A plum tree, master.   98

GLOUCESTER   How long hast thou been blind?

SIMPCOX   O, born so, master.

GLOUCESTER   What, and wouldst climb a tree?

SIMPCOX   But that in all my life, when I was a youth.   102

WIFE

Too true, and bought his climbing very dear.

GLOUCESTER   Mass, thou lov'dst plums well, that wouldst   104
venture so.

SIMPCOX   Alas, good master, my wife desired some
damsons and made me climb, with danger of my life.   107

GLOUCESTER

A subtle knave! But yet it shall not serve.   108
Let me see thine eyes. Wink now. Now open them.   109
In my opinion yet thou seest not well.

SIMPCOX   Yes, master, clear as day, I thank God and Saint
Alban.

GLOUCESTER

Sayst thou me so? What color is this cloak of?

SIMPCOX   Red, master, red as blood.

---

90 Simon (His proper name; *Simpcox* is a variant.)   **91 offer** make an
offering   **98 plum tree** (A slang phrase for the female pudenda that sets
up an elaborate ribald joke here about a husband risking his life to try
to satisfy his wife's craving.)   **102 But that** only that once   **104 Mass** by
the Mass. (An oath.)   **107 damsons** a variety of plum (commonly used as
a slang phrase for testicles)   **108 shall not serve** won't serve to fool
me   **109 Wink** close your eyes

GLOUCESTER
   Why, that's well said. What color is my gown of?
SIMPCOX   Black, forsooth, coal black as jet.
KING
   Why, then, thou know'st what color jet is of?
SUFFOLK
   And yet, I think, jet did he never see.
GLOUCESTER
   But cloaks and gowns, before this day, a many.   119
WIFE
   Never, before this day, in all his life.
GLOUCESTER   Tell me, sirrah, what's my name?
SIMPCOX   Alas, master, I know not.
GLOUCESTER [*Pointing*]   What's his name?
SIMPCOX   I know not.
GLOUCESTER [*Pointing to another*]   Nor his?
SIMPCOX   No, indeed, master.
GLOUCESTER   What's thine own name?
SIMPCOX   Sander Simpcox, an if it please you, master.
GLOUCESTER   Then, Sander, sit there, the lying'st
   knave in Christendom. If thou hadst been born
   blind, thou mightst as well have known all our names
   as thus to name the several colors we do wear. Sight
   may distinguish of colors, but suddenly to nominate   133
   them all, it is impossible. My lords, Saint Alban here
   hath done a miracle; and would ye not think his cunning to be great that could restore this cripple to his
   legs again?
SIMPCOX   O master, that you could!
GLOUCESTER   My masters of Saint Albans, have you not
   beadles in your town, and things called whips?   140
MAYOR   Yes, my lord, if it please Your Grace.
GLOUCESTER   Then send for one presently.   142
MAYOR   Sirrah, go fetch the beadle hither straight.   143
                              Exit [an Attendant].
GLOUCESTER   Now fetch me a stool hither by and by. [*A*   144
   stool is brought.] Now, sirrah, if you mean to save

---

119 many multitude   **133 nominate** call by name   **140 beadles** minor
parish officers who might punish petty offenses   **142 presently** immediately   **143 straight** immediately   **144 by and by** at once

yourself from whipping, leap me over this stool and 146
run away.
SIMPCOX   Alas, master, I am not able to stand alone. You
go about to torture me in vain.

        Enter a Beadle with whips.

GLOUCESTER   Well, sir, we must have you find your legs.
Sirrah beadle, whip him till he leap over that same
stool.
BEADLE   I will, my lord. Come on, sirrah, off with your
doublet quickly.   154
SIMPCOX   Alas, master, what shall I do? I am not able to
stand.

        *After the Beadle hath hit him once, he leaps over
        the stool and runs away; and they follow and cry,
        "A miracle!"*

KING
O God, seest Thou this, and bearest so long?
QUEEN
It made me laugh to see the villain run.
GLOUCESTER [*To the Beadle*]
Follow the knave, and take this drab away.   159
WIFE   Alas, sir, we did it for pure need.
GLOUCESTER   Let them be whipped through every mar-
ket town till they come to Berwick, from whence they
came.
                Exit [Wife, with Beadle, Mayor, etc.].
CARDINAL
Duke Humphrey has done a miracle today.
SUFFOLK
True; made the lame to leap and fly away.
GLOUCESTER
But you have done more miracles than I;
You made in a day, my lord, whole towns to fly.   167

        Enter Buckingham.

146 me for me   154 doublet close-fitting jacket   159 drab slut
167 You . . . fly i.e., you gave away French towns in a day, as part of
Queen Margaret's dowry

KING
  What tidings with our cousin Buckingham?
BUCKINGHAM
  Such as my heart doth tremble to unfold:
  A sort of naughty persons, lewdly bent,   170
  Under the countenance and confederacy   171
  Of Lady Eleanor, the Protector's wife,
  The ringleader and head of all this rout,   173
  Have practiced dangerously against your state,   174
  Dealing with witches and with conjurers,
  Whom we have apprehended in the fact,   176
  Raising up wicked spirits from under ground,
  Demanding of King Henry's life and death   178
  And other of Your Highness' Privy Council,
  As more at large Your Grace shall understand.   180
CARDINAL
  And so, my Lord Protector, by this means
  Your lady is forthcoming yet at London.   182
  [*Aside to Gloucester.*] This news, I think, hath turned
    your weapon's edge;
  'Tis like, my lord, you will not keep your hour.   184
GLOUCESTER
  Ambitious churchman, leave to afflict my heart.   185
  Sorrow and grief have vanquished all my powers;
  And, vanquished as I am, I yield to thee
  Or to the meanest groom.   188
KING
  O God, what mischiefs work the wicked ones,
  Heaping confusion on their own heads thereby!   190
QUEEN
  Gloucester, see here the tainture of thy nest,   191
  And look thyself be faultless, thou wert best.   192

---

170 sort lot, gang. **naughty** wicked. **lewdly** evilly **171 Under . . .
confederacy** with the authorization and even complicity **173 rout**
crew **174 practiced** conspired **176 fact** deed **178 Demanding of**
inquiring about **180 at large** in detail **182 forthcoming** ready to
appear (in court) **184 like** likely. **hour** appointment (for the duel
between Gloucester and the Cardinal) **185 leave to afflict** cease afflict-
ing **188 meanest** of lowest degree **190 confusion** destruction
191 tainture defilement **192 look** take care, see to it. **thou wert best**
you'd be well advised

GLOUCESTER
  Madam, for myself, to heaven I do appeal   193
  How I have loved my king and commonweal;
  And, for my wife, I know not how it stands.   195
  Sorry I am to hear what I have heard.
  Noble she is; but if she have forgot
  Honor and virtue, and conversed with such   198
  As, like to pitch, defile nobility,
  I banish her my bed and company
  And give her as a prey to law and shame
  That hath dishonored Gloucester's honest name.

KING
  Well, for this night we will repose us here;
  Tomorrow toward London back again,
  To look into this business thoroughly,
  And call these foul offenders to their answers,
  And poise the cause in Justice' equal scales,   207
  Whose beam stands sure, whose rightful cause
      prevails.   *Flourish. Exeunt.* 208

❖

2.2   *Enter York, Salisbury, and Warwick.*

YORK
  Now, my good lords of Salisbury and Warwick,
  Our simple supper ended, give me leave,
  In this close walk, to satisfy myself   3
  In craving your opinion of my title,
  Which is infallible, to England's crown.
SALISBURY   My lord, I long to hear it at full.
WARWICK
  Sweet York, begin; and if thy claim be good,
  The Nevilles are thy subjects to command.
YORK   Then thus:

193, 195 **for** as for   198 **conversed** had to do with   **207 poise** weigh
208 **beam** bar on which the scales are suspended.   **stands sure** is
perfectly level

2.2. Location: London. The Duke of York's garden.
3 **close** private

Edward the Third, my lords, had seven sons:
The first, Edward the Black Prince, Prince of Wales;
The second, William of Hatfield, and the third,
Lionel, Duke of Clarence; next to whom
Was John of Gaunt, the Duke of Lancaster;
The fifth was Edmund Langley, Duke of York;
The sixth was Thomas of Woodstock, Duke of
  Gloucester;
William of Windsor was the seventh and last.
Edward the Black Prince died before his father
And left behind him Richard, his only son,   19
Who after Edward the Third's death reigned as king
Till Henry Bolingbroke, Duke of Lancaster,
The eldest son and heir of John of Gaunt,
Crowned by the name of Henry the Fourth,
Seized on the realm, deposed the rightful king,
Sent his poor queen to France, from whence she came,
And him to Pomfret; where, as all you know,
Harmless Richard was murdered traitorously.

WARWICK
Father, the Duke hath told the truth.
Thus got the house of Lancaster the crown.

YORK
Which now they hold by force and not by right;
For Richard, the first son's heir, being dead,
The issue of the next son should have reigned.   32

SALISBURY
But William of Hatfield died without an heir.

YORK
The third son, Duke of Clarence, from whose line
I claim the crown, had issue, Philippe, a daughter,
Who married Edmund Mortimer, Earl of March.
Edmund had issue, Roger, Earl of March;
Roger had issue, Edmund, Anne, and Eleanor.

SALISBURY
This Edmund, in the reign of Bolingbroke,   39

---

19 Richard i.e., Richard II   **32 issue** offspring   **39 This Edmund** (A
historical error, found also in the chronicles, of confusing Edmund
Mortimer, fifth Earl of March, who was named heir to the throne by
Richard II, with his uncle Edmund, brother of Roger, who married
Glendower's daughter. See *1 Henry VI*, 2.5, and *1 Henry IV*, 1.3.)

As I have read, laid claim unto the crown,
And, but for Owen Glendower, had been king,
Who kept him in captivity till he died.   42
But to the rest.

YORK   His eldest sister, Anne,
My mother, being heir unto the crown,
Married Richard, Earl of Cambridge, who was son
To Edmund Langley, Edward the Third's fifth son.
By her I claim the kingdom. She was heir
To Roger, Earl of March, who was the son
Of Edmund Mortimer, who married Philippe,
Sole daughter unto Lionel, Duke of Clarence.
So, if the issue of the elder son
Succeed before the younger, I am king.

WARWICK
What plain proceeding is more plain than this?
Henry doth claim the crown from John of Gaunt,
The fourth son; York claims it from the third.
Till Lionel's issue fails, his should not reign.   56
It fails not yet, but flourishes in thee   57
And in thy sons, fair slips of such a stock.   58
Then, father Salisbury, kneel we together,
And in this private plot be we the first   60
That shall salute our rightful sovereign
With honor of his birthright to the crown.

BOTH [*Kneeling*]
Long live our sovereign Richard, England's king!

YORK
We thank you, lords. [*They rise.*] But I am not your king   64
Till I be crowned, and that my sword be stained   65
With heart-blood of the house of Lancaster;
And that's not suddenly to be performed,
But with advice and silent secrecy.   68
Do you as I do in these dangerous days:
Wink at the Duke of Suffolk's insolence,   70
At Beaufort's pride, at Somerset's ambition,
At Buckingham, and all the crew of them,

---

42 Who i.e., Glendower   **56 his** i.e., John of Gaunt's   **57 It fails not** i.e.,
Lionel's line of descent has not died out   **58 slips** cuttings   **60 plot** plot
of ground   **64 We** (The royal "we"!)   **65 and that** and until the time
that   **68 advice** careful reflection   **70 Wink at** shut your eyes to

Till they have snared the shepherd of the flock,
That virtuous prince, the good Duke Humphrey.
'Tis that they seek, and they in seeking that
Shall find their deaths, if York can prophesy.

SALISBURY
My lord, break we off. We know your mind at full.

WARWICK
My heart assures me that the Earl of Warwick
Shall one day make the Duke of York a king.

YORK
And, Neville, this I do assure myself:
Richard shall live to make the Earl of Warwick
The greatest man in England but the King.   *Exeunt.*

✣

2.3   *Sound trumpets. Enter the King and state, [the
Queen, Gloucester, York, Suffolk, Salisbury,
and others,] with guard, to banish the Duchess
[of Gloucester, who is brought on under guard
with Margery Jourdain, Southwell, Hume, and
Bolingbroke].*

KING
Stand forth, Dame Eleanor Cobham, Gloucester's wife.
In sight of God and us, your guilt is great.
Receive the sentence of the law for sins
Such as by God's book are adjudged to death.   4
[*To Margery and the others.*] You four, from hence to
    prison back again;
From thence unto the place of execution.
The witch in Smithfield shall be burnt to ashes,
And you three shall be strangled on the gallows.
[*To the Duchess.*] You, madam, for you are more
    nobly born,   9

2.3. Location: London. A hall of justice.
s.d. and others (In the quarto, the Cardinal, Buckingham, and Warwick
are also named. Warwick, York, and Salisbury enter "to them," i.e.,
meeting the royal party.)   4 by God's book i.e., according to the commandments in the Bible against witches, Exodus 22:18, and enchant-
ments, Leviticus 19:26, among other passages   9 for because

Despoilèd of your honor in your life,   10
Shall, after three days' open penance done,
Live in your country here in banishment
With Sir John Stanley in the Isle of Man.   13

DUCHESS
Welcome is banishment. Welcome were my death.   14

GLOUCESTER
Eleanor, the law, thou seest, hath judged thee.
I cannot justify whom the law condemns.
      [*Exeunt Duchess and other prisoners, guarded.*]
Mine eyes are full of tears, my heart of grief.
Ah, Humphrey, this dishonor in thine age
Will bring thy head with sorrow to the grave!
I beseech Your Majesty, give me leave to go;
Sorrow would solace and mine age would ease.   21

KING
Stay, Humphrey, Duke of Gloucester. Ere thou go,
Give up thy staff. Henry will to himself   23
Protector be; and God shall be my hope,
My stay, my guide, and lantern to my feet.
And go in peace, Humphrey, no less beloved
Than when thou wert Protector to thy king.

QUEEN
I see no reason why a king of years   28
Should be to be protected like a child.   29
God and King Henry govern England's realm!
Give up your staff, sir, and the King his realm.   31

GLOUCESTER
My staff? Here, noble Henry, is my staff.
                   [*He surrenders his staff.*]
As willingly do I the same resign
As ere thy father Henry made it mine;   34
And even as willingly at thy feet I leave it
As others would ambitiously receive it.

---

10 Despoilèd deprived.   **in your life** during the remainder of your life
13 With . . . Stanley (An error for Sir Thomas Stanley, the Duchess's
custodian and the Lord Stanley of *Richard III*.)   **14 were** would be
21 would wishes to have   **23 staff** staff of office   **28 of years** who is of
age   **29 be to be** need to be   **31 King his** King's   **34 ere** at an earlier
time. (The quarto reading, "erst," conveys the same meaning.)

Farewell, good King. When I am dead and gone,
May honorable peace attend thy throne!

Exit Gloucester.

QUEEN
Why, now is Henry king and Margaret queen,
And Humphrey, Duke of Gloucester, scarce himself,
That bears so shrewd a maim. Two pulls at once: 41
His lady banished, and a limb lopped off.   42
This staff of honor raught, there let it stand   43
Where it best fits to be, in Henry's hand.

SUFFOLK
Thus droops this lofty pine and hangs his sprays;   45
Thus Eleanor's pride dies in her youngest days.   46

YORK
Lords, let him go. Please it Your Majesty,
This is the day appointed for the combat,
And ready are the appellant and defendant—   49
The armorer and his man—to enter the lists,
So please Your Highness to behold the fight.

QUEEN
Ay, good my lord, for purposely therefor
Left I the court, to see this quarrel tried.

KING
I' God's name, see the lists and all things fit.
Here let them end it, and God defend the right!

YORK
I never saw a fellow worse bestead,   56
Or more afraid to fight, than is the appellant,
The servant of this armorer, my lords.   58

Enter at one door, the Armorer [Horner] and his
Neighbors, drinking to him so much that he is
drunk; and he enters with a drum before him
and his staff with a sandbag fastened to it; and

---

41 **bears . . . maim** endures so grievous a mutilation.   **pulls** pluckings
42 **a limb lopped off** i.e., his staff of office taken away, so much a part
of him that the severing was like an amputation   43 **raught** attained,
seized   45 **lofty pine** (An emblem adopted by Henry IV, Gloucester's
father.)   **sprays** branches   46 **her youngest days** i.e., when her ambition
and pride are at their height   49 **appellant** challenger   56 **bestead**
prepared   58 s.d. **drinking to him** offering toasts to him (to which he is
obliged to drink in return, drink for drink).   **drum** drummer

at the other door his man [Peter], with a drum
and sandbag, and Prentices drinking to him.

FIRST NEIGHBOR   Here, neighbor Horner, I drink to you
in a cup of sack; and fear not, neighbor, you shall do   60
well enough.

SECOND NEIGHBOR   And here, neighbor, here's a cup of
charneco.   63

THIRD NEIGHBOR   And here's a pot of good double beer,   64
neighbor. Drink, and fear not your man.

HORNER   Let it come, i' faith, and I'll pledge you all; and   66
a fig for Peter!   67

FIRST PRENTICE   Here, Peter, I drink to thee, and be not
afraid.

SECOND PRENTICE   Be merry, Peter, and fear not thy
master. Fight for credit of the prentices.   71

PETER   I thank you all. Drink, and pray for me, I pray
you, for I think I have taken my last draft in this
world. Here, Robin, an if I die, I give thee my apron;
and Will, thou shalt have my hammer; and here,
Tom, take all the money that I have. [*He gives away his*
things.] O Lord bless me, I pray God, for I am never
able to deal with my master, he hath learned so much
fence already.   79

SALISBURY   Come, leave your drinking and fall to
blows. Sirrah, what's thy name?

PETER   Peter, forsooth.

SALISBURY   Peter? What more?

PETER   Thump.

SALISBURY   Thump? Then see thou thump thy master
well.

HORNER   Masters, I am come hither, as it were, upon
my man's instigation, to prove him a knave and myself an honest man; and touching the Duke of York, I
will take my death, I never meant him any ill, nor the   90

---

60 sack a dry Spanish or Canary wine   **63 charneco** a sweet Portuguese
wine   **64 double** strong   **66 Let it come** i.e., let the drink be passed
around.   **pledge you** drink your health   **67 a fig** (An obscene insult,
accompanied by the gesture of putting the thumb between the first and
second fingers.)   **71 credit** reputation, good name   **79 fence** skill in
fencing   **90 take my death** i.e., take an oath on pain of death

King, nor the Queen. And therefore, Peter, have at 91
thee with a downright blow!   92

YORK
Dispatch. This knave's tongue begins to double.   93
Sound, trumpets, alarum to the combatants!   94
     [*Alarum.*] *They fight, and Peter strikes him down.*
HORNER   Hold, Peter, hold! I confess, I confess treason.
                                            [*He dies.*]
YORK   Take away his weapon. Fellow, thank God and
the good wine in thy master's way.   97
PETER   O God, have I overcome mine enemies in this
presence? O Peter, thou hast prevailed in right!
KING
Go, take hence that traitor from our sight;   100
For by his death we do perceive his guilt,
And God in justice hath revealed to us
The truth and innocence of this poor fellow,
Which he had thought to have murdered wrongfully.   104
[*To Peter.*] Come, fellow, follow us for thy reward.
                       Sound a flourish. Exeunt
                       [*with Horner's body*].

❖

2.4   *Enter Duke Humphrey [of Gloucester] and his
          Men in mourning cloaks.*

GLOUCESTER
Thus sometimes hath the brightest day a cloud,
And after summer evermore succeeds
Barren winter, with his wrathful nipping cold;
So cares and joys abound, as seasons fleet.   4
Sirs, what's o'clock?
SERVANT   Ten, my lord.
GLOUCESTER
Ten is the hour that was appointed me

91–92 have at thee here I come at you
intoxication)   **94 alarum** call to arms
marred your master's fighting ability
104 Which he i.e., whom Horner

93 double thicken and slur (with
97 in thy master's way i.e., that
100 that traitor i.e., Horner

2.4. Location: London. A street.
4 fleet flow by

To watch the coming of my punished duchess.
Uneath may she endure the flinty streets,   9
To tread them with her tender-feeling feet.
Sweet Nell, ill can thy noble mind abrook   11
The abject people gazing on thy face,   12
With envious looks laughing at thy shame,   13
That erst did follow thy proud chariot wheels   14
When thou didst ride in triumph through the streets.
But soft! I think she comes, and I'll prepare   16
My tearstained eyes to see her miseries.   17

> *Enter the Duchess [of Gloucester, barefoot], in a*
> *white sheet, [with verses pinned upon her back,]*
> *and a taper burning in her hand; with [Sir John*
> *Stanley,] the Sheriff, and officers [with bills and*
> *halberds].*

SERVANT
So please Your Grace, we'll take her from the sheriff.   18
GLOUCESTER
No, stir not for your lives. Let her pass by.
DUCHESS
Come you, my lord, to see my open shame?
Now thou dost penance too. Look how they gaze!   21
See how the giddy multitude do point
And nod their heads and throw their eyes on thee!
Ah, Gloucester, hide thee from their hateful looks   24
And, in thy closet pent up, rue my shame   25
And ban thine enemies, both mine and thine!   26
GLOUCESTER
Be patient, gentle Nell. Forget this grief.
DUCHESS
Ah, Gloucester, teach me to forget myself!
For whilst I think I am thy married wife
And thou a prince, Protector of this land,
Methinks I should not thus be led along,

---

9 **Uneath** with difficulty, scarcely   11 **abrook** endure   12 **abject** lowly
born   13 **envious** full of malice   14 **erst** formerly   16 **soft** wait a
minute   17 **s.d. with bills and halberds** with long-handled axlike weapons. (The bracketed stage directions are derived from the quarto.)
18 **take her** rescue her by force   21 **Look how they gaze** (The crowd of
commoners may be represented onstage, or the Duchess may gesture
offstage.)   24 **hateful** full of hate   25 **closet** private room   26 **ban** curse

Mailed up in shame, with papers on my back,   32
And followed with a rabble that rejoice   33
To see my tears and hear my deep-fet groans.   34
The ruthless flint doth cut my tender feet,
And when I start, the envious people laugh   36
And bid me be advisèd how I tread.   37
Ah, Humphrey, can I bear this shameful yoke?
Trowest thou that e'er I'll look upon the world,   39
Or count them happy that enjoy the sun?
No, dark shall be my light and night my day;
To think upon my pomp shall be my hell.
Sometimes I'll say I am Duke Humphrey's wife,
And he a prince and ruler of the land;
Yet so he ruled, and such a prince he was,
As he stood by whilst I, his forlorn duchess,   46
Was made a wonder and a pointing-stock   47
To every idle rascal follower.
But be thou mild and blush not at my shame,
Nor stir at nothing till the ax of death
Hang over thee, as, sure, it shortly will.
For Suffolk, he that can do all in all
With her that hateth thee and hates us all,   53
And York, and impious Beaufort, that false priest,
Have all limed bushes to betray thy wings,   55
And fly thou how thou canst, they'll tangle thee.   56
But fear not thou until thy foot be snared,   57
Nor never seek prevention of thy foes.   58
GLOUCESTER
Ah, Nell, forbear! Thou aimest all awry.
I must offend before I be attainted;   60
And had I twenty times so many foes,

---

32 Mailed up enveloped. (Used in hawking to prevent the hawk from
struggling, just as Eleanor is wrapped in a white sheet.) **papers on my
back** (The verses pinned upon her back describe the sin for which she is
doing penance.) **33 with** by **34 deep-fet** fetched from the depths
36 start flinch, wince. **envious** malicious **37 advisèd** careful
39 Trowest thou do you believe **46 As** that **47 pointing-stock** one
pointed at in scorn **53 her** i.e., Queen Margaret **55 limed** put out
sticky birdlime as a trap on **56 fly . . . thee** no matter how you try to
fly away, they will ensnare you **57 fear not thou** i.e., you are not properly wary. (Or the Duchess may be ironically urging him to wait until it
is too late.) **58 prevention** forestalling **60 attainted** condemned for
treason or other serious wrongdoing

And each of them had twenty times their power,
All these could not procure me any scathe   63
So long as I am loyal, true, and crimeless.
Wouldst have me rescue thee from this reproach?
Why, yet thy scandal were not wiped away,   66
But I in danger for the breach of law.
Thy greatest help is quiet, gentle Nell.   68
I pray thee, sort thy heart to patience;   69
These few days' wonder will be quickly worn.   70

    Enter a Herald.

HERALD
  I summon Your Grace to His Majesty's Parliament,
  Holden at Bury the first of this next month.   72
GLOUCESTER
  And my consent ne'er asked herein before?
  This is close dealing. Well, I will be there.   74
                          [Exit Herald.]
  My Nell, I take my leave. And, Master Sheriff,
  Let not her penance exceed the King's commission.
SHERIFF
  An 't please Your Grace, here my commission stays, 77
  And Sir John Stanley is appointed now
  To take her with him to the Isle of Man.
GLOUCESTER
  Must you, Sir John, protect my lady here?
STANLEY
  So am I given in charge, may 't please Your Grace. 81
GLOUCESTER
  Entreat her not the worse in that I pray   82
  You use her well. The world may laugh again,   83
  And I may live to do you kindness if
  You do it her. And so, Sir John, farewell.
DUCHESS
  What, gone, my lord, and bid me not farewell?

---

63 scathe injury   **66 were not** would not be   **68 quiet** i.e., patient
endurance   **69 sort** adapt   **70 These . . . wonder** i.e., this passing
notoriety (as in the phrase "a nine-days' wonder").   **worn** worn out, i.e.,
forgotten   **72 Holden at Bury** to be held at Bury St. Edmunds (in
Suffolk)   **74 close** secret, underhand   **77 stays** stops, ends   **81 given in
charge** commanded   **82 Entreat** treat. **in that** merely because   **83 The
world . . . again** i.e., we may see happier times. (Proverbial.)

GLOUCESTER
  Witness my tears, I cannot stay to speak.
                   Exit Gloucester [with his Men].

DUCHESS
  Art thou gone too? All comfort go with thee!
  For none abides with me. My joy is death—
  Death, at whose name I oft have been afeard,
  Because I wished this world's eternity.   · 91
  Stanley, I prithee, go, and take me hence.
  I care not whither, for I beg no favor;
  Only convey me where thou art commanded.

STANLEY
  Why, madam, that is to the Isle of Man,
  There to be used according to your state.   96

DUCHESS
  That's bad enough, for I am but reproach;   97
  And shall I then be used reproachfully?

STANLEY
  Like to a duchess and Duke Humphrey's lady,
  According to that state you shall be used.

DUCHESS
  Sheriff, farewell, and better than I fare,   101
  Although thou hast been conduct of my shame. 102

SHERIFF
  It is my office; and, madam, pardon me.

DUCHESS
  Ay, ay, farewell. Thy office is discharged.
  Come, Stanley, shall we go?

STANLEY
  Madam, your penance done, throw off this sheet,
  And go we to attire you for our journey.

DUCHESS
  My shame will not be shifted with my sheet.   108
  No, it will hang upon my richest robes
  And show itself, attire me how I can.
  Go, lead the way. I long to see my prison.   *Exeunt.*

❖

91 this world's eternity endless worldly success **96 state** noble rank.
(But Eleanor plays on *state* in the sense of "condition.") **97 I . . .
reproach** I am the embodiment of reproach or disgrace, deserve only
my shame **101 better . . . fare** may you fare better than I **102 conduct**
conductor **108 shifted** changed (with a pun on *shift,* a chemise)

3.1   *Sound a sennet. Enter King, Queen, Cardinal*
[Beaufort], Suffolk, York, Buckingham,
Salisbury, and Warwick to the Parliament.

KING
　I muse my lord of Gloucester is not come.　　　　　1
　'Tis not his wont to be the hindmost man,　　　　　2
　Whate'er occasion keeps him from us now.

QUEEN
　Can you not see, or will ye not observe,
　The strangeness of his altered countenance?　　　　5
　With what a majesty he bears himself,
　How insolent of late he is become,
　How proud, how peremptory, and unlike himself?
　We know the time since he was mild and affable,　　9
　And if we did but glance a far-off look,
　Immediately he was upon his knee,
　That all the court admired him for submission;　　12
　But meet him now, and, be it in the morn,
　When everyone will give the time of day,　　　　　14
　He knits his brow and shows an angry eye
　And passeth by with stiff unbowèd knee,
　Disdaining duty that to us belongs.　　　　　　　17
　Small curs are not regarded when they grin,　　　18
　But great men tremble when the lion roars—
　And Humphrey is no little man in England.
　First note that he is near you in descent,
　And should you fall, he is the next will mount.　　22
　Me seemeth then it is no policy,　　　　　　　　23
　Respecting what a rancorous mind he bears　　　24
　And his advantage following your decease,
　That he should come about your royal person

**3.1. Location: A hall for a session of Parliament at Bury St. Edmunds
(historically, the Abbey).**
s.d. Sound a sennet (The quarto stage direction specifies that two
heralds enter first, leading a formal procession.)　**1 muse** wonder
2 wont custom　**5 strangeness** aloofness　**9 know** remember.　**since**
when　**12 admired** wondered at　**14 give . . . day** say good morning
17 Disdaining . . . belongs disdaining to show the ceremonial respect
that is our (or my) due　**18 grin** bare their teeth　**22 will mount** who
will mount the throne　**23 Me seemeth** it seems to me.　**policy** prudent
course　**24 Respecting** considering

Or be admitted to Your Highness' Council.
By flattery hath he won the commons' hearts;
And when he please to make commotion,   29
'Tis to be feared they all will follow him.
Now 'tis the spring, and weeds are shallow-rooted;
Suffer them now, and they'll o'ergrow the garden
And choke the herbs for want of husbandry.   33
The reverent care I bear unto my lord
Made me collect these dangers in the Duke.   35
If it be fond, call it a woman's fear—   36
Which fear, if better reasons can supplant,   37
I will subscribe and say I wronged the Duke.   38
My lord of Suffolk, Buckingham, and York,
Reprove my allegation if you can,   40
Or else conclude my words effectual.   41

SUFFOLK
Well hath Your Highness seen into this duke,
And, had I first been put to speak my mind,
I think I should have told Your Grace's tale.
The Duchess by his subornation,   45
Upon my life, began her devilish practices;   46
Or if he were not privy to those faults,   47
Yet, by reputing of his high descent—   48
As next the King he was successive heir,
And such high vaunts of his nobility—   50
Did instigate the bedlam brainsick Duchess   51
By wicked means to frame our sovereign's fall.   52
Smooth runs the water where the brook is deep,
And in his simple show he harbors treason.   54
The fox barks not when he would steal the lamb.
No, no, my sovereign, Gloucester is a man
Unsounded yet and full of deep deceit.   57

---

29 make commotion foment unrest   **33 husbandry** proper cultivation
35 collect gather, infer   **36 fond** foolish   **37 Which . . . supplant** if
better reasons can supplant which fear   **38 subscribe** agree. (Literally,
"undersign.")   **40 Reprove** disprove   **41 effectual** decisive
45 subornation instigation   **46 Upon my life** i.e., I swear this on pain of
death.   **practices** intrigues   **47 privy to those faults** informed as to
those crimes   **48 reputing** boasting, overvaluing   **50 vaunts** boasts
51 bedlam crazy   **52 frame** devise   **54 simple show** innocent outward
appearance   **57 Unsounded** with depths still undiscovered

CARDINAL
Did he not, contrary to form of law,
Devise strange deaths for small offenses done?

YORK
And did he not, in his protectorship,
Levy great sums of money through the realm
For soldiers' pay in France, and never sent it,
By means whereof the towns each day revolted?   63

BUCKINGHAM
Tut, these are petty faults to faults unknown,   64
Which time will bring to light in smooth Duke
Humphrey.

KING
My lords, at once: the care you have of us   66
To mow down thorns that would annoy our foot   67
Is worthy praise; but, shall I speak my conscience,   68
Our kinsman Gloucester is as innocent
From meaning treason to our royal person
As is the sucking lamb or harmless dove.
The Duke is virtuous, mild, and too well given   72
To dream on evil or to work my downfall.

QUEEN
Ah, what's more dangerous than this fond affiance?   74
Seems he a dove? His feathers are but borrowed,
For he's disposèd as the hateful raven.   76
Is he a lamb? His skin is surely lent him,
For he's inclined as is the ravenous wolves.
Who cannot steal a shape that means deceit?   79
Take heed, my lord. The welfare of us all
Hangs on the cutting short that fraudful man.   81

    Enter Somerset.

SOMERSET
All health unto my gracious sovereign!

---

63 By means whereof on which account **64 to** compared to **66 at
once** answering all of you; or, without more ado; or, once and for all
67 annoy injure **68 shall I speak** if I may speak in accordance with
72 well given kindly disposed **74 fond affiance** foolish confidence
76 disposèd as has the disposition of **79 Who . . . deceit** who is there,
intending to deceive, that cannot assume an appropriate disguise
81 cutting short (with a grisly suggestion of beheading)

KING
Welcome, Lord Somerset. What news from France?

SOMERSET
That all your interest in those territories
Is utterly bereft you. All is lost.

KING
Cold news, Lord Somerset; but God's will be done!

YORK [*Aside*]
Cold news for me, for I had hope of France
As firmly as I hope for fertile England.
Thus are my blossoms blasted in the bud,
And caterpillars eat my leaves away;
But I will remedy this gear ere long,   91
Or sell my title for a glorious grave.

Enter Gloucester.

GLOUCESTER
All happiness unto my lord the King!
Pardon, my liege, that I have stayed so long.   94

SUFFOLK
Nay, Gloucester, know that thou art come too soon,
Unless thou wert more loyal than thou art.
I do arrest thee of high treason here.

GLOUCESTER
Well, Suffolk, thou shalt not see me blush
Nor change my countenance for this arrest.
A heart unspotted is not easily daunted.
The purest spring is not so free from mud
As I am clear from treason to my sovereign.
Who can accuse me? Wherein am I guilty?

YORK
'Tis thought, my lord, that you took bribes of France
And, being Protector, stayed the soldiers' pay,   105
By means whereof His Highness hath lost France.

GLOUCESTER
Is it but thought so? What are they that think it?   107
I never robbed the soldiers of their pay,
Nor ever had one penny bribe from France.
So help me God as I have watched the night,   110

91 **gear** business   94 **stayed** delayed   105 **stayed** held back   107 **What**
who   110 **watched the night** remained awake all night

Ay, night by night, in studying good for England!
That doit that e'er I wrested from the King,   112
Or any groat I hoarded to my use,   113
Be brought against me at my trial day!   114
No, many a pound of mine own proper store,   115
Because I would not tax the needy commons,
Have I dispursèd to the garrisons   117
And never asked for restitution.

CARDINAL
It serves you well, my lord, to say so much.

GLOUCESTER
I say no more than truth, so help me God!

YORK
In your protectorship you did devise
Strange tortures for offenders, never heard of,
That England was defamed by tyranny.   123

GLOUCESTER
Why, 'tis well known that, whiles I was Protector,
Pity was all the fault that was in me;
For I should melt at an offender's tears,   126
And lowly words were ransom for their fault.   127
Unless it were a bloody murderer,
Or foul felonious thief that fleeced poor passengers,   129
I never gave them condign punishment.   130
Murder indeed, that bloody sin, I tortured
Above the felon or what trespass else.   132

SUFFOLK
My lord, these faults are easy, quickly answered;   133
But mightier crimes are laid unto your charge
Whereof you cannot easily purge yourself.
I do arrest you in His Highness' name,
And here commit you to my Lord Cardinal
To keep until your further time of trial.   138

KING
My lord of Gloucester, 'tis my special hope

112, 113 doit, groat coins of small value **114 Be** may it be. **trial day**
i.e., Day of Judgment before God **115 proper** personal **117 dispursèd**
disbursed **123 That** so that. **was defamed by** became notorious for
126 should would **127 lowly** humble. **their fault** the offenders'
crimes **129 fleeced poor passengers** robbed unfortunate travelers
130 condign worthily deserved **132 Above . . . else** beyond any other
kind of felony or misdemeanor **133 easy** slight **138 further** future

That you will clear yourself from all suspense.   140
My conscience tells me you are innocent.

GLOUCESTER
Ah, gracious lord, these days are dangerous!
Virtue is choked with foul ambition
And charity chased hence by rancor's hand;
Foul subornation is predominant,   145
And equity exiled Your Highness' land.   146
I know their complot is to have my life,   147
And if my death might make this island happy
And prove the period of their tyranny,   149
I would expend it with all willingness.
But mine is made the prologue to their play;   151
For thousands more, that yet suspect no peril,
Will not conclude their plotted tragedy.   153
Beaufort's red sparkling eyes blab his heart's malice,
And Suffolk's cloudy brow his stormy hate;   155
Sharp Buckingham unburdens with his tongue
The envious load that lies upon his heart;
And dogged York, that reaches at the moon,   158
Whose overweening arm I have plucked back,
By false accuse doth level at my life.   160
[To the Queen.] And you, my sovereign lady, with the rest,
Causeless have laid disgraces on my head,
And with your best endeavor have stirred up
My liefest liege to be mine enemy.   164
Ay, all of you have laid your heads together—
Myself had notice of your conventicles—   166
And all to make away my guiltless life.
I shall not want false witness to condemn me   168
Nor store of treasons to augment my guilt.
The ancient proverb will be well effected: 170
"A staff is quickly found to beat a dog."

---

140 suspense i.e., doubt as to your innocence   **145 subornation** instigating others to commit crimes, including perjury   **146 exiled** exiled from   **147 complot** plot, conspiracy   **149 prove the period** turn out to be the end   **151 mine** i.e., my death   **153 Will . . . tragedy** i.e., will not suffice to bring to an end this tragedy they have devised (with a suggestion of plotting a play)   **155 cloudy** threatening   **158 dogged** (1) relentless (2) currish   **160 accuse** accusation.   **level** aim   **164 liefest liege** dearest sovereign   **166 conventicles** private or secret meetings   **168 want** lack   **170 effected** fulfilled, realized

CARDINAL
My liege, his railing is intolerable.
If those that care to keep your royal person   173
From treason's secret knife and traitors' rage
Be thus upbraided, chid, and rated at,   175
And the offender granted scope of speech,   176
'Twill make them cool in zeal unto Your Grace.

SUFFOLK
Hath he not twit our sovereign lady here   178
With ignominious words, though clerkly couched,   179
As if she had subornèd some to swear
False allegations to o'erthrow his state?

QUEEN
But I can give the loser leave to chide.   182

GLOUCESTER
Far truer spoke than meant. I lose, indeed;
Beshrew the winners, for they played me false!   184
And well such losers may have leave to speak.

BUCKINGHAM
He'll wrest the sense and hold us here all day.   186
Lord Cardinal, he is your prisoner.

CARDINAL [*To his attendants*]
Sirs, take away the Duke and guard him sure.

GLOUCESTER
Ah, thus King Henry throws away his crutch
Before his legs be firm to bear his body.
Thus is the shepherd beaten from thy side,
And wolves are gnarling who shall gnaw thee first.   192
Ah, that my fear were false; ah, that it were!
For, good King Henry, thy decay I fear.   194
                                        Exit Gloucester [guarded].

KING [*Rising*]
My lords, what to your wisdoms seemeth best,
Do or undo, as if ourself were here.

QUEEN
What, will Your Highness leave the Parliament?

---

173 care take care   **175 rated** scolded   **176 scope** freedom   **178 twit**
twitted   **179 clerkly couched** learnedly and cleverly phrased   **182 leave**
permission   **184 Beshrew** curse   **186 wrest the sense** twist the meaning   **192 gnarling** snarling over   **194 decay** downfall

KING

Ay, Margaret. My heart is drowned with grief,
Whose flood begins to flow within mine eyes,
My body round engirt with misery;
For what's more miserable than discontent?
Ah, uncle Humphrey, in thy face I see
The map of honor, truth, and loyalty;
And yet, good Humphrey, is the hour to come
That e'er I proved thee false or feared thy faith.   205
What louring star now envies thy estate,
That these great lords and Margaret our queen
Do seek subversion of thy harmless life?
Thou never didst them wrong nor no man wrong.
And as the butcher takes away the calf
And binds the wretch and beats it when it strains,   211
Bearing it to the bloody slaughterhouse,
Even so remorseless have they borne him hence;
And as the dam runs lowing up and down,   214
Looking the way her harmless young one went,
And can do naught but wail her darling's loss,
Even so myself bewails good Gloucester's case
With sad unhelpful tears, and with dimmed eyes
Look after him and cannot do him good,
So mighty are his vowèd enemies.
His fortunes I will weep, and twixt each groan
Say "Who's a traitor? Gloucester he is none."   222

           Exeunt [King, Buckingham, Salisbury,
                  and Warwick with attendants;
                    Somerset remains apart].

QUEEN

Free lords, cold snow melts with the sun's hot beams.   223
Henry my lord is cold in great affairs,   224
Too full of foolish pity; and Gloucester's show   225

---

205 feared thy faith doubted your loyalty   **211 strains** strives. (The
Folio reading, *strays,* is perhaps possible if *binds* means "pens in.")
214 dam mother   **222 s.d. Exeunt** (The quarto version has Salisbury
and Warwick exit here with the King. Buckingham, with no further role
in the scene, possibly leaves too. But the Folio reads *Exit,* and it is
possible the King departs alone, leaving the others in little groups,
trying to conduct a parliament without a king.)   **223 Free** noble
224 cold i.e., faint, neglectful, and ready to melt or give way   **225 show**
false appearance

Beguiles him, as the mournful crocodile   226
With sorrow snares relenting passengers,   227
Or as the snake, rolled in a flowering bank,   228
With shining checkered slough, doth sting a child   229
That for the beauty thinks it excellent.
Believe me, lords, were none more wise than I—   231
And yet herein I judge mine own wit good—   232
This Gloucester should be quickly rid the world,
To rid us from the fear we have of him.

CARDINAL
That he should die is worthy policy,   235
But yet we want a color for his death.   236
'Tis meet he be condemned by course of law.

SUFFOLK
But, in my mind, that were no policy.   238
The King will labor still to save his life,   239
The commons haply rise to save his life;   240
And yet we have but trivial argument,   241
More than mistrust, that shows him worthy death.   242

YORK
So that, by this, you would not have him die.   243

SUFFOLK
Ah, York, no man alive so fain as I!   244

YORK
'Tis York that hath more reason for his death.
But, my Lord Cardinal, and you, my lord of Suffolk,
Say as you think, and speak it from your souls:
Were 't not all one an empty eagle were set   248
To guard the chicken from a hungry kite   249
As place Duke Humphrey for the King's Protector?

QUEEN
So the poor chicken should be sure of death.

226 mournful crocodile i.e., the animal famous for its "crocodile tears" **227 relenting passengers** i.e., gullible passersby **228 rolled** coiled **229 slough** skin **231 were . . . than I** i.e., I would venture my opinion, were there not wiser heads than I **232 wit** intelligence **235 is worthy policy** is a sound scheme **236 color** pretext **238 were no policy** would be a poor stratagem **239 still** continually **240 haply** perhaps **241 argument** evidence **242 More than mistrust** other than suspicion **243 by this** i.e., by this reasoning **244 fain** glad, eager **248 all one** all the same, the same thing that. **empty** hungry **249 kite** scavenger bird, a kind of hawk

SUFFOLK
Madam, 'tis true; and were 't not madness then
To make the fox surveyor of the fold?   253
Who, being accused a crafty murderer,
His guilt should be but idly posted over   255
Because his purpose is not executed.
No, let him die in that he is a fox,
By nature proved an enemy to the flock,
Before his chaps be stained with crimson blood,   259
As Humphrey, proved by reasons, to my liege.   260
And do not stand on quillets how to slay him—   261
Be it by gins, by snares, by subtlety,   262
Sleeping or waking, 'tis no matter how,
So he be dead. For that is good deceit   264
Which mates him first that first intends deceit.   265

QUEEN
Thrice-noble Suffolk, 'tis resolutely spoke.

SUFFOLK
Not resolute, except so much were done,   267
For things are often spoke and seldom meant;
But that my heart accordeth with my tongue,   269
Seeing the deed is meritorious,
And to preserve my sovereign from his foe,
Say but the word and I will be his priest.   272

CARDINAL
But I would have him dead, my lord of Suffolk,
Ere you can take due orders for a priest.   274
Say you consent and censure well the deed,   275
And I'll provide his executioner,
I tender so the safety of my liege.   277

253 surveyor guardian   **255 idly posted over** foolishly ignored or has-
tened over. (Suffolk argues that it would be foolish to place a fox in
charge of a chicken coop and then exonerate him of being a killer
simply because he hasn't yet killed the chickens.)   **259 chaps** jaws
260 proved i.e., proved to be an enemy.   **by reasons** by arguments
261 quillets subtle distinctions or disputes   **262 gins** engines, traps
264 So so long as   **265 mates** checkmates, foils (i.e., strikes quickly
before the enemy can move first)   **267 except . . . done** unless what I've
spoken is converted into action   **269 that** i.e., to prove that   **272 be his
priest** i.e., perform the last rites for him, preside over his death
274 take . . . priest (1) make arrangements to have a priest there (2) prepare yourself for the priesthood   **275 censure well** approve   **277 tender**
am concerned for, care for

SUFFOLK
Here is my hand. The deed is worthy doing.

QUEEN   And so say I.

YORK
And I. And now we three have spoke it,
It skills not greatly who impugns our doom.   281

Enter a Post.

POST
Great lords, from Ireland am I come amain   282
To signify that rebels there are up   283
And put the Englishmen unto the sword.
Send succors, lords, and stop the rage betimes,   285
Before the wound do grow uncurable;
For, being green, there is great hope of help.   *[Exit.]* 287

CARDINAL
A breach that craves a quick expedient stop!
What counsel give you in this weighty cause?

YORK
That Somerset be sent as regent thither.
'Tis meet that lucky ruler be employed—   291
Witness the fortune he hath had in France.

SOMERSET *[Coming forward]*
If York, with all his far-fet policy,   293
Had been the regent there instead of me,
He never would have stayed in France so long.

YORK
No, not to lose it all, as thou hast done.
I rather would have lost my life betimes   297
Than bring a burden of dishonor home
By staying there so long till all were lost.   299
Show me one scar charactered on thy skin.   300
Men's flesh preserved so whole do seldom win.   301

---

281 skills not makes no great difference.   **impugns our doom** questions
our decision   **s.d. Post** messenger   **282 amain** with full speed
283 signify report.   **up** up in arms   **285 betimes** early, swiftly
287 green fresh   **291 meet** fitting. (Said ironically; York is hostile
toward Somerset.)   **293 far-fet** farfetched, artful, deep. (Said ironically;
Somerset comes forward to defend himself against York's insulting way
of speaking as though Somerset were not there.)   **297 betimes** forthwith, sooner   **299 staying . . . long** temporizing   **300 charactered**
inscribed   **301 Men's . . . win** men who can show no wounds are seldom victors

QUEEN
   Nay, then, this spark will prove a raging fire
   If wind and fuel be brought to feed it with.
   No more, good York; sweet Somerset, be still.
   Thy fortune, York, hadst thou been regent there,
   Might happily have proved far worse than his.   306
YORK
   What, worse than naught? Nay, then a shame take all!
SOMERSET
   And, in the number, thee that wishest shame!   308
CARDINAL
   My lord of York, try what your fortune is.
   Th' uncivil kerns of Ireland are in arms   310
   And temper clay with blood of Englishmen.   311
   To Ireland will you lead a band of men,
   Collected choicely, from each county some,
   And try your hap against the Irishmen?   314
YORK
   I will, my lord, so please His Majesty.
SUFFOLK
   Why, our authority is his consent,
   And what we do establish he confirms.
   Then, noble York, take thou this task in hand.
YORK
   I am content. Provide me soldiers, lords,
   Whiles I take order for mine own affairs.   320
SUFFOLK
   A charge, Lord York, that I will see performed.
   But now return we to the false Duke Humphrey.
CARDINAL
   No more of him; for I will deal with him
   That henceforth he shall trouble us no more.
   And so, break off. The day is almost spent.   325
   Lord Suffolk, you and I must talk of that event.   326
YORK
   My lord of Suffolk, within fourteen days

---

306 happily haply, perhaps   **308 in . . . shame** i.e., among the "all" to
whom you wish shame, may you be included   **310 uncivil kerns** disorderly and irregular light-armed Irish soldiers   **311 temper clay** moisten
the soil   **314 hap** fortune   **320 take order for** arrange   **325 break off**
cease conversation   **326 event** affair, business

At Bristol I expect my soldiers,
For there I'll ship them all for Ireland.

SUFFOLK
I'll see it truly done, my lord of York.   330

Exeunt. Manet York.

YORK
Now, York, or never, steel thy fearful thoughts   331
And change misdoubt to resolution.   332
Be that thou hop'st to be, or what thou art   333
Resign to death; it is not worth th' enjoying.
Let pale-faced fear keep with the mean-born man   335
And find no harbor in a royal heart.
Faster than springtime showers comes thought on
  thought,
And not a thought but thinks on dignity.   338
My brain, more busy than the laboring spider,
Weaves tedious snares to trap mine enemies.   340
Well, nobles, well, 'tis politicly done,   341
To send me packing with an host of men.   342
I fear me you but warm the starvèd snake,   343
Who, cherished in your breasts, will sting your hearts.
'Twas men I lacked, and you will give them me;
I take it kindly. Yet be well assured
You put sharp weapons in a madman's hands.
Whiles I in Ireland nourish a mighty band,
I will stir up in England some black storm
Shall blow ten thousand souls to heaven or hell;   350
And this fell tempest shall not cease to rage   351
Until the golden circuit on my head,   352
Like to the glorious sun's transparent beams,
Do calm the fury of this mad-bred flaw.   354
And, for a minister of my intent,   355
I have seduced a headstrong Kentishman,

---

330 s.d. Manet he remains onstage **331 fearful** timid **332 misdoubt**
suspicion, fear **333 that** that which **335 keep** dwell. **mean-born**
lowly-born **338 dignity** i.e., the dignity of high office—kingship
340 tedious intricate **341 politicly** shrewdly. (Said ironically.)
342 packing away, a-journeying **343 starvèd** i.e., deathlike with cold.
(One of Aesop's fables is about a man who puts a snake next to his
chest to warm it and is stung by it.) **350 Shall** that shall **351 fell**
fierce **352 circuit** circlet, crown **354 mad-bred** produced by madness. **flaw** squall, tempest **355 minister** agent

John Cade of Ashford,
To make commotion, as full well he can,
Under the title of John Mortimer.   359
In Ireland have I seen this stubborn Cade
Oppose himself against a troop of kerns,
And fought so long till that his thighs with darts   362
Were almost like a sharp-quilled porpentine;   363
And in the end being rescued, I have seen
Him caper upright like a wild Morisco,   365
Shaking the bloody darts as he his bells.   366
Full often, like a shag-haired crafty kern,
Hath he conversèd with the enemy,
And undiscovered come to me again
And given me notice of their villainies.
This devil here shall be my substitute,
For that John Mortimer, which now is dead,   372
In face, in gait, in speech, he doth resemble.
By this I shall perceive the commons' mind,
How they affect the house and claim of York.   375
Say he be taken, racked, and torturèd,
I know no pain they can inflict upon him
Will make him say I moved him to those arms.   378
Say that he thrive, as 'tis great like he will,   379
Why then from Ireland come I with my strength
And reap the harvest which that rascal sowed.
For Humphrey being dead, as he shall be,
And Henry put apart, the next for me.   *Exit.*

❖

359 Mortimer (The name of a powerful family claiming descent from
Lionel, Duke of Clarence, and hence entitled to the crown. See
1 Henry VI, 2.5.)   **362 till that** until.   **darts** light spears or arrows
363 porpentine porcupine   **365 Morisco** morris dancer, always fancily
or grotesquely dressed; or the dance itself   **366 he** i.e., the morris
dancer   **372 For that** because   **375 affect** incline toward   **378 Will**
that will.   **moved** incited, prompted   **379 great like** very likely

3.2   *Enter two or three running over the stage, from
the murder of Duke Humphrey.*

FIRST MURDERER
    Run to my lord of Suffolk. Let him know
    We have dispatched the Duke, as he commanded.
SECOND MURDERER
    O, that it were to do! What have we done?   3
    Didst ever hear a man so penitent?

        Enter Suffolk.

FIRST MURDERER   Here comes my lord.
SUFFOLK
    Now, sirs, have you dispatched this thing?
FIRST MURDERER   Ay, my good lord, he's dead.
SUFFOLK
    Why, that's well said. Go get you to my house.   8
    I will reward you for this venturous deed.
    The King and all the peers are here at hand.
    Have you laid fair the bed? Is all things well,   11
    According as I gave directions?
FIRST MURDERER   'Tis, my good lord.
SUFFOLK   Away! Begone.   *Exeunt [Murderers].*

        *Sound trumpets. Enter the King, the Queen,
        Cardinal [Beaufort], Somerset, with attendants.*

KING
    Go call our uncle to our presence straight.   15
    Say we intend to try His Grace today,
    If he be guilty, as 'tis publishèd.   17
SUFFOLK
    I'll call him presently, my noble lord.   *Exit.* 18

**3.2. Location: Bury St. Edmunds, in a room of state adjoining the
place of imprisonment where Gloucester has been murdered. Seats
are prepared, as for his trial.**
s.d. from the murder (In the quarto version, "the curtains being drawn,
Duke Humphrey is discovered in his bed, and two men lying on his
breast and smothering him in his bed." Suffolk enters to them. The
curtains are closed as the Murderers exit at l. 14.)   **3 that . . . do** i.e.,
that it were not yet done and thus could be avoided   **8 well said** well
done   **11 laid fair the bed** i.e., straightened the bed linen to conceal the
signs of struggle   **15 straight** straightway   **17 If** whether.   **publishèd**
publicly proclaimed   **18 presently** at once

KING
  Lords, take your places; and, I pray you all,
  Proceed no straiter 'gainst our uncle Gloucester   20
  Than from true evidence of good esteem   21
  He be approved in practice culpable.   22
                    [*They take their places.*]
QUEEN
  God forbid any malice should prevail
  That faultless may condemn a nobleman!   24
  Pray God he may acquit him of suspicion!   25
KING
  I thank thee, Meg. These words content me much.

        Enter Suffolk.

  How now? Why look'st thou pale? Why tremblest thou?
  Where is our uncle? What's the matter, Suffolk?
SUFFOLK
  Dead in his bed, my lord. Gloucester is dead.
QUEEN   Marry, God forfend!   30
CARDINAL
  God's secret judgment. I did dream tonight   31
  The Duke was dumb and could not speak a word.
                        King swoons.
QUEEN
  How fares my lord? Help, lords, the King is dead!
SOMERSET
  Rear up his body. Wring him by the nose.   34
QUEEN
  Run, go, help, help! O Henry, ope thine eyes!
                    [*They revive the King.*]
SUFFOLK
  He doth revive again. Madam, be patient.
KING
  O heavenly God!
QUEEN   How fares my gracious lord?
SUFFOLK
  Comfort, my sovereign! Gracious Henry, comfort!

---

20 straiter more severely   **21 of good esteem** worthy of belief   **22 approved
in** proved guilty of   **24 faultless** (Modifies *nobleman.*)   **25 acquit him**
exonerate himself   **30 forfend** forbid   **31 tonight** this past night
34 Wring . . . nose (Evidently a common first-aid remedy for restoring
consciousness; cf. *Venus and Adonis*, l. 475.)

KING
   What, doth my lord of Suffolk comfort me?
   Came he right now to sing a raven's note,   40
   Whose dismal tune bereft my vital powers,
   And thinks he that the chirping of a wren,
   By crying comfort from a hollow breast,   43
   Can chase away the first-conceivèd sound?   44
   Hide not thy poison with such sugared words.
   Lay not thy hands on me. Forbear, I say!
   Their touch affrights me as a serpent's sting.
   Thou baleful messenger, out of my sight!
   Upon thy eyeballs murderous Tyranny
   Sits in grim majesty to fright the world.
   Look not upon me, for thine eyes are wounding.
   Yet do not go away. Come, basilisk,   52
   And kill the innocent gazer with thy sight;
   For in the shade of death I shall find joy,
   In life but double death, now Gloucester's dead.
QUEEN
   Why do you rate my lord of Suffolk thus?   56
   Although the Duke was enemy to him,
   Yet he most Christian-like laments his death.
   And for myself, foe as he was to me,   59
   Might liquid tears or heart-offending groans   60
   Or blood-consuming sighs recall his life,   61
   I would be blind with weeping, sick with groans,
   Look pale as primrose with blood-drinking sighs,   63
   And all to have the noble Duke alive.
   What know I how the world may deem of me?   65
   For it is known we were but hollow friends.
   It may be judged I made the Duke away;
   So shall my name with slander's tongue be wounded,
   And princes' courts be filled with my reproach.
   This get I by his death. Ay me, unhappy,
   To be a queen, and crowned with infamy!

---

40 right now just now. **raven's note** a supposed omen of death
43 hollow deceitful **44 first-conceivèd sound** sound that was perceived
first **52 basilisk** fabulous reptile, said to kill by its look **56 rate**
berate **59 for** as for **60, 61, 63 heart-offending, blood-consuming,
blood-drinking** (It was commonly believed that groans and sighs cost
the heart a drop of blood.) **65 deem** judge

KING
    Ah, woe is me for Gloucester, wretched man!
QUEEN
    Be woe for me, more wretched than he is.   73
    What, dost thou turn away and hide thy face?
    I am no loathsome leper. Look on me.
    What? Art thou, like the adder, waxen deaf?   76
    Be poisonous too and kill thy forlorn queen.
    Is all thy comfort shut in Gloucester's tomb?
    Why, then, Dame Margaret was ne'er thy joy.
    Erect his statue and worship it,
    And make my image but an alehouse sign.
    Was I for this nigh wrecked upon the sea,
    And twice by awkward wind from England's bank   83
    Drove back again unto my native clime?   84
    What boded this, but well forewarning wind   85
    Did seem to say, "Seek not a scorpion's nest,
    Nor set no footing on this unkind shore"?
    What did I then but cursed the gentle gusts
    And he that loosed them forth their brazen caves,   89
    And bid them blow towards England's blessèd shore
    Or turn our stern upon a dreadful rock?
    Yet Aeolus would not be a murderer,
    But left that hateful office unto thee.
    The pretty-vaulting sea refused to drown me,   94
    Knowing that thou wouldst have me drowned on shore
    With tears as salt as sea, through thy unkindness.
    The splitting rocks cow'red in the sinking sands   97
    And would not dash me with their ragged sides,
    Because thy flinty heart, more hard than they,   99
    Might in thy palace perish Margaret.   100
    As far as I could ken thy chalky cliffs,   101
    When from thy shore the tempest beat us back,

---

73 woe sorry   **76 waxen deaf** grown deaf. (Snakes were popularly
supposed to be deaf.)   **83 awkward** adverse.   **bank** shore   **84 Drove**
driven.   **clime** country   **85 but** but that   **89 he** i.e., Aeolus, god of the
winds.   **forth** forth from.   **brazen** (In Homer's *Odyssey*, 10.3–4,
the floating island of Aeolus is enclosed by a rampart of bronze.)
94 pretty-vaulting handsomely rising and falling   **97 splitting rocks**
rocks on which ships split.   **sinking sands** sandbars on which ships
founder and sink   **99 Because** so that   **100 perish** cause to perish
101 ken discern

I stood upon the hatches in the storm,
And when the dusky sky began to rob
My earnest-gaping sight of thy land's view,   105
I took a costly jewel from my neck—
A heart it was, bound in with diamonds—
And threw it towards thy land. The sea received it,
And so I wished thy body might my heart.
And even with this I lost fair England's view,
And bid mine eyes be packing with my heart,   111
And called them blind and dusky spectacles   112
For losing ken of Albion's wishèd coast.   113
How often have I tempted Suffolk's tongue,   114
The agent of thy foul inconstancy,   115
To sit and witch me, as Ascanius did   116
When he to madding Dido would unfold   117
His father's acts commenced in burning Troy!
Am I not witched like her, or thou not false like him?   119
Ay me, I can no more. Die, Margaret!
For Henry weeps that thou dost live so long.

*Noise within. Enter Warwick, [Salisbury,] and
many Commons.*

WARWICK
  It is reported, mighty sovereign,
  That good Duke Humphrey traitorously is murdered
  By Suffolk and the Cardinal Beaufort's means.
  The commons, like an angry hive of bees
  That want their leader, scatter up and down   126
  And care not who they sting in his revenge.   127

105 My earnest-gaping . . . view my ardently peering eyesight of the
view of your land   111 be packing begone.   my heart (1) my affection,
left behind in England (2) my heart-shaped jewel   112 spectacles instruments of sight   113 Albion's England's.   wishèd longed-for
114 tempted (Queen Margaret's point is that, by her beauty, she has
innocently induced Suffolk to practice witchcraft on her in behalf of
King Henry.)   115 agent i.e., arranger of the marriage agreement
between Henry and Margaret   116 witch bewitch.   Ascanius young son
of Aeneas. (In Virgil's *Aeneid*, Book 1, during Aeneas' narration of his
adventures and misfortunes to Queen Dido, Aeneas' mother Venus sends
Cupid disguised as Ascanius to afflict the Queen with love for
Aeneas.)   117 madding becoming frantic (with love).   unfold disclose,
narrate   119 witched bewitched.   him i.e., Aeneas   126 want lack
127 his revenge revenge of him

Myself have calmed their spleenful mutiny,   128
Until they hear the order of his death.   129

KING
That he is dead, good Warwick, 'tis too true;
But how he died God knows, not Henry.
Enter his chamber, view his breathless corpse,
And comment then upon his sudden death.   133

WARWICK
That shall I do, my liege.—Stay, Salisbury,
With the rude multitude till I return.   [*Exit.*] 135
          [*Exit Salisbury with the Commons.*]

KING
O Thou that judgest all things, stay my thoughts,   136
My thoughts that labor to persuade my soul
Some violent hands were laid on Humphrey's life!
If my suspect be false, forgive me, God,   139
For judgment only doth belong to Thee.
Fain would I go to chafe his paly lips   141
With twenty thousand kisses, and to drain
Upon his face an ocean of salt tears,
To tell my love unto his dumb deaf trunk
And with my fingers feel his hand unfeeling.
But all in vain are these mean obsequies.   146

     Bed put forth [*bearing Gloucester's body. Enter
     Warwick*].

And to survey his dead and earthy image,
What were it but to make my sorrow greater?

WARWICK
Come hither, gracious sovereign. View this body.

KING
That is to see how deep my grave is made.
For with his soul fled all my worldly solace;
For seeing him I see my life in death.   152

128 spleenful mutiny wrathful uprising   **129 order** manner
133 comment . . . upon explain   **135 rude** turbulent, unpolished
136 stay hold back   **139 suspect** suspicion   **141 Fain** gladly.   **chafe**
rub, warm.   **paly** pale   **146 mean obsequies** deficient funeral rites
s.d. Bed put forth (In the quarto version, Warwick need not leave the
stage [see l. 135] to view Gloucester's dead body; he simply "draws the
curtain and shows Duke Humphrey in his bed." In the present Folio
version the bed must be thrust forth onto the stage with Humphrey in
it.)   **152 For . . . death** i.e., for in his death I see an image of my own

WARWICK
As surely as my soul intends to live
With that dread King that took our state upon Him   154
To free us from His Father's wrathful curse,
I do believe that violent hands were laid
Upon the life of this thrice-famèd duke.   157

SUFFOLK
A dreadful oath, sworn with a solemn tongue!
What instance gives Lord Warwick for his vow?   159

WARWICK
See how the blood is settled in his face.
Oft have I seen a timely-parted ghost,   161
Of ashy semblance, meager, pale, and bloodless,
Being all descended to the laboring heart,   163
Who, in the conflict that it holds with death,   164
Attracts the same for aidance 'gainst the enemy,   165
Which with the heart there cools and ne'er returneth   166
To blush and beautify the cheek again.   167
But see, his face is black and full of blood;
His eyeballs further out than when he lived,
Staring full ghastly, like a strangled man;
His hair upreared, his nostrils stretched with
    struggling;   171
His hands abroad displayed, as one that grasped   172
And tugged for life and was by strength subdued.
Look, on the sheets his hair, you see, is sticking;
His well-proportioned beard made rough and rugged,
Like to the summer's corn by tempest lodged.   176
It cannot be but he was murdered here.
The least of all these signs were probable.   178

SUFFOLK
Why, Warwick, who should do the Duke to death?
Myself and Beaufort had him in protection,
And we, I hope, sir, are no murderers.

154 King i.e., Christ. state i.e., human nature   157 thrice-famèd very
famous   159 instance proof   161 a timely-parted ghost the remains of
one having died in the natural course of events   163 Being all descended i.e., the blood having all descended   164 Who i.e., the heart
165 the same i.e., the blood. aidance aid. the enemy i.e., death
166 Which i.e., the blood   167 blush cause to blush, take on sanguine
color   171 upreared standing on end   172 abroad displayed i.e., spread
out   176 corn grain. lodged beaten down   178 were probable would
be sufficient confirmation

WARWICK

But both of you were vowed Duke Humphrey's foes,
[*To Cardinal*] And you, forsooth, had the good Duke
   to keep.   183
'Tis like you would not feast him like a friend,   184
And 'tis well seen he found an enemy.   185

QUEEN

Then you, belike, suspect these noblemen   186
As guilty of Duke Humphrey's timeless death.   187

WARWICK

Who finds the heifer dead and bleeding fresh
And sees fast by a butcher with an ax,   189
But will suspect 'twas he that made the slaughter?
Who finds the partridge in the puttock's nest   191
But may imagine how the bird was dead,
Although the kite soar with unbloodied beak?
Even so suspicious is this tragedy.

QUEEN

Are you the butcher, Suffolk? Where's your knife?
Is Beaufort termed a kite? Where are his talons?

SUFFOLK

I wear no knife to slaughter sleeping men;
But here's a vengeful sword, rusted with ease,   198
That shall be scourèd in his rancorous heart
That slanders me with murder's crimson badge.
Say, if thou dar'st, proud lord of Warwickshire,
That I am faulty in Duke Humphrey's death.   202
      [*Exeunt Cardinal, Somerset, and others.*]

WARWICK

What dares not Warwick, if false Suffolk dare him?

QUEEN

He dares not calm his contumelious spirit,   204

---

183 **to keep** in your custody   184 **like** likely   185 **well seen** obvious
186 **belike** perchance   187 **timeless** untimely   189 **fast by** close by
191 **puttock's** kite's   198 **ease** i.e., disuse   202 **faulty in** guilty of
s.d. Exeunt . . . others (The Cardinal's exit is marked in the quarto, not
in the Folio. Somerset's exit here is even more uncertain, but he is not
needed for the ensuing quarrel and may help the ailing and guilt-ridden
Cardinal offstage. Also, at some point the bed and its dead occupant
must be withdrawn or concealed by curtains.)   204 **contumelious**
contemptuous, contentious

Nor cease to be an arrogant controller,   205
Though Suffolk dare him twenty thousand times.

WARWICK
Madam, be still—with reverence may I say—
For every word you speak in his behalf
Is slander to your royal dignity.

SUFFOLK
Blunt-witted lord, ignoble in demeanor!
If ever lady wronged her lord so much,
Thy mother took into her blameful bed
Some stern untutored churl, and noble stock   213
Was graft with crab-tree slip—whose fruit thou art 214
And never of the Nevilles' noble race.

WARWICK
But that the guilt of murder bucklers thee   216
And I should rob the deathsman of his fee,   217
Quitting thee thereby of ten thousand shames,   218
And that my sovereign's presence makes me mild,   219
I would, false murderous coward, on thy knee
Make thee beg pardon for thy passèd speech   221
And say it was thy mother that thou meant'st,   222
That thou thyself wast born in bastardy;
And after all this fearful homage done,   224
Give thee thy hire and send thy soul to hell,   225
Pernicious bloodsucker of sleeping men!   226

SUFFOLK
Thou shalt be waking while I shed thy blood,   227
If from this presence thou dar'st go with me.   228

WARWICK
Away even now, or I will drag thee hence!

205 controller critic, detractor   **213 stern** rough   **214 graft** grafted.
slip cutting (with a possible play on the sense of "moral lapse")
216 But that were it not that.   **bucklers** shields   **217 deathsman** executioner   **218 Quitting** ridding   **219 that** were it not that   **221 passèd** just spoken   **222 And . . . thy mother** i.e., and force you to admit it was your own mother. (The emphasis is on *thy*.)   **224 fearful homage** craven submission   **225 Give** i.e., I would give.   **hire** reward (i.e., death)
226 bloodsucker . . . men (Warwick accuses Suffolk of killing Gloucester in his sleep, suggesting further that he is a sort of vampire.)
227 waking (Suffolk responds sarcastically to the accusation of killing sleeping men.)   **228 this presence** (Drawing swords is not allowed in the King's presence, as also at ll. 237–238.)

Unworthy though thou art, I'll cope with thee   230
And do some service to Duke Humphrey's ghost.
                    Exeunt [Suffolk and Warwick].

KING
    What stronger breastplate than a heart untainted!
    Thrice is he armed that hath his quarrel just,
    And he but naked, though locked up in steel,   234
    Whose conscience with injustice is corrupted.
                              A noise within.

QUEEN   What noise is this?

    *Enter Suffolk and Warwick with their weapons
    drawn.*

KING
    Why, how now, lords? Your wrathful weapons drawn
    Here in our presence? Dare you be so bold?
    Why, what tumultuous clamor have we here?
SUFFOLK
    The traitorous Warwick, with the men of Bury,
    Set all upon me, mighty sovereign.

    Enter Salisbury.

SALISBURY [*To the Commons, within*]
    Sirs, stand apart. The King shall know your mind.—
    Dread lord, the commons send you word by me,
    Unless Lord Suffolk straight be done to death   244
    Or banishèd fair England's territories,
    They will by violence tear him from your palace
    And torture him with grievous lingering death.
    They say, by him the good Duke Humphrey died;
    They say, in him they fear Your Highness' death;
    And mere instinct of love and loyalty,   250
    Free from a stubborn opposite intent,   251
    As being thought to contradict your liking,   252
    Makes them thus forward in his banishment.   253
    They say, in care of your most royal person,
    That if Your Highness should intend to sleep,

230 cope with encounter   **234 naked** i.e., unarmed   **244 straight** at
once   **250 mere instinct** pure impulse   **251–252 Free . . . liking** innocent of any stubborn willfulness that might be interpreted as crossing
your wishes   **253 forward in** bold, insistent upon

And charge that no man should disturb your rest
In pain of your dislike or pain of death,
Yet, notwithstanding such a strait edict,   258
Were there a serpent seen with forkèd tongue
That slyly glided towards Your Majesty,
It were but necessary you were waked,
Lest, being suffered in that harmful slumber,   262
The mortal worm might make the sleep eternal.   263
And therefore do they cry, though you forbid,
That they will guard you, whe'er you will or no,   265
From such fell serpents as false Suffolk is—   266
With whose envenomèd and fatal sting   267
Your loving uncle, twenty times his worth,   268
They say, is shamefully bereft of life.   269

COMMONS (*Within*)
An answer from the King, my lord of Salisbury!

SUFFOLK
'Tis like the commons, rude unpolished hinds,   271
Could send such message to their sovereign!
[*To Salisbury.*] But you, my lord, were glad to be
    employed,
To show how quaint an orator you are.   274
But all the honor Salisbury hath won
Is that he was the lord ambassador
Sent from a sort of tinkers to the King.   277

COMMONS (*Within*)
An answer from the King, or we will all break in!

KING
Go, Salisbury, and tell them all from me,
I thank them for their tender loving care;
And had I not been cited so by them,   281
Yet did I purpose as they do entreat.
For, sure, my thoughts do hourly prophesy
Mischance unto my state by Suffolk's means.   284
And therefore, by His majesty I swear,   285

---

258 strait strict   **262 being suffered** you being permitted to remain
263 mortal worm deadly serpent   **265 whe'er** whether   **266 fell** cruel
267–269 With . . . life with whose venomous and fatal sting, they say,
your uncle (who is twenty times more worthy than Suffolk) is deprived
of life   **271 like** likely. (Said ironically.)   **hinds** boors, rustics
274 quaint skilled, clever   **277 sort** gang   **281 cited** incited, urged
284 Mischance disaster   **285 His** i.e., God's

Whose far unworthy deputy I am,
He shall not breathe infection in this air   287
But three days longer, on the pain of death.

                                    [Exit Salisbury.]

QUEEN
O Henry, let me plead for gentle Suffolk!   289
KING
Ungentle queen, to call him gentle Suffolk!
No more, I say! If thou dost plead for him,
Thou wilt but add increase unto my wrath.
Had I but said, I would have kept my word,   293
But when I swear, it is irrevocable.
[To Suffolk.] If, after three days' space, thou here
   be'st found
On any ground that I am ruler of,
The world shall not be ransom for thy life.
Come, Warwick, come, good Warwick, go with me.
I have great matters to impart to thee.   299

                  Exit [with all but Queen and Suffolk].

QUEEN
Mischance and sorrow go along with you!
Heart's discontent and sour affliction
Be playfellows to keep you company!
There's two of you; the devil make a third,   303
And threefold vengeance tend upon your steps!   304
SUFFOLK
Cease, gentle Queen, these execrations,
And let thy Suffolk take his heavy leave.   306
QUEEN
Fie, coward woman and softhearted wretch!
Hast thou not spirit to curse thine enemy?
SUFFOLK
A plague upon them, wherefore should I curse them?
Would curses kill, as doth the mandrake's groan,   310

---

287 breathe breathe out, spread   **289 gentle** noble   **293 but said** merely
spoken, without an oath   **299 s.d. Exit** (Possibly the bed and Gloucester's body are concealed or withdrawn at this point; see l. 202 s.d., note.)
303 two i.e., the King and Warwick   **304 tend upon** follow   **306 heavy**
sorrowful   **310 mandrake's groan** (Folk belief held that when the
forked and man-shaped mandrake root was pulled from the ground, it
uttered a shriek that was fatal to the hearer or would drive him mad; cf.
Romeo and Juliet, 4.3.47–48.)

I would invent as bitter searching terms,   311
As curst, as harsh, and horrible to hear,   312
Delivered strongly through my fixèd teeth,
With full as many signs of deadly hate,
As lean-faced Envy in her loathsome cave.
My tongue should stumble in mine earnest words,
Mine eyes should sparkle like the beaten flint,
Mine hair be fixed on end, as one distract;   318
Ay, every joint should seem to curse and ban;   319
And even now my burdened heart would break,
Should I not curse them. Poison be their drink!
Gall, worse than gall, the daintiest that they taste!
Their sweetest shade a grove of cypress trees!   323
Their chiefest prospect murdering basilisks!   324
Their softest touch as smart as lizards' stings!   325
Their music frightful as the serpent's hiss,
And boding screech owls make the consort full!   327
All the foul terrors in dark-seated hell—

QUEEN
Enough, sweet Suffolk. Thou torment'st thyself,
And these dread curses, like the sun 'gainst glass,
Or like an overchargèd gun, recoil,   331
And turns the force of them upon thyself.

SUFFOLK
You bade me ban, and will you bid me leave?   333
Now, by the ground that I am banished from,
Well could I curse away a winter's night,
Though standing naked on a mountain top,
Where biting cold would never let grass grow,
And think it but a minute spent in sport.

QUEEN
O, let me entreat thee cease! Give me thy hand,
That I may dew it with my mournful tears;
Nor let the rain of heaven wet this place
To wash away my woeful monuments.   342

              [*She kisses his hand.*]

311 searching probing, cutting **312 curst** malignant **318 distract**
mad **319 ban** curse **323 cypress trees** (Associated with death because
they were often planted near graveyards.) **324 prospect** view. **basilisks**
(See l. 52 above.) **325 smart** stinging **327 boding** portending evil.
consort ensemble of musicians **331 overchargèd** overloaded **333 leave**
leave off **342 monuments** i.e., traces of her tears

O, could this kiss be printed in thy hand,
That thou mightst think upon these by the seal,   344
Through whom a thousand sighs are breathed for thee!   345
So, get thee gone, that I may know my grief;   346
'Tis but surmised whiles thou art standing by,
As one that surfeits thinking on a want.   348
I will repeal thee, or, be well assured,   349
Adventure to be banishèd myself;   350
And banishèd I am, if but from thee.
Go, speak not to me. Even now, begone!
O, go not yet! Even thus two friends condemned
Embrace and kiss and take ten thousand leaves,
Loather a hundred times to part than die.
                              [*They embrace.*]
Yet now farewell, and farewell life with thee!
SUFFOLK
Thus is poor Suffolk ten times banishèd,
Once by the King, and three times thrice by thee.
'Tis not the land I care for, wert thou thence.
A wilderness is populous enough,
So Suffolk had thy heavenly company;   361
For where thou art, there is the world itself,
With every several pleasure in the world,   363
And where thou art not, desolation.
I can no more. Live thou to joy thy life;   365
Myself no joy in naught but that thou liv'st.

          Enter Vaux.

QUEEN
Whither goes Vaux so fast? What news, I prithee?
VAUX
To signify unto His Majesty   368
That Cardinal Beaufort is at point of death;
For suddenly a grievous sickness took him,
That makes him gasp and stare and catch the air,
Blaspheming God and cursing men on earth.

344 these i.e., my lips. seal imprint 345 Through whom i.e., through
which lips 346 know fully comprehend 348 As . . . want like a person
(such as myself) who, enjoying plenty, anticipates a time of depriva-
tion 349 repeal thee bring about your recall 350 Adventure risk
361 So so long as 363 several distinct 365 joy enjoy 368 signify
report

Sometimes he talks as if Duke Humphrey's ghost
Were by his side; sometimes he calls the King,
And whispers to his pillow as to him
The secrets of his overchargèd soul;   376
And I am sent to tell His Majesty
That even now he cries aloud for him.

QUEEN
Go tell this heavy message to the King.   *Exit* [*Vaux*].
Ay me, what is this world? What news are these!
But wherefore grieve I at an hour's poor loss,   381
Omitting Suffolk's exile, my soul's treasure?   382
Why only, Suffolk, mourn I not for thee,
And with the southern clouds contend in tears—   384
Theirs for the earth's increase, mine for my sorrows?
Now get thee hence. The King, thou know'st, is coming.
If thou be found by me, thou art but dead.   387

SUFFOLK
If I depart from thee, I cannot live,
And in thy sight to die, what were it else
But like a pleasant slumber in thy lap?
Here could I breathe my soul into the air,
As mild and gentle as the cradle babe
Dying with mother's dug between its lips—   393
Where, from thy sight, I should be raging mad   394
And cry out for thee to close up mine eyes,
To have thee with thy lips to stop my mouth.
So shouldst thou either turn my flying soul,   397
Or I should breathe it so into thy body,
And then it lived in sweet Elysium.   399
To die by thee were but to die in jest;   400
From thee to die were torture more than death.   401
O, let me stay, befall what may befall!

---

376 overchargèd overburdened with guilt   **381 an hour's** (i.e., the
Cardinal has figuratively but an hour left to live in any case)
382 Omitting neglecting   **384 southern** i.e., especially moist   **387 by me**
near me   **393 dug** breast   **394 from** out of   **397 turn** turn back, i.e.,
prevent the soul's escape, preserve my life. (The soul was thought to
leave the body through the mouth.)   **399 lived** would live.   **Elysium**
classical abode after death of those favored by the gods   **400 in jest** i.e.,
not truly to die at all. (*To die* carries the suggestion of experiencing
orgasm.)   **401 From** away from

QUEEN
  Away! Though parting be a fretful corrosive,   403
  It is applièd to a deathful wound.   404
  To France, sweet Suffolk. Let me hear from thee,
  For wheresoe'er thou art in this world's globe,
  I'll have an Iris that shall find thee out.   407
SUFFOLK I go.
QUEEN And take my heart with thee.   [*She kisses him.*]
SUFFOLK
  A jewel, locked into the woefull'st cask   410
  That ever did contain a thing of worth.
  Even as a splitted bark, so sunder we;   412
  This way fall I to death.
QUEEN   This way for me.   413
                            Exeunt [*separately*].

✛

3.3 *Enter the King, Salisbury, and Warwick,*
      to the Cardinal in bed, [*raving and staring*
      as if he were mad].

KING
  How fares my lord? Speak, Beaufort, to thy sovereign.
CARDINAL
  If thou be'st Death, I'll give thee England's treasure,
  Enough to purchase such another island,
  So thou wilt let me live and feel no pain.   4
KING
  Ah, what a sign it is of evil life,
  Where death's approach is seen so terrible!
WARWICK
  Beaufort, it is thy sovereign speaks to thee.

403 fretful corrosive painful and caustic course of treatment
404 deathful fatal (since Suffolk's remaining would prove fatal)
407 Iris Juno's messenger **410 cask** casket **412 splitted bark** sailing
vessel split in two **413 s.d. Exeunt** (Gloucester's body in its bed is
probably concealed or removed earlier, perhaps at l. 202 or l. 299; since
the bed is needed immediately in the next scene, it almost certainly
does not remain onstage until the end of this scene.)

3.3. Location: The Cardinal's bedchamber.
s.d. in bed (In the quarto version, the curtains are drawn and the Cardinal "is discovered in his bed," raving and staring. Cf. 3.2.0 s.d.) **4 So**
provided

CARDINAL
  Bring me unto my trial when you will.
  Died he not in his bed? Where should he die?   9
  Can I make men live, whe'er they will or no?   10
  O, torture me no more! I will confess.
  Alive again? Then show me where he is.
  I'll give a thousand pound to look upon him.
  He hath no eyes! The dust hath blinded them.
  Comb down his hair. Look, look! It stands upright,
  Like lime-twigs set to catch my wingèd soul.   16
  Give me some drink, and bid the apothecary
  Bring the strong poison that I bought of him.   18
KING
  O thou eternal mover of the heavens,
  Look with a gentle eye upon this wretch!
  O, beat away the busy meddling fiend
  That lays strong siege unto this wretch's soul
  And from his bosom purge this black despair!
WARWICK
  See how the pangs of death do make him grin!
SALISBURY
  Disturb him not. Let him pass peaceably.
KING
  Peace to his soul, if God's good pleasure be!
  Lord Cardinal, if thou think'st on heaven's bliss,
  Hold up thy hand. Make signal of thy hope.
                       [*The Cardinal dies.*]
  He dies and makes no sign. O God, forgive him!
WARWICK
  So bad a death argues a monstrous life.
KING
  Forbear to judge, for we are sinners all.
  Close up his eyes and draw the curtain close,   32
  And let us all to meditation. [*The curtains are closed.*]
                           Exeunt.

❖

9 he i.e., Gloucester   **10 whe'er** whether   **16 lime-twigs** twigs smeared with sticky lime to trap birds   **18 of** from   **32 curtain** (The bed itself, presumably "thrust out" onstage for this brief scene, would have to be removed at this point; the curtains here are presumably bed curtains, although in the quarto version they are drawn open at l. 1 in such a way as to discover the Cardinal to view without having to bring on a bed, i.e., using a curtained area backstage.)

4.1   *Alarum [within]. Fight at sea. Ordnance goes*
off. Enter Lieutenant, [a Master, a Master's
Mate, Walter Whitmore, and others; with them]
Suffolk [disguised], and others, [prisoners].

LIEUTENANT
  The gaudy, blabbing, and remorseful day   1
  Is crept into the bosom of the sea,
  And now loud-howling wolves arouse the jades   3
  That drag the tragic melancholy night,
  Who, with their drowsy, slow, and flagging wings
  Clip dead men's graves, and from their misty jaws   6
  Breathe foul contagious darkness in the air.
  Therefore bring forth the soldiers of our prize;   8
  For, whilst our pinnace anchors in the Downs,   9
  Here shall they make their ransom on the sand,
  Or with their blood stain this discolored shore.   11
  Master, this prisoner freely give I thee;   12
  And thou that art his mate, make boot of this;   13
  The other, Walter Whitmore, is thy share.   14
        [*Three gentlemen prisoners, one of them Suffolk,*
                  are apportioned and handed over.]

FIRST GENTLEMAN
  What is my ransom, Master? Let me know.
MASTER
  A thousand crowns, or else lay down your head.
MATE [*To the Second Gentleman*]
  And so much shall you give, or off goes yours.
LIEUTENANT
  What, think you much to pay two thousand crowns,

4.1. Location: The coast of Kent.
1 s.p. **Lieutenant** i.e., captain in charge of the fighting; see ll. 65 and
107. (He is called "Captain of the ship" in the quarto stage direction,
but the Master is the mariner in charge of sailing the vessel.)
1 **blabbing** telltale, revealing.   **remorseful** causing remorse   **3 the jades**
i.e., the dragons of Hecate that draw the chariot of the night   **6 Clip**
embrace   **8 soldiers . . . prize** i.e., those we have captured   **9 pinnace**
one-masted vessel.   **Downs** anchorage off the Kentish coast
11 discolored i.e., to be discolored by blood   **12 this prisoner** i.e., the
First Gentleman   **13 his** i.e., the ship master's.   **make . . . this** i.e.,
make a profit by ransoming this Second Gentleman   **14 The other** i.e.,
Suffolk

And bear the name and port of gentlemen?   19
Cut both the villains' throats, for die you shall.
The lives of those which we have lost in fight   21
Be counterpoised with such a petty sum?   22

FIRST GENTLEMAN
I'll give it, sir, and therefore spare my life.

SECOND GENTLEMAN
And so will I, and write home for it straight.

WHITMORE [*To Suffolk*]
I lost mine eye in laying the prize aboard,   25
And therefore to revenge it shalt thou die;
And so should these, if I might have my will.

LIEUTENANT
Be not so rash. Take ransom, let him live.   28

SUFFOLK
Look on my George; I am a gentleman.   29
Rate me at what thou wilt, thou shalt be paid.   30

WHITMORE
And so am I. My name is Walter Whitmore.   31
                              [*Suffolk starts.*]
How now, why starts thou? What, doth death affright?

SUFFOLK
Thy name affrights me, in whose sound is death.   33
A cunning man did calculate my birth   34
And told me that by water I should die.
Yet let not this make thee be bloody-minded;
Thy name is Gualtier, being rightly sounded.

19 port demeanor   **21–22 The lives . . . sum** (An indignant question,
and one that should perhaps be spoken by Whitmore rather than the
Lieutenant; see ll. 25–28.)   **25 laying . . . aboard** boarding the captured
ship   **28 Be . . . live** (The Lieutenant's caution about killing the prisoners
seems to contradict his threatening speech at ll. 20–22. Perhaps those
lines should be assigned to Whitmore, but it's also possible that the
Lieutenant is simply being pragmatic in l. 28, advising against killing
the goose with the golden egg.)   **29 George** the gold or jeweled figure of
Saint George, worn as the insignium of the Order of the Knights of the
Garter   **30 Rate** value, assess   **31 am I** i.e., am I a gentleman. (Whitmore
denies Suffolk's assertion of distinction in rank.)   **33 Thy name** (i.e.,
Walter, pronounced like "water." In l. 37 below, Suffolk tries to avert the
prophecy referred to in ll. 34–35 [cf. 1.4.33–34] by urging the French
form of the name, *Gualtier* or *Gaultier.*)   **34 A . . . birth** a fortune-teller
cast my horoscope

WHITMORE
  Gualtier or Walter, which it is, I care not.
  Never yet did base dishonor blur our name
  But with our sword we wiped away the blot.
  Therefore, when merchantlike I sell revenge,   41
  Broke be my sword, my arms torn and defaced,   42
  And I proclaimed a coward through the world!
SUFFOLK [*Revealing his face*]
  Stay, Whitmore, for thy prisoner is a prince,
  The Duke of Suffolk, William de la Pole.
WHITMORE
  The Duke of Suffolk muffled up in rags?
SUFFOLK
  Ay, but these rags are no part of the Duke.
  Jove sometime went disguised, and why not I?
LIEUTENANT
  But Jove was never slain, as thou shalt be.
SUFFOLK
  Obscure and lousy swain, King Henry's blood,   50
  The honorable blood of Lancaster,
  Must not be shed by such a jaded groom.   52
  Hast thou not kissed thy hand and held my stirrup?
  Bareheaded plodded by my footcloth mule   54
  And thought thee happy when I shook my head?   55
  How often hast thou waited at my cup,
  Fed from my trencher, kneeled down at the board,   57
  When I have feasted with Queen Margaret?
  Remember it and let it make thee crestfall'n,   59
  Ay, and allay this thy abortive pride,   60
  How in our voiding lobby hast thou stood   61
  And duly waited for my coming forth.   62

41 sell revenge i.e., give up revenge (for my lost eye) in return for ransom money   **42 arms** coat of arms   **50 lousy** louse-infested.   **King Henry's blood** (Suffolk's claim to be connected to the house of Lancaster is a dubious one.)   **52 jaded** ignoble (with a play in the next line on one who deals with *jades*, or horses)   **54 footcloth** with a large, richly ornamented cloth laid over the back of a horse or mule, hanging down to the ground on each side   **55 happy** fortunate.   **shook** i.e., nodded   **57 trencher** wooden dish or plate.   **board** dining table   **59 it** all this.   **crestfall'n** (1) downcast, abashed (2) deprived of the coat of arms boasted of in l. 42   **60 abortive** monstrous   **61 our voiding lobby** my anteroom   **62 duly** dutifully

This hand of mine hath writ in thy behalf,   63
And therefore shall it charm thy riotous tongue.   64

WHITMORE
Speak, Captain, shall I stab the forlorn swain?   65

LIEUTENANT
First let my words stab him, as he hath me.

SUFFOLK
Base slave, thy words are blunt and so art thou.   67

LIEUTENANT
Convey him hence, and on our longboat's side
Strike off his head.

SUFFOLK   Thou dar'st not, for thy own.   69

LIEUTENANT
Yes, Pole.

SUFFOLK   Pole?

LIEUTENANT   Pool! Sir Pool! Lord!   70
Ay, kennel, puddle, sink, whose filth and dirt   71
Troubles the silver spring where England drinks.
Now will I dam up this thy yawning mouth
For swallowing the treasure of the realm.   74
Thy lips that kissed the Queen shall sweep the ground,
And thou that smiledst at good Duke Humphrey's death
Against the senseless winds shalt grin in vain,   77
Who in contempt shall hiss at thee again.   78
And wedded be thou to the hags of hell   79
For daring to affy a mighty lord   80
Unto the daughter of a worthless king,
Having neither subject, wealth, nor diadem.   82
By devilish policy art thou grown great,   83
And, like ambitious Sylla, overgorged   84

63 writ . . . behalf i.e., written to recommend you, or because you
cannot write   **64 charm** put a spell on, silence   **65 Captain** (Appropriate courtesy title for the Lieutenant, since he is the military commander.)   **forlorn swain** desolate, wretched fellow   **67 blunt** blunted like an
arrow with no point, harmless   **69 for thy own** i.e., for fear of losing
your own head   **70 Pole, Pool** (with verbal play on *poll*, head, *Pole*,
Suffolk's family name, and *pool*, a pool of water, all similar in pronunci-
ation)   **71 kennel** gutter.   **sink** cesspool   **74 For swallowing** lest it
swallow   **77 senseless** insensible. (Suffolk's head is to be put up on
display.)   **78 Who** which, i.e., the winds.   **again** in return   **79 the hags
of hell** i.e., the Furies   **80 affy** betroth.   **lord** i.e., King Henry
82 Having i.e., he, Reignier, having   **83 policy** political cunning
84 ambitious Sylla i.e., Sulla, Roman dictator of the second century
B.C., notorious for his cruel proceedings against his adversaries

With gobbets of thy mother's bleeding heart.   85
By thee Anjou and Maine were sold to France.
The false revolting Normans thorough thee   87
Disdain to call us lord, and Picardy
Hath slain their governors, surprised our forts,
And sent the ragged soldiers wounded home.
The princely Warwick, and the Nevilles all,
Whose dreadful swords were never drawn in vain,
As hating thee, are rising up in arms;
And now the house of York, thrust from the crown
By shameful murder of a guiltless king   95
And lofty, proud, encroaching tyranny,
Burns with revenging fire, whose hopeful colors
Advance our half-faced sun, striving to shine,   98
Under the which is writ *"Invitis nubibus."*   99
The commons here in Kent are up in arms,
And, to conclude, reproach and beggary
Is crept into the palace of our King,
And all by thee.—Away! Convey him hence.

SUFFOLK
O, that I were a god, to shoot forth thunder
Upon these paltry, servile, abject drudges!
Small things make base men proud. This villain here,
Being captain of a pinnace, threatens more
Than Bargulus, the strong Illyrian pirate.   108
Drones suck not eagles' blood, but rob beehives.   109
It is impossible that I should die
By such a lowly vassal as thyself.
Thy words move rage and not remorse in me.
I go of message from the Queen to France;   113
I charge thee waft me safely cross the Channel.   114

---

85 gobbets pieces of raw flesh. **mother's** i.e., England's **87 thorough**
through, because of **95 shameful . . . king** i.e., the murder of Richard
II by Bolingbroke, who thereupon sidestepped the Yorkist claim and
became King Henry IV **98 Advance** raise, display. **half-faced sun** (Edward III's and Richard II's banner displayed the rays of the sun dispersing themselves out of a cloud.) **99 Invitis nubibus** in spite of the
clouds **108 Bargulus** (A pirate, Bardulis, mentioned in Cicero's *De
Officiis*, 2.11.) **109 Drones** beetles, worthless parasites. (The legends
referred to here, that beetles suck the blood of eagles and rob beehives
of honey, are typical of much imaginary natural history in the
Renaissance.) **113 of message** as messenger **114 waft** transport,
convey

LIEUTENANT   Walter—

WHITMORE
Come, Suffolk, I must waft thee to thy death.

SUFFOLK
Paene gelidus timor occupat artus.   117
It is thee I fear.

WHITMORE
Thou shalt have cause to fear before I leave thee.
What, are ye daunted now? Now will ye stoop.

FIRST GENTLEMAN [*To Suffolk*]
My gracious lord, entreat him, speak him fair.   121

SUFFOLK
Suffolk's imperial tongue is stern and rough,
Used to command, untaught to plead for favor.
Far be it we should honor such as these
With humble suit. No, rather let my head
Stoop to the block than these knees bow to any
Save to the God of heaven and to my king;
And sooner dance upon a bloody pole   128
Than stand uncovered to the vulgar groom.   129
True nobility is exempt from fear.
More can I bear than you dare execute.

LIEUTENANT
Hale him away, and let him talk no more.   132

SUFFOLK
Come, soldiers, show what cruelty ye can,
That this my death may never be forgot!
Great men oft die by vile bezonians: 135
A Roman sworder and banditto slave   136
Murdered sweet Tully; Brutus' bastard hand   137
Stabbed Julius Caesar; savage islanders   138
Pompey the Great; and Suffolk dies by pirates.

117 **Paene . . . artus** cold fear takes hold of my limbs almost entirely
121 **fair** courteously   128 **And . . . pole** i.e., and rather have my head
stuck on a bloodstained pole on London Bridge for treason
129 **uncovered** bareheaded   132 **Hale** haul   135 **bezonians** needy
beggars, rascals   136 **sworder** gladiator.   **banditto** bandit   137 **Tully**
Cicero.   **bastard** (According to an unreliable tradition, Brutus was
thought to be Caesar's bastard son.)   138 **savage islanders** i.e., inhabitants of Lesbos. (But Plutarch reports, quite to the contrary, that Pompey
the Great was stabbed by his former officers at the instigation of Ptol-
emy, in Egypt after his defeat by Caesar at Pharsalus.)

Exit Walter [Whitmore and others] with Suffolk.

LIEUTENANT
And as for these whose ransom we have set,
It is our pleasure one of them depart;
Therefore [*To the Second Gentleman*] come you with us
and let him go.   142

Exeunt Lieutenant and the rest.
Manet the First Gentleman.

Enter Walter [Whitmore] with the body
[and severed head of Suffolk].

WHITMORE
There let his head and lifeless body lie,
Until the Queen his mistress bury it.   *Exit Walter.*
FIRST GENTLEMAN
O barbarous and bloody spectacle!
His body will I bear unto the King.
If he revenge it not, yet will his friends;   147
So will the Queen, that living held him dear.   148

[*Exit with the body and head.*]

❖

4.2   *Enter [George] Bevis and John Holland, [with*
long staves].

BEVIS   Come, and get thee a sword, though made of a
lath. They have been up these two days.   2
HOLLAND   They have the more need to sleep now, then.   3
BEVIS   I tell thee, Jack Cade the clothier means to dress   4
the commonwealth, and turn it, and set a new nap   5
upon it.

142 him i.e., the First Gentleman   **s.d. Manet** he remains onstage
147 his i.e., Suffolk's   **148 living** while he was living

4.2. Location: Blackheath, a heath in Kent near London.
s.d. John Holland (The name of the actor assigned to a bit part in this
scene; probably *George Bevis* is similarly a hired man in the company.)   **2 lath** wood strip (often used by the comic Vice character in
morality plays).   **up** i.e., up in arms   **3 They . . . then** (Holland's joke is
that if they've been *up*, awake, for two days, they must be sleepy.)
4 dress (1) clothe, array (2) remedy   **5 turn** (1) turn inside out (as a way
of refurbishing old cloth) (2) turn upside down socially.   **nap** (1) fuzz
or down on the surface of cloth (2) surface of the social structure

HOLLAND   So he had need, for 'tis threadbare. Well, I 7
say it was never merry world in England since gentlemen came up. 9

BEVIS   O miserable age! Virtue is not regarded in handi- 10
craftsmen.

HOLLAND   The nobility think scorn to go in leather 12
aprons.

BEVIS   Nay, more, the King's Council are no good work- 14
men. 15

HOLLAND   True. And yet it is said, "Labor in thy vocation,"
which is as much to say as, "Let the magistrates be laboring men." And therefore should we be magistrates.

BEVIS   Thou hast hit it, for there's no better sign of a 19
brave mind than a hard hand. 20

HOLLAND   I see them, I see them! There's Best's son, the
tanner of Wingham— 22

BEVIS   He shall have the skins of our enemies to make
dog's leather of. 24

HOLLAND   And Dick the butcher—

BEVIS   Then is sin struck down like an ox, and iniquity's
throat cut like a calf.

HOLLAND   And Smith the weaver—

BEVIS   Argo, their thread of life is spun. 29

HOLLAND   Come, come, let's fall in with them. 30

*Drum. Enter Cade, Dick [the] butcher, Smith the
weaver, and a Sawyer, with infinite numbers,
[bearing long staves].*

CADE   We, John Cade, so termed of our supposed 31
father—

DICK [*Aside*]   Or rather, of stealing a cade of herrings. 33

CADE   For our enemies shall fall before us, inspired with 34

---

7 threadbare (1) shabby (2) down-at-heels   **9 came up** came into fashion,
rose to prominence   **10 regarded** esteemed   **12 think scorn** disdain
14–15 workmen (1) laborers (2) masters of their calling   **19 hit it** hit
the nail on the head   **20 brave** noble.   **hard** callused   **22 Wingham** a
village near Canterbury   **24 dog's leather** (Used in the manufacture of
gloves.)   **29 Argo** i.e., ergo, therefore   **30 s.d. infinite numbers** i.e., as
many supers as the theater can provide   **31 We** (The royal "we," fatu-
ously misappropriated.)   **so termed of** named after   **33 of** on account
of.   **cade** barrel, cask   **34 For** because.   **fall** (with a pun on the Latin
cado, I fall)

the spirit of putting down kings and princes—command silence.

DICK   Silence!

CADE   My father was a Mortimer—   38

DICK [*Aside*]   He was an honest man and a good brick-   39
layer.   40

CADE   My mother a Plantagenet—

DICK [*Aside*]   I knew her well. She was a midwife.

CADE   My wife descended of the Lacys—   43

DICK [*Aside*]   She was, indeed, a peddler's daughter, and
sold many laces.

SMITH [*Aside*]   But now of late, not able to travel with   46
her furred pack, she washes bucks here at home.   47

CADE   Therefore am I of an honorable house.

DICK [*Aside*]   Ay, by my faith, the field is honorable;   49
and there was he born, under a hedge, for his father
had never a house but the cage.   51

CADE   Valiant I am.

SMITH [*Aside*]   'A must needs, for beggary is valiant.   53

CADE   I am able to endure much.

DICK [*Aside*]   No question of that; for I have seen him
whipped three market days together.   56

CADE   I fear neither sword nor fire.

SMITH [*Aside*]   He need not fear the sword, for his coat
is of proof.   59

DICK [*Aside*]   But methinks he should stand in fear of
fire, being burnt i' the hand for stealing of sheep.   61

CADE   Be brave, then, for your captain is brave, and
vows reformation. There shall be in England seven

---

38 Mortimer (See 3.1.359 and note.)   **39–40 bricklayer** (with a play on
mortarer, Mortimer)   **43 Lacys** the family name of the Earls of Lincoln.
(But Dick makes an obvious pun on *laces*.)   **46 travel** (suggesting also
travail, work)   **47 furred pack** peddler's pack made of hides turned hair
outward (with a pun on "herd of deer").   **bucks** soiled clothes treated
with *buck* or lye. (There is a bawdy suggestion of a loose woman, a
vagabond's daughter, who has given up streetwalking with her *furred
pack*, her genital organs, to service men [*bucks*] at home.)   **49 field**
(1) field in a coat of arms (2) out in the fields   **51 cage** prison for petty
malefactors   **53 'A must needs** he must be.   **valiant** sturdy, able to
work. (Ordnances forbade those who were sturdy to beg.)   **56 whipped**
i.e., for vagabondage   **59 of proof** (1) impenetrable, tried by experience
and hence reliable (2) well-worn   **61 burnt i' the hand** branded

halfpenny loaves sold for a penny, the three-hooped 64
pot shall have ten hoops, and I will make it felony to 65
drink small beer. All the realm shall be in common, 66
and in Cheapside shall my palfry go to grass. And 67
when I am king, as king I will be—

ALL   God save Your Majesty!

CADE   I thank you, good people—there shall be no
money; all shall eat and drink on my score; and I will 71
apparel them all in one livery, that they may agree like
brothers and worship me their lord.

DICK   The first thing we do, let's kill all the lawyers.

CADE   Nay, that I mean to do. Is not this a lamentable
thing, that of the skin of an innocent lamb should be
made parchment? That parchment, being scribbled
o'er, should undo a man? Some say the bee stings, but
I say 'tis the bee's wax; for I did but seal once to a 79
thing, and I was never mine own man since. How
now? Who's there?

*Enter [some, bringing forward] a Clerk [of
Chartham].*

SMITH   The clerk of Chartham. He can write and read 82
and cast account.   83

CADE   O, monstrous!

SMITH   We took him setting of boys' copies.   85

CADE   Here's a villain!

SMITH   H'as a book in his pocket with red letters in 't. 87

CADE   Nay, then, he is a conjurer.

DICK   Nay, he can make obligations and write court 89
hand.   90

64–65 three-hooped pot wooden quart-pot made with three metal bands
or staves. (A ten-hooped pot would presumably hold a lot more.)
66 small weak. (Cade intends that everyone shall drink strong beer.) **be
in common** belong to everyone, be free from enclosure. (See 1.3.23–24
and note.) **67 Cheapside** chief location for markets in London (which
Cade wishes to abolish) **71 on my score** at my expense **79 seal** i.e.,
sign and seal (with sealing wax) a legal agreement **82 Chartham** a
town near Canterbury **83 cast account** i.e., do arithmetic
85 setting . . . copies writing out words, etc., as models to be repro-
duced by schoolboys **87 H'as** he has. **book . . . in 't** a schoolbook,
probably a primer, with "rubricated" or red-lettered capitals **89 make
obligations** draw up bonds **89–90 court hand** professional hand, used
in preparing legal documents

CADE   I am sorry for 't. The man is a proper man, of   91
mine honor; unless I find him guilty, he shall not die.
Come hither, sirrah, I must examine thee. What is thy
name?

CLERK   Emmanuel.   95

DICK   They use to write it on the top of letters. 'Twill go
hard with you.

CADE   Let me alone.—Dost thou use to write thy name?
Or hast thou a mark to thyself, like an honest, plain-
dealing man?

CLERK   Sir, I thank God, I have been so well brought up
that I can write my name.

ALL   He hath confessed. Away with him! He's a villain
and a traitor.

CADE   Away with him, I say! Hang him with his pen
and inkhorn about his neck.   *Exit one with the Clerk.*

     Enter Michael.

MICHAEL   Where's our general?

CADE   Here I am, thou particular fellow.   108

MICHAEL   Fly, fly, fly! Sir Humphrey Stafford and his
brother are hard by, with the King's forces.

CADE   Stand, villain, stand, or I'll fell thee down. He
shall be encountered with a man as good as himself.
He is but a knight, is 'a?

MICHAEL   No.   114

CADE   To equal him, I will make myself a knight pres-   115
ently. [*He kneels.*] Rise up Sir John Mortimer. [*He rises.*]   116
Now have at him!   117

     Enter Sir Humphrey Stafford and his Brother,
     with drum and soldiers.

STAFFORD
Rebellious hinds, the filth and scum of Kent,   118
Marked for the gallows, lay your weapons down!

---

91 proper handsome-looking.   **of** upon   **95 Emmanuel** i.e., God with us.
(Used frequently as heading for letters and documents.)   **108 particular**
private (as opposed to *general* in the previous line)   **114 No** i.e., he is
only a knight   **115–116 presently** immediately   **117 have at him** let me
at him   **s.d. drum** drummer   **118 hinds** peasants

Home to your cottages; forsake this groom.   120
The King is merciful, if you revolt.   121

BROTHER
But angry, wrathful, and inclined to blood
If you go forward. Therefore yield, or die.

CADE
As for these silken-coated slaves, I pass not.   124
It is to you, good people, that I speak,
Over whom, in time to come, I hope to reign;
For I am rightful heir unto the crown.

STAFFORD
Villain, thy father was a plasterer,
And thou thyself a shearman, art thou not?   129

CADE   And Adam was a gardener.
BROTHER   And what of that?

CADE
Marry, this: Edmund Mortimer, Earl of March,
Married the Duke of Clarence' daughter, did he not?

STAFFORD   Ay, sir.

CADE
By her he had two children at one birth.

BROTHER   That's false.

CADE
Ay, there's the question. But I say 'tis true.
The elder of them, being put to nurse,
Was by a beggar-woman stolen away,
And, ignorant of his birth and parentage,
Became a bricklayer when he came to age.
His son am I. Deny it if you can.

DICK
Nay, 'tis too true. Therefore he shall be king.   142

SMITH   Sir, he made a chimney in my father's house, 143
and the bricks are alive at this day to testify it. Therefore deny it not.

STAFFORD
And will you credit this base drudge's words,
That speaks he knows not what?

---

120 groom i.e., low wretch   **121 revolt** turn back   **124 pass** care
129 shearman one who shears the excess nap (see l. 5) from woolen
cloth during its manufacture   **142 too** very   **143 he** i.e., Cade's father

ALL
   Ay, marry, will we. Therefore get ye gone.
BROTHER
   Jack Cade, the Duke of York hath taught you this.
CADE [*Aside*] He lies, for I invented it myself.—Go to,
   sirrah, tell the King from me that for his father's sake,
   Henry the Fifth, in whose time boys went to span-   152
   counter for French crowns, I am content he shall reign;   153
   but I'll be Protector over him.
DICK   And furthermore, we'll have the Lord Saye's head   155
   for selling the dukedom of Maine.
CADE   And good reason; for thereby is England mained   157
   and fain to go with a staff, but that my puissance holds   158
   it up. Fellow kings, I tell you that that Lord Saye hath
   gelded the commonwealth and made it an eunuch;
   and more than that, he can speak French, and there-
   fore he is a traitor.
STAFFORD
   O gross and miserable ignorance!
CADE   Nay, answer, if you can. The Frenchmen are our
   enemies. Go to, then, I ask but this: can he that speaks
   with the tongue of an enemy be a good counselor,
   or no?
ALL   No, no! And therefore we'll have his head.
BROTHER [*To Stafford*]
   Well, seeing gentle words will not prevail,
   Assail them with the army of the King.
STAFFORD
   Herald, away, and throughout every town
   Proclaim them traitors that are up with Cade,
   That those which fly before the battle ends   173
   May, even in their wives' and children's sight,
   Be hanged up for example at their doors.
   And you that be the King's friends, follow me.
                  Exeunt [*the two Staffords, and soldiers*].

152–153 span-counter a boys' game in which one throws a counter or
piece of money that the other wins if he can throw another that hits it
or falls within a span (nine inches) of it   **153 crowns** (1) coins (2) kingdoms   **155 Lord Saye** (A peer implicated with Suffolk in the loss of
Anjou and Maine.)   **157 mained** maimed (with a pun on *Maine*)
158 fain obliged.   **go** walk   **173 That . . . fly** i.e., so that those cowardly
traitors who will surely flee

CADE
  And you that love the commons, follow me.
  Now show yourselves men; 'tis for liberty!
  We will not leave one lord, one gentleman;
  Spare none but such as go in clouted shoon,   180
  For they are thrifty honest men and such
  As would, but that they dare not, take our parts.
DICK   They are all in order and march toward us.
CADE   But then are we in order when we are most out
  of order. Come, march forward.   [*Exeunt.*]

4.3   *Alarums to the fight, wherein both the*
       Staffords are slain. Enter Cade and the rest.

CADE   Where's Dick, the butcher of Ashford?
DICK   Here, sir.
CADE   They fell before thee like sheep and oxen, and
  thou behavedst thyself as if thou hadst been in thine
  own slaughterhouse. Therefore thus will I reward
  thee: the Lent shall be as long again as it is, and thou   6
  shalt have a license to kill for a hundred lacking one.   7
DICK   I desire no more.
CADE   And, to speak truth, thou deserv'st no less. This
  monument of the victory will I bear [*Putting on Sir*   10
  Humphrey's armor]; and the bodies shall be dragged at
  my horse heels till I do come to London, where we
  will have the Mayor's sword borne before us.
DICK   If we mean to thrive and do good, break open the   14
  jails and let out the prisoners.
CADE   Fear not that, I warrant thee. Come, let's march   16
  towards London.   *Exeunt* [*with the Staffords' bodies*].

❖

180 **clouted shoon** hobnailed or patched shoes
4.3. Location: Scene continues at Blackheath.
s.d. (The bodies of the slain Staffords must be removed at some
point.) 6–7 **Lent . . . one** (For Dick the butcher's benefit, Cade proposes to double the length of Lent, during which animals could be
butchered only by special license in order to supply the sick and others
with particular needs; and during this period, Dick is to have license to
kill 99 animals a week, or to supply 99 persons, or for 99 years
10 **monument** memorial   14 **do good** succeed   16 **Fear** doubt

4.4   *Enter the King with a supplication, and*
            the Queen with Suffolk's head, the Duke
            of Buckingham, and the Lord Saye.

QUEEN [*To herself*]
　Oft have I heard that grief softens the mind
　And makes it fearful and degenerate.
　Think therefore on revenge and cease to weep.
　But who can cease to weep and look on this?
　Here may his head lie on my throbbing breast,
　But where's the body that I should embrace?
BUCKINGHAM　What answer makes Your Grace to the
　rebels' supplication?
KING
　I'll send some holy bishop to entreat,
　For God forbid so many simple souls
　Should perish by the sword! And I myself,
　Rather than bloody war shall cut them short,
　Will parley with Jack Cade their general.
　But stay, I'll read it over once again.
QUEEN [*To herself*]
　Ah, barbarous villains! Hath this lovely face
　Ruled, like a wandering planet, over me,   16
　And could it not enforce them to relent
　That were unworthy to behold the same?
KING
　Lord Saye, Jack Cade hath sworn to have thy head.
SAYE
　Ay, but I hope Your Highness shall have his.
KING　How now, madam?
　Still lamenting and mourning for Suffolk's death?
　I fear me, love, if that I had been dead,
　Thou wouldst not have mourned so much for me.
QUEEN
　No, my love, I should not mourn, but die for thee.

　　　Enter a Messenger.

KING
　How now, what news? Why com'st thou in such haste?

4.4. Location: London. The royal court.
16 wandering i.e., not fixed, like the stars

FIRST MESSENGER

    The rebels are in Southwark. Fly, my lord!   27
    Jack Cade proclaims himself Lord Mortimer,
    Descended from the Duke of Clarence' house,
    And calls Your Grace usurper, openly,
    And vows to crown himself in Westminster.
    His army is a ragged multitude
    Of hinds and peasants, rude and merciless.
    Sir Humphrey Stafford and his brother's death
    Hath given them heart and courage to proceed.
    All scholars, lawyers, courtiers, gentlemen,
    They call false caterpillars and intend their death.

KING

    O graceless men! They know not what they do.

BUCKINGHAM

    My gracious lord, retire to Killingworth   39
    Until a power be raised to put them down.   40

QUEEN

    Ah, were the Duke of Suffolk now alive,
    These Kentish rebels would be soon appeased!   42

KING

    Lord Saye, the traitors hateth thee;
    Therefore away with us to Killingworth.

SAYE

    So might Your Grace's person be in danger.
    The sight of me is odious in their eyes;
    And therefore in this city will I stay
    And live alone as secret as I may.

      Enter another Messenger.

SECOND MESSENGER

    Jack Cade hath gotten London Bridge!
    The citizens fly and forsake their houses.
    The rascal people, thirsting after prey,
    Join with the traitor, and they jointly swear
    To spoil the city and your royal court.   53

BUCKINGHAM

    Then linger not, my lord. Away, take horse!

---

27 Southwark suburb on the south bank of the Thames, just across the
river from London **39 Killingworth** Kenilworth (in Warwickshire)
40 power army **42 appeased** pacified **53 spoil** despoil, sack

KING
   Come, Margaret. God, our hope, will succor us.
QUEEN
   My hope is gone, now Suffolk is deceased.
KING [*To Saye*]
   Farewell, my lord. Trust not the Kentish rebels.
BUCKINGHAM
   Trust nobody, for fear you be betrayed.
SAYE
   The trust I have is in mine innocence,
   And therefore am I bold and resolute.   *Exeunt.*

❖

4.5   *Enter Lord Scales upon the Tower, walking.*
         Then enter two or three Citizens below.

SCALES   How now, is Jack Cade slain?
FIRST CITIZEN   No, my lord, nor likely to be slain; for
   they have won the bridge, killing all those that with-
   stand them. The Lord Mayor craves aid of your honor
   from the Tower to defend the city from the rebels.
SCALES
   Such aid as I can spare you shall command.
   But I am troubled here with them myself;
   The rebels have assayed to win the Tower.
   But get you to Smithfield and gather head,   9
   And thither I will send you Matthew Gough.
   Fight for your king, your country, and your lives.
   And so, farewell, for I must hence again.   *Exeunt.*

❖

4.5. Location: The Tower of London.
s.d. upon the Tower i.e., probably in the rear gallery above the main
stage   **9 Smithfield** area of open fields to the northwest, just outside
London's walls.   **head** an armed force

4.6 *Enter Jack Cade and the rest, and strikes his staff on London Stone.*

CADE Now is Mortimer lord of this city. And here, sitting upon London Stone, I charge and command that, of the city's cost, the Pissing Conduit run nothing but 3 claret wine this first year of our reign. And now henceforward it shall be treason for any that calls me other than Lord Mortimer.

Enter a Soldier, running.

SOLDIER Jack Cade! Jack Cade!
CADE Knock him down there.   *They kill him.*
SMITH If this fellow be wise, he'll never call ye Jack Cade more. I think he hath a very fair warning.
DICK My lord, there's an army gathered together in Smithfield.
CADE Zounds, then, let's go fight with them. But first go and set London Bridge on fire, and, if you can, burn down the Tower too. Come, let's away. *Exeunt omnes.*

4.7 *Alarums. Matthew Gough is slain, and all the rest. Then enter Jack Cade, with his company.*

CADE So, sirs. Now go some and pull down the Savoy; 1 others to th' Inns of Court. Down with them all. 2
DICK I have a suit unto your lordship.

4.6. Location: London.
s.d. London Stone ancient landmark, located in Cannon Street **3 of** at. **Pissing Conduit** popular name of a conduit, or common fountain, near the Royal Exchange

4.7. Location: London. The rebellion continues. (The historical location moves from Cannon Street to Smithfield, but onstage the action is continuous.)
s.d. all the rest i.e., the King's forces. (The bodies of Gough and other slain must be removed at some point.) **1 the Savoy** (This palace, residence of the Duke of Lancaster, was actually destroyed during Wat Tyler's rebellion in 1381 and not rebuilt until the sixteenth century.)
2 Inns of Court sets of buildings in London belonging to legal societies training persons in the law

CADE Be it a lordship, thou shalt have it for that word. 4
DICK Only that the laws of England may come out of
your mouth.
HOLLAND [*Aside*] Mass, 'twill be sore law then, for he
was thrust in the mouth with a spear, and 'tis not
whole yet.
SMITH [*Aside*] Nay, John, it will be stinking law, for his
breath stinks with eating toasted cheese.
CADE I have thought upon it. It shall be so. Away! Burn
all the records of the realm. My mouth shall be the
Parliament of England.
HOLLAND [*Aside*] Then we are like to have biting stat-
utes, unless his teeth be pulled out.
CADE And henceforward all things shall be in common.

Enter a Messenger.

MESSENGER My lord, a prize, a prize! Here's the Lord
Saye, which sold the towns in France; he that made us
pay one-and-twenty fifteens, and one shilling to the 20
pound, the last subsidy.   21

Enter George [Bevis], with the Lord Saye.

CADE Well, he shall be beheaded for it ten times. Ah,
thou say, thou serge, nay, thou buckram lord! Now art 23
thou within point-blank of our jurisdiction regal. 24
What canst thou answer to My Majesty for giving up
of Normandy unto Monsieur Basimecu, the Dau- 26
phin of France? Be it known unto thee by these 27
presence, even the presence of Lord Mortimer, that I 28
am the besom that must sweep the court clean of such 29
filth as thou art. Thou hast most traitorously corrupted
the youth of the realm in erecting a grammar school;
and whereas, before, our forefathers had no other

4 lordship title and estates of a noble lord (playing on the honorific *your
lordship* in l. 3, by which Cade is flattered)   **20–21 one . . . pound** (An
exaggeratedly inflated estimate of personal property.)   **21 subsidy** tax
levied on special occasions; see 1.1.131–134.)   **23 say, serge, buckram**
kinds of cloth, respectively of silk, wool, and coarse linen (with a pun on
say/Saye)   **24 point-blank** so close that a missile will travel straight to
the target   **26 Basimecu** *baise mon cul* (French), kiss my ass
27–28 these presence i.e., Cade's error, or joke, for "these presents, this
present document." (A legal phrase.)   **29 besom** broom

books but the score and the tally, thou hast caused 33
printing to be used, and, contrary to the King his crown 34
and dignity, thou hast built a paper mill. It will be
proved to thy face that thou hast men about thee that
usually talk of a noun and a verb and such abomina- 37
ble words as no Christian ear can endure to hear. Thou
hast appointed justices of peace to call poor men before them about matters they were not able to answer.
Moreover, thou hast put them in prison, and because
they could not read thou hast hanged them, when in- 42
deed only for that cause they have been most worthy to 43
live. Thou dost ride in a footcloth, dost thou not? 44

SAYE   What of that?

CADE   Marry, thou oughtst not to let thy horse wear a
cloak, when honester men than thou go in their hose 47
and doublets. 48

DICK   And work in their shirt too—as myself, for example, that am a butcher.

SAYE   You men of Kent—

DICK   What say you of Kent?

SAYE   Nothing but this: 'tis *bona terra, mala gens*. 53

CADE   Away with him, away with him! He speaks
Latin.

SAYE
Hear me but speak, and bear me where you will.
Kent, in the *Commentaries* Caesar writ,
Is termed the civil'st place of all this isle.
Sweet is the country, because full of riches,
The people liberal, valiant, active, wealthy, 60
Which makes me hope you are not void of pity.
I sold not Maine, I lost not Normandy,

---

33 score . . . tally means of reckoning accounts or keeping score, in
which a stick was notched and then split lengthwise, thereby giving
both debtor and creditor a record of what was owed   **34 printing** (An
anachronism; the first printing press was set up in England twenty-
seven years after Cade's rebellion, and the first paper mill in 1495.)
King his King's   **37 usually** habitually   **42 could not read** i.e., could
not demonstrate their literacy in Latin and thereby claim exemption
from civil prosecution through "benefit of clergy"   **43 only . . . cause**
for that reason alone   **44 footcloth** richly ornamented horse covering;
see 4.1.54 note   **47–48 hose and doublets** breeches and jacket (without
a cloak)   **53 bona . . . gens** good land, bad people   **60 liberal** generous,
free, refined

Yet to recover them would lose my life.
Justice with favor have I always done;   64
Prayers and tears have moved me, gifts could never.
When have I aught exacted at your hands   66
But to maintain the King, the realm, and you?
Large gifts have I bestowed on learnèd clerks,   68
Because my book preferred me to the King;   69
And, seeing ignorance is the curse of God,
Knowledge the wing wherewith we fly to heaven,
Unless you be possessed with devilish spirits
You cannot but forbear to murder me.
This tongue hath parleyed unto foreign kings   74
For your behoof—   75
CADE   Tut, when struck'st thou one blow in the field?
SAYE
Great men have reaching hands. Oft have I struck   77
Those that I never saw, and struck them dead.
BEVIS   O monstrous coward! What, to come behind
folks?
SAYE
These cheeks are pale for watching for your good.   81
CADE   Give him a box o' the ear and that will make 'em
red again.
SAYE
Long sitting to determine poor men's causes   84
Hath made me full of sickness and diseases.
CADE   Ye shall have a hempen caudle, then, and the help 86
of hatchet.   87
DICK   Why dost thou quiver, man?
SAYE
The palsy, and not fear, provokes me.
CADE   Nay, he nods at us, as who should say, "I'll be   90

---

64 **favor** compassion   66 **aught . . . hands** taken any taxes from you (in
my capacity as Lord Treasurer)   68 **clerks** scholars   69 **book** learning.   **preferred . . . King** gave me advancement at court   74 **parleyed
unto** entered into negotiations with   75 **behoof** benefit   77 **reaching**
far-reaching   81 **for watching** from remaining awake, on watch
84 **sitting** i.e., on the judge's bench.   **determine** settle, decide
86 **caudle** warm gruel, given to sick people. (*Hempen caudle* means that
his restorative is to be a hanging.)   86–87 **the help of hatchet** i.e., the
assistance of the executioner's ax. (Possibly a variant of or error for
"pap with a hatchet," the administering of punishment under the
ironical guise of kindly correction.)   90 **as who should** as one might

even with you." I'll see if his head will stand steadier
on a pole, or no. Take him away and behead him.

SAYE

Tell me wherein have I offended most?
Have I affected wealth or honor? Speak.   94
Are my chests filled up with extorted gold?
Is my apparel sumptuous to behold?
Whom have I injured, that ye seek my death?
These hands are free from guiltless blood-shedding,   98
This breast from harboring foul deceitful thoughts.
O, let me live!

CADE [*Aside*]   I feel remorse in myself with his words,
but I'll bridle it. He shall die, an it be but for pleading   102
so well for his life.—Away with him! He has a familiar   103
under his tongue; he speaks not i' God's name. Go,
take him away, I say, and strike off his head presently;   105
and then break into his son-in-law's house, Sir James
Cromer, and strike off his head, and bring them both
upon two poles hither.

ALL   It shall be done.

SAYE

Ah, countrymen! If when you make your prayers,
God should be so obdurate as yourselves,
How would it fare with your departed souls?   112
And therefore yet relent, and save my life.

CADE

Away with him! And do as I command ye.
                    [*Exeunt some with Lord Saye.*]
The proudest peer in the realm shall not wear a head
on his shoulders, unless he pay me tribute. There shall
not a maid be married but she shall pay to me her
maidenhead ere they have it. Men shall hold of me *in*   118
capite; and we charge and command that their wives   119
be as free as heart can wish or tongue can tell.   120

---

94 affected preferred, striven for   **98 guiltless blood-shedding** shedding
of guiltless blood   **102 an it be but** if only   **103 familiar** familiar spirit,
attendant demon   **105 presently** immediately   **112 your departed souls**
your souls when you die   **118 maidenhead** (Cade claims the *droit de
seigneur,* presumed customary right of a feudal lord to be the first to
enjoy a bride sexually on her marriage night.)   **118–119 in capite** as
tenant in chief, i.e., directly from the crown. The Latin *caput,* head, also
puns on *maidenhead.*)   **120 free** (1) legally unencumbered (2) licentious

DICK   My lord, when shall we go to Cheapside and take   121
up commodities upon our bills?   122

CADE   Marry, presently.

ALL   O, brave!   124

*Enter one with the heads [of Lord Saye and Sir
John Cromer upon two poles].*

CADE   But is not this braver? Let them kiss one another,
for they loved well when they were alive. [*The heads
are made to touch one another.*] Now part them again,
lest they consult about the giving up of some more
towns in France. Soldiers, defer the spoil of the city   129
until night, for with these borne before us, instead of
maces, will we ride through the streets, and at every   131
corner have them kiss. Away!   *Exeunt.*

❖

4.8   *Alarum and retreat. Enter again Cade and all
his rabblement.*

CADE   Up Fish Street! Down Saint Magnus' Corner! Kill   1
and knock down! Throw them into Thames! (*Sound a
parley.*) What noise is this I hear? Dare any be so bold   3
to sound retreat or parley when I command them kill?

Enter Buckingham and old Clifford [attended].

BUCKINGHAM
Ay, here they be that dare and will disturb thee.
Know, Cade, we come ambassadors from the King

121–122 take . . . bills obtain goods on credit (with a pun on *bills*,
military weapons having wooden handles and a blade or ax-shaped
head)   **124 brave** fine, splendid   **129 spoil** plundering   **131 maces**
staves of office carried by sergeants

**4.8. Location: Southwark. The rebellion continues. (The historical
location moves from Smithfield to Southwark, but the onstage action
is uninterrupted.)**
s.d. retreat signal to cease attack   **1 Fish Street, Saint Magnus' Corner**
locations in London near London Bridge, directly across from Southwark   **3 s.d. parley** trumpet signal requesting a conference between the
contending forces (also in l. 4)

Unto the commons whom thou hast misled,
And here pronounce free pardon to them all   8
That will forsake thee and go home in peace.

CLIFFORD
What say ye, countrymen? Will ye relent,
And yield to mercy whilst 'tis offered you,
Or let a rebel lead you to your deaths?
Who loves the King and will embrace his pardon,   13
Fling up his cap and say "God save His Majesty!"
Who hateth him and honors not his father,
Henry the Fifth, that made all France to quake,
Shake he his weapon at us and pass by.   17

ALL   God save the King! God save the King!
                    [*They fling up their caps.*]

CADE   What, Buckingham and Clifford, are ye so brave?   19
And you, base peasants, do ye believe him? Will you
needs be hanged with your pardons about your necks?   21
Hath my sword therefore broke through London
gates, that you should leave me at the White Hart in   23
Southwark? I thought ye would never have given out   24
these arms till you had recovered your ancient freedom. But you are all recreants and dastards, and de-   26
light to live in slavery to the nobility. Let them break
your backs with burdens, take your houses over your
heads, ravish your wives and daughters before your
faces. For me, I will make shift for one, and so God's   30
curse light upon you all!

ALL   We'll follow Cade, we'll follow Cade!

CLIFFORD
Is Cade the son of Henry the Fifth,
That thus you do exclaim you'll go with him?
Will he conduct you through the heart of France
And make the meanest of you earls and dukes?   36
Alas, he hath no home, no place to fly to,
Nor knows he how to live but by the spoil,   38

---

8 pronounce proclaim   **13 Who** anyone who (also in l. 15)   **17 Shake he**
let him shake (in a gesture of defiance)   **19 brave** haughty
21 pardons . . . necks (because the pardons would be not only worthless
but also the very means of their hanging)   **23 that** to the end that.
White Hart a famous inn in Southwark   **24 out** up   **26 recreants** those
who break faith, cowards   **30 make shift for one** manage for myself
36 meanest lowest born   **38 the spoil** pillaging

Unless by robbing of your friends and us.
Were 't not a shame that, whilst you live at jar,   40
The fearful French, whom you late vanquishèd,   41
Should make a start o'er seas and vanquish you?   42
Methinks already in this civil broil
I see them lording it in London streets,
Crying *"Villiago!"* unto all they meet.   45
Better ten thousand baseborn Cades miscarry   46
Than you should stoop unto a Frenchman's mercy.
To France, to France, and get what you have lost!
Spare England, for it is your native coast.
Henry hath money; you are strong and manly;
God on our side, doubt not of victory.

ALL   A Clifford! A Clifford! We'll follow the King and 52
Clifford!

CADE [*Aside*]   Was ever feather so lightly blown to and
fro as this multitude? The name of Henry the Fifth
hales them to an hundred mischiefs and makes them   56
leave me desolate. I see them lay their heads together
to surprise me. My sword make way for me, for here   58
is no staying.—In despite of the devils and hell, have 59
through the very middest of you! And heavens and   60
honor be witness that no want of resolution in me, but
only my followers' base and ignominious treasons,
makes me betake me to my heels.   63

    Exit [*Cade, running through the crowd*
        with drawn sword].

BUCKINGHAM
What, is he fled? Go some, and follow him,
And he that brings his head unto the King
Shall have a thousand crowns for his reward.

        Exeunt some of them.

Follow me, soldiers. We'll devise a means
To reconcile you all unto the King.   *Exeunt omnes.*

        ❧

40 at jar in discord   **41 fearful** timid.   **late** lately   **42 make a start**
suddenly arouse themselves   **45 Villiago** rascal, villain. (Italian.)
46 miscarry encounter misfortune   **52 A Clifford** rally to Clifford
56 hales draws   **58 surprise** capture   **59 despite** spite   **59–60 have
through** i.e., here I come through   **63 s.d. Exit** (In the quarto version,
Cade "runs through them with his staff and flies away.")

4.9   *Sound trumpets. Enter King, Queen, and*
            Somerset, on the terrace [aloft].

KING

Was ever king that joyed an earthly throne   1
And could command no more content than I?
No sooner was I crept out of my cradle
But I was made a king at nine months old.
Was never subject longed to be a king
As I do long and wish to be a subject.

        Enter Buckingham and [old] Clifford.

BUCKINGHAM

Health and glad tidings to Your Majesty!

KING

Why, Buckingham, is the traitor Cade surprised?   8
Or is he but retired to make him strong?

        Enter [below] multitudes, with halters about
        their necks.

CLIFFORD

He is fled, my lord, and all his powers do yield,   10
And humbly thus, with halters on their necks,
Expect Your Highness' doom, of life or death.   12

KING

Then, heaven, set ope thy everlasting gates
To entertain my vows of thanks and praise!   14
Soldiers, this day have you redeemed your lives
And showed how well you love your prince and country.
Continue still in this so good a mind,
And Henry, though he be infortunate,
Assure yourselves, will never be unkind.
And so, with thanks and pardon to you all,
I do dismiss you to your several countries.   21

4.9. Location: A castle, historically identified as Kenilworth Castle
in Warwickshire, though in the theater we only know that the King
receives the submission of the rebels shortly after the fighting in
London.
s.d. terrace i.e., probably in the gallery to the rear above the main
stage **1 joyed** enjoyed **8 surprised** captured **10 powers** troops (also
in l. 25) **12 Expect** await. **doom** judgment **14 entertain** receive
21 several countries various localities

ALL   God save the King! God save the King!

> [*Exeunt the multitudes.*]

    Enter a Messenger.

MESSENGER
Please it Your Grace to be advertisèd   23
The Duke of York is newly come from Ireland,
And with a puissant and a mighty power
Of gallowglasses and stout kerns   26
Is marching hitherward in proud array,
And still proclaimeth, as he comes along,   28
His arms are only to remove from thee
The Duke of Somerset, whom he terms a traitor.

KING
Thus stands my state, twixt Cade and York distressed,
Like to a ship that, having scaped a tempest,
Is straightway calmed and boarded with a pirate.   33
But now is Cade driven back, his men dispersed,   34
And now is York in arms to second him.
I pray thee, Buckingham, go and meet him,
And ask him what's the reason of these arms.
Tell him I'll send Duke Edmund to the Tower;   38
And, Somerset, we will commit thee thither,
Until his army be dismissed from him.

SOMERSET   My lord,
I'll yield myself to prison willingly,
Or unto death, to do my country good.

KING [*To Buckingham*]
In any case, be not too rough in terms,
For he is fierce and cannot brook hard language.   45

BUCKINGHAM
I will, my lord, and doubt not so to deal
As all things shall redound unto your good.

KING
Come, wife, let's in, and learn to govern better,
For yet may England curse my wretched reign.   49

         Flourish. Exeunt.

❖

23 **advertisèd** informed   26 **gallowglasses, kerns** Irish horsemen and foot-
soldiers, armed with heavy and light weapons respectively   28 **still** continually   33 **calmed** becalmed.   **with** by   34 **But now** even now, just now
38 **Duke Edmund** i.e., Edmund Beaufort, the Duke of Somerset   45 **brook**
endure   49 **yet** until now

4.10   *Enter Cade.*

CADE Fie on ambitions! Fie on myself, that have a
sword and yet am ready to famish! These five days
have I hid me in these woods and durst not peep out,
for all the country is laid for me. But now am I so hun- 4
gry that, if I might have a lease of my life for a thousand years, I could stay no longer. Wherefore, o'er a 6
brick wall have I climbed into this garden, to see if I
can eat grass, or pick a sallet another while, which is 8
not amiss to cool a man's stomach this hot weather.
And I think this word "sallet" was born to do me
good; for many a time, but for a sallet, my brainpan
had been cleft with a brown bill; and many a time, 12
when I have been dry and bravely marching, it hath
served me instead of a quart pot to drink in; and now
the word "sallet" must serve me to feed on. 15

Enter Iden [and his men].

IDEN
Lord, who would live turmoilèd in the court,
And may enjoy such quiet walks as these?
This small inheritance my father left me
Contenteth me, and worth a monarchy.
I seek not to wax great by others' waning,
Or gather wealth, I care not with what envy.
Sufficeth that I have maintains my state 22
And sends the poor well pleasèd from my gate. 23

CADE [*Aside*] Zounds, here's the lord of the soil come to
seize me for a stray, for entering his fee simple without 25
leave.—Ah, villain, thou wilt betray me and get a

4.10. Location: Kent. Iden's garden.
4 is laid is lying in wait **6 stay** wait **8 sallet** salad greens (with a pun
in the following lines on *sallet*, light helmet) **12 brown bill** brown-
handled weapon with a blade or ax-shaped head **15 s.d. and his men**
(The quarto reads, "Enter Jack Cade at me door, and at the other Master Alexander Eyden and his men," and at ll. 38–39 Cade refers to
Iden's "five men.") **22 Sufficeth . . . state** it suffices that what I have
supports my manner of life **23 And . . . gate** i.e., and also provides
enough to feed the poor who come to my gate **25 stray** trespasser. **fee
simple** estate belonging to an owner and his heirs forever

thousand crowns of the King by carrying my head to
him; but I'll make thee eat iron like an ostrich and
swallow my sword like a great pin, ere thou and I part.

IDEN
Why, rude companion, whatsoe'er thou be,   30
I know thee not. Why then should I betray thee?
Is 't not enough to break into my garden,
And like a thief to come to rob my grounds,
Climbing my walls in spite of me the owner,
But thou wilt brave me with these saucy terms?   35

CADE   Brave thee? Ay, by the best blood that ever was 36
broached, and beard thee too. Look on me well. I have 37
eat no meat these five days, yet come thou and thy 38
five men, and if I do not leave you all as dead as a
doornail, I pray God I may never eat grass more.

IDEN
Nay, it shall ne'er be said, while England stands,
That Alexander Iden, an esquire of Kent,
Took odds to combat a poor famished man.   43
Oppose thy steadfast-gazing eyes to mine;
See if thou canst outface me with thy looks.
Set limb to limb, and thou art far the lesser;   46
Thy hand is but a finger to my fist,
Thy leg a stick comparèd with this truncheon;   48
My foot shall fight with all the strength thou hast;
And if mine arm be heavèd in the air,   50
Thy grave is digged already in the earth.   51
As for words, whose greatness answers words,   52
Let this my sword report what speech forbears.   53

CADE   By my valor, the most complete champion that 54
ever I heard! Steel, if thou turn the edge, or cut not out 55
the burly-boned clown in chines of beef ere thou sleep 56

---

30 rude companion base fellow   **35 brave** defy, taunt.   **saucy** insolent
36 best blood i.e., Christ's blood   **37 broached** tapped, shed.   **beard**
defy   **38 eat** eaten. (Pronounced "et.")   **43 odds** advantage   **46 Set**
compare   **48 truncheon** heavy staff (i.e., Iden's leg)   **50–51 And . . .**
earth i.e., if I but lift my arm, you're as good as dead already
52 whose . . . words i.e., I whose might is more than a match for your
words   **53 report . . . forbears** i.e., speak through actions in place of
words   **54 complete** accomplished   **55 turn the edge** fail to cut
56 chines roasts

in thy sheath, I beseech God on my knees thou mayst
be turned to hobnails.   *Here they fight.* [*Cade falls.*] 58
O, I am slain! Famine and no other hath slain me. Let
ten thousand devils come against me, and give me but
the ten meals I have lost, and I'd defy them all. Wither,
garden, and be henceforth a burying place to all that
do dwell in this house, because the unconquered soul
of Cade is fled.

IDEN
Is 't Cade that I have slain, that monstrous traitor?
Sword, I will hallow thee for this thy deed
And hang thee o'er my tomb when I am dead.
Ne'er shall this blood be wipèd from thy point
But thou shalt wear it as a herald's coat
To emblaze the honor that thy master got.   70

CADE   Iden, farewell, and be proud of thy victory. Tell
Kent from me she hath lost her best man, and exhort
all the world to be cowards; for I, that never feared any,
am vanquished by famine, not by valor.   *Dies.*

IDEN
How much thou wrong'st me, heaven be my judge.
Die, damnèd wretch, the curse of her that bare thee! 76
And as I thrust thy body in with my sword,
                    [*Stabbing Cade's body*]
So wish I, I might thrust thy soul to hell.
Hence will I drag thee headlong by the heels   79
Unto a dunghill, which shall be thy grave,
And there cut off thy most ungracious head,
Which I will bear in triumph to the King,
Leaving thy trunk for crows to feed upon.
                    Exeunt, [*dragging out the body*].

✤

58 turned to hobnails i.e., melted down and recast as nails   **70 emblaze**
proclaim as by a heraldic device   **76 bare** bore, gave birth to
79 headlong at full length

5.1   *Enter York and his army of Irish, with drum
and colors.*

YORK

  From Ireland thus comes York to claim his right
  And pluck the crown from feeble Henry's head.
  Ring, bells, aloud! Burn, bonfires, clear and bright
  To entertain great England's lawful king!   4
  Ah, *sancta maiestas*, who would not buy thee dear? 5
  Let them obey that knows not how to rule;
  This hand was made to handle naught but gold.
  I cannot give due action to my words
  Except a sword or scepter balance it.   9
  A scepter shall it have, have I a soul,   10
  On which I'll toss the flower-de-luce of France. 11

    Enter Buckingham.

  Whom have we here? Buckingham, to disturb me?
  The King hath sent him, sure. I must dissemble.

BUCKINGHAM

  York, if thou meanest well, I greet thee well.

YORK

  Humphrey of Buckingham, I accept thy greeting.
  Art thou a messenger, or come of pleasure?

BUCKINGHAM

  A messenger from Henry, our dread liege,
  To know the reason of these arms in peace;
  Or why thou, being a subject as I am,
  Against thy oath and true allegiance sworn
  Should raise so great a power without his leave, 21
  Or dare to bring thy force so near the court.

5.1. Location: In the theater, Act 5 appears to take place in one continuous sweep, though historically the action begins between Dartford and Blackheath just southeast of London in 1452–1453 (see l. 46) and then shifts to a battlefield between London and St. Albans, near the Castle Inn, in 1455.
s.d. drum and colors drummer and flagbearer **4 entertain** welcome
5 sancta maiestas sacred majesty **9 Except** unless. **balance it** i.e., give due weight to my action **10 have I** i.e., just as sure as I have **11 On which** i.e., my sword-holding hand, my action. (The *it* of l. 10.) **toss** carry aloft on the point of a sword. **flower-de-luce** France's national emblem **21 power** armed force

YORK [*Aside*]
  Scarce can I speak, my choler is so great.
  O, I could hew up rocks and fight with flint,
  I am so angry at these abject terms!   25
  And now, like Ajax Telamonius,   26
  On sheep or oxen could I spend my fury.
  I am far better born than is the King,
  More like a king, more kingly in my thoughts.
  But I must make fair weather yet awhile,   30
  Till Henry be more weak and I more strong.—
  Buckingham, I prithee, pardon me,
  That I have given no answer all this while;
  My mind was troubled with deep melancholy.
  The cause why I have brought this army hither
  Is to remove proud Somerset from the King,
  Seditious to His Grace and to the state.

BUCKINGHAM
  That is too much presumption on thy part.
  But if thy arms be to no other end,
  The King hath yielded unto thy demand;
  The Duke of Somerset is in the Tower.

YORK
  Upon thine honor, is he prisoner?

BUCKINGHAM
  Upon mine honor, he is prisoner.

YORK
  Then, Buckingham, I do dismiss my powers.
  Soldiers, I thank you all. Disperse yourselves.
  Meet me tomorrow in Saint George's field;   46
  You shall have pay and everything you wish.
                       [*Exeunt soldiers.*]
  And let my sovereign, virtuous Henry,
  Command my eldest son, nay, all my sons,   49
  As pledges of my fealty and love;   50

25 abject terms degrading, insulting words   **26 Ajax Telamonius** Ajax the son of Telamon, one of the Greek heroes of the Trojan War who, when the weapons of Achilles were allotted to Odysseus, slaughtered in his fury a flock of sheep, mistaking them for the enemy   **30 make fair weather** i.e., dissemble   **46 Saint George's field** an open area south of the Thames River near Southwark   **49 Command** hold under his authority   **50 pledges** hostages

I'll send them all as willing as I live.
Lands, goods, horse, armor, anything I have,
Is his to use, so Somerset may die.   53

BUCKINGHAM
York, I commend this kind submission.
We twain will go into His Highness' tent.

> [*They walk arm in arm.*]

Enter King and Attendants.

KING
Buckingham, doth York intend no harm to us,
That thus he marcheth with thee arm in arm?

YORK
In all submission and humility
York doth present himself unto Your Highness.

KING
Then what intends these forces thou dost bring?

YORK
To heave the traitor Somerset from hence
And fight against that monstrous rebel Cade,
Who since I heard to be discomfited.   63

Enter Iden, with Cade's head.

IDEN
If one so rude and of so mean condition   64
May pass into the presence of a king,
Lo, I present Your Grace a traitor's head,
The head of Cade, whom I in combat slew.

KING
The head of Cade? Great God, how just art Thou!
O, let me view his visage, being dead,
That living wrought me such exceeding trouble.
Tell me, my friend, art thou the man that slew him?

IDEN   I was, an 't like Your Majesty.   72

KING
How art thou called, and what is thy degree?   73

IDEN
Alexander Iden, that's my name,
A poor esquire of Kent that loves his king.

___

53 so as long as   **63 discomfited** routed   **64 rude** uncultivated.   **mean
condition** low rank   **72 an 't like** if it please   **73 degree** social rank

BUCKINGHAM [*To the King*]
  So please it you, my lord, 'twere not amiss
  He were created knight for his good service.
KING
  Iden, kneel down. [*He kneels.*] Rise up a knight.
                                      [*Iden rises.*]
  We give thee for reward a thousand marks,   79
  And will that thou henceforth attend on us.   80
IDEN
  May Iden live to merit such a bounty,
  And never live but true unto his liege!

      Enter Queen and Somerset.

KING
  See, Buckingham, Somerset comes with the Queen.
  Go bid her hide him quickly from the Duke.   84
QUEEN
  For thousand Yorks he shall not hide his head,
  But boldly stand and front him to his face.   86
YORK
  How now? Is Somerset at liberty?
  Then, York, unloose thy long-imprisoned thoughts
  And let thy tongue be equal with thy heart.
  Shall I endure the sight of Somerset?
  False king, why hast thou broken faith with me,
  Knowing how hardly I can brook abuse?   92
  "King" did I call thee? No, thou art not king,
  Not fit to govern and rule multitudes,
  Which dar'st not—no, nor canst not—rule a traitor.   95
  That head of thine doth not become a crown;
  Thy hand is made to grasp a palmer's staff,   97
  And not to grace an awful princely scepter.   98
  That gold must round engirt these brows of mine,
  Whose smile and frown, like to Achilles' spear,   100
  Is able with the change to kill and cure.

79 marks (Valued at two thirds of a pound.)   **80 will** command   **84 the
Duke** i.e., of York   **86 front** confront   **92 brook abuse** tolerate deception   **95 Which** who   **97 palmer's** pilgrim's   **98 awful** awe-inspiring
100 Achilles' spear (Telephus, wounded by Achilles' spear, learned from
an oracle that he could be cured only by the wounder. He was eventually cured by an application of rust from the point of the spear.)

Here is a hand to hold a scepter up
And with the same to act controlling laws.   103
Give place. By heaven, thou shalt rule no more
O'er him whom heaven created for thy ruler.

SOMERSET
O monstrous traitor! I arrest thee, York,
Of capital treason 'gainst the King and crown.
Obey, audacious traitor. Kneel for grace.

YORK
Wouldst have me kneel? First let me ask of these,   109
If they can brook I bow a knee to man.   110
[*To an Attendant.*] Sirrah, call in my sons to be my bail.
                                          [*Exit Attendant.*]
I know, ere they will have me go to ward,   112
They'll pawn their swords for my enfranchisement.   113

QUEEN [*To Buckingham*]
Call hither Clifford. Bid him come amain,   114
To say if that the bastard boys of York
Shall be the surety for their traitor father.   116
                                          [*Exit Buckingham.*]

YORK [*To the Queen*]
O blood-bespotted Neapolitan,   117
Outcast of Naples, England's bloody scourge!
The sons of York, thy betters in their birth,
Shall be their father's bail, and bane to those   120
That for my surety will refuse the boys!   121

*Enter Edward and Richard [Plantagenet, with
drum and soldiers, at one door].*

See where they come. I'll warrant they'll make it good.

*Enter [old] Clifford [and his Son, with drum and
soldiers, at the other door].*

---

103 act enact   **109 these** i.e., his sons, who are waiting outside, or
attendants, or possibly his hands or weapons   **110 brook . . . man**
tolerate that I should bow my knee in submission to anyone   **112 to
ward** into custody   **113 pawn** pledge.   **enfranchisement** freedom
114 amain swiftly   **116 s.d. Exit Buckingham** (Buckingham must exit
somewhere before an attendant is sent to find him at l. 192, and here
seems a likely place.)   **117 Neapolitan** (Margaret's father Reignier or
René was titular King of Naples.)   **120 bane** destruction   **121 s.d. drum**
drummer.   **at one door** (The quarto version is explicit that Plantagenet's sons enter "at one door" and Clifford with his son and forces "at
the other.")

QUEEN
  And here comes Clifford to deny their bail.
CLIFFORD [*Kneeling before King Henry*]
  Health and all happiness to my lord the King!
                                        [*He rises.*]
YORK
  I thank thee, Clifford. Say, what news with thee?
  Nay, do not fright us with an angry look.
  We are thy sovereign, Clifford, kneel again.
  For thy mistaking so, we pardon thee.
CLIFFORD
  This is my king, York. I do not mistake,
  But thou mistakes me much to think I do.—
  To Bedlam with him! Is the man grown mad?   131
KING
  Ay, Clifford, a bedlam and ambitious humor   132
  Makes him oppose himself against his king.
CLIFFORD
  He is a traitor. Let him to the Tower,
  And chop away that factious pate of his.   135
QUEEN
  He is arrested, but will not obey.
  His sons, he says, shall give their words for him.
YORK   Will you not, sons?
EDWARD
  Ay, noble Father, if our words will serve.
RICHARD
  And if words will not, then our weapons shall.
CLIFFORD
  Why, what a brood of traitors have we here!
YORK
  Look in a glass, and call thy image so.   142
  I am thy king, and thou a false-heart traitor.
  Call hither to the stake my two brave bears,   144

131 Bedlam hospital of St. Mary of Bethlehem in London, used as an
asylum for the mentally deranged   **132 bedlam** mad.   **humor** disposition   **135 factious pate** rebellious head   **142 glass** looking glass
144 brave bears i.e., Salisbury and his son Warwick. (Cf. ll. 202–203
below, where Warwick describes the badge of his house as a *rampant
bear chained to the ragged staff.* The image is from bearbaiting, in
which bears were chained to a stake and attacked by *fell-lurking curs,*
cruelly waiting dogs, l. 146.)

That with the very shaking of their chains
They may astonish these fell-lurking curs.—
Bid Salisbury and Warwick come to me.
           [*An Attendant goes to summon them.*]

     Enter the Earls of Warwick and Salisbury, [*with
     drum and soldiers*].

CLIFFORD
  Are these thy bears? We'll bait thy bears to death
  And manacle the bearherd in their chains,   149
  If thou dar'st bring them to the baiting place.   150
RICHARD
  Oft have I seen a hot o'erweening cur   151
  Run back and bite, because he was withheld,   152
  Who, being suffered with the bear's fell paw,   153
  Hath clapped his tail between his legs and cried;
  And such a piece of service will you do,
  If you oppose yourselves to match Lord Warwick.   156
CLIFFORD
  Hence, heap of wrath, foul indigested lump,   157
  As crooked in thy manners as thy shape!
YORK
  Nay, we shall heat you thoroughly anon.   159
CLIFFORD
  Take heed, lest by your heat you burn yourselves.
KING
  Why, Warwick, hath thy knee forgot to bow?
  Old Salisbury, shame to thy silver hair,
  Thou mad misleader of thy brainsick son!
  What, wilt thou on thy deathbed play the ruffian,
  And seek for sorrow with thy spectacles?   165

149 bearherd bear handler, keeper (i.e., York)   **150 baiting place** bear-baiting pit   **151 hot o'erweening** hot-tempered and overconfident   **152 bite** i.e., at his trainer, who is restraining him   **153 suffered with** permitted to do battle with, or, injured by.   **fell** fierce, terrible   **156 oppose yourselves** set yourselves up as opponents   **157 indigested** ill-formed.   **lump** (Bear cubs were supposedly born unformed and had to be licked into shape by their mother. See *3 Henry VI*, 3.2.161, where Richard's hunched back and other deformities are compared with those of *an unlicked bear whelp*.)   **159 heat you** i.e., warm you in the fighting   **165 spectacles** (A sign of advanced age, like *silver hair*, l. 162, and *frosty*, white-haired, l. 167.)

O, where is faith? O, where is loyalty?
If it be banished from the frosty head,
Where shall it find a harbor in the earth?
Wilt thou go dig a grave to find out war,
And shame thine honorable age with blood?
Why art thou old and want'st experience?   171
Or wherefore dost abuse it if thou hast it?   172
For shame! In duty bend thy knee to me
That bows unto the grave with mickle age.   174

SALISBURY
My lord, I have considered with myself
The title of this most renownèd duke,
And in my conscience do repute His Grace
The rightful heir to England's royal seat.

KING
Hast thou not sworn allegiance unto me?

SALISBURY   I have.

KING
Canst thou dispense with heaven for such an oath?   181

SALISBURY
It is great sin to swear unto a sin,
But greater sin to keep a sinful oath.
Who can be bound by any solemn vow
To do a murderous deed, to rob a man,
To force a spotless virgin's chastity,
To reave the orphan of his patrimony,   187
To wring the widow from her customed right,   188
And have no other reason for this wrong
But that he was bound by a solemn oath?

QUEEN
A subtle traitor needs no sophister.   191

KING [To an Attendant]
Call Buckingham, and bid him arm himself.
                              [Exit Attendant.]

---

171 want'st lack. (Why are you old before you are wise?)   **172 Or . . . it**
or why do you put wisdom and experience to such bad use if you have
them   **174 That bows** you that bow or your knee that bows.   **mickle**
great   **181 dispense with heaven for** expect or obtain dispensation from
heaven for breaking   **187 reave** bereave   **188 customed right** i.e., right
to inherit a portion of her husband's estate   **191 sophister** equivocator,
expert in casuistry

YORK [*To King Henry*]
 Call Buckingham and all the friends thou hast,   193
 I am resolved for death or dignity.   194
CLIFFORD
 The first, I warrant thee, if dreams prove true.
WARWICK
 You were best to go to bed and dream again,   196
 To keep thee from the tempest of the field.
CLIFFORD
 I am resolved to bear a greater storm
 Than any thou canst conjure up today;
 And that I'll write upon thy burgonet,   200
 Might I but know thee by thy household badge.
WARWICK
 Now, by my father's badge, old Neville's crest,   202
 The rampant bear chained to the ragged staff,
 This day I'll wear aloft my burgonet,   204
 As on a mountaintop the cedar shows
 That keeps his leaves in spite of any storm,
 Even to affright thee with the view thereof.
CLIFFORD
 And from thy burgonet I'll rend thy bear
 And tread it underfoot with all contempt,
 Despite the bearherd that protects the bear.
YOUNG CLIFFORD
 And so to arms, victorious Father,
 To quell the rebels and their complices.   212
RICHARD
 Fie! Charity, for shame! Speak not in spite,
 For you shall sup with Jesu Christ tonight.
YOUNG CLIFFORD
 Foul stigmatic, that's more than thou canst tell.   215
RICHARD
 If not in heaven, you'll surely sup in hell.
            Exeunt [*separately*].

---

193 Call even if you call   **194 dignity** exalted rank   **196 You were best**
you had better   **200 burgonet** light helmet or steel cap (upon which the
wearer's heraldic device was often mounted)   **202 old Neville's crest**
(The Nevilles' crest was in fact a bull; Warwick inherited his badge of a
chained bear from his wife's family, the Beauchamps.)   **204 aloft** on top
of   **212 complices** accomplices   **215 stigmatic** one branded with the
mark of his crime (just as Richard is marked by his deformities)

5.2   [*Alarums to the battle.*] *Enter Warwick.*

WARWICK
Clifford of Cumberland, 'tis Warwick calls!
And if thou dost not hide thee from the bear,
Now, when the angry trumpet sounds alarum
And dead men's cries do fill the empty air,   4
Clifford, I say, come forth and fight with me!
Proud northern lord, Clifford of Cumberland,
Warwick is hoarse with calling thee to arms.

    Enter York.

How now, my noble lord? What, all afoot?
YORK
The deadly-handed Clifford slew my steed,
But match to match I have encountered him
And made a prey for carrion kites and crows
Even of the bonny beast he loved so well.

    Enter [*old*] *Clifford.*

WARWICK
Of one or both of us the time is come.
YORK
Hold, Warwick, seek thee out some other chase,   14
For I myself must hunt this deer to death.
WARWICK
Then, nobly, York! 'Tis for a crown thou fight'st.—
As I intend, Clifford, to thrive today,
It grieves my soul to leave thee unassailed.
                Exit Warwick.
CLIFFORD
What seest thou in me, York? Why dost thou pause?
YORK
With thy brave bearing should I be in love,   20
But that thou art so fast mine enemy.   21
CLIFFORD
Nor should thy prowess want praise and esteem,   22
But that 'tis shown ignobly and in treason.

5.2. Location: Scene continues at the battlefield near the Castle Inn.
4 dead dying   **14 chase** game, prey   **20 bearing** demeanor   **21 fast**
completely   **22 want** lack

YORK
  So let it help me now against thy sword
  As I in justice and true right express it.
CLIFFORD
  My soul and body on the action both!   26
YORK
  A dreadful lay! Address thee instantly.   27
                          [*They fight, and Clifford falls.*]
CLIFFORD
  La fin couronne les oeuvres.   [*He dies.*] 28
YORK
  Thus war hath given thee peace, for thou art still.
  Peace with his soul, heaven, if it be thy will!   [*Exit.*]

      Enter young Clifford.

YOUNG CLIFFORD
  Shame and confusion! All is on the rout.   31
  Fear frames disorder, and disorder wounds   32
  Where it should guard. O war, thou son of hell,
  Whom angry heavens do make their minister,
  Throw in the frozen bosoms of our part   35
  Hot coals of vengeance! Let no soldier fly.
  He that is truly dedicate to war   37
  Hath no self-love, nor he that loves himself   38
  Hath not essentially but by circumstance   39
  The name of valor. [*Seeing his dead father.*] O, let the
      vile world end
  And the premisèd flames of the last day   41
  Knit earth and heaven together!
  Now let the general trumpet blow his blast,
  Particularities and petty sounds   44
  To cease! Wast thou ordained, dear Father,   45
  To lose thy youth in peace, and to achieve   46

26 action outcome of action   **27 lay** wager, oath.   **Address thee** prepare
yourself   **28 La . . . oeuvres** the end crowns the work   **31 confusion**
destruction.   **on the rout** in disorderly retreat   **32 frames** causes
35 frozen i.e., unwarmed by wrathful courage.   **part** party, faction
37 dedicate dedicated   **38 nor** conversely   **39 not . . . circumstance** not
by any virtue of his own, but only outwardly and by happenstance
41 premisèd foreordained.   **last day** Day of Judgment   **44 Particularities**
individual affairs   **45 cease** bring to an end.   **ordained** chosen, fated
46 lose expend

The silver livery of advisèd age,   47
And, in thy reverence and thy chair days, thus   48
To die in ruffian battle? Even at this sight
My heart is turned to stone, and while 'tis mine
It shall be stony. York not our old men spares;
No more will I their babes. Tears virginal   52
Shall be to me even as the dew to fire,   53
And beauty, that the tyrant oft reclaims,   54
Shall to my flaming wrath be oil and flax.
Henceforth I will not have to do with pity.
Meet I an infant of the house of York,   57
Into as many gobbets will I cut it   58
As wild Medea young Absyrtus did.   59
In cruelty will I seek out my fame.
Come, thou new ruin of old Clifford's house.
As did Aeneas old Anchises bear,   62
So bear I thee upon my manly shoulders;
But then Aeneas bare a living load,   64
Nothing so heavy as these woes of mine.   65
                    [*Exit, bearing off his father.*]

Enter Richard and Somerset to fight. [*Somerset
is killed under the sign of the Castle Inn.*]

RICHARD   So, lie thou there;
For underneath an alehouse' paltry sign,
The Castle in Saint Albans, Somerset
Hath made the wizard famous in his death.   69
Sword, hold thy temper; heart, be wrathful still.   70
Priests pray for enemies, but princes kill.   [*Exit.*] 71

---

47 silvery livery i.e., white hair, worn as though part of a uniform.
advisèd wise, prudent   **48 reverence** revered old age.   **chair days** i.e.,
inactive years of old age   **52 virginal** of young maidens   **53 dew to fire**
(Water finely sprayed on a fire was thought to cause it to burn hotter.)
54 that . . . reclaims which often softens the temper of the tyrant   **57 Meet
I** if I should meet   **58 gobbets** pieces, lumps of flesh   **59 Medea** daughter
of Aeetes, King of Colchis, who helped Jason recover the Golden Fleece
and fled with him. (To delay her father's pursuit, she killed her brother
Absyrtus and left pieces of his dismembered body in the father's path.)
62 Aeneas, Anchises (In Virgil's *Aeneid*, Aeneas, fleeing from Troy, carried
his aged father on his shoulders.)   **64 bare** bore   **65 Nothing** not at all.
heavy (1) weighty (2) sorrowful   **69 Hath . . . death** i.e., has confirmed by
his death the prophecy that he would die *where castles mounted stand.*
(See 1.4.36–38.)   **70 still** always   **71 s.d. Exit** (The body of the slain Somerset must be removed at some point.)

Fight. Excursions. Enter King, Queen, and others.

QUEEN
  Away, my lord! You are slow. For shame, away!

KING
  Can we outrun the heavens? Good Margaret, stay.

QUEEN
  What are you made of? You'll nor fight nor fly.   74
  Now is it manhood, wisdom, and defense
  To give the enemy way, and to secure us   76
  By what we can, which can no more but fly.   77
                    Alarum afar off.
  If you be ta'en, we then should see the bottom
  Of all our fortunes; but if we haply scape,
  As well we may, if not through your neglect,   80
  We shall to London get, where you are loved
  And where this breach now in our fortunes made
  May readily be stopped.

      Enter [young] Clifford.

YOUNG CLIFFORD
  But that my heart's on future mischief set,
  I would speak blasphemy ere bid you fly;
  But fly you must. Uncurable discomfit   86
  Reigns in the hearts of all our present parts.   87
  Away, for your relief! And we will live
  To see their day and them our fortune give.   89
  Away, my lord, away!   *Exeunt.*

5.3   *Alarum. Retreat. Enter York, Richard,*
          Warwick, and soldiers, with drum
          and colors.

YORK
  Of Salisbury, who can report of him,

---

71 s.d. Excursions sorties **74 nor . . . nor** neither . . . nor **76 secure us**
save ourselves **77 what** whatever means. **which** (we) who **80 if not**
unless **86 Uncurable discomfit** hopeless discouragement **87 our present
parts** those forces still remaining to us **89 To . . . give** to see a day of
success like theirs and let them experience our misfortune

5.3. Location: Scene continues at the battlefield.

That winter lion, who in rage forgets   2
Agèd contusions and all brush of time,   3
And like a gallant in the brow of youth   4
Repairs him with occasion? This happy day   5
Is not itself, nor have we won one foot,
If Salisbury be lost.

RICHARD   My noble Father,
Three times today I holp him to his horse,   8
Three times bestrid him; thrice I led him off,   9
Persuaded him from any further act.
But still, where danger was, still there I met him,   11
And like rich hangings in a homely house,   12
So was his will in his old feeble body.
But, noble as he is, look where he comes.

  Enter Salisbury.

SALISBURY
Now, by my sword, well hast thou fought today!
By th' Mass, so did we all. I thank you, Richard.
God knows how long it is I have to live,
And it hath pleased Him that three times today
You have defended me from imminent death.
Well, lords, we have not got that which we have;   20
'Tis not enough our foes are this time fled,
Being opposites of such repairing nature.   22

YORK
I know our safety is to follow them;
For, as I hear, the King is fled to London
To call a present court of Parliament.
Let us pursue him ere the writs go forth.   26
What says Lord Warwick? Shall we after them?

WARWICK
After them? Nay, before them, if we can.

---

2 winter i.e., aged   **3 brush** assault, collision   **4 gallant** young man of
fashion.   **brow** i.e., crown, height   **5 Repairs . . . occasion** i.e., renews
his strength with the opportunity of further military action   **8 holp**
helped   **9 bestrid him** i.e., stood over him to defend him when he was
down   **11 still** continually   **12 hangings** tapestries.   **homely** modest
20 not . . . have i.e., not decisively overwhelmed the forces we today
defeated in order to secure the whole country   **22 Being . . . nature**
they being adversaries with such ability to recover quickly   **26 writs**
official summonses issued by the King to members of Parliament

Now, by my faith, lords, 'twas a glorious day.
Saint Albans battle won by famous York
Shall be eternized in all age to come.   31
Sound drum and trumpets, and to London all,
And more such days as these to us befall!

                              [*Flourish.*] *Exeunt.*

31 eternized immortalized

Date and Text

A shortened and memorially reconstructed text of *Henry VI, Part Two* was published in quarto in 1594 with the title, *The First Part of the Contention Betwixt the Two Famous Houses of York and Lancaster*. The play appears to have been written about 1590–1591. The First Folio text seems to have been based on an authorial manuscript with some reference to the third quarto, which in turn may have been corrected by reference to a theatrical manuscript. For a more extensive discussion of date and textual situation in all three *Henry VI* plays, see "Date and Text" to *Henry VI, Part One* in this volume.

Textual Notes

These textual notes are not a historical collation, either of the early quartos and folios or of more recent editions; they are simply a record of departures in this edition from the copy text. The reading adopted in this edition appears in boldface, followed by the rejected reading from the copy text, i.e., the First Folio. Only major alterations in punctuation are noted. Changes in lineation are not indicated, nor are some minor and obvious typographical errors.

Abbreviations used:
F the First Folio
Q the quarto of 1594
s.d. stage direction
s.p. speech prefix

Copy text: the First Folio.

1.1. 4 Princess Princes   **37 s.d. Kneeling** kneel   **56 s.p. Cardinal** [Q] Win
57 duchies Dutchesse   **72 s.d. Exeunt** Exit   **Manent** Manet   **91 had** hath
99 Rasing Racing   **107 roast** rost   **130 s.p. [and elsewhere] Gloucester** Hum
167 hoist hoyse   **176 Protector** [Q] Protectors   **177 s.d. Exeunt** Exit   **206 let's
away** lets make hast away   **211 s.d. Exeunt** Exit   **254 in** [Q1] in in

1.2. 1 s.p. [and elsewhere] Duchess Elia   **19 hour** thought   **22 dream**
dreames   **38 are** wer   **60 s.d. Exit Humphrey** [at l. 59 in F]

1.3. 6 s.p. First Petitioner Peter   **32 master** Mistresse   **41 s.d. Exeunt** Exit
100 [F has "Exit" here]   **104 denied** denay'd   **142 I'd** I could   **187 s.p. [and
throughout scene] Horner** Armorer   **212–213 King. Then . . . French** [Q; not
in F]

1.4. 25 s.p. Margery Jourdain Witch   **25 Asnath** Asmath   **62 Aio te** Aio
63 posse posso

2.1. 30 Lord-Protectorship Lords Protectorship   **48 Cardinal [Aside to
Gloucester] I am with you** Cardinall, I am with you [as part of Gloucester's
speech]   **59 s.p. Townsman** One [also at l. 61]   **111 Alban** Albones   **135 his**
[Q] it

2.2. 45 was son was   **46 son** Sonnes Sonne

2.3. 3 sins sinne   **19 grave** ground   **74 apron** Aporne

2.4. 88 too to

3.1. 211 strains strayes   **218–219 eyes . . . good,** eyes; . . . good:
222 s.d. Exeunt Exit   **333–334 art . . . death; it** art; . . . death, it

3.2. 14 s.d. Somerset Suffolke, Somerset   **26 Meg** Nell   **79 Margaret** Elianor
[also at ll. 100 and 120]   **113 losing** loosing   **116 witch** watch
278 s.p. Commons [not in F]   **391 breathe** breath

3.3. 8 s.p. Cardinal [Q] Beau   **10 whe'er** where

4.1. 6 Clip Cleape   **7 Breathe** Breath   **48 Jove . . . I** [Q; not in F]

50 s.p. Suffolk [Q; at l. 51 in F]   **70 Lieutenant. Yes, Pole. Suffolk. Pole?**
[Q; not in F]   **85 mother's bleeding** Mother-bleeding   **93 are** and
115–116 Lieutenant. Walter– / Whitmore Lieu. Water: W.   **117 Paene** Pine
119 s.p. Whitmore Wal [also at l. 143]   **133 s.p. Suffolk** [at l. 134 in F]
142 s.d. Exeunt Exit

4.2. 33 s.p. [and elsewhere] Dick [Q] But [or "Butch"]   **34 fall** faiĺe
46 s.p. [and elsewhere] Smith Weauer [or "Wea"]   **99 an** a   **131 this:** this
176 s.d. Exeunt Exit

4.4. 19 have huae   **27 s.p. First Messenger** Mess   **49 s.p. Second Messenger**
Mess   **58 you be** you

4.5 s.d. enter enters

4.6. 9 s.p. Smith But   **13 Zounds** Come

4.7. 7 s.p. Holland Iohn [also at l. 15]   **63 lose** loose   **66 hands** hands?
67 But Kent you?   **79 s.p. Bevis** Geo   **86 caudle** Candle
132 s.d. Exeunt Exit

4.8. 12 rebel rabble

4.9. 0 s.d. terrace Tarras   **33 calmed** calme

4.10. 6 o'er on   **20 waning** warning   **24 Zounds** [Q; not in F]   **28 I'll** He
57 God Ioue

5.1. 109 these thee   **111 sons** [Q] sonne   **113 for** of   **149 bearherd** Berard
[also at l. 210]   **194 or** and   **195 s.p. Clifford** Old Clif [and at ll. 198 and 208]
201 household [Q] housed

5.2. 8 [F repeats s.p. "War"]   **28 oeuvres** eumenes   **31 s.p. Young Clifford**
Clif [also at l. 84]   **46 lose** loose

5.3. 29 faith [Q] hand

HENRY VI,
PART THREE

Introduction

Henry VI, Part Three must be seen not only as a part of Shakespeare's first historical four-play series but as a play in its own right, presumably seen on its first showing by an Elizabethan audience who, though aware of a larger context, witnessed this dramatic action as a self-contained event. Because *3 Henry VI* represents nearly the entire military phase of the civil war, it is the most crowded and bustling play of the series. Historically it covers the period from the battles of Wakefield and second St. Albans (1460–1461) to the decisive Yorkist victories at Barnet and Tewkesbury (1471). These and other battles are actually represented onstage. The conventional method of representing armed conflict is by means of alarums and excursions (i.e., sudden assaults and forays by armed soldiers in response to a signal to attack), employing as many soldiers as the acting company could muster, with martial music and numerous entrances and exits in rapid succession. Battles are usually preceded by florid boastful rhetorical exchanges, or *flytings*, between the combatants. The military contests focus on heroic confrontations between individual leaders. Staging of battles often uses the Elizabethan playhouse to its physical capacity, with appearances "on the walls" of some town (i.e., from the upper gallery), scaling operations, sieges, and the like. *3 Henry VI* abounds in spectacular deaths, often performed as gruesome rituals. Young Rutland is dragged from his tutor by the implacable Clifford, and Richard of York is mocked with a paper crown by Queen Margaret; Clifford dies with an arrow in his neck, and Warwick the kingmaker dies lamenting the vanity of all earthly achievement; King Henry dies in the Tower, a defenseless prisoner in the hands of Richard of Gloucester. The play is perhaps confusing to the reader, but it breathes with violent energy onstage.

Symbolic of the chaos is the lack of a single central character. The title of the 1595 octavo edition pairs the deaths of Richard of York and of King Henry as the play's most memorable episodes; and in this dual focus we see the dominant motif of reciprocity, a Yorkist death for a Lancastrian death.

This pattern will continue into *Richard III,* for *3 Henry VI* ends with an ominous amount of unfinished business; Clarence, for example, later sees that he must die in atonement for his part in the slaughter of Edward, the Lancastrian Prince of Wales. Just as the deaths are balanced and contrasted with one another, the military action also seesaws back and forth. Both Henry VI and Edward IV are at times imprisoned. The wheel of fortune elevates one side and then the other. Political alliances shift the balance of power one way and then the other. The action is painfully indecisive, the carnage leading pointlessly only to further violence. The spectacle is made infinitely more agonizing by the realization that all this is a family quarrel. The commoners suffer accordingly: we witness the grief of a father who has mistakenly killed his son in battle, and a son who has killed his father (2.5). The people, seldom seen, are no longer political troublemakers but mere victims, waiting patiently for an end. A recurrent emblem used to convey the utter futility of this war is the molehill. York is mockingly crowned before his execution on a molehill, and King Henry retires from a battle to a molehill in order to meditate on the happy contemplative life he has been denied. The molehill suggests the ironic perversity of the quest for worldly power, whereby those who possess power are incapable of exercising it wisely, and those who burn with ambition are denied legitimate opportunity.

One sure sign of moral chaos throughout this play is the phenomenon of oath breaking. In the opening scene, Richard of York accepts under oath an obligation to honor Henry VI as his king in return for being named king after Henry's death, but is soon talked out of his promise by his son Richard on the specious grounds that the oath was not made before "a true and lawful magistrate" (1.2.23). This masterful equivocation prepares us for Richard's later perfidies. (In Shakespeare's sources, Hall and Holinshed Parliament plays a major role in working out the compromise between York and Henry; Shakespeare shows us instead a personal agreement made between two contending leaders on the basis of private will and assertion of military power, and easily broken on the same pragmatic grounds.) King Henry is no less forsworn in denying to his own son the crown bestowed on him as birthright by sacred law and custom. Lewis the French King excuses his shifting of alliance from King Henry to the Yorkists on the grounds of simple expediency. Clarence forswears his oaths made to his brother Edward and changes sides in the wars, offended at Edward's perfidy in having renounced his intent to marry the French King's sister-in-law. Soon Clarence is back again in the Yorkist camp, having now betrayed the promises he made to the Lancastrians. Warwick the king-maker forswears his oaths to Edward because Edward has undermined Warwick's embassy to France. Where in fact do truth and justice reside, now that England is governed by two kings who are both forsworn? The common people sense this dilemma, as revealed in the attitudes of two game-keepers: they capture Henry to whom they were once loyal because they are now "sworn in all allegiance" to Edward, but would be true subjects again to Henry "If he were seated as King Edward is" (3.1.70, 95). Political and military reality governs political ethics; the ruler to be acknowledged is he who can establish control.

Another sign of moral decay in this play is the dominance of vengeful purpose. *3 Henry VI* indeed can be viewed as a kind of revenge play in which Richard of Gloucester finally emerges as the consummate avenger in a society of avengers. In the opening confrontation between the Yorkists and Lancastrians, Warwick taunts the Lancastrians with having lost many of their fathers in the recent military action at St. Albans; the fathers of Northumberland, Westmorland, and Clifford have all fallen in that one battle. The sons of course vow vengeance. Clifford, renowned as "the butcher" for his cruelty, exacts a terrible price for his father's death through the slaughter of the defenseless young Rutland and the mocking execution of Rutland's father, the Duke of York. York's surviving sons take vengeance not only on Clifford but on King Henry, his son Edward, and many others. Warwick turns against Edward of York more to avenge an insult than to aid Henry, and is himself cut down by the Yorkists at Barnet (4.2). The implacable pattern of an eye for an eye eventually takes on a providential meaning, especially as seen from the hindsight of *Richard III*, but as we experience this play in the theater the reality is chiefly one of brutality and horror.

As in earlier plays of the series, the relationships between men and women echo the discord of the English nation, and contribute in turn to further discord. Margaret of Anjou, the remorseless defender of her son Edward's claim, acts with increasingly masculine authority, while her ineffectual husband abdicates responsibility. She is the Lancastrian general, resourceful in battle and often victorious, implacable in vengeance. This inversion of male and female roles is reflected on the Yorkist side by Edward IV's disastrous marriage with Lady Elizabeth Grey. She is the widow of a Lancastrian soldier with no family position or political power to bring to the marriage—nothing, in fact, but her ambition on behalf of her kinsmen. Edward's attraction to her is fleshly and imprudent. To make matters worse, Warwick is at that very moment negotiating a highly favorable marriage treaty for Edward with the King of France. Edward IV thus unconsciously apes the earlier willfulness of his counterpart, Henry VI. Edward IV's snubbing of Warwick leads to the defection of that powerful leader, and through him the defection of Edward's brother Clarence, who has succumbed to the charms of Warwick's daughter Isabel. And whereas *1 Henry VI* at least counterbalances the uxoriousness of Henry with the positive example of Lord Talbot, *3 Henry VI* fails to discover any such central noble character. (To be sure, we are briefly introduced to the young Earl of Richmond, who is to be Henry VII, but only as a glimpse of a hopeful future.) The almost total lack of any distinctly virtuous character gives to *3 Henry VI* its predominantly dismaying and helpless mood. The heroes have been destroyed.

Richard of Gloucester alone seems to profit from England's decline. Like his father, York, his strategy has been to let England flay herself into anarchic vulnerability. Once the father York has disappeared from the scene, young Richard's malevolent character becomes increasingly apparent. No longer merely one of York's brave sons, Richard is the new genius of discord. His bravura soliloquy in scene 2 of Act 3 is often included in performances of *Richard III*, for it yields rich clues to his emerging character: he is ambitious, ruthless, deformed from birth, and above all a consummate deceiver. To the audience he boasts of his ability, claiming that as a hypocrite he will excel the combined talents of Nestor, Ulysses, Sinon, Proteus, and Machiavelli.

The superb self-assurance is arresting, the heartless consistency admirable even though despicable. In a second soliloquy, virtually at the end of the play, having already dispatched Henry VI and his son Edward, Richard confides to the audience that Clarence is to be his next victim. And although Richard pledges fealty to his young nephew Edward, the Yorkist crown prince, at the Yorkist victory celebration with which the play ends, we know that Richard's kiss of peace is no more trustworthy than Judas' kiss given to Christ. All those standing between Richard and the throne are to be eliminated. Clearly, the pious longings for peace expressed by King Edward IV are to be cruelly violated.

HENRY VI,
PART THREE

MAYOR OF COVENTRY
A SON *that has killed his father*
A FATHER *that has killed his son*
MESSENGERS
POSTS

KING LEWIS *of France*
LADY BONA, *his sister-in-law*
LORD BOURBON, *French Admiral*

*English and French Soldiers, Attendants, Aldermen, a Nurse to
Prince Edward*

SCENE: *England and France*]

1.1   *Alarum. Enter [Richard] Plantagenet, [Duke*
of York,] Edward, Richard, Norfolk, Montague,
Warwick, [with drum] and soldiers, [wearing
white roses in their hats].

WARWICK
  I wonder how the King escaped our hands.
YORK
  While we pursued the horsemen of the north,
  He slyly stole away and left his men;
  Whereat the great lord of Northumberland,
  Whose warlike ears could never brook retreat,   5
  Cheered up the drooping army, and himself,
  Lord Clifford, and Lord Stafford, all abreast,
  Charged our main battle's front and, breaking in,   8
  Were by the swords of common soldiers slain.   9
EDWARD
  Lord Stafford's father, Duke of Buckingham,
  Is either slain or wounded dangerous;   11
  I cleft his beaver with a downright blow.   12
  That this is true, Father, behold his blood.
                    [*He shows his bloody sword.*]
MONTAGUE [*To York*]
  And, brother, here's the Earl of Wiltshire's blood,   14
  Whom I encountered as the battles joined.   15
                    [*He shows his sword.*]
RICHARD [*Showing the Duke of Somerset's head*]
  Speak thou for me and tell them what I did.

1.1. Location: London. The Parliament House (see ll. 35–39, 71, etc.),
but also referred to as King Henry VI's palace; see l. 25. The throne
is onstage, seemingly on a raised platform.
s.d. Alarum trumpet call to arms. (York and his followers, in hot pursuit
of King Henry, have just arrived from St. Albans.) **drum** drummer.
white roses (The badge of the house of York.) **5 brook** endure. **retreat**
the call sounding withdrawal from the attack **8 battle's** army's
9 Were . . . slain (In *2 Henry VI*, 5.2, it is York who kills old Clifford.)
11 dangerous dangerously **12 beaver** face guard of a helmet, i.e., here
the helmet itself **14 brother** (Montague was actually brother to
Warwick, but his father, Salisbury of *2 Henry VI*, was brother-in-law of
York.) **15 battles joined** battalions joined in combat

YORK
  Richard hath best deserved of all my sons.
  But is Your Grace dead, my lord of Somerset?   18

NORFOLK
  Such hap have all the line of John of Gaunt!   19

RICHARD
  Thus do I hope to shake King Henry's head.

WARWICK
  And so do I. Victorious prince of York,
  Before I see thee seated in that throne   22
  Which now the house of Lancaster usurps,
  I vow by heaven these eyes shall never close.
  This is the palace of the fearful King,   25
  And this the regal seat. Possess it, York,
  For this is thine and not King Henry's heirs'.

YORK
  Assist me, then, sweet Warwick, and I will,
  For hither we have broken in by force.

NORFOLK
  We'll all assist you. He that flies shall die.

YORK
  Thanks, gentle Norfolk. Stay by me, my lords;
  And soldiers, stay and lodge by me this night.   32
                          They go up [to the chair of state].

WARWICK
  And when the King comes, offer him no violence,
  Unless he seek to thrust you out perforce.   34

YORK
  The Queen this day here holds her Parliament,
  But little thinks we shall be of her council.   36
  By words or blows here let us win our right.

---

18 But . . . Somerset i.e., are you really dead, my lord. (Like his son,
York contemptuously addresses his slain enemy.) **19 Such . . . Gaunt**
(The descendants of John of Gaunt, to whom Norfolk wishes ill luck,
include King Henry VI as well as Somerset who is already dead.)
22 Before i.e., until **25 fearful** timid **32 s.d. They go up** i.e., Plantagenet, his sons, Norfolk, Montague, and Warwick, all seemingly go up
onto the dais or raised platform supporting the throne. (The soldiers
may withdraw at this point; they must reenter later at l. 169.) **34 perforce** by force **36 of her council** (1) taking part in the Privy Council
meeting (2) serving as confidential advisers

RICHARD
  Armed as we are, let's stay within this house.

WARWICK
  "The Bloody Parliament" shall this be called,
  Unless Plantagenet, Duke of York, be king   40
  And bashful Henry deposed, whose cowardice
  Hath made us bywords to our enemies.   42

YORK
  Then leave me not, my lords. Be resolute.
  I mean to take possession of my right.

WARWICK
  Neither the King, nor he that loves him best,
  The proudest he that holds up Lancaster,   46
  Dares stir a wing if Warwick shake his bells.   47
  I'll plant Plantagenet, root him up who dares.
  Resolve thee, Richard; claim the English crown.   49
              [*York seats himself in the throne.*]

  Flourish. Enter King Henry, Clifford,
  Northumberland, Westmorland, Exeter,
  and the rest. [*All wear red roses.*]

KING HENRY
  My lords, look where the sturdy rebel sits,
  Even in the chair of state! Belike he means,   51
  Backed by the power of Warwick, that false peer,
  To aspire unto the crown and reign as king.
  Earl of Northumberland, he slew thy father,
  And thine, Lord Clifford, and you both have vowed
      revenge
  On him, his sons, his favorites, and his friends.

NORTHUMBERLAND
  If I be not, heavens be revenged on me!   57

CLIFFORD
  The hope thereof makes Clifford mourn in steel.   58

---

40 be become   **42 bywords** i.e., objects of scorn.   **our enemies** i.e., the
French   **46 he . . . up** person that supports   **47 shake his bells** (Bells
were sometimes fastened to the legs of a falcon to incite it to greater
ferocity.)   **49 Resolve thee** be resolute   **s.d. Flourish** trumpet fanfare.
red roses (The badge of the house of Lancaster.)   **51 chair of state**
throne.   **Belike** evidently   **57 be not** i.e., be not avenged   **58 in steel**
i.e., in armor, not in mourning attire

WESTMORLAND
    What, shall we suffer this? Let's pluck him down.
    My heart for anger burns. I cannot brook it.
KING HENRY
    Be patient, gentle Earl of Westmorland.
CLIFFORD
    Patience is for poltroons, such as he.   62
    He durst not sit there, had your father lived.
    My gracious lord, here in the Parliament
    Let us assail the family of York.
NORTHUMBERLAND
    Well hast thou spoken, cousin. Be it so.   66
KING HENRY
    Ah, know you not the city favors them,   67
    And they have troops of soldiers at their beck?
EXETER
    But when the Duke is slain, they'll quickly fly.
KING HENRY
    Far be the thought of this from Henry's heart,
    To make a shambles of the Parliament House!   71
    Cousin of Exeter, frowns, words, and threats
    Shall be the war that Henry means to use.—
    Thou factious Duke of York, descend my throne
    And kneel for grace and mercy at my feet!
    I am thy sovereign.
YORK   I am thine.
EXETER
    For shame, come down. He made thee Duke of York.   77
YORK
    It was my inheritance, as the earldom was.   78
EXETER
    Thy father was a traitor to the crown.   79

---

62 poltroons arrant cowards. **he** i.e., York, who must not be impatient
for the throne, in Clifford's view **66 cousin** kinsman (also in l. 72)
67 the city i.e., London **71 shambles** slaughterhouse **77–78 He . . .
was** (Cf. *1 Henry VI*, 3.1.161–174, where the King restored to Richard
the whole inheritance of the house of York, which included the earldom
of March.) **79 Thy . . . crown** (On the execution of Richard, Earl of
Cambridge, for treason by Henry V, see *Henry V*, 2.2, and *1 Henry VI*,
2.4.90–94, 2.5.84–91.)

WARWICK
  Exeter, thou art a traitor to the crown
  In following this usurping Henry.
CLIFFORD
  Whom should he follow but his natural king?
WARWICK
  True, Clifford. That's Richard, Duke of York.
KING HENRY [*To York*]
  And shall I stand, and thou sit in my throne?
YORK
  It must and shall be so. Content thyself.
WARWICK [*To King Henry*]
  Be Duke of Lancaster. Let him be King.
WESTMORLAND
  He is both King and Duke of Lancaster,
  And that the lord of Westmorland shall maintain.
WARWICK
  And Warwick shall disprove it. You forget
  That we are those which chased you from the field
  And slew your fathers, and with colors spread   91
  Marched through the city to the palace gates.
NORTHUMBERLAND
  Yes, Warwick, I remember it to my grief;
  And, by his soul, thou and thy house shall rue it.   94
WESTMORLAND
  Plantagenet, of thee and these thy sons,
  Thy kinsmen and thy friends, I'll have more lives
  Than drops of blood were in my father's veins.   97
CLIFFORD
  Urge it no more, lest that, instead of words,
  I send thee, Warwick, such a messenger
  As shall revenge his death before I stir.   100

---

91 colors battle flags   **94 his** i.e., the second Earl of Northumberland's, who fell at St. Albans on the Lancastrian side. (This event is not shown in *2 Henry VI*.) The speaker is the third earl.   **97 my father's** (Three noble fathers died on the Lancastrian side at St. Albans, according to Hall: Northumberland, old Clifford, and Somerset. Westmorland's father was not a casualty in that battle, but Shakespeare may be replacing Somerset here to keep the symmetry of three.)   **100 his** i.e., old Clifford's; see previous note

WARWICK
    Poor Clifford, how I scorn his worthless threats!
YORK
    Will you we show our title to the crown?   102
    If not, our swords shall plead it in the field.
KING HENRY
    What title hast thou, traitor, to the crown?
    Thy father was, as thou art, Duke of York,   105
    Thy grandfather, Roger Mortimer, Earl of March.
    I am the son of Henry the Fifth,
    Who made the Dauphin and the French to stoop
    And seized upon their towns and provinces.
WARWICK
    Talk not of France, sith thou hast lost it all.   110
KING HENRY
    The Lord Protector lost it, and not I.   111
    When I was crowned I was but nine months old.
RICHARD
    You are old enough now, and yet, methinks, you lose.
    Father, tear the crown from the usurper's head.
EDWARD
    Sweet father, do so. Set it on your head.
MONTAGUE [*To York*]
    Good brother, as thou lov'st and honorest arms,
    Let's fight it out and not stand caviling thus.
RICHARD
    Sound drums and trumpets, and the King will fly.
YORK   Sons, peace!
NORTHUMBERLAND
    Peace, thou! And give King Henry leave to speak.
WARWICK
    Plantagenet shall speak first. Hear him, lords,
    And be you silent and attentive too,
    For he that interrupts him shall not live.
KING HENRY
    Think'st thou that I will leave my kingly throne,

---

102 Will you do you desire   **105 Thy . . . York** (Shakespeare's historical
inaccuracy; Richard's father was never Duke of York. That title be-
longed to his oldest brother, Edward, who died at Agincourt; it was
given by Henry VI to Richard.)   **110 sith** since   **111 Lord Protector** i.e.,
Humphrey, Duke of Gloucester

Wherein my grandsire and my father sat?
No! First shall war unpeople this my realm;
Ay, and their colors, often borne in France,
And now in England to our heart's great sorrow,
Shall be my winding-sheet. Why faint you, lords?   129
My title's good, and better far than his.

WARWICK
Prove it, Henry, and thou shalt be king.

KING HENRY
Henry the Fourth by conquest got the crown.

YORK
'Twas by rebellion against his king.

KING HENRY [*Aside*]
I know not what to say; my title's weak.—
Tell me, may not a king adopt an heir?

YORK   What then?

KING HENRY
An if he may, then am I lawful king;   137
For Richard, in the view of many lords,
Resigned the crown to Henry the Fourth,
Whose heir my father was, and I am his.

YORK
He rose against him, being his sovereign,   141
And made him to resign his crown perforce.

WARWICK
Suppose, my lords, he did it unconstrained,
Think you 'twere prejudicial to his crown?   144

EXETER
No, for he could not so resign his crown
But that the next heir should succeed and reign.

KING HENRY
Art thou against us, Duke of Exeter?

EXETER
His is the right, and therefore pardon me.   148

YORK
Why whisper you, my lords, and answer not?

---

129 winding-sheet sheet in which a corpse was wrapped.   **faint** lose
heart   **137 An if** if   **141 him, being** i.e., Richard, who was
144 'twere . . . crown it would invalidate his, Richard's, entitlement to
the throne   **148 His** i.e., York's

EXETER
  My conscience tells me he is lawful king.
KING HENRY [*Aside*]
  All will revolt from me and turn to him.
NORTHUMBERLAND
  Plantagenet, for all the claim thou lay'st,
  Think not that Henry shall be so deposed.
WARWICK
  Deposed he shall be, in despite of all.   154
NORTHUMBERLAND
  Thou art deceived. 'Tis not thy southern power   155
  Of Essex, Norfolk, Suffolk, nor of Kent,
  Which makes thee thus presumptuous and proud,
  Can set the Duke up in despite of me.
CLIFFORD
  King Henry, be thy title right or wrong,
  Lord Clifford vows to fight in thy defense.
  May that ground gape and swallow me alive
  Where I shall kneel to him that slew my father!
KING HENRY
  O Clifford, how thy words revive my heart!
YORK
  Henry of Lancaster, resign thy crown.
  What mutter you, or what conspire you, lords?
WARWICK
  Do right unto this princely Duke of York,   166
  Or I will fill the house with armèd men,
  And over the chair of state, where now he sits,
  Write up his title with usurping blood.   169
                          He stamps with his foot, and the
                               soldiers show themselves.
KING HENRY
  My lord of Warwick, hear but one word:
  Let me for this my lifetime reign as king.
YORK
  Confirm the crown to me and to mine heirs,
  And thou shalt reign in quiet while thou liv'st.   173

---

154 despite spite (also in l. 158)   **155 deceived** mistaken   **166 Do right
unto** deal justly with   **169 usurping blood** i.e., the blood of usurping
Henry VI   **173 while** as long as

KING HENRY
I am content. Richard Plantagenet,
Enjoy the kingdom after my decease.

CLIFFORD
What wrong is this unto the Prince your son!

WARWICK
What good is this to England and himself!   177

WESTMORLAND
Base, fearful, and despairing Henry!

CLIFFORD
How hast thou injured both thyself and us!

WESTMORLAND
I cannot stay to hear these articles.   180

NORTHUMBERLAND   Nor I.

CLIFFORD
Come, cousin, let us tell the Queen these news.

WESTMORLAND
Farewell, fainthearted and degenerate King,
In whose cold blood no spark of honor bides.   184
                         [Exit with his men.]

NORTHUMBERLAND
Be thou a prey unto the house of York
And die in bonds for this unmanly deed!   186
                         [Exit with his men.]

CLIFFORD
In dreadful war mayst thou be overcome,
Or live in peace abandoned and despised!
                         [Exit with his men.]

WARWICK
Turn this way, Henry, and regard them not.

EXETER
They seek revenge and therefore will not yield.   190

KING HENRY
Ah, Exeter!

WARWICK   Why should you sigh, my lord?

KING HENRY
Not for myself, Lord Warwick, but my son,

---

177 What . . . to i.e., what a good thing for. (Warwick welcomes Henry's decision.)   **180 articles** terms of agreement   **184 cold** listless, cowardly   **186 bonds** fetters   **190 revenge** i.e., for their fathers' deaths

Whom I unnaturally shall disinherit.
But be it as it may: [*To York*] I here entail   194
The crown to thee and to thine heirs forever,
Conditionally, that here thou take an oath
To cease this civil war, and whilst I live
To honor me as thy king and sovereign,
And neither by treason nor hostility
To seek to put me down and reign thyself.

YORK
This oath I willingly take and will perform.

WARWICK
Long live King Henry! Plantagenet, embrace him.
          [*York descends and embraces Henry.*]

KING HENRY
And long live thou and these thy forward sons!   203

YORK
Now York and Lancaster are reconciled.

EXETER
Accurst be he that seeks to make them foes!   205
          Sennet. Here they come down.

YORK
Farewell, my gracious lord. I'll to my castle.   206
          [*Exeunt York and his sons with their men.*]

WARWICK
And I'll keep London with my soldiers.
          [*Exit Warwick with his men.*]

NORFOLK
And I to Norfolk with my followers.
          [*Exit Norfolk with his men.*]

MONTAGUE
And I unto the sea, from whence I came.   209
          [*Exit Montague with his men.*]

---

194 entail bequeath irrevocably   **203 forward** precocious, zealous,
promising   **205 s.d. Sennet** trumpet notes signaling a procession.   **Here
they come down** (York and his sons, together with Norfolk, Montague,
and Warwick, have evidently been on the dais around the throne since
l. 32. Once York has descended and embraced Henry, formalizing their
agreement, the rest of the York faction can descend and prepare to
depart.)   **206 castle** i.e., Sandal Castle in Yorkshire. (See next scene.)
209 unto the sea (Actually, Montague appears in scene 2 at Sandal
Castle, not at the sea; possibly he is confused here with his uncle,
William Neville, Baron Falconbridge. See l. 239 below.)

KING HENRY
  And I, with grief and sorrow, to the court.

    Enter the Queen [Margaret and Edward,
    Prince of Wales].

EXETER
  Here comes the Queen, whose looks bewray her anger. 211
  I'll steal away.
KING HENRY   Exeter, so will I.   *[They start to leave.]*
QUEEN MARGARET
  Nay, go not from me. I will follow thee.
KING HENRY
  Be patient, gentle Queen, and I will stay.
QUEEN MARGARET
  Who can be patient in such extremes?
  Ah, wretched man! Would I had died a maid
  And never seen thee, never borne thee son,
  Seeing thou hast proved so unnatural a father!   218
  Hath he deserved to lose his birthright thus?
  Hadst thou but loved him half so well as I,
  Or felt that pain which I did for him once,
  Or nourished him as I did with my blood,
  Thou wouldst have left thy dearest heart-blood there,
  Rather than have made that savage duke thine heir
  And disinherited thine only son.
PRINCE
  Father, you cannot disinherit me.
  If you be king, why should not I succeed?
KING HENRY
  Pardon me, Margaret. Pardon me, sweet son.
  The Earl of Warwick and the Duke enforced me.
QUEEN MARGARET
  Enforced thee? Art thou king, and wilt be forced?
  I shame to hear thee speak. Ah, timorous wretch!
  Thou hast undone thyself, thy son, and me,
  And given unto the house of York such head   233
  As thou shalt reign but by their sufferance.   234
  To entail him and his heirs unto the crown,
  What is it but to make thy sepulcher

211 bewray betray, reveal   **218 unnatural** i.e., showing no feeling for a
son   **233 head** i.e., free rein   **234 As** that

And creep into it far before thy time?
Warwick is Chancellor and the lord of Calais;
Stern Falconbridge commands the narrow seas,   239
The Duke is made Protector of the realm,   240
And yet shalt thou be safe? Such safety finds
The trembling lamb environèd with wolves.   242
Had I been there, which am a silly woman,   243
The soldiers should have tossed me on their pikes   244
Before I would have granted to that act.   245
But thou preferr'st thy life before thine honor;
And seeing thou dost, I here divorce myself
Both from thy table, Henry, and thy bed,
Until that act of Parliament be repealed
Whereby my son is disinherited.
The northern lords that have forsworn thy colors   251
Will follow mine, if once they see them spread;
And spread they shall be, to thy foul disgrace
And utter ruin of the house of York.
Thus do I leave thee. Come, son, let's away.
Our army is ready. Come, we'll after them.

KING HENRY
Stay, gentle Margaret, and hear me speak.

QUEEN MARGARET
Thou hast spoke too much already. Get thee gone.

KING HENRY
Gentle son Edward, thou wilt stay with me?

QUEEN MARGARET
Ay, to be murdered by his enemies!

PRINCE
When I return with victory from the field,
I'll see Your Grace. Till then I'll follow her.

QUEEN MARGARET
Come, son, away. We may not linger thus.
        [*Exeunt Queen Margaret and the Prince.*]

KING HENRY
Poor Queen! How love to me and to her son

---

239 Falconbridge i.e., William Neville or his son Thomas. (See l. 209
above, and note.)   **narrow seas** i.e., English Channel   **240 Duke** i.e.,
Duke of York   **242 environèd** surrounded   **243 silly** helpless
244 tossed impaled.   **pikes** long steel-pointed or axlike weapons
245 granted yielded   **251 The northern lords** i.e., Northumberland,
Westmorland, and Clifford (as also in the *three lords* of l. 270)

Hath made her break out into terms of rage!   265
Revenged may she be on that hateful duke,
Whose haughty spirit, wingèd with desire,
Will cost my crown, and like an empty eagle   268
Tire on the flesh of me and of my son!   269
The loss of those three lords torments my heart.
I'll write unto them and entreat them fair.   271
Come, cousin, you shall be the messenger.

EXETER
And I, I hope, shall reconcile them all.

Flourish. Exeunt.

❖

1.2   *Enter Richard, Edward, and Montague.*

RICHARD
Brother, though I be youngest, give me leave.   1

EDWARD
No, I can better play the orator.

MONTAGUE
But I have reasons strong and forcible.

Enter the Duke of York.

YORK
Why, how now, sons and brother, at a strife?   4
What is your quarrel? How began it first?

EDWARD
No quarrel, but a slight contention.

YORK   About what?

RICHARD
About that which concerns Your Grace and us:
The crown of England, Father, which is yours.

YORK
Mine, boy? Not till King Henry be dead.

---

265 terms words **268 cost** i.e., deprive me of (with a pun on *coast*, attack, fly from the straight course, a metaphor that generates the image of the eagle). **empty** hungry **269 Tire** feed ravenously **271 fair** civilly, kindly

1.2. Location: Sandal Castle (the Duke of York's castle) in Yorkshire.
1 give me leave permit me (to speak first) **4 brother** (See 1.1.14, note.)

RICHARD
Your right depends not on his life or death.
EDWARD
Now you are heir; therefore enjoy it now.
By giving the house of Lancaster leave to breathe,   13
It will outrun you, Father, in the end.
YORK
I took an oath that he should quietly reign.
EDWARD
But for a kingdom any oath may be broken.
I would break a thousand oaths to reign one year.
RICHARD
No. God forbid Your Grace should be forsworn.
YORK
I shall be, if I claim by open war.
RICHARD
I'll prove the contrary, if you'll hear me speak.
YORK
Thou canst not, son. It is impossible.
RICHARD
An oath is of no moment, being not took   22
Before a true and lawful magistrate
That hath authority over him that swears.
Henry had none, but did usurp the place.
Then, seeing 'twas he that made you to depose,   26
Your oath, my lord, is vain and frivolous.
Therefore, to arms! And, Father, do but think
How sweet a thing it is to wear a crown,
Within whose circuit is Elysium   30
And all that poets feign of bliss and joy.   31
Why do we linger thus? I cannot rest
Until the white rose that I wear be dyed
Even in the lukewarm blood of Henry's heart.
YORK
Richard, enough. I will be king, or die.
[*To Montague.*] Brother, thou shalt to London presently   36
And whet on Warwick to this enterprise.

---

13 to breathe i.e., to enjoy a respite   **22 moment** significance
26 depose take an oath   **30 Elysium** the classical abode after life of
those beloved of the gods   **31 feign** portray imaginatively   **36 presently**
immediately

Thou, Richard, shalt to the Duke of Norfolk
And tell him privily of our intent.   39
You, Edward, shall unto my Lord Cobham,
With whom the Kentishmen will willingly rise.
In them I trust, for they are soldiers,
Witty, courteous, liberal, full of spirit.   43
While you are thus employed, what resteth more   44
But that I seek occasion how to rise,
And yet the King not privy to my drift,   46
Nor any of the house of Lancaster?

    Enter a Messenger.

But stay, what news? Why com'st thou in such post?   48
MESSENGER
  The Queen, with all the northern earls and lords,
  Intend here to besiege you in your castle.
  She is hard by with twenty thousand men,
  And therefore fortify your hold, my lord.   52
YORK
  Ay, with my sword. What, think'st thou that we
    fear them?
  Edward and Richard, you shall stay with me;
  My brother Montague shall post to London.
  Let noble Warwick, Cobham, and the rest,
  Whom we have left protectors of the King,
  With powerful policy strengthen themselves   58
  And trust not simple Henry nor his oaths.
MONTAGUE
  Brother, I go. I'll win them, fear it not.
  And thus most humbly I do take my leave.
                        Exit Montague.

    Enter [Sir John] Mortimer and [Sir Hugh,]
    his brother.

YORK
  Sir John and Sir Hugh Mortimer, mine uncles,

---

39 privily secretly   **43 Witty** intelligent.   **liberal** large-minded   **44 what resteth more** what else remains   **46 privy to** aware of   **48 post** haste   **52 hold** stronghold, castle   **58 policy** stratagem, cunning

You are come to Sandal in a happy hour.   63
The army of the Queen mean to besiege us.

SIR JOHN
She shall not need. We'll meet her in the field.

YORK   What, with five thousand men?

RICHARD
Ay, with five hundred, Father, for a need.   67
A woman's general. What should we fear?

A march afar off.

EDWARD
I hear their drums. Let's set our men in order,
And issue forth and bid them battle straight.   70

YORK
Five men to twenty! Though the odds be great,
I doubt not, uncle, of our victory.
Many a battle have I won in France
Whenas the enemy hath been ten to one.   74
Why should I not now have the like success?   75

Alarum. Exeunt.

1.3   [*Alarums.*] *Enter Rutland and his Tutor.*

RUTLAND
Ah, whither shall I fly to scape their hands?
Ah, tutor, look where bloody Clifford comes!

Enter Clifford [and soldiers].

CLIFFORD
Chaplain, away! Thy priesthood saves thy life.
As for the brat of this accursèd duke,   4
Whose father slew my father, he shall die.

TUTOR
And I, my lord, will bear him company.

---

63 **in a happy hour** opportunely   67 **for a need** if necessary
70 **straight** immediately   74 **Whenas** when   75 **the like** a similar

1.3. Location: Field of battle between Sandal Castle and Wakefield. The
action follows continuously from the previous scene.
s.d. Alarums calls to arms (signaling by sound effects a battle fought
offstage)   **4 duke** i.e., Duke of York, who killed old Clifford in
2 Henry VI, 5.2

CLIFFORD Soldiers, away with him!

TUTOR
 Ah, Clifford, murder not this innocent child,
 Lest thou be hated both of God and man!
       Exit [*dragged off by soldiers*].

CLIFFORD
 How now, is he dead already? Or is it fear
 That makes him close his eyes? I'll open them.

RUTLAND
 So looks the pent-up lion o'er the wretch   12
 That trembles under his devouring paws;
 And so he walks, insulting o'er his prey,   14
 And so he comes, to rend his limbs asunder.
 Ah, gentle Clifford, kill me with thy sword   16
 And not with such a cruel threatening look!
 Sweet Clifford, hear me speak before I die!
 I am too mean a subject for thy wrath.   19
 Be thou revenged on men, and let me live.

CLIFFORD
 In vain thou speak'st, poor boy. My father's blood
 Hath stopped the passage where thy words should enter.

RUTLAND
 Then let my father's blood open it again.
 He is a man, and, Clifford, cope with him.   24

CLIFFORD
 Had I thy brethren here, their lives and thine
 Were not revenge sufficient for me;
 No, if I digged up thy forefathers' graves
 And hung their rotten coffins up in chains,
 It could not slake mine ire nor ease my heart. 29
 The sight of any of the house of York
 Is as a fury to torment my soul;
 And till I root out their accursèd line
 And leave not one alive, I live in hell.
 Therefore—   [*Lifting his sword.*]

---

12 pent-up caged, hence fierce and hungry **14 insulting** gloating,
exulting **16 gentle** noble (with ironic suggestion of "free from harsh-
ness") **19 mean** lowly. (Rutland appeals to the popular notion that
because the lion was a royal beast it would show compassion to women
and children. See 2.2.11–12.) **24 cope with** engage in combat with
29 slake lessen

RUTLAND
O, let me pray before I take my death!
To thee I pray. Sweet Clifford, pity me!
CLIFFORD
Such pity as my rapier's point affords.
RUTLAND
I never did thee harm. Why wilt thou slay me?
CLIFFORD
Thy father hath.
RUTLAND   But 'twas ere I was born.
Thou hast one son. For his sake pity me,
Lest in revenge thereof, sith God is just,   41
He be as miserably slain as I.
Ah, let me live in prison all my days,
And when I give occasion of offense,
Then let me die, for now thou hast no cause.
CLIFFORD   No cause?
Thy father slew my father. Therefore, die.

                              [*He stabs him.*]

RUTLAND
Di faciant laudis summa sit ista tuae!   [*He dies.*] 48
CLIFFORD
Plantagenet, I come, Plantagenet!
And this thy son's blood cleaving to my blade
Shall rust upon my weapon, till thy blood,
Congealed with this, do make me wipe off both.
                              Exit [*with soldiers, bearing
                                   off Rutland's body*].

1.4   *Alarum. Enter Richard, Duke of York.*

YORK
The army of the Queen hath got the field.   1
My uncles both are slain in rescuing me,   2
And all my followers to the eager foe   3
Turn back and fly, like ships before the wind   4

---

41 sith since   **48 Di ... tuae** The gods grant that this may be the height
of your glory. (Ovid, *Heroides*, 2.66.)

1.4. Location: The battle of Wakefield continues.
1 got the field won the battle   **2 uncles** i.e., Sir John and Sir Hugh
Mortimer   **3 eager** fierce, zealous   **4 Turn back** turn their backs

Or lambs pursued by hunger-starvèd wolves.
My sons—God knows what hath bechancèd them;
But this I know, they have demeaned themselves   7
Like men born to renown by life or death.
Three times did Richard make a lane to me,
And thrice cried "Courage, Father, fight it out!"
And full as oft came Edward to my side,
With purple falchion painted to the hilt   12
In blood of those that had encountered him.
And when the hardiest warriors did retire,
Richard cried "Charge, and give no foot of ground!"
And cried "A crown, or else a glorious tomb!   16
A scepter, or an earthly sepulcher!"
With this, we charged again, but out, alas!   18
We budged again, as I have seen a swan   19
With bootless labor swim against the tide   20
And spend her strength with overmatching waves.   21
                              A short alarum within.
Ah, hark! The fatal followers do pursue,   22
And I am faint and cannot fly their fury;
And, were I strong, I would not shun their fury.
The sands are numbered that makes up my life.   25
Here must I stay, and here my life must end.

          *Enter the Queen [Margaret], Clifford,
          Northumberland, the young Prince,
          and soldiers.*

Come, bloody Clifford, rough Northumberland,
I dare your quenchless fury to more rage.   28
I am your butt, and I abide your shot.   29
NORTHUMBERLAND
Yield to our mercy, proud Plantagenet.   30
CLIFFORD
Ay, to such mercy as his ruthless arm,
With downright payment, showed unto my father.

---

7 demeaned conducted   **12 purple** purple with blood.   **falchion** curved
sword   **16 And cried** (Some text may be missing here; the parallelism of
ll. 9–13 suggests that Edward is quoted as speaking after Richard.)
18 out (An expression of reproach.)   **19 budged** gave way   **20 bootless**
fruitless   **21 with** against   **22 followers** pursuing troops   **25 sands** (of
the hourglass)   **28 dare** defy.   **more** even more   **29 butt** target
30 Yield . . . mercy put yourself at our mercy

Now Phaëthon hath tumbled from his car   33
And made an evening at the noontide prick.   34

YORK
My ashes, as the phoenix, may bring forth   35
A bird that will revenge upon you all;
And in that hope I throw mine eyes to heaven,
Scorning whate'er you can afflict me with.
Why come you not? What? Multitudes, and fear?

CLIFFORD
So cowards fight when they can fly no further;
So doves do peck the falcon's piercing talons;
So desperate thieves, all hopeless of their lives,
Breathe out invectives 'gainst the officers.

YORK
O Clifford, but bethink thee once again,   44
And in thy thought o'errun my former time;   45
And, if thou canst for blushing, view this face,   46
And bite thy tongue, that slanders him with cowardice
Whose frown hath made thee faint and fly ere this!

CLIFFORD
I will not bandy with thee word for word,   49
But buckler with thee blows, twice two for one.   50
                  [*He threatens with his sword.*]

QUEEN MARGARET
Hold, valiant Clifford! For a thousand causes
I would prolong awhile the traitor's life.—
Wrath makes him deaf. Speak thou, Northumberland.   53

NORTHUMBERLAND
Hold, Clifford! Do not honor him so much
To prick thy finger, though to wound his heart.
What valor were it, when a cur doth grin,   56
For one to thrust his hand between his teeth,
When he might spurn him with his foot away?   58

---

33 Phaëthon son of the sun god, who begged his father to allow him to
drive the chariot of the sun; he drove it so near the earth that Zeus
destroyed him with a thunderbolt   **34 noontide prick** exact point of
noon on a sundial   **35 phoenix** fabulous bird that was consumed
through spontaneous combustion and was reborn from its own ashes
44 but bethink thee only call to mind   **45 o'errun** review   **46 for**
despite   **49 bandy** exchange   **50 buckler** join in close combat, grapple
53 him i.e., Clifford   **56 grin** show its teeth   **58 spurn** kick

It is war's prize to take all vantages, 59
And ten to one is no impeach of valor. 60
[*They capture York, who struggles.*]

CLIFFORD
Ay, ay, so strives the woodcock with the gin. 61

NORTHUMBERLAND
So doth the coney struggle in the net. 62

YORK
So triumph thieves upon their conquered booty;
So true men yield, with robbers so o'ermatched. 64

NORTHUMBERLAND [*To the Queen*]
What would Your Grace have done unto him now?

QUEEN MARGARET
Brave warriors, Clifford and Northumberland,
Come, make him stand upon this molehill here,
That raught at mountains with outstretchèd arms 68
Yet parted but the shadow with his hand. 69
What, was it you that would be England's king?
Was 't you that reveled in our Parliament 71
And made a preachment of your high descent?
Where are your mess of sons to back you now, 73
The wanton Edward and the lusty George?
And where's that valiant crookback prodigy, 75
Dicky, your boy, that with his grumbling voice
Was wont to cheer his dad in mutinies?
Or, with the rest, where is your darling Rutland?
Look, York, I stained this napkin with the blood 79
That valiant Clifford, with his rapier's point,
Made issue from the bosom of the boy;
And if thine eyes can water for his death,
I give thee this to dry thy cheeks withal. 83
[*She gives him the bloodstained cloth.*]
Alas, poor York, but that I hate thee deadly, 84
I should lament thy miserable state.
I prithee, grieve, to make me merry, York.

---

59 prize reward, benefit   **60 impeach** calling in question   **61 woodcock**
(A proverbially stupid bird.) **gin** snare, trap   **62 coney** rabbit   **64 true**
honest   **68 That raught** he that reached   **69 parted but** only divided.
(The prize York reached for turned out to be illusory.)   **71 reveled** rioted
73 mess group of four   **75 prodigy** monster   **79 napkin** handkerchief
83 withal with   **84 but** were it not

What, hath thy fiery heart so parched thine entrails
That not a tear can fall for Rutland's death?
Why art thou patient, man? Thou shouldst be mad;
And I, to make thee mad, do mock thee thus.
Stamp, rave, and fret, that I may sing and dance.
Thou wouldst be fee'd, I see, to make me sport.   92
York cannot speak, unless he wear a crown.—
A crown for York! And, lords, bow low to him.
Hold you his hands, whilst I do set it on.
          [*She puts a paper crown on his head.*]
Ay, marry, sir, now looks he like a king!   96
Ay, this is he that took King Henry's chair,   97
And this is he was his adopted heir.
But how is it that great Plantagenet
Is crowned so soon, and broke his solemn oath?
As I bethink me, you should not be king
Till our King Henry had shook hands with death.
And will you pale your head in Henry's glory,   103
And rob his temples of the diadem,
Now, in his life, against your holy oath?   105
O, 'tis a fault too-too unpardonable!
Off with the crown, and, with the crown, his head!
And whilst we breathe, take time to do him dead.   108

CLIFFORD
That is my office, for my father's sake.

QUEEN MARGARET
Nay, stay. Let's hear the orisons he makes.   110

YORK
She-wolf of France, but worse than wolves of France,
Whose tongue more poisons than the adder's tooth!
How ill-beseeming is it in thy sex
To triumph, like an Amazonian trull,   114
Upon their woes whom fortune captivates!   115
But that thy face is, vizardlike, unchanging,   116
Made impudent with use of evil deeds,

92 **fee'd** paid   96 **marry** i.e., indeed. (Originally an oath, "by the Virgin Mary.")   97 **chair** throne   103 **pale** encircle   105 **life** lifetime   108 **breathe** rest.   **do him dead** kill him   110 **orisons** prayers   114 **triumph** exult.   **Amazonian** from the race of legendary female warriors.   **trull** wench, whore   115 **Upon . . . captivates** upon the woes of those whom fortune takes captive   116 **But that** were it not that.   **vizardlike** masklike

I would essay, proud Queen, to make thee blush.   118
To tell thee whence thou cam'st, of whom derived,
Were shame enough to shame thee, wert thou not
    shameless.
Thy father bears the type of King of Naples,   121
Of both the Sicils and Jerusalem,   122
Yet not so wealthy as an English yeoman.   123
Hath that poor monarch taught thee to insult?
It needs not, nor it boots thee not, proud Queen,   125
Unless the adage must be verified
That beggars mounted run their horse to death.
'Tis beauty that doth oft make women proud;
But, God he knows, thy share thereof is small.
'Tis virtue that doth make them most admired;
The contrary doth make thee wondered at.
'Tis government that makes them seem divine;   132
The want thereof makes thee abominable.   133
Thou art as opposite to every good
As the Antipodes are unto us,   135
Or as the south to the Septentrion.   136
O tiger's heart wrapped in a woman's hide!
How couldst thou drain the lifeblood of the child,
To bid the father wipe his eyes withal,
And yet be seen to bear a woman's face?
Women are soft, mild, pitiful, and flexible;   141
Thou stern, obdurate, flinty, rough, remorseless.
Bidd'st thou me rage? Why, now thou hast thy wish.
Wouldst have me weep? Why, now thou hast thy will.
For raging wind blows up incessant showers,
And, when the rage allays, the rain begins. [*He weeps.*] 146
These tears are my sweet Rutland's obsequies,   147
And every drop cries vengeance for his death
'Gainst thee, fell Clifford, and thee, false Frenchwoman. 149

---

118 essay attempt   **121 type** title   **122 both the Sicils** i.e., Sicily and
Naples (known as the Kingdom of the Two Sicilies)   **123 yeoman** land-
owner below rank of gentleman   **125 needs not** is unnecessary.   **boots**
profits   **132 government** self-government   **133 want** lack   **135 Antipodes** people dwelling on the opposite side of the world   **136 Septentrion** the seven stars, i.e., the Big Dipper, representing the north
141 pitiful capable of pity   **146 allays** abates   **147 obsequies** funeral
observances   **149 fell** cruel

NORTHUMBERLAND
  Beshrew me, but his passions moves me so   150
  That hardly can I check my eyes from tears.   151
YORK
  That face of his the hungry cannibals
  Would not have touched, would not have stained with
    blood.
  But you are more inhuman, more inexorable,
  O, ten times more, than tigers of Hyrcania.   155
  See, ruthless Queen, a hapless father's tears!
  This cloth thou dippedst in blood of my sweet boy,
  And I with tears do wash the blood away.
  Keep thou the napkin, and go boast of this;
  And if thou tell'st the heavy story right,   160
  Upon my soul, the hearers will shed tears.
  Yea, even my foes will shed fast-falling tears
  And say, "Alas, it was a piteous deed!"
  There, take the crown, and with the crown my curse;   164
  And in thy need such comfort come to thee
  As now I reap at thy too cruel hand!
  Hardhearted Clifford, take me from the world.
  My soul to heaven, my blood upon your heads!
NORTHUMBERLAND
  Had he been slaughterman to all my kin,
  I should not for my life but weep with him,
  To see how inly sorrow gripes his soul.   171
QUEEN MARGARET
  What, weeping-ripe, my Lord Northumberland?   172
  Think but upon the wrong he did us all,
  And that will quickly dry thy melting tears.
CLIFFORD [*Stabbing him*]
  Here's for my oath. Here's for my father's death.
QUEEN MARGARET [*Stabbing him*]
  And here's to right our gentlehearted king.

---

150 Beshrew curse   **151 check** restrain   **155 Hyrcania** region of the
ancient Persian empire, reputed to abound in wild beasts. (See *Aeneid*,
4.366–367.)   **160 heavy** sorrowful   **164 There . . . crown** (Unless his
hands are restrained, as at l. 95, York probably removes his paper
crown and throws it to them, as with the handkerchief at l. 159.)
171 inly inward.   **gripes** grieves (with suggestion also of *grips*, seizes)
172 weeping-ripe ready to weep

YORK
  Open Thy gate of mercy, gracious God!
  My soul flies through these wounds to seek out Thee.
                                              [*He dies.*]
QUEEN MARGARET
  Off with his head and set it on York gates,
  So York may overlook the town of York.
                          Flourish. Exeunt [*with the body*].

✣

2.1 *A march. Enter Edward, Richard,*
and their power.

EDWARD

I wonder how our princely father scaped,
Or whether he be scaped away or no
From Clifford's and Northumberland's pursuit.
Had he been ta'en, we should have heard the news;
Had he been slain, we should have heard the news;
Or had he scaped, methinks we should have heard
The happy tidings of his good escape.
How fares my brother? Why is he so sad?

RICHARD

I cannot joy until I be resolved   9
Where our right valiant father is become.   10
I saw him in the battle range about
And watched him how he singled Clifford forth.
Methought he bore him in the thickest troop   13
As doth a lion in a herd of neat,   14
Or as a bear encompassed round with dogs,
Who having pinched a few and made them cry,   16
The rest stand all aloof and bark at him.
So fared our father with his enemies;
So fled his enemies my warlike father.   19
Methinks 'tis prize enough to be his son.
See how the morning opes her golden gates
And takes her farewell of the glorious sun!   22
How well resembles it the prime of youth,
Trimmed like a younker prancing to his love!   24

EDWARD

Dazzle mine eyes, or do I see three suns?   25

2.1. Location: Fields near the Welsh border or marches (l. 140), historically identified as near Mortimer's Cross in Herefordshire, several days
after the battle of Wakefield.
s.d. power army   9 resolved informed   10 Where . . . become what is
become of our very valiant father   13 bore him conducted himself
14 neat cattle   16 pinched bit   19 fled his enemies his enemies fled
from   22 farewell (The dawn is pictured as remaining behind while the
sun ascends the sky.)   24 Trimmed dressed up.   younker young man
25 three suns (According to the chronicles, it was because Edward saw
three suns as a favorable omen before the battle of Mortimer's Cross,
in which he triumphed, that he chose the bright sun as his badge.)

RICHARD

Three glorious suns, each one a perfect sun,
Not separated with the racking clouds,   27
But severed in a pale clear-shining sky.
See, see! They join, embrace, and seem to kiss,
As if they vowed some league inviolable.
Now are they but one lamp, one light, one sun.
In this the heaven figures some event.   32

EDWARD

'Tis wondrous strange, the like yet never heard of.
I think it cites us, brother, to the field,   34
That we, the sons of brave Plantagenet,
Each one already blazing by our meeds,   36
Should notwithstanding join our lights together
And overshine the earth as this the world.   38
Whate'er it bodes, henceforward will I bear
Upon my target three fair-shining suns.   40

RICHARD

Nay, bear three daughters. By your leave I speak it,   41
You love the breeder better than the male.   42

Enter one [a Messenger] blowing [a horn].

But what art thou, whose heavy looks foretell   43
Some dreadful story hanging on thy tongue?

MESSENGER

Ah, one that was a woeful looker-on
Whenas the noble Duke of York was slain,   46
Your princely father and my loving lord!

EDWARD

O, speak no more, for I have heard too much.

RICHARD

Say how he died, for I will hear it all.

MESSENGER

Environèd he was with many foes,   50

---

27 with by.   **racking** driving, scudding   **32 figures** prefigures   **34 cites**
incites, impels   **36 meeds** worth, deserts   **38 overshine** (1) shine upon
(2) surpass in shining.   **this** i.e., this phenomenon   **40 target** shield
41 daughters i.e., instead of sons or *suns*   **42 breeder** female. (Richard
jokes about Edward's weakness for women, to be demonstrated in 3.2
and following.)   **s.d. blowing a horn** (Express riders thus announced
themselves.)   **43 heavy** sorrowful   **46 Whenas** when   **50 Environèd**
surrounded

And stood against them, as the hope of Troy   51
Against the Greeks that would have entered Troy.
But Hercules himself must yield to odds;
And many strokes, though with a little ax,
Hews down and fells the hardest-timbered oak.
By many hands your father was subdued,
But only slaughtered by the ireful arm   57
Of unrelenting Clifford and the Queen,
Who crowned the gracious Duke in high despite,
Laughed in his face; and when with grief he wept,
The ruthless Queen gave him to dry his cheeks
A napkin steepèd in the harmless blood
Of sweet young Rutland, by rough Clifford slain.
And after many scorns, many foul taunts,
They took his head, and on the gates of York
They set the same; and there it doth remain,
The saddest spectacle that e'er I viewed.

EDWARD
Sweet Duke of York, our prop to lean upon,
Now thou art gone, we have no staff, no stay.   69
O Clifford, boisterous Clifford! Thou hast slain   70
The flower of Europe for his chivalry;
And treacherously hast thou vanquished him,
For hand to hand he would have vanquished thee.
Now my soul's palace is become a prison.   74
Ah, would she break from hence, that this my body
Might in the ground be closèd up in rest!
For never henceforth shall I joy again.
Never, O, never, shall I see more joy!   78

RICHARD
I cannot weep, for all my body's moisture
Scarce serves to quench my furnace-burning heart;
Nor can my tongue unload my heart's great burden,
For selfsame wind that I should speak withal   82
Is kindling coals that fires all my breast,
And burns me up with flames that tears would quench.
To weep is to make less the depth of grief.

51 **the hope of Troy** i.e., Hector 57 **ireful** angry 69 **stay** support
70 **boisterous** savage 74 **soul's palace** i.e., body 78 **see more joy** see
joy any more 82 **For . . . withal** for that very breath that I should use
in speaking

Tears, then, for babes; blows and revenge for me!
Richard, I bear thy name. I'll venge thy death,
Or die renownèd by attempting it.

EDWARD
His name that valiant duke hath left with thee;
His dukedom and his chair with me is left.   90

RICHARD
Nay, if thou be that princely eagle's bird,   91
Show thy descent by gazing 'gainst the sun;   92
For "chair" and "dukedom," "throne" and "kingdom"
      say;
Either that is thine, or else thou wert not his.   94

> *March. Enter Warwick, Marquess Montague,
> and their army.*

WARWICK
How now, fair lords? What fare? What news abroad?   95

RICHARD
Great lord of Warwick, if we should recount
Our baleful news, and at each word's deliverance
Stab poniards in our flesh till all were told,   98
The words would add more anguish than the wounds.
O valiant lord, the Duke of York is slain!

EDWARD
O Warwick, Warwick! That Plantagenet,
Which held thee dearly as his soul's redemption,
Is by the stern Lord Clifford done to death.

WARWICK
Ten days ago I drowned these news in tears;
And now, to add more measure to your woes,   105
I come to tell you things sith then befallen.   106
After the bloody fray at Wakefield fought,
Where your brave father breathed his latest gasp,   108
Tidings, as swiftly as the posts could run,   109

---

90 his chair i.e., his ducal seat, but also the claim to the throne   **91 bird**
i.e., offspring   **92 gazing . . . sun** (According to Pliny and other writers,
eagles could gaze unblinkingly at the sun and would test their young by
forcing them to do so.)   **94 that** i.e., the throne, symbolized by the sun.
his i.e., Plantagenet's son   **s.d. army** (The octavo text specifies drum,
i.e., drummer, and ensign along with soldiers.)   **95 What fare** how are
things faring   **98 poniards** daggers   **105 measure** quantity   **106 sith**
since   **108 latest** last   **109 posts** messengers

Were brought me of your loss and his depart.   110
I, then in London, keeper of the King,   111
Mustered my soldiers, gathered flocks of friends,
And very well appointed, as I thought,   113
Marched toward Saint Albans to intercept the Queen,
Bearing the King in my behalf along;   115
For by my scouts I was advertisèd   116
That she was coming with a full intent
To dash our late decree in Parliament   118
Touching King Henry's oath and your succession.   119
Short tale to make, we at Saint Albans met,
Our battles joined, and both sides fiercely fought.   121
But whether 'twas the coldness of the King,
Who looked full gently on his warlike queen,
That robbed my soldiers of their heated spleen,   124
Or whether 'twas report of her success,
Or more than common fear of Clifford's rigor,   126
Who thunders to his captives blood and death,
I cannot judge; but, to conclude with truth,
Their weapons like to lightning came and went;
Our soldiers', like the night owl's lazy flight,
Or like an idle thresher with a flail,   131
Fell gently down, as if they struck their friends.
I cheered them up with justice of our cause,
With promise of high pay and great rewards,
But all in vain. They had no heart to fight,
And we in them no hope to win the day,
So that we fled: the King unto the Queen;
Lord George your brother, Norfolk, and myself   138
In haste, posthaste, are come to join with you.
For in the marches here we heard you were,   140
Making another head to fight again.   141

110 depart departure, i.e., death   **111 keeper** jailer   **113 appointed**
equipped   **115 in my behalf** for my advantage   **116 advertisèd** informed   **118 dash** overthrow.   **late** recent   **119 Touching** regarding
121 battles armies   **124 heated spleen** i.e., courage roused to a high
pitch   **126 rigor** fierceness   **131 flail** threshing tool   **138 Lord George**
i.e., George, later Duke of Clarence, brother to Edward and Richard
140 marches borders (of Wales)   **141 Making another head** raising
another armed force

EDWARD
Where is the Duke of Norfolk, gentle Warwick?   142
And when came George from Burgundy to England?

WARWICK
Some six miles off the Duke is with the soldiers;
And for your brother, he was lately sent   145
From your kind aunt, Duchess of Burgundy,   146
With aid of soldiers to this needful war.

RICHARD
'Twas odds, belike, when valiant Warwick fled.   148
Oft have I heard his praises in pursuit,   149
But ne'er till now his scandal of retire.   150

WARWICK
Nor now my scandal, Richard, dost thou hear;
For thou shalt know this strong right hand of mine
Can pluck the diadem from faint Henry's head
And wring the awful scepter from his fist,   154
Were he as famous and as bold in war
As he is famed for mildness, peace, and prayer.

RICHARD
I know it well, Lord Warwick. Blame me not.
'Tis love I bear thy glories make me speak.   158
But in this troublous time what's to be done?
Shall we go throw away our coats of steel
And wrap our bodies in black mourning gowns,
Numb'ring our Ave Marys with our beads?   162
Or shall we on the helmets of our foes
Tell our devotion with revengeful arms?   164
If for the last, say ay, and to it, lords.

WARWICK
Why, therefore Warwick came to seek you out,

---

142 gentle noble   **145 for** as for   **146 Duchess of Burgundy** (A granddaughter of John of Gaunt and distant relative of Richard of York, to
whom, according to the chroniclers, both George and Richard were sent
for protection after York's execution.)   **148 'Twas odds, belike** i.e., no
doubt the odds were very heavy   **149 in pursuit** i.e., for pursuing the
enemy   **150 his . . . retire** i.e., condemnation of him for retreating
154 awful awe-inspiring   **158 make** that makes   **162 beads** rosary
beads (used in reciting *Ave Marys*, i.e., Ave Marias or Hail Marys)
164 Tell our devotion (1) count off our prayers (2) proclaim our love.
(Said ironically.)

And therefore comes my brother Montague.
Attend me, lords. The proud insulting Queen,
With Clifford and the haught Northumberland,   169
And of their feather many more proud birds,
Have wrought the easy-melting King like wax.   171
He swore consent to your succession,
His oath enrollèd in the Parliament,   173
And now to London all the crew are gone
To frustrate both his oath and what besides   175
May make against the house of Lancaster.   176
Their power, I think, is thirty thousand strong.
Now, if the help of Norfolk and myself,
With all the friends that thou, brave Earl of March, 179
Amongst the loving Welshmen canst procure,   180
Will but amount to five-and-twenty thousand,
Why, *via*! To London will we march,   182
And once again bestride our foaming steeds,
And once again cry "Charge!" upon our foes,
But never once again turn back and fly.   185

RICHARD
Ay, now methinks I hear great Warwick speak.
Ne'er may he live to see a sunshine day   187
That cries "Retire!" if Warwick bid him stay.   188

EDWARD
Lord Warwick, on thy shoulder will I lean;
And when thou fail'st—as God forbid the hour!—
Must Edward fall, which peril heaven forfend!   191

WARWICK
No longer Earl of March, but Duke of York;
The next degree is England's royal throne.   193
For King of England shalt thou be proclaimed
In every borough as we pass along;
And he that throws not up his cap for joy
Shall for the fault make forfeit of his head.
King Edward, valiant Richard, Montague,

169 **haught** haughty 171 **wrought** worked on, manipulated
173 **enrollèd** recorded on official rolls 175 **frustrate** annul. **what besides** anything else 176 **make** be effective 179 **Earl of March** i.e., Edward, who at his father's death inherited this with other titles
180 **loving** loyal, friendly 182 **via** forward 185 **turn back** turn our backs 187 **he** i.e., anyone 188 **stay** stand firm 191 **forfend** forbid
193 **degree** step, rank

Stay we no longer, dreaming of renown,   199
But sound the trumpets and about our task.

RICHARD
Then, Clifford, were thy heart as hard as steel,
As thou hast shown it flinty by thy deeds,
I come to pierce it or to give thee mine.

EDWARD
Then strike up drums. God and Saint George for us!   204

    Enter a Messenger.

WARWICK   How now? What news?

MESSENGER
The Duke of Norfolk sends you word by me
The Queen is coming with a puissant host;   207
And craves your company for speedy counsel.

WARWICK
Why then it sorts, brave warriors. Let's away.   209
                      Exeunt omnes.

✣

2.2   *Flourish. Enter the King [Henry], the Queen
      [Margaret], Clifford, Northumberland, and
      young Prince, with drum and trumpets.
      [York's head is set above the gates.]*

QUEEN MARGARET
Welcome, my lord, to this brave town of York.   1
Yonder's the head of that archenemy
That sought to be encompassed with your crown.
Doth not the object cheer your heart, my lord?

KING HENRY
Ay, as the rocks cheer them that fear their wreck.   5
To see this sight, it irks my very soul.
Withhold revenge, dear God! 'Tis not my fault,
Nor wittingly have I infringed my vow.

---

199 Stay we let us remain   **204 Saint George** patron saint of England
207 puissant powerful   **209 sorts** is fitting, is working out

2.2. Location: Before the walls of York.
s.d. drum drummer.   **trumpets** trumpeters   **1 brave** fine   **5 wreck**
shipwreck, destruction

CLIFFORD
My gracious liege, this too much lenity
And harmful pity must be laid aside.
To whom do lions cast their gentle looks?
Not to the beast that would usurp their den.
Whose hand is that the forest bear doth lick?
Not his that spoils her young before her face.   14
Who scapes the lurking serpent's mortal sting?
Not he that sets his foot upon her back.
The smallest worm will turn, being trodden on,
And doves will peck in safeguard of their brood.   18
Ambitious York did level at thy crown,   19
Thou smiling while he knit his angry brows.
He, but a duke, would have his son a king
And raise his issue, like a loving sire;   22
Thou, being a king, blest with a goodly son,
Didst yield consent to disinherit him,
Which argued thee a most unloving father.   25
Unreasonable creatures feed their young;   26
And though man's face be fearful to their eyes,   27
Yet, in protection of their tender ones,
Who hath not seen them, even with those wings
Which sometimes they have used with fearful flight,
Make war with him that climbed unto their nest,
Offering their own lives in their young's defense?
For shame, my liege, make them your precedent!
Were it not pity that this goodly boy
Should lose his birthright by his father's fault,
And long hereafter say unto his child,
"What my great-grandfather and grandsire got,
My careless father fondly gave away"?   38
Ah, what a shame were this! Look on the boy,
And let his manly face, which promiseth
Successful fortune, steel thy melting heart
To hold thine own and leave thine own with him.
KING HENRY
Full well hath Clifford played the orator,

---

14 spoils destroys, seizes as prey   **18 safeguard of** safeguarding
19 level aim   **22 raise** raise in dignity   **25 argued thee** showed you to
be   **26 Unreasonable** not endowed with reason   **27 fearful** causing fear
38 fondly foolishly

Inferring arguments of mighty force.   44
But, Clifford, tell me, didst thou never hear
That things ill got had ever bad success?   46
And happy always was it for that son   47
Whose father for his hoarding went to hell?   48
I'll leave my son my virtuous deeds behind;
And would my father had left me no more!
For all the rest is held at such a rate   51
As brings a thousandfold more care to keep
Than in possession any jot of pleasure.
Ah, cousin York, would thy best friends did know
How it doth grieve me that thy head is here!

QUEEN MARGARET
My lord, cheer up your spirits. Our foes are nigh,
And this soft courage makes your followers faint.   57
You promised knighthood to our forward son.   58
Unsheathe your sword and dub him presently.   59
Edward, kneel down.   [*The Prince kneels.*]

KING HENRY
Edward Plantagenet, arise a knight,
And learn this lesson: Draw thy sword in right.

PRINCE [*Rising*]
My gracious Father, by your kingly leave,
I'll draw it as apparent to the crown,   64
And in that quarrel use it to the death.

CLIFFORD
Why, that is spoken like a toward prince.   66

    Enter a Messenger.

MESSENGER
Royal commanders, be in readiness,
For with a band of thirty thousand men
Comes Warwick, backing of the Duke of York,   69
And in the towns, as they do march along,

44 Inferring alleging, adducing **46 success** outcome **47–48 And . . .
hell** i.e., the son may be fortunate in inheriting wealth, but the father
who obtained that wealth by hoarding and miserly grasping will go to
hell **51 rate** cost **57 faint** fainthearted **58 forward** promising
59 presently at once **64 apparent** heir **66 toward** ready, bold, promising **69 Duke of York** i.e., Edward

Proclaims him king, and many fly to him.
Darraign your battle, for they are at hand.   72

CLIFFORD
I would Your Highness would depart the field.
The Queen hath best success when you are absent.

QUEEN MARGARET
Ay, good my lord, and leave us to our fortune.

KING HENRY
Why, that's my fortune too. Therefore I'll stay.

NORTHUMBERLAND
Be it with resolution then to fight.

PRINCE
My royal Father, cheer these noble lords
And hearten those that fight in your defense.
Unsheathe your sword, good Father; cry "Saint
    George!"   80

    *March. Enter Edward, Warwick, Richard, [George
    of] Clarence, Norfolk, Montague, and soldiers.*

EDWARD
Now, perjured Henry, wilt thou kneel for grace   81
And set thy diadem upon my head,
Or bide the mortal fortune of the field?   83

QUEEN MARGARET
Go rate thy minions, proud insulting boy!   84
Becomes it thee to be thus bold in terms   85
Before thy sovereign and thy lawful king?

EDWARD
I am his king, and he should bow his knee.
I was adopted heir by his consent.
Since when, his oath is broke; for, as I hear,
You, that are king, though he do wear the crown,   90
Have caused him, by new act of Parliament,
To blot out me and put his own son in.

CLIFFORD   And reason too.
Who should succeed the father but the son?

72 Darraign your battle set your army in battle array   **80 s.d. George of
Clarence** (Actually, George is not made Duke of Clarence until 2.6.104.)
81 grace mercy, pardon   **83 bide** wait for.   **mortal** fatal   **84 rate thy
minions** chide your followers or favorites   **85 terms** language   **90 You,
that are king** i.e., you, Margaret, who in fact rule

RICHARD
Are you there, butcher? O, I cannot speak!   95

CLIFFORD
Ay, crookback, here I stand to answer thee,
Or any he the proudest of thy sort.   97

RICHARD
'Twas you that killed young Rutland, was it not?

CLIFFORD
Ay, and old York, and yet not satisfied.

RICHARD
For God's sake, lords, give signal to the fight.

WARWICK
What sayst thou, Henry, wilt thou yield the crown?

QUEEN MARGARET
Why, how now, long-tongued Warwick, dare you speak?
When you and I met at Saint Albans last,
Your legs did better service than your hands.

WARWICK
Then 'twas my turn to fly, and now 'tis thine.

CLIFFORD
You said so much before, and yet you fled.

WARWICK
'Twas not your valor, Clifford, drove me thence.

NORTHUMBERLAND
No, nor your manhood that durst make you stay.

RICHARD
Northumberland, I hold thee reverently.   109
Break off the parley, for scarce I can refrain   110
The execution of my big-swollen heart   111
Upon that Clifford, that cruel child-killer.

CLIFFORD
I slew thy father. Call'st thou him a child?

RICHARD
Ay, like a dastard and a treacherous coward,
As thou didst kill our tender brother Rutland;
But ere sunset I'll make thee curse the deed.

95 butcher (Clifford was nicknamed "the butcher" for his cruelty.)
97 any he any man. **sort** gang **109 hold thee reverently** hold you in
the greatest respect **110 refrain** give up, hold back **111 execution** i.e.,
giving practical effect to my passion

KING HENRY
Have done with words, my lords, and hear me speak.

QUEEN MARGARET
Defy them, then, or else hold close thy lips.

KING HENRY
I prithee, give no limits to my tongue.
I am a king, and privileged to speak.

CLIFFORD
My liege, the wound that bred this meeting here
Cannot be cured by words. Therefore be still.

RICHARD
Then, executioner, unsheathe thy sword.
By Him that made us all, I am resolved   124
That Clifford's manhood lies upon his tongue.   125

EDWARD
Say, Henry, shall I have my right or no?
A thousand men have broke their fasts today   127
That ne'er shall dine unless thou yield the crown.

WARWICK
If thou deny, their blood upon thy head,   129
For York in justice puts his armor on.

PRINCE
If that be right which Warwick says is right,
There is no wrong, but everything is right.

RICHARD
Whoever got thee, there thy mother stands;   133
For, well I wot, thou hast thy mother's tongue.   134

QUEEN MARGARET
But thou art neither like thy sire nor dam,
But like a foul misshapen stigmatic,   136
Marked by the destinies to be avoided,
As venom toads or lizards' dreadful stings.   138

RICHARD
Iron of Naples hid with English gilt,   139
Whose father bears the title of a king—

---

124 resolved convinced   **125 lies . . . tongue** i.e., consists only in words
127 broke their fasts i.e., had breakfast   **129 deny** refuse. **upon** be
upon   **133 got** begot, sired   **134 wot** know   **136 stigmatic** one branded
with the mark of his crime or deformity. (See *2 Henry VI*, 5.1.215.)
138 venom venomous   **139 Iron . . . gilt** i.e., you cheap product of
Naples (being daughter of the titular King of Naples), being gilded over
by an English marriage

As if a channel should be called the sea—   141
Sham'st thou not, knowing whence thou art extraught,   142
To let thy tongue detect thy baseborn heart?   143

EDWARD

A wisp of straw were worth a thousand crowns   144
To make this shameless callet know herself.   145
Helen of Greece was fairer far than thou,
Although thy husband may be Menelaus;   147
And ne'er was Agamemnon's brother wronged   148
By that false woman, as this king by thee.
His father reveled in the heart of France,   150
And tamed the King, and made the Dauphin stoop;
And had he matched according to his state,   152
He might have kept that glory to this day.
But when he took a beggar to his bed
And graced thy poor sire with his bridal day,   155
Even then that sunshine brewed a shower for him
That washed his father's fortunes forth of France   157
And heaped sedition on his crown at home.
For what hath broached this tumult but thy pride?   159
Hadst thou been meek, our title still had slept,   160
And we, in pity of the gentle King,
Had slipped our claim until another age.   162

GEORGE

But when we saw our sunshine made thy spring,   163
And that thy summer bred us no increase,   164
We set the ax to thy usurping root;
And though the edge hath something hit ourselves,   166
Yet know thou, since we have begun to strike,

---

141 As . . . sea i.e., comparing your father to a king is like comparing
a gutter (*channel*) to the sea   **142 extraught** descended, extracted
143 detect expose   **144 wisp of straw** (A traditional way of marking or
branding a scolding woman.)   **145 callet** lewd woman   **147 Menelaus**
husband of Helen of Greece, whose abduction led to the Trojan War. (By
implication, King Henry is the cuckolded husband just as Menelaus
was.)   **148 Agamemnon** brother of Menelaus and leader of the Greeks
in the Trojan War   **150 His father** i.e., Henry V   **152 had . . . state** i.e.,
if Henry VI had married someone equal to him in social position
155 graced honored.   **thy poor sire** i.e., Reignier, King of Naples.   **his**
i.e., Henry VI's   **157 of** out of   **159 broached** set flowing, started
160 title claim to the throne   **162 Had slipped** would have postponed
163 But . . . spring i.e., but when we saw you reaping all the benefit of
what should be ours   **164 increase** harvest   **166 something** somewhat

We'll never leave till we have hewn thee down   168
Or bathed thy growing with our heated bloods.   169

EDWARD
And in this resolution I defy thee,
Not willing any longer conference,
Since thou deniedst the gentle King to speak.
Sound trumpets! Let our bloody colors wave!
And either victory, or else a grave.

QUEEN MARGARET   Stay, Edward.

EDWARD
No, wrangling woman, we'll no longer stay.
These words will cost ten thousand lives this day.   177

                                        Exeunt omnes.

2.3   *Alarum. Excursions. Enter Warwick.*

WARWICK
Forspent with toil, as runners with a race,   1
I lay me down a little while to breathe;   2
For strokes received and many blows repaid
Have robbed my strong-knit sinews of their strength,
And, spite of spite, needs must I rest awhile.   5

     Enter Edward, running.

EDWARD
Smile, gentle heaven, or strike, ungentle death!   6
For this world frowns, and Edward's sun is clouded.

WARWICK
How now, my lord, what hap? What hope of good?

     Enter [George of] Clarence.

GEORGE
Our hap is loss, our hope but sad despair;

---

168 leave leave off   **169 bathed thy growing** watered your growth
177 s.d. omnes all

**2.3. Location: The field of battle near York, immediately following the
preceding scene. (Historically, the field of battle was between Towton
and Saxton in Yorkshire.)**
s.d. Excursions sorties, forays of armed soldiers   **1 Forspent** exhausted
2 breathe rest   **5 spite of spite** i.e., come what may.   **needs must I** I
must   **6 ungentle** ignoble

Our ranks are broke, and ruin follows us.
What counsel give you? Whither shall we fly?

EDWARD
Bootless is flight. They follow us with wings,   12
And weak we are and cannot shun pursuit.

Enter Richard.

RICHARD
Ah, Warwick, why hast thou withdrawn thyself?
Thy brother's blood the thirsty earth hath drunk,   15
Broached with the steely point of Clifford's lance;   16
And in the very pangs of death he cried,
Like to a dismal clangor heard from far,
"Warwick, revenge! Brother, revenge my death!"
So, underneath the belly of their steeds,
That stained their fetlocks in his smoking blood,
The noble gentleman gave up the ghost.

WARWICK
Then let the earth be drunken with our blood!
I'll kill my horse, because I will not fly.
Why stand we like softhearted women here,
Wailing our losses, whiles the foe doth rage,
And look upon, as if the tragedy   27
Were played in jest by counterfeiting actors?   28
Here on my knee I vow to God above   [*Kneeling*]
I'll never pause again, never stand still,
Till either death hath closed these eyes of mine
Or fortune given me measure of revenge.   32

EDWARD [*Kneeling*]
O Warwick, I do bend my knee with thine,
And in this vow do chain my soul to thine!
And, ere my knee rise from the earth's cold face,
I throw my hands, mine eyes, my heart to Thee,   36
Thou setter-up and plucker-down of kings,
Beseeching Thee, if with Thy will it stands   38

---

12 Bootless useless   **15 Thy brother's blood** (Warwick's half brother,
the Bastard of Salisbury, not among the *Dramatis Personae* of this play,
was killed at Ferrybridge shortly before the battle of Towton.)
16 Broached with set flowing by   **27 upon** on   **28 counterfeiting actors**
actors performing roles   **32 measure** full quantity   **36 Thee** i.e., God
38 stands agrees

That to my foes this body must be prey,
Yet that Thy brazen gates of heaven may ope
And give sweet passage to my sinful soul!

                                    [*They rise.*]
Now, lords, take leave until we meet again,
Where'er it be, in heaven or in earth.

RICHARD
Brother, give me thy hand; and, gentle Warwick,   44
Let me embrace thee in my weary arms.

                                    [*They embrace.*]
I, that did never weep, now melt with woe
That winter should cut off our springtime so.

WARWICK
Away, away! Once more, sweet lords, farewell.

GEORGE
Yet let us all together to our troops,
And give them leave to fly that will not stay,
And call them pillars that will stand to us;   51
And, if we thrive, promise them such rewards
As victors wear at the Olympian games.
This may plant courage in their quailing breasts,
For yet is hope of life and victory.
Forslow no longer! Make we hence amain.   *Exeunt.* 56

2.4   *Excursions. Enter Richard and Clifford*
         [*meeting*].

RICHARD
Now, Clifford, I have singled thee alone.   1
Suppose this arm is for the Duke of York,
And this for Rutland—both bound to revenge,
Wert thou environed with a brazen wall.   4

CLIFFORD
Now, Richard, I am with thee here alone.
This is the hand that stabbed thy father York,
And this the hand that slew thy brother Rutland,
And here's the heart that triumphs in their death

---

44 gentle noble   **51 stand to** support   **56 Forslow** delay.   **amain**
with full speed

2.4. Location: Scene continues at the battlefield.
1 singled singled out, chosen   **4 environed** surrounded

And cheers these hands that slew thy sire and brother 9
To execute the like upon thyself.
And so, have at thee!   11
          They fight. Warwick comes; Clifford flies.

RICHARD
  Nay, Warwick, single out some other chase,   12
  For I myself will hunt this wolf to death.

                             Exeunt.

2.5   *Alarum. Enter King Henry alone.*

KING HENRY
  This battle fares like to the morning's war,
  When dying clouds contend with growing light,
  What time the shepherd, blowing of his nails,   3
  Can neither call it perfect day nor night.
  Now sways it this way, like a mighty sea
  Forced by the tide to combat with the wind;
  Now sways it that way, like the selfsame sea
  Forced to retire by fury of the wind.
  Sometimes the flood prevails, and then the wind;
  Now one the better, then another best;
  Both tugging to be victors, breast to breast,
  Yet neither conqueror nor conquerèd.
  So is the equal poise of this fell war.   13
  Here on this molehill will I sit me down.   *[He sits.]*
  To whom God will, there be the victory!
  For Margaret my queen, and Clifford too,
  Have chid me from the battle, swearing both
  They prosper best of all when I am thence.
  Would I were dead, if God's good will were so!
  For what is in this world but grief and woe?
  O God! Methinks it were a happy life
  To be no better than a homely swain,   22
  To sit upon a hill, as I do now,
  To carve out dials quaintly, point by point,   24

---

9 cheers urges on   **11 have at thee** i.e., on guard, here I come   **12 chase**
prey

2.5. Location: The battlefield, as before.
3 What time when.   **of** on (to warm them)   **13 poise** balance. **fell** cruel
22 homely simple   **24 dials** sundials. **quaintly** artfully, intricately

Thereby to see the minutes how they run:
How many makes the hour full complete,
How many hours brings about the day,
How many days will finish up the year,
How many years a mortal man may live.
When this is known, then to divide the times:
So many hours must I tend my flock,
So many hours must I take my rest,
So many hours must I contemplate,
So many hours must I sport myself,   34
So many days my ewes have been with young,
So many weeks ere the poor fools will ean,   36
So many years ere I shall shear the fleece.
So minutes, hours, days, months, and years,
Passed over to the end they were created,   39
Would bring white hairs unto a quiet grave.
Ah, what a life were this, how sweet, how lovely!
Gives not the hawthorn bush a sweeter shade
To shepherds looking on their silly sheep   43
Than doth a rich embroidered canopy
To kings that fear their subjects' treachery?
O, yes, it doth, a thousandfold it doth.
And to conclude, the shepherd's homely curds,
His cold thin drink out of his leather bottle,
His wonted sleep under a fresh tree's shade,   49
All which secure and sweetly he enjoys,
Is far beyond a prince's delicates—   51
His viands sparkling in a golden cup,
His body couchèd in a curious bed—   53
When care, mistrust, and treason waits on him.

> *Alarum. Enter a Son that hath killed his father,
> at one door [bearing in the dead body].*

SON
  Ill blows the wind that profits nobody.
  This man, whom hand to hand I slew in fight,
  May be possessèd with some store of crowns;   57

34 sport amuse   **36 ean** bring forth (lambs)   **39 end they** end for which
they   **43 silly** innocent, helpless   **49 wonted** accustomed   **51 delicates**
luxuries   **53 curious** skillfully and daintily made, decorated   **57 crowns**
i.e., coins, money

And I, that haply take them from him now,   58
May yet ere night yield both my life and them
To some man else, as this dead man doth me.—
Who's this? O God! It is my father's face,
Whom in this conflict I unwares have killed.
O, heavy times, begetting such events!   63
From London by the King was I pressed forth;   64
My father, being the Earl of Warwick's man,   65
Came on the part of York, pressed by his master;   66
And I, who at his hands received my life,
Have by my hands of life bereavèd him.
Pardon me, God, I knew not what I did!   69
And pardon, Father, for I knew not thee!
My tears shall wipe away these bloody marks;
And no more words till they have flowed their fill.
                                        [*He weeps.*]

KING HENRY
O piteous spectacle! O bloody times!
Whiles lions war and battle for their dens,
Poor harmless lambs abide their enmity.   75
Weep, wretched man. I'll aid thee tear for tear;
And let our hearts and eyes, like civil war,
Be blind with tears, and break o'ercharged with
    grief.   [*He weeps.*] 78

*Enter at another door a Father that hath killed
his son, bearing of his son.*

FATHER
Thou that so stoutly hast resisted me,
Give me thy gold, if thou hast any gold;
For I have bought it with an hundred blows.
But let me see. Is this our foeman's face?
Ah, no, no, no, it is mine only son!
Ah, boy, if any life be left in thee,
Throw up thine eye! See, see what showers arise,
Blown with the windy tempest of my heart,

---

58 haply by chance   **63 heavy** sorrowful   **64 pressed forth** impressed
into military service   **65 man** retainer, servant   **66 part** party, side
69 Pardon . . . did (An echo of Luke 23:34, "Father, forgive them,
for they know not what they do.")   **75 abide** endure, pay for
78 o'ercharged overfilled

Upon thy wounds, that kills mine eye and heart!

> [*He weeps.*]

O, pity, God, this miserable age!
What stratagems, how fell, how butcherly, 89
Erroneous, mutinous, and unnatural, 90
This deadly quarrel daily doth beget!
O boy, thy father gave thee life too soon,
And hath bereft thee of thy life too late! 93

KING HENRY
Woe above woe, grief more than common grief! 94
O, that my death would stay these ruthful deeds! 95
O, pity, pity, gentle heaven, pity!
The red rose and the white are on his face,
The fatal colors of our striving houses.
The one his purple blood right well resembles;
The other his pale cheeks, methinks, presenteth. 100
Wither one rose, and let the other flourish;
If you contend, a thousand lives must wither.

SON
How will my mother for a father's death
Take on with me and ne'er be satisfied! 104

FATHER
How will my wife for slaughter of my son
Shed seas of tears and ne'er be satisfied!

KING HENRY
How will the country for these woeful chances 107
Misthink the King and not be satisfied! 108

SON
Was ever son so rued a father's death?

FATHER
Was ever father so bemoaned his son?

KING HENRY
Was ever king so grieved for subjects' woe?
Much is your sorrow; mine ten times so much.

SON
I'll bear thee hence, where I may weep my fill.

> [*Exit with the body.*]

---

89 stratagems deeds of violence.　**fell** cruel　**90 Erroneous** criminal
93 late lately　**94 above** piled on　**95 stay** put a halt to.　**ruthful** pitiful
100 presenteth represents　**104 Take on with** cry out against.　**satisfied**
comforted　**107 chances** happenings　**108 Misthink** think ill of

FATHER
These arms of mine shall be thy winding-sheet;   114
My heart, sweet boy, shall be thy sepulcher,
For from my heart thine image ne'er shall go.
My sighing breast shall be thy funeral bell;
And so obsequious will thy father be,   118
E'en for the loss of thee, having no more,
As Priam was for all his valiant sons.   120
I'll bear thee hence, and let them fight that will,
For I have murdered where I should not kill.
          Exit [with the body].

KING HENRY
Sad-hearted men, much overgone with care,   123
Here sits a king more woeful than you are.

          *Alarums. Excursions. Enter the Queen
          [Margaret], the Prince, and Exeter.*

PRINCE
Fly, Father, fly! For all your friends are fled,
And Warwick rages like a chafèd bull.   126
Away! For death doth hold us in pursuit.

QUEEN MARGARET
Mount you, my lord. Towards Berwick post amain.   128
Edward and Richard, like a brace of greyhounds   129
Having the fearful flying hare in sight,
With fiery eyes sparkling for very wrath,
And bloody steel grasped in their ireful hands,
Are at our backs; and therefore hence amain.

EXETER
Away! For vengeance comes along with them.
Nay, stay not to expostulate, make speed!
Or else come after. I'll away before.

KING HENRY
Nay, take me with thee, good sweet Exeter.
Not that I fear to stay, but love to go
Whither the Queen intends. Forward! Away!   *Exeunt.*

---

114 winding-sheet shroud, burial cloth   **118 obsequious** dutiful in mani-
festing regard for the dead   **120 Priam** King of Troy, whose fifty sons fell
in the war against the Greeks   **123 overgone** overcome   **126 chafèd** enraged   **128 Berwick** Berwick-on-Tweed, on the Scottish border at the
North Sea shore.   **post amain** hasten with full speed   **129 brace** pair

2.6   *A loud alarum. Enter Clifford, wounded, [with*
        an arrow in his neck].

CLIFFORD
  Here burns my candle out; ay, here it dies,
  Which, whiles it lasted, gave King Henry light.
  O Lancaster, I fear thy overthrow
  More than my body's parting with my soul!
  My love and fear glued many friends to thee;   5
  And, now I fall, thy tough commixture melts,   6
  Impairing Henry, strengthening misproud York.   7
  The common people swarm like summer flies;
  And whither fly the gnats but to the sun?   9
  And who shines now but Henry's enemies?
  O Phoebus, hadst thou never given consent
  That Phaëthon should check thy fiery steeds,   12
  Thy burning car never had scorched the earth!   13
  And, Henry, hadst thou swayed as kings should do, 14
  Or as thy father and his father did,
  Giving no ground unto the house of York,
  They never then had sprung like summer flies;
  I and ten thousand in this luckless realm
  Had left no mourning widows for our death,   19
  And thou this day hadst kept thy chair in peace. 20
  For what doth cherish weeds but gentle air?   21
  And what makes robbers bold but too much lenity?
  Bootless are plaints, and cureless are my wounds; 23
  No way to fly, nor strength to hold out flight.   24
  The foe is merciless, and will not pity,
  For at their hands I have deserved no pity.
  The air hath got into my deadly wounds,
  And much effuse of blood doth make me faint.   28
  Come, York and Richard, Warwick and the rest;

2.6. Location: The battlefield, as before.
5 My love and fear love and fear of me **6 now** now that. **commixture**
compound (i.e., the *glue* that held many friends) **7 Impairing** weakening. **misproud** falsely proud **9 the sun** (Refers to Edward's emblem.)
12 Phaëthon (See 1.4.33, note.) **check** control, manage **13 car** chariot
14 swayed reigned **19 mourning widows** widows mourning **20 chair**
throne **21 cherish** foster, encourage **23 Bootless** fruitless. **plaints**
lamentations **24 hold out** sustain **28 effuse** effusion

I stabbed your fathers' bosoms. Split my breast.   30
                              [He faints.]

   Alarum and retreat. Enter Edward, Warwick,
   Richard, and soldiers, Montague, and [*George of*]
   Clarence.

EDWARD
Now breathe we, lords. Good fortune bids us pause   31
And smooth the frowns of war with peaceful looks.
Some troops pursue the bloody-minded Queen,
That led calm Henry, though he were a king,
As doth a sail, filled with a fretting gust,   35
Command an argosy to stem the waves.   36
But think you, lords, that Clifford fled with them?

WARWICK
No, 'tis impossible he should escape;
For, though before his face I speak the words,   39
Your brother Richard marked him for the grave,
And wheresoe'er he is, he's surely dead.
                       Clifford groans [*and dies*].

EDWARD
Whose soul is that which takes her heavy leave?

RICHARD
A deadly groan, like life and death's departing.   43

EDWARD
See who it is. And, now the battle's ended,
If friend or foe, let him be gently used.   45

RICHARD
Revoke that doom of mercy, for 'tis Clifford,   46
Who not contented that he lopped the branch   47
In hewing Rutland when his leaves put forth,
But set his murdering knife unto the root
From whence that tender spray did sweetly spring—   50
I mean our princely father, Duke of York.

---

30 s.d. retreat signal to cease the attack   **31 breathe we** let us pause for
breath   **35 fretting** blowing in gusts (with a suggestion also of "nag-
ging")   **36 Command** compel forward.   **argosy** large merchant vessel.
stem make headway against, cut through   **39 his** i.e., Richard's
43 departing parting   **45 If** whether.   **gently used** treated in death with
dignity   **46 doom** judgment   **47 Who not contented** who did not rest
contented   **50 spray** small and tender twig

WARWICK
From off the gates of York fetch down the head,
Your father's head, which Clifford placèd there;
Instead whereof let this supply the room.   54
Measure for measure must be answerèd.   55

EDWARD
Bring forth that fatal screech owl to our house,   56
That nothing sung but death to us and ours.

                    [*Soldiers drag Clifford's body
                        in front of York gates.*]

Now death shall stop his dismal threatening sound,
And his ill-boding tongue no more shall speak.

WARWICK
I think his understanding is bereft.   60
Speak, Clifford, dost thou know who speaks to thee?—
Dark cloudy death o'ershades his beams of life,
And he nor sees nor hears us what we say.   63

RICHARD
O, would he did! And so perhaps he doth.
'Tis but his policy to counterfeit,   65
Because he would avoid such bitter taunts
Which in the time of death he gave our father.

GEORGE
If so thou think'st, vex him with eager words.   68

RICHARD
Clifford, ask mercy and obtain no grace.

EDWARD
Clifford, repent in bootless penitence.

WARWICK
Clifford, devise excuses for thy faults.

GEORGE
While we devise fell tortures for thy faults.   72

RICHARD
Thou didst love York, and I am son to York.

EDWARD
Thou pitiedst Rutland. I will pity thee.

54 this i.e., Clifford's head. **supply the room** take the place
55 answerèd given in return **56 screech owl** (A conventional omen of
death, here likened to Clifford.) **house** family **60 bereft** taken from
him **63 nor . . . nor** neither . . . nor **65 policy** stratagem **68 eager**
biting, bitter **72 fell** cruel

GEORGE
  Where's Captain Margaret to fence you now?   75
WARWICK
  They mock thee, Clifford. Swear as thou wast wont.   76
RICHARD
  What, not an oath? Nay, then the world goes hard
  When Clifford cannot spare his friends an oath.
  I know by that he's dead; and, by my soul,
  If this right hand would buy two hours' life,
  That I in all despite might rail at him,   81
  This hand should chop it off, and with the issuing blood   82
  Stifle the villain whose unstanchèd thirst   83
  York and young Rutland could not satisfy.
WARWICK
  Ay, but he's dead. Off with the traitor's head,
  And rear it in the place your father's stands.
  And now to London with triumphant march,
  There to be crownèd England's royal king;
  From whence shall Warwick cut the sea to France
  And ask the Lady Bona for thy queen.   90
  So shalt thou sinew both these lands together,   91
  And, having France thy friend, thou shalt not dread   92
  The scattered foe that hopes to rise again;
  For though they cannot greatly sting to hurt,
  Yet look to have them buzz to offend thine ears.
  First will I see the coronation,
  And then to Brittany I'll cross the sea
  To effect this marriage, so it please my lord.
EDWARD
  Even as thou wilt, sweet Warwick, let it be;
  For in thy shoulder do I build my seat,   100
  And never will I undertake the thing
  Wherein thy counsel and consent is wanting.
  Richard, I will create thee Duke of Gloucester,
  And George, of Clarence. Warwick, as ourself,
  Shall do and undo as him pleaseth best.

---

75 fence defend **76 wont** accustomed **81 despite** spite, contempt
82 This hand i.e., this left hand **83 unstanchèd** unquenchable **90 Lady Bona** daughter of the Duke of Savoy and sister to the Queen of France
91 sinew join (as with sinew) **92 France** the King of France **100 in thy shoulder** i.e., with your support. **seat** throne

RICHARD
  Let me be Duke of Clarence, George of Gloucester;
  For Gloucester's dukedom is too ominous.   107
WARWICK
  Tut, that's a foolish observation.
  Richard, be Duke of Gloucester. Now to London,
  To see these honors in possession.   *Exeunt.*   110

♣

---

107 Gloucester's . . . ominous (Three dukes of Gloucester had met with
violent deaths: Hugh Spenser, a favorite of Edward II, Thomas of Woodstock, youngest son of Edward III [see *Richard II*, 1.1], and Humphrey,
uncle of Henry VI [see *2 Henry VI*, 3.2].)   **110 in possession** i.e., in our
possession

3.1   *Enter two Keepers with crossbows in*
         their hands.

FIRST KEEPER
  Under this thick-grown brake we'll shroud ourselves,   1
  For through this laund anon the deer will come;   2
  And in this covert will we make our stand,
  Culling the principal of all the deer.   4
SECOND KEEPER
  I'll stay above the hill, so both may shoot.
FIRST KEEPER
  That cannot be. The noise of thy crossbow
  Will scare the herd, and so my shoot is lost.
  Here stand we both, and aim we at the best;   8
  And, for the time shall not seem tedious,   9
  I'll tell thee what befell me on a day
  In this self place where now we mean to stand.   11
SECOND KEEPER
  Here comes a man. Let's stay till he be past.
                        [*They remain concealed.*]

     Enter the King [*Henry, disguised,*] *with*
     a prayer book.

KING HENRY
  From Scotland am I stol'n, even of pure love,   13
  To greet mine own land with my wishful sight.   14
  No, Harry, Harry, 'tis no land of thine!
  Thy place is filled, thy scepter wrung from thee,
  Thy balm washed off wherewith thou wast anointed.
  No bending knee will call thee Caesar now,
  No humble suitors press to speak for right,   19
  No, not a man comes for redress of thee;   20
  For how can I help them, and not myself?

3.1. Location: A forest in the north of England, near the Scottish border.
s.d. Keepers gamekeepers   1 brake thicket   2 laund glade   4 Culling
. . . deer selecting the best deer   8 at the best as best we can   9 for
so that   11 self same, very   13 of out of   14 wishful longing   19 speak
for right plead for justice   20 of from

FIRST KEEPER [*Aside to Second Keeper*]
　　Ay, here's a deer whose skin's a keeper's fee:　　22
　　This is the quondam king. Let's seize upon him.　　23
KING HENRY
　　Let me embrace thee, sour adversity,
　　For wise men say it is the wisest course.
SECOND KEEPER [*Aside*]
　　Why linger we? Let us lay hands upon him.
FIRST KEEPER [*Aside*]
　　Forbear awhile. We'll hear a little more.
KING HENRY
　　My queen and son are gone to France for aid;
　　And, as I hear, the great commanding Warwick
　　Is thither gone, to crave the French King's sister
　　To wife for Edward. If this news be true,　　31
　　Poor Queen and son, your labor is but lost,
　　For Warwick is a subtle orator,
　　And Lewis a prince soon won with moving words.
　　By this account, then, Margaret may win him,
　　For she's a woman to be pitied much.
　　Her sighs will make a battery in his breast;　　37
　　Her tears will pierce into a marble heart.
　　The tiger will be mild whiles she doth mourn,
　　And Nero will be tainted with remorse　　40
　　To hear and see her plaints, her brinish tears.　　41
　　Ay, but she's come to beg, Warwick to give;
　　She, on his left side, craving aid for Henry,
　　He, on his right, asking a wife for Edward.
　　She weeps, and says her Henry is deposed;
　　He smiles, and says his Edward is installed;
　　That she, poor wretch, for grief can speak no more,　　47
　　Whiles Warwick tells his title, smooths the wrong,　　48
　　Inferreth arguments of mighty strength,　　49
　　And in conclusion wins the King from her

22 fee perquisite. (The gamekeeper will get a reward for capturing the
King, just as gamekeepers were customarily awarded the horn and
skins of a slain deer.)　　**23 quondam** onetime, former　　**31 To** as a
37 battery breach　　**40 Nero** Roman emperor famed for his cruelty.
tainted touched, affected　　**41 brinish** salty　　**47 That** so that　　**48 his title**
i.e., Edward's royal claim.　　**smooths** explains away　　**49 Inferreth**
adduces

With promise of his sister, and what else,   51
To strengthen and support King Edward's place.
O Margaret, thus 'twill be, and thou, poor soul,
Art then forsaken, as thou went'st forlorn!
                    [*The Keepers come forward.*]
SECOND KEEPER
  Say, what art thou that talk'st of kings and queens?   55
KING HENRY
  More than I seem, and less than I was born to.
  A man at least, for less I should not be;
  And men may talk of kings, and why not I?
SECOND KEEPER
  Ay, but thou talk'st as if thou wert a king.
KING HENRY
  Why, so I am, in mind, and that's enough.
SECOND KEEPER
  But, if thou be a king, where is thy crown?
KING HENRY
  My crown is in my heart, not on my head;
  Not decked with diamonds and Indian stones,   63
  Nor to be seen. My crown is called content;
  A crown it is that seldom kings enjoy.
SECOND KEEPER
  Well, if you be a king crowned with content,
  Your crown content and you must be contented
  To go along with us. For, as we think,
  You are the king King Edward hath deposed;
  And we his subjects sworn in all allegiance
  Will apprehend you as his enemy.   71
KING HENRY
  But did you never swear, and break an oath?
SECOND KEEPER
  No, never such an oath, nor will not now.
KING HENRY
  Where did you dwell when I was King of England?
SECOND KEEPER
  Here in this country where we now remain.   75

51 **what else** other things also   55 **what** who   63 **Indian stones** gems
71 **apprehend** arrest   75 **country** region

KING HENRY

  I was anointed king at nine months old;

  My father and my grandfather were kings,

  And you were sworn true subjects unto me.

  And tell me, then, have you not broke your oaths?

FIRST KEEPER

  No, for we were subjects but while you were king.   80

KING HENRY

  Why, am I dead? Do I not breathe a man?

  Ah, simple men, you know not what you swear!   82

  Look as I blow this feather from my face,   83

  And as the air blows it to me again,

  Obeying with my wind when I do blow,   85

  And yielding to another when it blows,

  Commanded always by the greater gust—

  Such is the lightness of you common men.

  But do not break your oaths, for of that sin

  My mild entreaty shall not make you guilty.

  Go where you will, the King shall be commanded;

  And be you kings, command, and I'll obey.

FIRST KEEPER

  We are true subjects to the King, King Edward.

KING HENRY

  So would you be again to Henry,

  If he were seated as King Edward is.

FIRST KEEPER

  We charge you, in God's name and the King's,

  To go with us unto the officers.

KING HENRY

  In God's name, lead. Your king's name be obeyed,

  And what God will, that let your king perform;

  And what he will, I humbly yield unto.   *Exeunt.*

❖

---

80 but only   **82 simple** foolish   **83 Look as** just as. **this feather**
(Henry may take a feather from his hat.)   **85 wind** breath

3.2   *Enter King Edward, Gloucester, Clarence, [and]*
         Lady Grey.

KING EDWARD
  Brother of Gloucester, at Saint Albans field
  This lady's husband, Sir Richard Grey, was slain,   2
  His land then seized on by the conqueror.
  Her suit is now to repossess those lands,
  Which we in justice cannot well deny,
  Because in quarrel of the house of York
  The worthy gentleman did lose his life.

GLOUCESTER
  Your Highness shall do well to grant her suit.
  It were dishonor to deny it her.

KING EDWARD
  It were no less, but yet I'll make a pause.

GLOUCESTER [*Aside to Clarence*]   Yea, is it so?
  I see the lady hath a thing to grant   12
  Before the King will grant her humble suit.

CLARENCE [*Aside to Gloucester*]
  He knows the game. How true he keeps the wind!   14

GLOUCESTER [*Aside to Clarence*]   Silence!

KING EDWARD
  Widow, we will consider of your suit;
  And come some other time to know our mind.

LADY GREY
  Right gracious lord, I cannot brook delay.   18
  May it please Your Highness to resolve me now,   19
  And what your pleasure is shall satisfy me.   20

GLOUCESTER [*Aside to Clarence*]
  Ay, widow? Then I'll warrant you all your lands,   21

3.2. **Location: London. The royal court.**
s.d. **Gloucester, Clarence** i.e., Richard and George, King Edward's brothers,
made dukes in 2.6.103–104   **2 Sir Richard Grey** (An error for Sir John
Grey, who fell at the second battle of St. Albans fighting on the Lancastrian
side; cf. *Richard III*, 1.3.127–130.)   **12 a thing** (with a sexual double enten-
dre that runs through much of this scene)   **14 game** (1) quarry in hunting
(2) game of seduction.   **keeps the wind** hunts downwind (to prevent the
game from catching the scent)   **19 resolve me** answer
me, end my uncertainty   **20 And . . . me** and whatever you please to grant
will content me. (But Richard, in the next speech, plays on sexual meanings of *pleasure* and *satisfy*.)   **21 warrant** guarantee

An if what pleases him shall pleasure you.   22
Fight closer or, good faith, you'll catch a blow.   23
CLARENCE [*Aside to Gloucester*]
I fear her not, unless she chance to fall.   24
GLOUCESTER [*Aside to Clarence*]
God forbid that, for he'll take vantages.
KING EDWARD
How many children hast thou, widow? Tell me.
CLARENCE [*Aside to Gloucester*]
I think he means to beg a child of her.   27
GLOUCESTER [*Aside to Clarence*]
Nay, whip me, then; he'll rather give her two.   28
LADY GREY   Three, my most gracious lord.
GLOUCESTER [*Aside to Clarence*]
You shall have four, if you'll be ruled by him.   30
KING EDWARD
'Twere pity they should lose their father's lands.
LADY GREY
Be pitiful, dread lord, and grant it then.
KING EDWARD
Lords, give us leave. I'll try this widow's wit.   33
GLOUCESTER [*Aside to Clarence*]
Ay, good leave have you; for you will have leave   34
Till youth take leave and leave you to the crutch. 35
               [*Gloucester and Clarence stand apart.*]
KING EDWARD
Now tell me, madam, do you love your children?
LADY GREY
Ay, full as dearly as I love myself.

22 An if if.   **pleasure** please   **23 Fight closer . . . catch a blow** (The
dueling terms here are used with sexual double meaning, as also in *fall*
and *vantages*, ll. 24, 25. See also *a thing*, l. 12, *beg a child*, l. 27, *crutch*,
i.e., crotch, l. 35, *service*, l. 43, *do*, l. 48, and *shift*, i.e., a woman's smock,
l. 108, for other sexual double entendres.)   **24 fear** i.e., fear for   **27 beg
a child** i.e., seek to be appointed guardian of her child, or to be guardian of some rich young ward—a lucrative sinecure (with sexual double
meaning)   **28 whip me** i.e., I'll bet a whipping the King has other
designs.   **give her two** make her pregnant twice   **30 have four** (Her
fourth child would be sired by Edward.)   **33 give us leave** pardon us,
i.e., leave us to confer alone.   **wit** intelligence   **34–35 Ay . . . crutch** yes,
may you be pardoned, for you will take liberties, until your youth bids
you farewell and leaves you hobbling on a crutch, too old for lovemak-
ing (with a pun on *crutch*, *crotch*, the loins)

KING EDWARD
  And would you not do much to do them good?
LADY GREY
  To do them good I would sustain some harm.
KING EDWARD
  Then get your husband's lands, to do them good.
LADY GREY
  Therefore I came unto Your Majesty.
KING EDWARD
  I'll tell you how these lands are to be got.
LADY GREY
  So shall you bind me to Your Highness' service.
KING EDWARD
  What service wilt thou do me if I give them?
LADY GREY
  What you command that rests in me to do.   45
KING EDWARD
  But you will take exceptions to my boon.   46
LADY GREY
  No, gracious lord, except I cannot do it.   47
KING EDWARD
  Ay, but thou canst do what I mean to ask.
LADY GREY
  Why, then I will do what Your Grace commands.
GLOUCESTER [*Aside to Clarence*]
  He plies her hard; and much rain wears the marble.
CLARENCE [*Aside to Gloucester*]
  As red as fire? Nay, then, her wax must melt.   51
LADY GREY
  Why stops my lord? Shall I not hear my task?
KING EDWARD
  An easy task. 'Tis but to love a king.
LADY GREY
  That's soon performed, because I am a subject.
KING EDWARD
  Why, then, thy husband's lands I freely give thee.
LADY GREY
  I take my leave with many thousand thanks.
                    [*She curtsies, preparing to go.*]

45 rests in me lies in my power   **46 take . . . boon** object to the request I
ask   **47 except** unless   **51 As red as fire** i.e., Edward is hotly importunate

GLOUCESTER [*Aside to Clarence*]
  The match is made; she seals it with a curtsy.   57
KING EDWARD
  But stay thee. 'Tis the fruits of love I mean.
LADY GREY
  The fruits of love I mean, my loving liege.   59
KING EDWARD
  Ay, but, I fear me, in another sense.
  What love, think'st thou, I sue so much to get?
LADY GREY
  My love till death, my humble thanks, my prayers—
  That love which virtue begs and virtue grants.
KING EDWARD
  No, by my troth, I did not mean such love.   64
LADY GREY
  Why then you mean not as I thought you did.
KING EDWARD
  But now you partly may perceive my mind.
LADY GREY
  My mind will never grant what I perceive
  Your Highness aims at, if I aim aright.   68
KING EDWARD
  To tell thee plain, I aim to lie with thee.
LADY GREY
  To tell you plain, I had rather lie in prison.   70
KING EDWARD
  Why, then, thou shalt not have thy husband's lands.
LADY GREY
  Why, then, mine honesty shall be my dower,   72
  For by that loss I will not purchase them.   73
KING EDWARD
  Therein thou wrong'st thy children mightily.
LADY GREY
  Herein Your Highness wrongs both them and me.
  But, mighty lord, this merry inclination

---

57 seals confirms (as in affixing a seal to a document)   **59 fruits of love**
(Lady Grey interprets the King's sexual phrase in the innocent sense of
"loyal feelings of affection toward the monarch.")   **64 troth** faith
68 aim guess   **70 lie** be confined (with a play on King Edward's *lie* in
sexual embrace)   **72 honesty** chastity, virtue   **73 that loss** loss of that

Accords not with the sadness of my suit.   77
Please you dismiss me, either with ay or no.

KING EDWARD
Ay, if thou wilt say ay to my request;
No, if thou dost say no to my demand.

LADY GREY
Then, no, my lord. My suit is at an end.

GLOUCESTER [*Aside to Clarence*]
The widow likes him not. She knits her brows.

CLARENCE [*Aside to Gloucester*]
He is the bluntest wooer in Christendom.

KING EDWARD [*Aside*]
Her looks doth argue her replete with modesty;   84
Her words doth show her wit incomparable;
All her perfections challenge sovereignty.   86
One way or other, she is for a king,
And she shall be my love, or else my queen.—
Say that King Edward take thee for his queen?

LADY GREY
'Tis better said than done, my gracious lord.
I am a subject fit to jest withal,
But far unfit to be a sovereign.

KING EDWARD
Sweet widow, by my state I swear to thee   93
I speak no more than what my soul intends,
And that is, to enjoy thee for my love.

LADY GREY
And that is more than I will yield unto.
I know I am too mean to be your queen,   97
And yet too good to be your concubine.

KING EDWARD
You cavil, widow. I did mean my queen.

LADY GREY
'Twill grieve Your Grace my sons should call you father.

KING EDWARD
No more than when my daughters call thee mother.
Thou art a widow, and thou hast some children;
And, by God's mother, I, being but a bachelor,

77 **sadness** seriousness   84 **argue her** show her to be   86 **challenge** lay
claim to   93 **state** i.e., kingship   97 **mean** low in social rank

Have other some. Why, 'tis a happy thing   104
To be the father unto many sons.
Answer no more, for thou shalt be my queen.

GLOUCESTER [*Aside to Clarence*]
The ghostly father now hath done his shrift.   107

CLARENCE [*Aside to Gloucester*]
When he was made a shriver, 'twas for shift.   108

KING EDWARD
Brothers, you muse what chat we two have had.   109
          [*Gloucester and Clarence come forward.*]

GLOUCESTER
The widow likes it not, for she looks very sad.   110

KING EDWARD
You'd think it strange if I should marry her.

CLARENCE
To who, my lord?

KING EDWARD   Why, Clarence, to myself.   112

GLOUCESTER
That would be ten days' wonder at the least.   113

CLARENCE
That's a day longer than a wonder lasts.

GLOUCESTER
By so much is the wonder in extremes.   115

KING EDWARD
Well, jest on, brothers. I can tell you both
Her suit is granted for her husband's lands.

          Enter a Nobleman.

NOBLEMAN
My gracious lord, Henry your foe is taken
And brought your prisoner to your palace gate.

KING EDWARD
See that he be conveyed unto the Tower.

---

104 other some some others.   **happy** fortunate   **107 ghostly father**
spiritual father, confessor.   **done his shrift** finished hearing confession
108 for shift (1) to serve a devious purpose (2) for a woman's smock or
chemise   **109 muse** wonder   **110 sad** serious   **112 To who** (Edward
might *marry her* in the sense of giving her in marriage to a wealthy
subject; he might then take her as his mistress.)   **113 ten days' wonder**
(One day longer than the proverbial "nine days' wonder," i.e., an event
of sudden notoriety. Clarence points out the exaggeration in the next
line.)   **115 in extremes** an unusual wonder indeed

And go we, brothers, to the man that took him,
To question of his apprehension.   122
Widow, go you along. Lords, use her honorably.
          Exeunt. Manet Richard [of Gloucester].

GLOUCESTER
Ay, Edward will use women honorably.
Would he were wasted, marrow, bones, and all,   125
That from his loins no hopeful branch may spring
To cross me from the golden time I look for!   127
And yet, between my soul's desire and me—
The lustful Edward's title burièd—   129
Is Clarence, Henry, and his son young Edward,
And all the unlooked-for issue of their bodies,   131
To take their rooms ere I can place myself.   132
A cold premeditation for my purpose!   133
Why, then, I do but dream on sovereignty,
Like one that stands upon a promontory
And spies a far-off shore where he would tread,
Wishing his foot were equal with his eye,   137
And chides the sea that sunders him from thence,
Saying he'll lade it dry to have his way.   139
So do I wish the crown, being so far off,
And so I chide the means that keeps me from it,   141
And so I say I'll cut the causes off,   142
Flattering me with impossibilities.   143
My eye's too quick, my heart o'erweens too much,   144
Unless my hand and strength could equal them.
Well, say there is no kingdom then for Richard;
What other pleasure can the world afford?
I'll make my heaven in a lady's lap,
And deck my body in gay ornaments,
And witch sweet ladies with my words and looks.   150
O miserable thought, and more unlikely

---

122 of his apprehension about his being taken   **125 wasted** wasted with disease—syphilis in particular   **127 cross** thwart, frustrate
129 The . . . burièd i.e., even after lustful Edward's title to the throne is eliminated by his death   **131 unlooked-for** unforeseeable and undesirable   **132 rooms** places   **133 cold premeditation** discouraging prospect
137 equal with his eye i.e., able to achieve what he views   **139 lade** empty (by ladling, scooping)   **141 means** obstacles   **142 causes** i.e., of my impatience   **143 Flattering . . . impossibilities** i.e., deceiving myself with vain hopes   **144 o'erweens** presumes   **150 witch** bewitch

Than to accomplish twenty golden crowns!   152
Why, love forswore me in my mother's womb;
And, for I should not deal in her soft laws,   154
She did corrupt frail nature with some bribe
To shrink mine arm up like a withered shrub;
To make an envious mountain on my back,   157
Where sits deformity to mock my body;
To shape my legs of an unequal size;
To disproportion me in every part,
Like to a chaos, or an unlicked bear whelp   161
That carries no impression like the dam.   162
And am I then a man to be beloved?
O monstrous fault, to harbor such a thought!
Then, since this earth affords no joy to me
But to command, to check, to o'erbear such   166
As are of better person than myself,
I'll make my heaven to dream upon the crown,
And, whiles I live, t' account this world but hell,
Until my misshaped trunk that bears this head
Be round impalèd with a glorious crown.   171
And yet I know not how to get the crown,
For many lives stand between me and home;   173
And I—like one lost in a thorny wood,
That rends the thorns and is rent with the thorns,
Seeking a way and straying from the way,
Not knowing how to find the open air,
But toiling desperately to find it out—
Torment myself to catch the English crown;
And from that torment I will free myself
Or hew my way out with a bloody ax.
Why, I can smile, and murder whiles I smile,
And cry "Content" to that which grieves my heart,
And wet my cheeks with artificial tears,
And frame my face to all occasions.
I'll drown more sailors than the mermaid shall;   186

---

152 accomplish get possession of **154 for** so that **157 envious** spiteful, detested **161 unlicked bear whelp** (It was a popular notion that bears licked their shapeless newly born cubs into a proper shape.) **162 impression** shape **166 check** control, rebuke. **o'erbear** dominate **171 impalèd** enclosed **173 home** i.e., the goal **186 mermaid** (Mermaids allegedly had the power to lure sailors to destruction by their singing or weeping.)

I'll slay more gazers than the basilisk;   187
I'll play the orator as well as Nestor,   188
Deceive more slyly than Ulysses could,   189
And, like a Sinon, take another Troy.   190
I can add colors to the chameleon,
Change shapes with Proteus for advantages,   192
And set the murderous Machiavel to school.   193
Can I do this, and cannot get a crown?
Tut, were it farther off, I'll pluck it down.   *Exit.*

❖

3.3   *Flourish. Enter Lewis the French King, his*
sister Bona, his Admiral, called Bourbon,
Prince Edward, Queen Margaret, and the Earl
of Oxford. Lewis sits, and riseth up again.

KING LEWIS
  Fair Queen of England, worthy Margaret,
  Sit down with us. It ill befits thy state   2
  And birth that thou shouldst stand while Lewis doth sit.
QUEEN MARGARET
  No, mighty King of France. Now Margaret
  Must strike her sail and learn awhile to serve   5
  Where kings command. I was, I must confess,
  Great Albion's queen in former golden days.   7
  But now mischance hath trod my title down   8
  And with dishonor laid me on the ground,

---

187 basilisk fabulous reptile said to kill by its gaze   **188–189 Nestor,
Ulysses** Greek leaders in the Trojan War, noted respectively for aged
wisdom and cunning   **190 Sinon** Greek warrior who allowed himself to
be taken captive by the Trojans, and then, feigning resentment toward
his Greek companions, persuaded Priam to bring the wooden horse
within the city walls by which Troy was taken   **192 Proteus** old man of
the sea, able to assume different shapes.   **for advantages** to suit my
purpose   **193 set . . . school** teach Machiavelli how to be ruthless. (In
the popular imagination, Machiavelli was the archetype of ruthless
political cunning and atheism.)

**3.3. Location: France. The royal court. A throne and a seat or seats are
provided.**
2 state rank   **5 strike her sail** lower her sail, i.e., act deferentially, as
the captain of a sea vessel does to one of higher rank   **7 Albion's**
England's   **8 mischance** misfortune

Where I must take like seat unto my fortune   10
And to my humble seat conform myself.

KING LEWIS
Why, say, fair Queen, whence springs this deep despair?

QUEEN MARGARET
From such a cause as fills mine eyes with tears
And stops my tongue, while heart is drowned in cares.

KING LEWIS
Whate'er it be, be thou still like thyself,   15
And sit thee by our side. (*Seats her by him.*) Yield not
     thy neck
To fortune's yoke, but let thy dauntless mind
Still ride in triumph over all mischance.
Be plain, Queen Margaret, and tell thy grief.   19
It shall be eased, if France can yield relief.   20

QUEEN MARGARET
Those gracious words revive my drooping thoughts
And give my tongue-tied sorrows leave to speak.
Now, therefore, be it known to noble Lewis
That Henry, sole possessor of my love,
Is, of a king, become a banished man   25
And forced to live in Scotland a forlorn,   26
While proud, ambitious Edward, Duke of York,
Usurps the regal title and the seat
Of England's true-anointed lawful king.
This is the cause that I, poor Margaret,
With this my son, Prince Edward, Henry's heir,
Am come to crave thy just and lawful aid;
And if thou fail us, all our hope is done.
Scotland hath will to help, but cannot help;
Our people and our peers are both misled,
Our treasure seized, our soldiers put to flight,
And, as thou seest, ourselves in heavy plight.

KING LEWIS
Renownèd Queen, with patience calm the storm,
While we bethink a means to break it off.   39

10 **like seat unto** a place befitting   15 **like thyself** i.e., as befits your
title   19 **grief** grievances   20 **France** i.e., the King of France   25 **of**
instead of   26 **forlorn** outcast   39 **break it off** i.e., cease the storm
of grief

QUEEN MARGARET
  The more we stay, the stronger grows our foe.   40
KING LEWIS
  The more I stay, the more I'll succor thee.   41
QUEEN MARGARET
  O, but impatience waiteth on true sorrow.   42
  And see where comes the breeder of my sorrow!

    Enter Warwick.

KING LEWIS
  What's he approacheth boldly to our presence?   44
QUEEN MARGARET
  Our Earl of Warwick, Edward's greatest friend.
KING LEWIS
  Welcome, brave Warwick! What brings thee to
    France?   *He descends. She ariseth.*
QUEEN MARGARET
  Ay, now begins a second storm to rise,
  For this is he that moves both wind and tide.
WARWICK
  From worthy Edward, King of Albion,
  My lord and sovereign, and thy vowèd friend,
  I come in kindness and unfeignèd love,
  First, to do greetings to thy royal person,
  And then to crave a league of amity;
  And lastly, to confirm that amity
  With nuptial knot, if thou vouchsafe to grant
  That virtuous Lady Bona, thy fair sister,   56
  To England's king in lawful marriage.
QUEEN MARGARET [*Aside*]
  If that go forward, Henry's hope is done.
WARWICK (*Speaking to Bona*)
  And, gracious madam, in our king's behalf
  I am commanded, with your leave and favor,   60
  Humbly to kiss your hand, and with my tongue
  To tell the passion of my sovereign's heart—

---

40 stay delay   **41 The . . . thee** i.e., the longer preparation I make, the greater help I can give you   **42 waiteth on** attends, accompanies   **44 he** he who   **56 sister** i.e., sister-in-law   **60 leave and favor** kind permission

Where fame, late entering at his heedful ears,   63
Hath placed thy beauty's image and thy virtue.

QUEEN MARGARET
King Lewis and Lady Bona, hear me speak
Before you answer Warwick. His demand
Springs not from Edward's well-meant honest love,
But from deceit bred by necessity.
For how can tyrants safely govern home
Unless abroad they purchase great alliance?
To prove him tyrant this reason may suffice,
That Henry liveth still; but were he dead,
Yet here Prince Edward stands, King Henry's son.
Look, therefore, Lewis, that by this league and marriage
Thou draw not on thy danger and dishonor.   75
For though usurpers sway the rule awhile,   76
Yet heavens are just, and time suppresseth wrongs.

WARWICK
Injurious Margaret!

PRINCE   And why not "Queen"?   78

WARWICK
Because thy father Henry did usurp,
And thou no more art prince than she is queen.

OXFORD
Then Warwick disannuls great John of Gaunt,   81
Which did subdue the greatest part of Spain;   82
And after John of Gaunt, Henry the Fourth,
Whose wisdom was a mirror to the wisest;   84
And after that wise prince, Henry the Fifth,
Who by his prowess conquerèd all France.
From these our Henry lineally descends.

WARWICK
Oxford, how haps it in this smooth discourse   88
You told not how Henry the Sixth hath lost
All that which Henry the Fifth had gotten?
Methinks these peers of France should smile at that.
But for the rest: you tell a pedigree

63 fame report. **late** lately **75 draw not on** do not bring about
76 sway exercise **78 Injurious** insulting **81 disannuls** cancels, takes
no account of **82 Which** who **84 a mirror** a model for emulation
88 haps it does it happen that

Of threescore-and-two years—a silly time   93
To make prescription for a kingdom's worth.   94

OXFORD
Why, Warwick, canst thou speak against thy liege,
Whom thou obeyèd'st thirty-and-six years,
And not bewray thy treason with a blush?   97

WARWICK
Can Oxford, that did ever fence the right,   98
Now buckler falsehood with a pedigree?   99
For shame! Leave Henry, and call Edward king.

OXFORD
Call him my king by whose injurious doom   101
My elder brother, the Lord Aubrey Vere,   102
Was done to death? And more than so, my father,   103
Even in the downfall of his mellowed years,
When nature brought him to the door of death?
No, Warwick, no! While life upholds this arm,
This arm upholds the house of Lancaster.

WARWICK   And I the house of York.

KING LEWIS
Queen Margaret, Prince Edward, and Oxford,
Vouchsafe, at our request, to stand aside
While I use further conference with Warwick.   111
                              They stand aloof.

QUEEN MARGARET
Heavens grant that Warwick's words bewitch him not!

KING LEWIS
Now, Warwick, tell me, even upon thy conscience,
Is Edward your true king? For I were loath
To link with him that were not lawful chosen.

WARWICK
Thereon I pawn my credit and mine honor.   116

93 threescore-and-two i.e., from 1399, the date of Henry IV's accession,
to 1461, that of Edward's.   **silly** i.e., ridiculously short   **94 prescription**
claim founded upon long use and de facto possession   **97 bewray** reveal
98 fence defend   **99 buckler** shield, protect   **101 doom** judgment
102 Lord Aubrey Vere the eldest son of the twelfth Earl of Oxford, John
de Vere. (Both he and his father were attainted and executed for treason
by the Yorkists in 1462.)   **103 more than so** even more than that
111 use further conference hold further conversation   **s.d. aloof** to one
side   **116 pawn my credit** stake my reputation

KING LEWIS
  But is he gracious in the people's eye?
WARWICK
  The more that Henry was unfortunate.
KING LEWIS
  Then further, all dissembling set aside,
  Tell me for truth the measure of his love   120
  Unto our sister Bona.
WARWICK   Such it seems
  As may beseem a monarch like himself.   122
  Myself have often heard him say and swear
  That this his love was an eternal plant,
  Whereof the root was fixed in virtue's ground,
  The leaves and fruit maintained with beauty's sun,
  Exempt from envy, but not from disdain,   127
  Unless the Lady Bona quit his pain.   128
KING LEWIS
  Now, sister, let us hear your firm resolve.
BONA
  Your grant, or your denial, shall be mine.   130
  (*Speaks to Warwick*.) Yet I confess that often ere this day,
  When I have heard your king's desert recounted,   132
  Mine ear hath tempted judgment to desire.   133
KING LEWIS
  Then, Warwick, thus: our sister shall be Edward's.
  And now forthwith shall articles be drawn   135
  Touching the jointure that your king must make,   136
  Which with her dowry shall be counterpoised.—   137
  Draw near, Queen Margaret, and be a witness
  That Bona shall be wife to the English King.
        [*Margaret, Edward, and Oxford come forward.*]
PRINCE
  To Edward, but not to the English King.

---

120 for truth truly   **122 beseem** befit   **127 envy** ill will, malice.   **but . . .
disdain** i.e., his love will wither if the lady disdains him. (Warwick uses
the stock hyperbole of Petrarchan devotion.)   **128 quit** requite, allevi-
ate   **130 grant** granting, agreeing   **132 desert** deserving   **133 Mine . . .
desire** what I have heard has prompted my judgment to desire him
135 articles i.e., articles of a marriage contract   **136 Touching** concerning.   **jointure** marriage settlement made by the groom in behalf of the
bride   **137 counterpoised** matched, balanced in amount

QUEEN MARGARET
  Deceitful Warwick! It was thy device   141
  By this alliance to make void my suit.
  Before thy coming, Lewis was Henry's friend.

KING LEWIS
  And still is friend to him and Margaret.
  But if your title to the crown be weak,
  As may appear by Edward's good success,
  Then 'tis but reason that I be released
  From giving aid which late I promisèd.
  Yet shall you have all kindness at my hand
  That your estate requires and mine can yield.   150

WARWICK [*To Queen Margaret*]
  Henry now lives in Scotland at his ease,
  Where, having nothing, nothing can he lose.
  And as for you yourself, our quondam queen,   153
  You have a father able to maintain you,
  And better 'twere you troubled him than France.

QUEEN MARGARET
  Peace, impudent and shameless Warwick,
  Proud setter-up and puller-down of kings!
  I will not hence till, with my talk and tears,
  Both full of truth, I make King Lewis behold
  Thy sly conveyance and thy lord's false love;   160
  For both of you are birds of selfsame feather.   161
                    Post blowing a horn within.

KING LEWIS
  Warwick, this is some post to us or thee.

  Enter the Post.

POST (*Speaks to Warwick*)
  My Lord Ambassador, these letters are for you,
  Sent from your brother, Marquess Montague.
  (*To Lewis.*) These from our king unto Your Majesty.
  (*To Margaret.*) And, madam, these for you; from whom I
    know not.   *They all read their letters.*

OXFORD [*To Edward*]
  I like it well that our fair queen and mistress
  Smiles at her news, while Warwick frowns at his.

141 device stratagem   **150 estate** rank, condition   **153 quondam** former
160 conveyance underhand dealing   **161 s.d. Post** messenger

PRINCE [*To Oxford*]
  Nay, mark how Lewis stamps, as he were nettled.   169
  I hope all's for the best.

KING LEWIS
  Warwick, what are thy news? And yours, fair Queen?

QUEEN MARGARET
  Mine, such as fill my heart with unhoped joys.

WARWICK
  Mine, full of sorrow and heart's discontent.

KING LEWIS
  What, has your king married the Lady Grey?
  And now, to soothe your forgery and his,   175
  Sends me a paper to persuade me patience?   176
  Is this th' alliance that he seeks with France?
  Dare he presume to scorn us in this manner?

QUEEN MARGARET
  I told Your Majesty as much before.
  This proveth Edward's love and Warwick's honesty.

WARWICK
  King Lewis, I here protest, in sight of heaven
  And by the hope I have of heavenly bliss,
  That I am clear from this misdeed of Edward's—   183
  No more my king, for he dishonors me,
  But most himself, if he could see his shame.
  Did I forget that by the house of York
  My father came untimely to his death?   187
  Did I let pass th' abuse done to my niece?   188
  Did I impale him with the regal crown?   189
  Did I put Henry from his native right?
  And am I guerdoned at the last with shame?   191
  Shame on himself! For my desert is honor;   192
  And to repair my honor lost for him,
  I here renounce him and return to Henry.
  My noble Queen, let former grudges pass,
  And henceforth I am thy true servitor.   196

---

169 as as if   **175 soothe** gloss over.   **forgery** deceit   **176 persuade**
advise   **183 clear from** innocent of   **187 My father** i.e., Salisbury (who,
according to the chronicles, was captured at Wakefield and beheaded by
the Lancastrians)   **188 abuse . . . niece** (The chronicles report that
Edward attempted to "deflower" Warwick's niece while a guest in his
house.)   **189 impale him** i.e., encircle his head   **191 guerdoned** rewarded   **192 my desert** what I deserve   **196 true servitor** loyal servant

I will revenge his wrong to Lady Bona
And replant Henry in his former state.

QUEEN MARGARET
Warwick, these words have turned my hate to love;
And I forgive and quite forget old faults,
And joy that thou becom'st King Henry's friend.

WARWICK
So much his friend, ay, his unfeignèd friend,
That, if King Lewis vouchsafe to furnish us
With some few bands of chosen soldiers,
I'll undertake to land them on our coast
And force the tyrant from his seat by war.   206
'Tis not his new-made bride shall succor him.   207
And as for Clarence, as my letters tell me,
He's very likely now to fall from him,   209
For matching more for wanton lust than honor,   210
Or than for strength and safety of our country.

BONA
Dear brother, how shall Bona be revenged
But by thy help to this distressèd queen?

QUEEN MARGARET
Renownèd prince, how shall poor Henry live,
Unless thou rescue him from foul despair?

BONA
My quarrel and this English queen's are one.

WARWICK
And mine, fair Lady Bona, joins with yours.

KING LEWIS
And mine with hers, and thine, and Margaret's.
Therefore at last I firmly am resolved
You shall have aid.

QUEEN MARGARET
Let me give humble thanks for all at once.

KING LEWIS
Then, England's messenger, return in post   222
And tell false Edward, thy supposèd king,
That Lewis of France is sending over maskers   224

---

206 tyrant usurper **207 'Tis . . . him** i.e., no newly chosen bride like
Lady Grey is going to be enough to save him **209 fall from** desert
210 matching marrying **222 in post** in haste **224 maskers** dancers in
a masque or court revels. (Said ironically.)

To revel it with him and his new bride.
Thou seest what's passed. Go fear thy king withal.   226
BONA
Tell him, in hope he'll prove a widower shortly,
I'll wear the willow garland for his sake.   228
QUEEN MARGARET
Tell him my mourning weeds are laid aside   229
And I am ready to put armor on.
WARWICK
Tell him from me that he hath done me wrong,
And therefore I'll uncrown him ere 't be long.
There's thy reward. [*He gives money.*] Begone.

                              Exit Post.
KING LEWIS   But, Warwick,
Thou and Oxford, with five thousand men,
Shall cross the seas and bid false Edward battle;
And, as occasion serves, this noble queen
And prince shall follow with a fresh supply.   237
Yet, ere thou go, but answer me one doubt: 238
What pledge have we of thy firm loyalty?
WARWICK
This shall assure my constant loyalty,
That, if our queen and this young prince agree,
I'll join mine eldest daughter and my joy   242
To him forthwith in holy wedlock bands.
QUEEN MARGARET
Yes, I agree, and thank you for your motion.   244
Son Edward, she is fair and virtuous;
Therefore delay not. Give thy hand to Warwick,
And, with thy hand, thy faith irrevocable
That only Warwick's daughter shall be thine.
PRINCE
Yes, I accept her, for she well deserves it;

---

226 fear frighten. **withal** with this **228 willow garland** (Symbol of a
forsaken lover; said here contemptuously. The leaves are from the great
willow herb, or loosestrife, not from the willow tree.) **229 weeds**
garments **237 supply** reinforcements **238 but** only **242 eldest daughter** (A historical inaccuracy; Prince Edward was betrothed to a younger
daughter of Warwick, Anne, who later married Richard of Gloucester;
the eldest daughter, Isabella, was already the wife of the Duke of Clarence.) **244 motion** proposal

And here, to pledge my vow, I give my hand.
                    He gives his hand to Warwick.

KING LEWIS
  Why stay we now? These soldiers shall be levied,   251
  And thou, Lord Bourbon, our high admiral,
  Shall waft them over with our royal fleet.   253
  I long till Edward fall by war's mischance
  For mocking marriage with a dame of France.   255
                    Exeunt. Manet Warwick.

WARWICK
  I came from Edward as ambassador,
  But I return his sworn and mortal foe.
  Matter of marriage was the charge he gave me,
  But dreadful war shall answer his demand.
  Had he none else to make a stale but me?   260
  Then none but I shall turn his jest to sorrow.
  I was the chief that raised him to the crown,
  And I'll be chief to bring him down again—
  Not that I pity Henry's misery,
  But seek revenge on Edward's mockery.   *Exit.*

❧

---

251 stay delay **253 waft** convey by water **255 s.d. Manet** he remains
onstage **260 stale** dupe, laughingstock

4.1 *Enter Richard, [Duke of Gloucester,] Clarence,*
Somerset, and Montague.

GLOUCESTER
  Now tell me, brother Clarence, what think you
  Of this new marriage with the Lady Grey?
  Hath not our brother made a worthy choice?
CLARENCE
  Alas, you know, 'tis far from hence to France.
  How could he stay till Warwick made return?   5
SOMERSET
  My lords, forbear this talk. Here comes the King.   6

    Flourish. Enter King Edward, Lady Grey [as
    Queen Elizabeth], Pembroke, Stafford, Hastings.
    Four stand on one side and four on the other.

GLOUCESTER And his well-chosen bride.
CLARENCE
  I mind to tell him plainly what I think.   8
KING EDWARD
  Now, brother of Clarence, how like you our choice,
  That you stand pensive, as half malcontent?   10
CLARENCE
  As well as Lewis of France, or the Earl of Warwick,
  Which are so weak of courage and in judgment   12
  That they'll take no offense at our abuse.   13
KING EDWARD
  Suppose they take offense without a cause;
  They are but Lewis and Warwick. I am Edward,
  Your king and Warwick's, and must have my will.   16
GLOUCESTER
  And shall have your will, because our king.
  Yet hasty marriage seldom proveth well.
KING EDWARD
  Yea, brother Richard, are you offended too?

4.1. Location: London. The royal court.
5 stay wait. (Clarence speaks ironically.) **6 s.d. Four stand** i.e., the four
already onstage. Edward is seemingly in the middle. **8 mind** intend
10 malcontent discontented **12 Which** who **13 abuse** insult. (Clarence
speaks scornfully, as does Gloucester in ll. 21–23.) **16 have my will**
(1) have my way (2) fulfill my lust

GLOUCESTER   Not I.
  No, God forbid that I should wish them severed
  Whom God hath joined together! Ay, and 'twere pity
  To sunder them that yoke so well together.   23

KING EDWARD
  Setting your scorns and your mislike aside,   24
  Tell me some reason why the Lady Grey
  Should not become my wife and England's queen.
  And you too, Somerset and Montague,
  Speak freely what you think.

CLARENCE
  Then this is mine opinion: that King Lewis
  Becomes your enemy for mocking him
  About the marriage of the Lady Bona.

GLOUCESTER
  And Warwick, doing what you gave in charge,   32
  Is now dishonorèd by this new marriage.

KING EDWARD
  What if both Lewis and Warwick be appeased
  By such invention as I can devise?   35

MONTAGUE
  Yet, to have joined with France in such alliance
  Would more have strengthened this our commonwealth
  'Gainst foreign storms than any homebred marriage.

HASTINGS
  Why, knows not Montague that of itself
  England is safe, if true within itself?

MONTAGUE
  But the safer when 'tis backed with France.

HASTINGS
  'Tis better using France than trusting France.
  Let us be backed with God and with the seas
  Which He hath given for fence impregnable,
  And with their helps only defend ourselves;   45
  In them and in ourselves our safety lies.

---

23 yoke are bound in marriage. (But Gloucester parodies the language
of the marriage service in such a way as to suggest sexual coupling and
the yoking of oxen.)   **24 mislike** displeasure   **32 gave in charge** commissioned   **35 invention** scheme, plan   **45 only** alone

CLARENCE
For this one speech Lord Hastings well deserves
To have the heir of the Lord Hungerford.   48

KING EDWARD
Ay, what of that? It was my will and grant,
And for this once my will shall stand for law.

GLOUCESTER
And yet methinks Your Grace hath not done well
To give the heir and daughter of Lord Scales
Unto the brother of your loving bride.   53
She better would have fitted me or Clarence.
But in your bride you bury brotherhood.

CLARENCE
Or else you would not have bestowed the heir
Of the Lord Bonville on your new wife's son,   57
And leave your brothers to go speed elsewhere.   58

KING EDWARD
Alas, poor Clarence! Is it for a wife
That thou art malcontent? I will provide thee.

CLARENCE
In choosing for yourself you showed your judgment,
Which being shallow, you shall give me leave
To play the broker in mine own behalf;   63
And to that end I shortly mind to leave you.   64

KING EDWARD
Leave me or tarry, Edward will be king,   65
And not be tied unto his brother's will.

QUEEN ELIZABETH
My lords, before it pleased His Majesty
To raise my state to title of a queen,
Do me but right, and you must all confess
That I was not ignoble of descent;
And meaner than myself have had like fortune.   71

---

48 To . . . Hungerford (Clarence objects to the marriage of Lord Hastings to the daughter of Lord Hungerford.)   **53 brother** i.e., Lord Anthony Rivers (whose marriage to the daughter of Lord Scales was one of
the advancements of Queen Elizabeth's kindred so much resented by
Edward's brothers and other noble supporters)   **57 son** i.e., Sir Thomas
Grey, Marquess Dorset, another of the Queen's upstart relatives advanced by Edward   **58 speed** prosper   **63 broker** agent, go-between
64 mind intend   **65 Leave** whether you leave   **71 meaner** more lowly

But as this title honors me and mine,
So your dislikes, to whom I would be pleasing,   73
Doth cloud my joys with danger and with sorrow.   74

KING EDWARD
My love, forbear to fawn upon their frowns.   75
What danger or what sorrow can befall thee
So long as Edward is thy constant friend
And their true sovereign, whom they must obey?
Nay, whom they shall obey, and love thee too,
Unless they seek for hatred at my hands;
Which if they do, yet will I keep thee safe,
And they shall feel the vengeance of my wrath.

GLOUCESTER [*Aside*]
I hear, yet say not much, but think the more.

    Enter a Post.

KING EDWARD
Now, messenger, what letters or what news
From France?

POST
My sovereign liege, no letters, and few words,
But such as I, without your special pardon,   87
Dare not relate.

KING EDWARD
Go to, we pardon thee. Therefore, in brief,   89
Tell me their words as near as thou canst guess them.   90
What answer makes King Lewis unto our letters?

POST
At my depart, these were his very words: 92
"Go tell false Edward, the supposèd king,
That Lewis of France is sending over maskers
To revel it with him and his new bride."

KING EDWARD
Is Lewis so brave? Belike he thinks me Henry.   96
But what said Lady Bona to my marriage?

POST
These were her words, uttered with mild disdain:

---

73 would wish to   **74 danger** apprehension   **75 forbear . . . frowns** stop
trying to overcome their disapproval by ingratiating yourself   **87 pardon**
i.e., permission   **89 Go to** (An expression of remonstrance.)   **90 guess** i.e.,
reproduce from memory   **92 depart** departure   **96 Belike** perhaps

"Tell him, in hope he'll prove a widower shortly,
I'll wear the willow garland for his sake."

KING EDWARD
I blame not her, she could say little less;
She had the wrong. But what said Henry's queen?
For I have heard that she was there in place.

POST
"Tell him," quoth she, "my mourning weeds are done,   104
And I am ready to put armor on."

KING EDWARD
Belike she minds to play the Amazon.   106
But what said Warwick to these injuries?   107

POST
He, more incensed against Your Majesty
Than all the rest, discharged me with these words: 109
"Tell him from me that he hath done me wrong,
And therefore I'll uncrown him ere 't be long."

KING EDWARD
Ha? Durst the traitor breathe out so proud words?
Well, I will arm me, being thus forewarned.
They shall have wars and pay for their presumption.
But say, is Warwick friends with Margaret?

POST
Ay, gracious sovereign, they are so linked in friendship
That young Prince Edward marries Warwick's
   daughter.

CLARENCE
Belike the elder; Clarence will have the younger.   118
Now, brother king, farewell, and sit you fast,   119
For I will hence to Warwick's other daughter,
That, though I want a kingdom, yet in marriage   121
I may not prove inferior to yourself.
You that love me and Warwick, follow me.
      Exit Clarence, and Somerset follows.

GLOUCESTER [*Aside*] Not I.
My thoughts aim at a further matter. I
Stay not for the love of Edward, but the crown.

---

104 done i.e., no longer needed   **106 Amazon** mythical female warrior
107 injuries insults   **109 discharged** dismissed   **118 the elder** (Cf.
3.3.242, note.)   **119 sit you fast** i.e., hold on tight to your throne
121 want lack

KING EDWARD

  Clarence and Somerset both gone to Warwick?

  Yet am I armed against the worst can happen;   128

  And haste is needful in this desperate case.

  Pembroke and Stafford, you in our behalf

  Go levy men and make prepare for war.   131

  They are already, or quickly will be, landed.

  Myself in person will straight follow you.   133

               Exeunt Pembroke and Stafford.

  But ere I go, Hastings and Montague,

  Resolve my doubt. You twain, of all the rest,

  Are near to Warwick by blood and by alliance.

  Tell me if you love Warwick more than me.

  If it be so, then both depart to him;

  I rather wish you foes than hollow friends.

  But if you mind to hold your true obedience,   140

  Give me assurance with some friendly vow,

  That I may never have you in suspect.   142

MONTAGUE

  So God help Montague as he proves true!

HASTINGS

  And Hastings as he favors Edward's cause!

KING EDWARD

  Now, brother Richard, will you stand by us?

GLOUCESTER

  Ay, in despite of all that shall withstand you.   146

KING EDWARD

  Why, so. Then am I sure of victory.

  Now therefore let us hence, and lose no hour

  Till we meet Warwick with his foreign power.

                       Exeunt.

❖

---

128 can that can   **131 prepare** preparation   **133 straight** immediately
140 mind intend   **142 suspect** suspicion   **146 despite** spite

4.2   *Enter Warwick and Oxford in England, with*
          French soldiers.

WARWICK
  Trust me, my lord, all hitherto goes well.
  The common people by numbers swarm to us.

    Enter Clarence and Somerset.

  But see where Somerset and Clarence comes!
  Speak suddenly, my lords, are we all friends?
CLARENCE   Fear not that, my lord.
WARWICK
  Then, gentle Clarence, welcome unto Warwick;   6
  And welcome, Somerset! I hold it cowardice
  To rest mistrustful where a noble heart   8
  Hath pawned an open hand in sign of love;   9
  Else might I think that Clarence, Edward's brother,
  Were but a feignèd friend to our proceedings.
  But welcome, sweet Clarence. My daughter shall be
    thine.
  And now what rests but, in night's coverture,   13
  Thy brother being carelessly encamped,
  His soldiers lurking in the towns about,   15
  And but attended by a simple guard,   16
  We may surprise and take him at our pleasure?   17
  Our scouts have found the adventure very easy;   18
  That as Ulysses and stout Diomed   19
  With sleight and manhood stole to Rhesus' tents   20
  And brought from thence the Thracian fatal steeds,   21
  So we, well covered with the night's black mantle,
  At unawares may beat down Edward's guard   23

4.2. Location: Fields in Warwickshire.
6 gentle noble   **8 rest** remain   **9 pawned** pledged   **13 rests** remains.
in night's coverture under cover of night   **15 lurking** idling, lodging
16 simple mere   **17 at our pleasure** whenever we wish   **18 adventure**
venturing (into Edward's camp)   **19–21 Ulysses . . . steeds** (In Book 10
of the *Iliad*, Ulysses and Diomedes under cover of night stealthily enter
the camp of the Thracian leader Rhesus, slay him and twelve of his
men, and lead away his horses. The horses are called *fatal steeds* because of a prophecy foretelling that Troy would not fall if once these
horses drank from the River Xanthus and grazed on the Trojan plain.)
19 stout brave   **20 sleight** cunning   **23 At unawares** unexpectedly,
suddenly

And seize himself. I say not "slaughter him,"
For I intend but only to surprise him.   25
You that will follow me to this attempt,
Applaud the name of Henry with your leader.

                They all cry "Henry!"

Why, then, let's on our way in silent sort.   28
For Warwick and his friends, God and Saint George!

                     Exeunt.

❖

4.3   *Enter three Watchmen to guard*
        the King's tent.

FIRST WATCH
   Come on, my masters, each man take his stand.
   The King by this is set him down to sleep.   2
SECOND WATCH   What, will he not to bed?
FIRST WATCH
   Why, no, for he hath made a solemn vow
   Never to lie and take his natural rest
   Till Warwick or himself be quite suppressed.
SECOND WATCH
   Tomorrow then belike shall be the day,
   If Warwick be so near as men report.
THIRD WATCH
   But say, I pray, what nobleman is that
   That with the King here resteth in his tent?
FIRST WATCH
   'Tis the Lord Hastings, the King's chiefest friend.
THIRD WATCH
   O, is it so? But why commands the King
   That his chief followers lodge in towns about him,   13
   While he himself keeps in the cold field?   14
SECOND WATCH
   'Tis the more honor, because more dangerous.

---

25 surprise capture   **28 sort** fashion

4.3. Location: Edward's camp near Warwick.
2 by this by this time.   **set him** settled himself   **13 about** round about
14 keeps lodges

THIRD WATCH
Ay, but give me worship and quietness;   16
I like it better than a dangerous honor.
If Warwick knew in what estate he stands,   18
'Tis to be doubted he would waken him.   19

FIRST WATCH
Unless our halberds did shut up his passage.   20

SECOND WATCH
Ay, wherefore else guard we his royal tent
But to defend his person from night foes?

Enter Warwick, Clarence, Oxford, Somerset,
and French soldiers, silent all.

WARWICK
This is his tent, and see where stand his guard.
Courage, my masters! Honor now or never!
But follow me, and Edward shall be ours.   25

FIRST WATCH   Who goes there?

SECOND WATCH   Stay, or thou diest!
                Warwick and the rest cry all "Warwick!
                Warwick!" and set upon the guard, who
                fly, crying "Arm! Arm!" Warwick and
                the rest following them.

The drum playing and trumpet sounding, enter
Warwick, Somerset, and the rest, bringing the
King [Edward] out in his gown, sitting in a chair.
Richard [of Gloucester] and Hastings fly over the
stage.

SOMERSET   What are they that fly there?

WARWICK
Richard and Hastings. Let them go. Here is
The Duke.

KING EDWARD   "The Duke"? Why, Warwick, when we
    parted
Thou calledst me King.

---

16 worship ease and dignity   **18 estate** situation.   **he** i.e., King Edward
19 doubted feared   **20 halberds** long-handled weapons bearing axlike
heads.   **shut up his passage** prevent Warwick's getting through
25 But only

WARWICK   Ay, but the case is altered.
  When you disgraced me in my ambassade,   32
  Then I degraded you from being king,
  And come now to create you Duke of York.
  Alas, how should you govern any kingdom,
  That know not how to use ambassadors,
  Nor how to be contented with one wife,
  Nor how to use your brothers brotherly,
  Nor how to study for the people's welfare,
  Nor how to shroud yourself from enemies?   40

KING EDWARD
  Yea, brother of Clarence, art thou here too?
  Nay, then I see that Edward needs must down.   42
  Yet, Warwick, in despite of all mischance,
  Of thee thyself and all thy complices,   44
  Edward will always bear himself as king.
  Though Fortune's malice overthrow my state,
  My mind exceeds the compass of her wheel.   47

WARWICK
  Then, for his mind, be Edward England's king.   48
                Takes off his crown.
  But Henry now shall wear the English crown
  And be true king indeed, thou but the shadow.
  My lord of Somerset, at my request
  See that forthwith Duke Edward be conveyed
  Unto my brother, Archbishop of York.   53
  When I have fought with Pembroke and his fellows,
  I'll follow you, and tell what answer
  Lewis and the Lady Bona send to him.
  Now, for a while farewell, good Duke of York.
          They [begin to] lead him out forcibly.

KING EDWARD
  What fates impose, that men must needs abide.
  It boots not to resist both wind and tide.   59
       Exeunt [Edward, Somerset, and soldiers].

---

32 **ambassade** ambassadorial mission   **40 shroud** conceal, shield
42 needs must down must fall of necessity   **44 complices** accomplices
47 My . . . wheel i.e., my spirit rises above the misery of Fortune and her
wheel.   **compass** range, circumference   **48 for his mind** i.e., in his own
thoughts   **53 Archbishop of York** i.e., George Neville   **59 boots** avails

OXFORD
> What now remains, my lords, for us to do
> But march to London with our soldiers?

WARWICK
> Ay, that's the first thing that we have to do,
> To free King Henry from imprisonment
> And see him seated in the regal throne. *Exeunt.*

❖

4.4 *Enter Rivers and Lady Grey [Queen Elizabeth].*

RIVERS
> Madam, what makes you in this sudden change?   1

QUEEN ELIZABETH
> Why, brother Rivers, are you yet to learn
> What late misfortune is befall'n King Edward?   3

RIVERS
> What? Loss of some pitched battle against Warwick?

QUEEN ELIZABETH
> No, but the loss of his own royal person.

RIVERS   Then is my sovereign slain?

QUEEN ELIZABETH
> Ay, almost slain, for he is taken prisoner,
> Either betrayed by falsehood of his guard
> Or by his foe surprised at unawares;
> And, as I further have to understand,   10
> Is new committed to the Bishop of York,   11
> Fell Warwick's brother, and by that our foe.   12

RIVERS
> These news I must confess are full of grief,
> Yet, gracious madam, bear it as you may.
> Warwick may lose, that now hath won the day.

QUEEN ELIZABETH
> Till then fair hope must hinder life's decay.   16
> And I the rather wean me from despair

4.4. Location: London. The royal court.
1 makes . . . change causes this sudden change (of mood) in you   **3 late**
recent   **10 have to** am given to   **11 new** newly.   **Bishop** i.e., Archbishop
12 Fell cruel.   **by that** i.e., by that token   **16 hope . . . decay** i.e., only
hope can hold off my downfall and death

For love of Edward's offspring in my womb.
This is it that makes me bridle passion   19
And bear with mildness my misfortune's cross.
Ay, ay, for this I draw in many a tear   21
And stop the rising of bloodsucking sighs,   22
Lest with my sighs or tears I blast or drown   23
King Edward's fruit, true heir to th' English crown.

RIVERS
But, madam, where is Warwick then become?

QUEEN ELIZABETH
I am informed that he comes towards London
To set the crown once more on Henry's head.
Guess thou the rest. King Edward's friends must down.   28
But, to prevent the tyrant's violence—   29
For trust not him that hath once broken faith—
I'll hence forthwith unto the sanctuary,   31
To save at least the heir of Edward's right.   32
There shall I rest secure from force and fraud.
Come, therefore, let us fly while we may fly.
If Warwick take us we are sure to die.   *Exeunt.*

✦

4.5   *Enter Richard, [Duke of Gloucester,] Lord*
        Hastings, and Sir William Stanley.

GLOUCESTER
Now, my Lord Hastings and Sir William Stanley,
Leave off to wonder why I drew you hither   2
Into this chiefest thicket of the park.   3
Thus stands the case: you know our king, my brother,
Is prisoner to the Bishop here, at whose hands
He hath good usage and great liberty,

---

19 bridle passion control my grief **21 draw in** hold back **22 bloodsucking sighs** (Sighs were thought to cost the heart a drop of blood.) **23 blast** wither, blight **28 must down** are destined to fall **29 prevent** forestall **31 the sanctuary** residence inside a church building, providing immunity from law **32 right** royal claim

4.5. Location: A park belonging to the Archbishop of York, historically identified as Middleham Castle in Yorkshire.
2 Leave off cease **3 chiefest thicket** thickest copse

And, often but attended with weak guard,   7
Comes hunting this way to disport himself.   8
I have advertised him by secret means   9
That if about this hour he make this way   10
Under the color of his usual game,   11
He shall here find his friends with horse and men
To set him free from his captivity.

Enter King Edward and a Huntsman with him.

HUNTSMAN
   This way, my lord, for this way lies the game.   14
KING EDWARD
   Nay, this way, man. See where the huntsmen stand.
   Now, brother of Gloucester, Lord Hastings, and the rest,
   Stand you thus close to steal the Bishop's deer?   17
GLOUCESTER
   Brother, the time and case requireth haste.   18
   Your horse stands ready at the park corner.
KING EDWARD
   But whither shall we then?
HASTINGS   To Lynn, my lord—   20
   And shipped from thence to Flanders?
GLOUCESTER
   Well guessed, believe me, for that was my meaning.
KING EDWARD
   Stanley, I will requite thy forwardness.   23
GLOUCESTER
   But wherefore stay we? 'Tis no time to talk.
KING EDWARD
   Huntsman, what sayst thou? Wilt thou go along?   25
HUNTSMAN
   Better do so than tarry and be hanged.
GLOUCESTER
   Come then, away. Let's ha' no more ado.

---

7 but attended with attended only by   **8 disport** amuse   **9 advertised**
notified   **10 make** come   **11 color** pretext.   **his usual game** his usual
custom of the hunt   **14 game** quarry   **17 close** concealed   **18 case**
circumstance   **20 Lynn** King's Lynn, a seaport in Norfolk   **23 requite**
repay.   **forwardness** zeal   **25 go along** come along with us

KING EDWARD
  Bishop, farewell! Shield thee from Warwick's frown,
  And pray that I may repossess the crown.   *Exeunt.*

❖

4.6   *Flourish. Enter King Henry the Sixth,*
           Clarence, Warwick, Somerset, young Henry
           [Earl of Richmond], Oxford, Montague, and
           Lieutenant [of the Tower].

KING HENRY
  Master Lieutenant, now that God and friends
  Have shaken Edward from the regal seat
  And turned my captive state to liberty,
  My fear to hope, my sorrows unto joys,
  At our enlargement what are thy due fees?   5
LIEUTENANT
  Subjects may challenge nothing of their sovereigns; 6
  But if an humble prayer may prevail,
  I then crave pardon of Your Majesty.
KING HENRY
  For what, Lieutenant? For well using me?
  Nay, be thou sure I'll well requite thy kindness,
  For that it made my imprisonment a pleasure—   11
  Ay, such a pleasure as encagèd birds
  Conceive when, after many moody thoughts,
  At last by notes of household harmony   14
  They quite forget their loss of liberty.
  But, Warwick, after God, thou sett'st me free,
  And chiefly therefore I thank God and thee.
  He was the author, thou the instrument.
  Therefore, that I may conquer fortune's spite
  By living low, where fortune cannot hurt me,   20

4.6. Location: The Tower of London.
s.d. Enter . . . Tower (In the octavo stage direction, Warwick and Clarence enter first "with the crown," then Henry, Oxford, Somerset, and "the young Earl of Richmond.") **5 enlargement** release from confinement **6 challenge** claim as a right **11 For that** because **14 household harmony** harmonious song suited to a domestic life **20 low** humbly

And that the people of this blessèd land
May not be punished with my thwarting stars,   22
Warwick, although my head still wear the crown,
I here resign my government to thee,
For thou art fortunate in all thy deeds.

WARWICK
Your Grace hath still been famed for virtuous,   26
And now may seem as wise as virtuous
By spying and avoiding fortune's malice,   28
For few men rightly temper with the stars.   29
Yet in this one thing let me blame Your Grace:
For choosing me when Clarence is in place.   31

CLARENCE
No, Warwick, thou art worthy of the sway,   32
To whom the heavens in thy nativity
Adjudged an olive branch and laurel crown,   34
As likely to be blest in peace and war;
And therefore I yield thee my free consent.   36

WARWICK
And I choose Clarence only for Protector.   37

KING HENRY
Warwick and Clarence, give me both your hands.
                    [*The King joins their hands.*]
Now join your hands, and with your hands your hearts,
That no dissension hinder government.
I make you both Protectors of this land,
While I myself will lead a private life
And in devotion spend my latter days,   43
To sin's rebuke and my Creator's praise.

WARWICK
What answers Clarence to his sovereign's will?

CLARENCE
That he consents, if Warwick yield consent;
For on thy fortune I repose myself.   47

---

22 thwarting crossing (in their astrological influence)   **26 still** always.
famed for virtuous reputed to be virtuous   **28 spying** spying out,
foreseeing   **29 temper . . . stars** i.e., blend or accord with their destiny
31 in place present   **32 sway** rule   **34 olive branch** (Symbol of peace.)
laurel crown (Symbol of honor in war.)   **36 free** freely given   **37 only
for** as sole   **43 latter** last   **47 repose myself** rely

WARWICK
    Why, then, though loath, yet must I be content.
    We'll yoke together, like a double shadow
    To Henry's body, and supply his place—
    I mean, in bearing weight of government
    While he enjoys the honor and his ease.
    And, Clarence, now then it is more than needful
    Forthwith that Edward be pronounced a traitor,
    And all his lands and goods be confiscate.

CLARENCE
    What else? And that succession be determined.   56

WARWICK
    Ay, therein Clarence shall not want his part.   57

KING HENRY
    But with the first of all your chief affairs,
    Let me entreat—for I command no more—
    That Margaret your queen and my son Edward
    Be sent for, to return from France with speed;
    For till I see them here, by doubtful fear
    My joy of liberty is half eclipsed.

CLARENCE
    It shall be done, my sovereign, with all speed.

KING HENRY
    My lord of Somerset, what youth is that
    Of whom you seem to have so tender care?

SOMERSET
    My liege, it is young Henry, Earl of Richmond.   67

KING HENRY
    Come hither, England's hope. (*Lays his hand on
      his head.*) If secret powers
    Suggest but truth to my divining thoughts,   69
    This pretty lad will prove our country's bliss.
    His looks are full of peaceful majesty,
    His head by nature framed to wear a crown,
    His hand to wield a scepter, and himself

56 What else i.e., yes, certainly.   **succession be determined** the order of succession to the throne (in view of Edward's removal) be definitely established   **57 want** lack. (Clarence would have an interest in the crown previously claimed by his brother and willed to him after Henry's death.)   **67 Henry . . . Richmond** Henry Tudor, later Henry VII and founder of the Tudor dynasty   **69 divining** foreseeing the future

Likely in time to bless a regal throne.
Make much of him, my lords, for this is he
Must help you more than you are hurt by me.

    Enter a Post.

WARWICK   What news, my friend?
POST
  That Edward is escapèd from your brother   78
  And fled, as he hears since, to Burgundy.   79
WARWICK
  Unsavory news! But how made he escape?
POST
  He was conveyed by Richard, Duke of Gloucester,   81
  And the Lord Hastings, who attended him   82
  In secret ambush on the forest side
  And from the Bishop's huntsmen rescued him;
  For hunting was his daily exercise.
WARWICK
  My brother was too careless of his charge.
  But let us hence, my sovereign, to provide
  A salve for any sore that may betide.   88
                    Exeunt. Manent Somerset,
                       Richmond, and Oxford.
SOMERSET [*To Oxford*]
  My lord, I like not of this flight of Edward's;   89
  For doubtless Burgundy will yield him help,
  And we shall have more wars before 't be long.
  As Henry's late presaging prophecy
  Did glad my heart with hope of this young Richmond,
  So doth my heart misgive me, in these conflicts
  What may befall him, to his harm and ours.
  Therefore, Lord Oxford, to prevent the worst,
  Forthwith we'll send him hence to Brittany,
  Till storms be past of civil enmity.
OXFORD
  Ay, for if Edward repossess the crown,

---

78 your brother i.e., the Archbishop of York **79 he** i.e., your brother
81 conveyed spirited away **82 attended** awaited **88 betide** occur,
develop **s.d. Manent** they remain onstage **89 like not of** am displeased by

'Tis like that Richmond with the rest shall down.   100
SOMERSET
  It shall be so. He shall to Brittany.
  Come, therefore, let's about it speedily.   *Exeunt.*

✢

4.7   *Flourish. Enter [King] Edward, Richard, [Duke*
        of Gloucester,] Hastings, and soldiers, [a troop
        of Hollanders].

KING EDWARD
  Now, brother Richard, Lord Hastings, and the rest,
  Yet thus far fortune maketh us amends
  And says that once more I shall interchange
  My wanèd state for Henry's regal crown.
  Well have we passed and now repassed the seas,
  And brought desirèd help from Burgundy.
  What then remains, we being thus arrived
  From Ravenspurgh haven before the gates of York,   8
  But that we enter, as into our dukedom?
GLOUCESTER
  The gates made fast? Brother, I like not this;
  For many men that stumble at the threshold
  Are well foretold that danger lurks within.
KING EDWARD
  Tush, man, abodements must not now affright us.   13
  By fair or foul means we must enter in,
  For hither will our friends repair to us.
HASTINGS
  My liege, I'll knock once more to summon them.   16

        Enter, on the walls, the Mayor of York and his
        brethren [the aldermen].

100 like likely.   **down** fall

4.7. Location: Before the walls of York.
8 Ravenspurgh former seaport on the Yorkshire coast, at the mouth of
the River Humber   **13 abodements** omens (such as stumbling at the
threshold, a conventional sign of bad luck)   **16 s.d. on the walls** (In this
scene, the back wall of the stage, or tiring-house facade, is imagined
to be the walls of York; a door in the facade represents the gates; and
persons in the rear gallery above the stage are *on the walls*.)

MAYOR

My lords, we were forewarnèd of your coming
And shut the gates for safety of ourselves;
For now we owe allegiance unto Henry.

KING EDWARD

But, Master Mayor, if Henry be your king,
Yet Edward at the least is Duke of York.

MAYOR

True, my good lord, I know you for no less.

KING EDWARD

Why, and I challenge nothing but my dukedom,   23
As being well content with that alone.

GLOUCESTER [*Aside*]

But when the fox hath once got in his nose,
He'll soon find means to make the body follow.

HASTINGS

Why, Master Mayor, why stand you in a doubt?
Open the gates. We are King Henry's friends.

MAYOR

Ay, say you so? The gates shall then be opened.   29
                    He descends [*with the aldermen*].

GLOUCESTER

A wise stout captain, and soon persuaded!   30

HASTINGS

The good old man would fain that all were well,   31
So 'twere not long of him; but being entered,   32
I doubt not, I, but we shall soon persuade
Both him and all his brothers unto reason.

Enter [*below*] *the Mayor and two aldermen.*

KING EDWARD

So, Master Mayor, these gates must not be shut
But in the night or in the time of war.
What, fear not, man, but yield me up the keys,
                    Takes his keys

---

23 **challenge** claim   29 s.d. **descends** (The Mayor and aldermen descend from the rear gallery behind the scenes, and then enter below through the door representing the gates of York.)   30 **stout** brave   31 **fain** be glad   32 **So . . . him** as long as he does not bear the responsibility

For Edward will defend the town and thee,
And all those friends that deign to follow me.   39

*March. Enter Montgomery, with drum
and Soldiers.*

GLOUCESTER
Brother, this is Sir John Montgomery,   40
Our trusty friend, unless I be deceived.
KING EDWARD
Welcome, Sir John! But why come you in arms?
MONTGOMERY
To help King Edward in his time of storm,
As every loyal subject ought to do.
KING EDWARD
Thanks, good Montgomery; but we now forget
Our title to the crown, and only claim
Our dukedom till God please to send the rest.
MONTGOMERY
Then fare you well, for I will hence again.
I came to serve a king and not a duke.
Drummer, strike up, and let us march away.   50
                    The drum begins to march.
KING EDWARD
Nay, stay, Sir John, awhile, and we'll debate
By what safe means the crown may be recovered.
MONTGOMERY
What talk you of debating? In few words,
If you'll not here proclaim yourself our king,
I'll leave you to your fortune and be gone
To keep them back that come to succor you.
Why shall we fight, if you pretend no title?   57
GLOUCESTER
Why, brother, wherefore stand you on nice points?   58
KING EDWARD
When we grow stronger, then we'll make our claim;
Till then, 'tis wisdom to conceal our meaning.   60

39 deign are willing   **s.d. drum** drummer   **40 Sir John Montgomery**
(Called "Sir Thomas" in the chronicles.)   **50 s.d. drum . . . march**
drummer strikes up a marching beat   **57 pretend** claim   **58 nice points**
overscrupulous details   **60 meaning** intentions

HASTINGS
    Away with scrupulous wit! Now arms must rule.   61
GLOUCESTER
    And fearless minds climb soonest unto crowns.
    Brother, we will proclaim you out of hand;   63
    The bruit thereof will bring you many friends.   64
KING EDWARD
    Then be it as you will. For 'tis my right,
    And Henry but usurps the diadem.
MONTGOMERY
    Ay, now my sovereign speaketh like himself,
    And now will I be Edward's champion.
HASTINGS
    Sound trumpet! Edward shall be here proclaimed.
    Come, fellow soldier, make thou proclamation.
                        [*He gives a Soldier a paper.*]
                            Flourish. Sound.
SOLDIER [*Reads*] "Edward the Fourth, by the grace of
    God, King of England and France, and lord of Ireland,
    etc."
MONTGOMERY
    And whosoe'er gainsays King Edward's right,   74
    By this I challenge him to single fight.
                            Throws down his gauntlet.
ALL   Long live Edward the Fourth!
KING EDWARD
    Thanks, brave Montgomery, and thanks unto you all.
    If fortune serve me, I'll requite this kindness.
    Now, for this night, let's harbor here in York;
    And when the morning sun shall raise his car   80
    Above the border of this horizon,
    We'll forward towards Warwick and his mates;
    For well I wot that Henry is no soldier.   83
    Ah, froward Clarence, how evil it beseems thee   84
    To flatter Henry and forsake thy brother!
    Yet, as we may, we'll meet both thee and Warwick.

---

61 scrupulous wit cautious or prudent reasoning   **63 out of hand** at
once   **64 bruit** rumor, report   **74 gainsays** denies   **80 his car** i.e.,
Phoebus' chariot   **83 wot** know   **84 froward** perverse.   **evil** ill

Come on, brave soldiers. Doubt not of the day,   87
And that once gotten, doubt not of large pay.
                                        Exeunt.

❧

4.8   *Flourish. Enter the King [Henry], Warwick,*
         Montague, Clarence, Oxford, and Exeter.

WARWICK
  What counsel, lords? Edward from Belgia,   1
  With hasty Germans and blunt Hollanders,   2
  Hath passed in safety through the narrow seas   3
  And with his troops doth march amain to London,   4
  And many giddy people flock to him.   5
KING HENRY
  Let's levy men and beat him back again.
CLARENCE
  A little fire is quickly trodden out
  Which, being suffered, rivers cannot quench.   8
WARWICK
  In Warwickshire I have truehearted friends,
  Not mutinous in peace, yet bold in war.
  Those will I muster up. And thou, son Clarence,   11
  Shalt stir up in Suffolk, Norfolk, and in Kent
  The knights and gentlemen to come with thee.
  Thou, brother Montague, in Buckingham,
  Northampton, and in Leicestershire, shalt find
  Men well inclined to hear what thou command'st.
  And thou, brave Oxford, wondrous well beloved,
  In Oxfordshire shalt muster up thy friends.
  My sovereign, with the loving citizens,
  Like to his island girt in with the ocean,
  Or modest Dian circled with her nymphs,   21

---

87 **the day** the day's outcome

4.8. Location: The Bishop of London's palace.
1 **Belgia** i.e., the Low Countries   2 **hasty** quick-tempered.   **blunt** harsh,
merciless   3 **narrow seas** English Channel   4 **amain** with full speed
5 **giddy** fickle   8 **suffered** allowed   11 **son** i.e., son-in-law   21 **modest**
Dian chaste Diana, goddess of the moon and of chastity

Shall rest in London till we come to him.   22
Fair lords, take leave and stand not to reply.   23
Farewell, my sovereign.

KING HENRY
Farewell, my Hector and my Troy's true hope.   25

CLARENCE [*Kissing the King's hand*]
In sign of truth, I kiss Your Highness' hand.

KING HENRY
Well-minded Clarence, be thou fortunate!   27

MONTAGUE [*Kissing the King's hand*]
Comfort, my lord; and so I take my leave.

OXFORD [*Kissing the King's hand*]
And thus I seal my truth, and bid adieu.   29

KING HENRY
Sweet Oxford, and my loving Montague,
And all at once, once more a happy farewell.   31

WARWICK
Farewell, sweet lords. Let's meet at Coventry.
                Exeunt [all but King Henry and Exeter].

KING HENRY
Here at the palace will I rest awhile.   33
Cousin of Exeter, what thinks your lordship?   34
Methinks the power that Edward hath in field
Should not be able to encounter mine.

EXETER
The doubt is that he will seduce the rest.   37

KING HENRY
That's not my fear. My meed hath got me fame.   38
I have not stopped mine ears to their demands,
Nor posted off their suits with slow delays.   40
My pity hath been balm to heal their wounds,
My mildness hath allayed their swelling griefs,

---

22 rest remain   **23 stand** wait   **25 Hector** i.e., chief protector of Troy.
(England derived its legendary descent from Troy, through Brutus,
great-grandson of Aeneas, supposed founder of the English nation.)
27 Well-minded virtuously inclined   **29 seal my truth** confirm my
loyalty (as though putting a seal to a document)   **31 at once** together
33 palace i.e., Bishop's palace   **34 Cousin** (Form of address from the
King to his peers.)   **37 doubt** fear, danger   **38 My . . . fame** my merits
(for dealing generously and justly) have established my reputation
40 posted off put off

My mercy dried their water-flowing tears.   43
I have not been desirous of their wealth,
Nor much oppressed them with great subsidies,   45
Nor forward of revenge, though they much erred.   46
Then why should they love Edward more than me?
No, Exeter, these graces challenge grace;   48
And when the lion fawns upon the lamb,
The lamb will never cease to follow him.   50
              Shout within, "A Lancaster!" "A York!"

EXETER
  Hark, hark, my lord! What shouts are these?

    *Enter [King] Edward and his soldiers [with
    Gloucester].*

KING EDWARD
  Seize on the shamefaced Henry. Bear him hence,   52
  And once again proclaim us king of England!
  You are the fount that makes small brooks to flow.
  Now stops thy spring; my sea shall suck them dry   55
  And swell so much the higher by their ebb.
  Hence with him to the Tower. Let him not speak.
              Exit [guard] with King Henry.
  And, lords, towards Coventry bend we our course,
  Where peremptory Warwick now remains.   59
  The sun shines hot, and, if we use delay,   60
  Cold biting winter mars our hoped-for hay.   61

GLOUCESTER
  Away betimes, before his forces join,   62
  And take the great-grown traitor unawares.
  Brave warriors, march amain towards Coventry.
                                    Exeunt.

✣

---

43 water-flowing tears tears flowing like water   **45 subsidies** taxes
46 forward of eager for   **48 challenge grace** claim favor   **50 s.d. A
Lancaster! A York** (Conflicting rallying cries for both sides.)   **52 shamefaced** shy, shamefast   **55 thy spring** i.e., the source of your power
59 peremptory overbearing   **60–61 The sun . . . hay** i.e., make hay while
the sun shines   **62 betimes** quickly.   **join** unite

5.1   *Enter Warwick, the Mayor of Coventry, two*
Messengers, and others upon the walls.

WARWICK
  Where is the post that came from valiant Oxford?—   1
  How far hence is thy lord, mine honest fellow?
FIRST MESSENGER
  By this at Dunsmore, marching hitherward.   3
WARWICK
  How far off is our brother Montague?
  Where is the post that came from Montague?
SECOND MESSENGER
  By this at Daintry, with a puissant troop.   6

    Enter [Sir John] Somerville [to them, aloft].

WARWICK
  Say, Somerville, what says my loving son?   7
  And, by thy guess, how nigh is Clarence now?
SOMERVILLE
  At Southam I did leave him with his forces,   9
  And do expect him here some two hours hence.
                  [A march afar off.]
WARWICK
  Then Clarence is at hand. I hear his drum.
SOMERVILLE
  It is not his, my lord. Here Southam lies.   *[He points.]*
  The drum your honor hears marcheth from Warwick.   13
WARWICK
  Who should that be? Belike unlooked-for friends.
SOMERVILLE
  They are at hand, and you shall quickly know.

    March. Flourish. Enter [King] Edward, Richard,
    [Duke of Gloucester,] and soldiers [below].

5.1. Location: Before the walls of Coventry.
s.d. upon the walls (As in 4.7, the *walls* of this town are the tiring-house
facade backstage, and those appearing *on the walls* are in the rear
gallery above the stage.)   **1 post** messenger (also in l. 5)   **3 By this** by
this time   **3, 6, 9, 13 Dunsmore, Daintry** (i.e., Daventry), **Southam,**
Warwick (Towns within a day's march of Coventry.)   **6 puissant** powerful   **7 son** i.e., son-in-law

KING EDWARD
Go, trumpet, to the walls and sound a parle.   16
                  [*A parley is sounded.*]

GLOUCESTER
See how the surly Warwick mans the wall!

WARWICK
O unbid spite! Is sportful Edward come?   18
Where slept our scouts, or how are they seduced,
That we could hear no news of his repair?   20

KING EDWARD
Now, Warwick, wilt thou ope the city gates,
Speak gentle words, and humbly bend thy knee,
Call Edward king, and at his hands beg mercy?
And he shall pardon thee these outrages.

WARWICK
Nay, rather, wilt thou draw thy forces hence,   25
Confess who set thee up and plucked thee down,
Call Warwick patron, and be penitent?
And thou shalt still remain the Duke of York.

GLOUCESTER
I thought at least he would have said "the King";
Or did he make the jest against his will?

WARWICK
Is not a dukedom, sir, a goodly gift?

GLOUCESTER
Ay, by my faith, for a poor earl to give.
I'll do thee service for so good a gift.   33

WARWICK
'Twas I that gave the kingdom to thy brother.

KING EDWARD
Why then, 'tis mine, if but by Warwick's gift.

WARWICK
Thou art no Atlas for so great a weight;   36
And, weakling, Warwick takes his gift again,
And Henry is my king, Warwick his subject.

---

16 trumpet trumpeter.   **parle** trumpet call for a parley   **18 unbid**
unwelcome.   **spite** vexatious circumstance.   **sportful** lascivious
20 repair approach   **25 draw** withdraw   **33 do thee service** i.e., pay
feudal homage. (Said ironically.)   **36 Atlas** the Titan's son in classical
myth who carried the world on his shoulders

KING EDWARD

  But Warwick's king is Edward's prisoner.
  And, gallant Warwick, do but answer this:
  What is the body when the head is off?

GLOUCESTER

  Alas, that Warwick had no more forecast,   42
  But, whiles he thought to steal the single ten,   43
  The King was slyly fingered from the deck!
  You left poor Henry at the Bishop's palace,
  And ten to one you'll meet him in the Tower.

KING EDWARD

  'Tis even so. Yet you are Warwick still.   47

GLOUCESTER

  Come, Warwick, take the time. Kneel down, kneel down. 48
  Nay, when? Strike now, or else the iron cools.   49

WARWICK

  I had rather chop this hand off at a blow,
  And with the other fling it at thy face,
  Than bear so low a sail to strike to thee.

KING EDWARD

  Sail how thou canst, have wind and tide thy friend,
  This hand, fast wound about thy coal black hair,
  Shall, whiles thy head is warm and new cut off,
  Write in the dust this sentence with thy blood:
  "Wind-changing Warwick now can change no more." 57

    Enter Oxford, with drum and colors.

WARWICK

  O cheerful colors! See where Oxford comes!

OXFORD

  Oxford, Oxford, for Lancaster!
                [He and his forces enter the city.]

---

42 forecast forethought **43 single ten** mere ten-card. (Less valuable
than the king-card.) **47 Yet . . . still** i.e., you are still the Duke of
Warwick and still have time to change before disaster strikes **48 time**
opportunity **49 when** i.e., when are you going to act. (An expression of
impatience.) **Strike . . . cools** i.e., strike while the iron is hot. (But
strike also means to lower sail, yield; hence Warwick's refusal to *bear so
low a sail*, i.e., offer tokens of submission, in l. 52. Cf. 3.3.5, note.)
57 Wind-changing i.e., shifting, like a weathervane **s.d. drum** drummer.
colors flags borne by flag carriers

GLOUCESTER
The gates are open. Let us enter too.

KING EDWARD
So other foes may set upon our backs.   61
Stand we in good array, for they no doubt
Will issue out again and bid us battle.
If not, the city being but of small defense,
We'll quickly rouse the traitors in the same.   65
                    [*Oxford appears above, on the walls.*]

WARWICK
O, welcome, Oxford, for we want thy help.

   Enter Montague, with drum and colors.

MONTAGUE
Montague, Montague, for Lancaster!
                    [*He and his forces enter the city.*]

GLOUCESTER
Thou and thy brother both shall buy this treason   68
Even with the dearest blood your bodies bear.

KING EDWARD
The harder matched, the greater victory.   70
My mind presageth happy gain and conquest.   71

   Enter Somerset, with drum and colors.

SOMERSET
Somerset, Somerset, for Lancaster!
                    [*He and his forces enter the city.*]

GLOUCESTER
Two of thy name, both Dukes of Somerset,   73
Have sold their lives unto the house of York,
And thou shalt be the third, if this sword hold.

   Enter Clarence, with drum and colors.

---

61 So in that case. **set . . . backs** attack us from the rear **65 rouse**
cause (an animal) to rise from its lair **68 buy** pay dearly for   **70 The
harder . . . victory** the more powerful the enemy, the greater the victory.
(Proverbial.) **71 happy** fortunate **73 Two of thy name** i.e., Edmund
Beaufort, second Duke of Somerset, killed at St. Albans in 1455, and his
son Henry (not a character in this play), beheaded in 1464 for his Lancastrian sympathies. (The duke addressed here is Henry's brother
Edmund, fourth duke.)

WARWICK
    And lo, where George of Clarence sweeps along,
    Of force enough to bid his brother battle;   77
    With whom an upright zeal to right prevails   78
    More than the nature of a brother's love!   79
            [*Gloucester and Clarence whisper together.*]
    Come, Clarence, come. Thou wilt, if Warwick call.
CLARENCE
    Father of Warwick, know you what this means?   81
            [*He takes his red rose out of his hat and
                      throws it at Warwick.*]
    Look here, I throw my infamy at thee.
    I will not ruinate my father's house,   83
    Who gave his blood to lime the stones together,   84
    And set up Lancaster. Why, trowest thou, Warwick,   85
    That Clarence is so harsh, so blunt, unnatural,
    To bend the fatal instruments of war   87
    Against his brother and his lawful king?
    Perhaps thou wilt object my holy oath.   89
    To keep that oath were more impiety
    Than Jephthah when he sacrificed his daughter.   91
    I am so sorry for my trespass made
    That, to deserve well at my brother's hands,
    I here proclaim myself thy mortal foe,
    With resolution, wheresoe'er I meet thee—
    As I will meet thee, if thou stir abroad—   96
    To plague thee for thy foul misleading me.
    And so, proudhearted Warwick, I defy thee,
    And to my brother turn my blushing cheeks.
    Pardon me, Edward, I will make amends;
    And, Richard, do not frown upon my faults,
    For I will henceforth be no more unconstant.

---

77 Of force enough with a powerful enough army   **78 to right** on behalf
of justice   **79 nature** natural feeling   **s.d. Gloucester . . . together** (This
stage direction, and that at l. 81, are basically from the octavo text.)
81 Father i.e., father-in-law   **83 ruinate** bring into ruin   **84 lime** cement
85 trowest thou do you think   **87 bend** direct   **89 object** urge   **91 Jephthah** (See Judges 11:30 ff. for the account of Jephthah's vow to sacrifice,
if victorious, the first living creature that came to meet him on his
return. His daughter was the victim.)   **96 abroad** from home, i.e.,
outside the city walls

KING EDWARD
Now welcome more, and ten times more beloved,
Than if thou never hadst deserved our hate!

GLOUCESTER
Welcome, good Clarence. This is brotherlike.

WARWICK
O passing traitor, perjured and unjust!   106

KING EDWARD
What, Warwick, wilt thou leave the town and fight?
Or shall we beat the stones about thine ears?

WARWICK
Alas, I am not cooped here for defense!
I will away towards Barnet presently,   110
And bid thee battle, Edward, if thou dar'st.

KING EDWARD
Yes, Warwick, Edward dares, and leads the way.
Lords, to the field! Saint George and victory!
                    Exeunt [King Edward and his company].
                    March. Warwick and his company
                    follows [out of the city].

5.2   *Alarum and excursions. Enter [King] Edward,*
        bringing forth Warwick wounded.

KING EDWARD
So, lie thou there. Die thou, and die our fear,
For Warwick was a bug that feared us all.   2
Now, Montague, sit fast. I seek for thee,   3
That Warwick's bones may keep thine company. *Exit.*

WARWICK
Ah, who is nigh? Come to me, friend or foe,
And tell me who is victor, York or Warwick?

---

106 passing surpassing **110 Barnet** a town in Hertfordshire, about ten
miles north of London. (Warwick's illogical proposal that the armies
meet at Barnet, some seventy-five miles from Coventry, is a result of
Shakespeare's telescoping and rearranging of historical events.) **presently** immediately

5.2. Location: A field of battle near Barnet. (Despite the distance from
Coventry to Barnet, the sense here is of virtually continuous action.)
2 bug bugbear, goblin. **feared** frightened **3 sit fast** position yourself
as securely as you can

Why ask I that? My mangled body shows,
My blood, my want of strength, my sick heart shows,
That I must yield my body to the earth
And, by my fall, the conquest to my foe.
Thus yields the cedar to the ax's edge,
Whose arms gave shelter to the princely eagle,   12
Under whose shade the ramping lion slept,   13
Whose top branch overpeered Jove's spreading tree   14
And kept low shrubs from winter's powerful wind.
These eyes, that now are dimmed with death's black veil,
Have been as piercing as the midday sun
To search the secret treasons of the world.
The wrinkles in my brows, now filled with blood,
Were likened oft to kingly sepulchers;
For who lived king, but I could dig his grave?
And who durst smile when Warwick bent his brow?   22
Lo, now my glory smeared in dust and blood!
My parks, my walks, my manors that I had,
Even now forsake me, and of all my lands
Is nothing left me but my body's length.
Why, what is pomp, rule, reign, but earth and dust?
And, live we how we can, yet die we must.

Enter Oxford and Somerset.

SOMERSET
Ah, Warwick, Warwick! Wert thou as we are,
We might recover all our loss again.
The Queen from France hath brought a puissant power;   31
Even now we heard the news. Ah, couldst thou fly!
WARWICK
Why, then I would not fly. Ah, Montague,
If thou be there, sweet brother, take my hand,
And with thy lips keep in my soul awhile!   35
Thou lov'st me not, for, brother, if thou didst,
Thy tears would wash this cold congealèd blood

12, 13 eagle, lion (Royal emblems; Warwick, the lofty *cedar* in this
metaphor, has at times given his protection to both Edward and Henry.)
13 ramping rampant, upreared. (A heraldic term.)   **14 Jove's spreading
tree** i.e., the oak   **22 bent his brow** frowned   **31 puissant** powerful
35 with thy lips i.e., with a kiss. (The soul was thought to leave the body
through the mouth.)

That glues my lips and will not let me speak.
Come quickly, Montague, or I am dead.

SOMERSET
Ah, Warwick, Montague hath breathed his last,
And to the latest gasp cried out for Warwick   41
And said "Commend me to my valiant brother."
And more he would have said, and more he spoke,
Which sounded like a cannon in a vault,
That mought not be distinguished; but at last   45
I well might hear, delivered with a groan,
"O, farewell, Warwick!"

WARWICK
Sweet rest his soul! Fly, lords, and save yourselves,
For Warwick bids you all farewell, to meet in heaven.
                                                     [*He dies.*]

OXFORD
Away, away, to meet the Queen's great power!
            Here they bear away his body. Exeunt.

5.3   *Flourish. Enter King Edward in triumph, with
           Richard, [Duke of Gloucester,] Clarence, and
           the rest.*

KING EDWARD
Thus far our fortune keeps an upward course,
And we are graced with wreaths of victory.
But in the midst of this bright-shining day
I spy a black, suspicious, threatening cloud
That will encounter with our glorious sun   5
Ere he attain his easeful western bed:
I mean, my lords, those powers that the Queen
Hath raised in Gallia have arrived our coast   8
And, as we hear, march on to fight with us.

CLARENCE
A little gale will soon disperse that cloud
And blow it to the source from whence it came.

41 latest last   45 mought might

5.3. Location: The field of battle near Barnet, as before.
5 sun i.e., the heraldic sun on the Yorkist coat of arms   8 Gallia France.
arrived reached

The very beams will dry those vapors up,   12
For every cloud engenders not a storm.
GLOUCESTER
The Queen is valued thirty thousand strong,
And Somerset, with Oxford, fled to her.
If she have time to breathe, be well assured   16
Her faction will be full as strong as ours.
KING EDWARD
We are advertised by our loving friends   18
That they do hold their course toward Tewkesbury.   19
We, having now the best at Barnet field,
Will thither straight, for willingness rids way;   21
And, as we march, our strength will be augmented
In every county as we go along.
Strike up the drum, cry "Courage!" and away.
                                                     Exeunt.

❖

5.4   *Flourish. March. Enter the Queen [Margaret],*
           young [Prince] Edward, Somerset, Oxford,
           and soldiers.

QUEEN MARGARET
Great lords, wise men ne'er sit and wail their loss,
But cheerly seek how to redress their harms.   2
What though the mast be now blown overboard,
The cable broke, the holding anchor lost,
And half our sailors swallowed in the flood?
Yet lives our pilot still. Is 't meet that he   6
Should leave the helm and, like a fearful lad,
With tearful eyes add water to the sea
And give more strength to that which hath too much,
Whiles, in his moan, the ship splits on the rock,   10

---

12 very mere   **16 breathe** i.e., pause and muster her strength   **18 advertised** notified   **19 Tewkesbury** a town in Gloucestershire   **21 straight**
immediately.   **rids way** annihilates distance, makes the way seem short

5.4. Location: Near Tewkesbury.
2 cheerly cheerfully   **6 our pilot** i.e., King Henry   **10 in his moan** as he
makes lamentation

Which industry and courage might have saved?
Ah, what a shame, ah, what a fault were this!
Say Warwick was our anchor. What of that?
And Montague our topmast. What of him?
Our slaughtered friends the tackles. What of these?   15
Why, is not Oxford here another anchor?
And Somerset another goodly mast?
The friends of France our shrouds and tacklings?   18
And, though unskillful, why not Ned and I
For once allowed the skillful pilot's charge?   20
We will not from the helm to sit and weep,   21
But keep our course, though the rough wind say no,
From shelves and rocks that threaten us with wreck.   23
As good to chide the waves as speak them fair.   24
And what is Edward but a ruthless sea?
What Clarence but a quicksand of deceit?
And Richard but a ragged fatal rock?
All these the enemies to our poor bark.
Say you can swim, alas, 'tis but a while;
Tread on the sand, why, there you quickly sink;
Bestride the rock, the tide will wash you off,
Or else you famish—that's a threefold death.
This speak I, lords, to let you understand,
If case some one of you would fly from us,   34
That there's no hoped-for mercy with the brothers
More than with ruthless waves, with sands and rocks.
Why, courage then! What cannot be avoided
'Twere childish weakness to lament or fear.

PRINCE
Methinks a woman of this valiant spirit
Should, if a coward heard her speak these words,
Infuse his breast with magnanimity
And make him, naked, foil a man at arms.   42
I speak not this as doubting any here;
For did I but suspect a fearful man,
He should have leave to go away betimes,   45

15 **tackles** rigging 18 **shrouds** ropes or cables supporting the mast
20 **charge** responsibility 21 **from** go away from 23 **shelves** sandbanks,
shoals 24 **As good to** i.e., one might as well. **speak them fair** address
them courteously 34 **If** in 42 **naked** unarmed. **foil** defeat. **man at
arms** armed soldier 45 **betimes** at once

Lest in our need he might infect another
And make him of like spirit to himself.
If any such be here—as God forbid!—
Let him depart before we need his help.

OXFORD
Women and children of so high a courage,
And warriors faint! Why, 'twere perpetual shame.
O brave young Prince! Thy famous grandfather   52
Doth live again in thee. Long mayst thou live
To bear his image and renew his glories!   54

SOMERSET
And he that will not fight for such a hope,
Go home to bed, and, like the owl by day,
If he arise, be mocked and wondered at.

QUEEN MARGARET
Thanks, gentle Somerset; sweet Oxford, thanks.

PRINCE
And take his thanks that yet hath nothing else.   59

Enter a Messenger.

MESSENGER
Prepare you, lords, for Edward is at hand,
Ready to fight. Therefore be resolute.

OXFORD
I thought no less. It is his policy   62
To haste thus fast, to find us unprovided.   63

SOMERSET
But he's deceived. We are in readiness.

QUEEN MARGARET
This cheers my heart, to see your forwardness.   65

OXFORD
Here pitch our battle. Hence we will not budge.   66

*Flourish and march. Enter [King] Edward,
Richard, [Duke of Gloucester,] Clarence,
and soldiers.*

---

52 grandfather i.e., Henry V   **54 image** likeness   **59 his . . . else** i e., my
thanks, I who as yet have nothing else to give   **62 policy** stratagem
63 unprovided unprepared   **65 forwardness** eagerness   **66 pitch our
battle** draw up our armies

KING EDWARD
　Brave followers, yonder stands the thorny wood
　Which, by the heavens' assistance and your strength,
　Must by the roots be hewn up yet ere night.
　I need not add more fuel to your fire,
　For well I wot ye blaze to burn them out.   71
　Give signal to the fight, and to it, lords!
QUEEN MARGARET
　Lords, knights, and gentlemen, what I should say
　My tears gainsay; for every word I speak,   74
　Ye see, I drink the water of mine eye.
　Therefore, no more but this: Henry, your sovereign,
　Is prisoner to the foe, his state usurped,   77
　His realm a slaughterhouse, his subjects slain,
　His statutes canceled, and his treasure spent;
　And yonder is the wolf that makes this spoil.   80
　You fight in justice. Then, in God's name, lords,
　Be valiant, and give signal to the fight.   82
　　　　　Alarum. Retreat. Excursions [in which
　　　　　Queen Margaret, Prince Edward, Oxford,
　　　　　　　　and Somerset are taken]. Exeunt.

5.5　　*Flourish. Enter [King] Edward, Richard, [Duke*
　　　　of Gloucester,] Queen [Margaret, as prisoner],
　　　　Clarence; Oxford, Somerset [as prisoners].

KING EDWARD
　Now here a period of tumultuous broils.   1
　Away with Oxford to Hames Castle straight.   2
　For Somerset, off with his guilty head.   3
　Go, bear them hence. I will not hear them speak.

71 wot know　**74 gainsay** forbid　**77 state** royal status as king　**80 spoil**
plunder, destruction　**82 s.d. Alarum** (The octavo version provides that
chambers or short cannon are "discharged," after which King Edward
and his brothers and allies enter with "a great shout," and cry "For
York! For York!" and take the Queen and her son.)

5.5. Location: Scene continues at the battlefield near Tewkesbury.
1 period termination　**2 Hames Castle** i.e., Hammes Castle near Calais
(where Oxford was indeed confined, but not until his capture some
three years after Tewkesbury).　**straight** at once　**3 For** as for

OXFORD
  For my part, I'll not trouble thee with words.
SOMERSET
  Nor I, but stoop with patience to my fortune.
                    Exeunt [*Oxford and Somerset, guarded*].
QUEEN MARGARET
  So part we sadly in this troublous world,
  To meet with joy in sweet Jerusalem.   8
KING EDWARD
  Is proclamation made that who finds Edward   9
  Shall have a high reward, and he his life?
GLOUCESTER
  It is. And lo, where youthful Edward comes!

          Enter [*soldiers, with*] *the Prince* [*Edward*].

KING EDWARD
  Bring forth the gallant. Let us hear him speak.
  What, can so young a thorn begin to prick?
  Edward, what satisfaction canst thou make   14
  For bearing arms, for stirring up my subjects,
  And all the trouble thou hast turned me to?
PRINCE
  Speak like a subject, proud ambitious York!
  Suppose that I am now my father's mouth;
  Resign thy chair, and where I stand kneel thou,   19
  Whilst I propose the selfsame words to thee,
  Which, traitor, thou wouldst have me answer to.
QUEEN MARGARET
  Ah, that thy father had been so resolved!
GLOUCESTER
  That you might still have worn the petticoat
  And ne'er have stol'n the breech from Lancaster.   24
PRINCE
  Let Aesop fable in a winter's night;   25
  His currish riddles sorts not with this place.   26

---

8 **sweet Jerusalem** i.e., the heavenly Jerusalem   9 **who** anyone who
14 **satisfaction** recompense   19 **chair** throne   24 **breech** breeches,
symbol of male authority   25 **Aesop** Greek teller of fables (who, like
Gloucester, was reputed to have been deformed).   **in . . . night** i.e., in a
setting fitted for such childish tales   26 **His . . . place** his mean riddles
are inappropriate to this place. (Prince Edward is retorting to Gloucester's jibe, denying the allegation that his father was henpecked.)

GLOUCESTER
By heaven, brat, I'll plague ye for that word.

QUEEN MARGARET
Ay, thou wast born to be a plague to men.

GLOUCESTER
For God's sake, take away this captive scold.

PRINCE
Nay, take away this scolding crookback rather.

KING EDWARD
Peace, willful boy, or I will charm your tongue.   31

CLARENCE
Untutored lad, thou art too malapert.   32

PRINCE
I know my duty. You are all undutiful.
Lascivious Edward, and thou perjured George,
And thou misshapen Dick, I tell ye all
I am your better, traitors as ye are,
And thou usurp'st my father's right and mine.

KING EDWARD
Take that, thou likeness of this railer here!   38
                                        Stabs him.

GLOUCESTER
Sprawl'st thou? Take that, to end thy agony.   39
                                        Richard stabs him.

CLARENCE
And there's for twitting me with perjury.
                    Clarence stabs him. [*Prince Edward dies.*]

QUEEN MARGARET   O, kill me too!

GLOUCESTER   Marry, and shall.   *Offers to kill her.* 42

KING EDWARD
Hold, Richard, hold, for we have done too much.

GLOUCESTER
Why should she live, to fill the world with words?
                                        [*Margaret swoons.*]

KING EDWARD
What, doth she swoon? Use means for her recovery.

---

31 charm cast a spell upon, i.e., silence   **32 malapert** saucy   **38 this
railer here** i.e., Queen Margaret   **39 Sprawl'st thou** i.e., are you twitch-
ing in the throes of death   **42 Marry, and shall** i.e., indeed, I will
s.d. Offers to is about to

GLOUCESTER [*Aside to Clarence*]
  Clarence, excuse me to the King my brother;
  I'll hence to London on a serious matter.
  Ere ye come there, be sure to hear some news.   48
CLARENCE [*Aside to Gloucester*] What? What?
GLOUCESTER [*Aside to Clarence*] The Tower, the Tower.
                                Exit.

QUEEN MARGARET [*Reviving*]
  O Ned, sweet Ned, speak to thy mother, boy!
  Canst thou not speak? O traitors, murderers!
  They that stabbed Caesar shed no blood at all,
  Did not offend, nor were not worthy blame,
  If this foul deed were by to equal it.   55
  He was a man; this, in respect, a child,   56
  And men ne'er spend their fury on a child.
  What's worse than murderer, that I may name it?
  No, no, my heart will burst, an if I speak;
  And I will speak, that so my heart may burst.
  Butchers and villains, bloody cannibals!
  How sweet a plant have you untimely cropped!
  You have no children, butchers; if you had,
  The thought of them would have stirred up remorse.
  But if you ever chance to have a child,
  Look in his youth to have him so cut off
  As, deathsmen, you have rid this sweet young prince! 67
KING EDWARD
  Away with her. Go, bear her hence perforce.   68
QUEEN MARGARET
  Nay, never bear me hence. Dispatch me here!
  Here sheathe thy sword. I'll pardon thee my death.
  What, wilt thou not? Then, Clarence, do it thou.
CLARENCE
  By heaven, I will not do thee so much ease.   72
QUEEN MARGARET
  Good Clarence, do. Sweet Clarence, do thou do it.
CLARENCE
  Didst thou not hear me swear I would not do it?

---

48 be sure expect **55 equal** compare with **56 respect** comparison
67 rid removed, killed **68 perforce** by force **72 ease** i.e., easing of
your grief in death

QUEEN MARGARET

  Ay, but thou usest to forswear thyself.   75

  'Twas sin before, but now 'tis charity.

  What, wilt thou not? Where is that devil's butcher,

  Hard-favored Richard? Richard, where art thou?   78

  Thou art not here. Murder is thy almsdeed;   79

  Petitioners for blood thou ne'er putt'st back.   80

KING EDWARD

  Away, I say! I charge ye, bear her hence.

QUEEN MARGARET

  So come to you and yours as to this prince!   82

                      Exit Queen, [guarded].

KING EDWARD Where's Richard gone?

CLARENCE

  To London, all in post—[*Aside*] and, as I guess,   84

  To make a bloody supper in the Tower.

KING EDWARD

  He's sudden, if a thing comes in his head.

  Now march we hence. Discharge the common sort   87

  With pay and thanks, and let's away to London

  And see our gentle queen how well she fares.

  By this, I hope, she hath a son for me.   *Exeunt.* 90

♣

5.6   *Enter Henry the Sixth and Richard, [Duke of*
        Gloucester,] with the Lieutenant [of the Tower],
        on the walls.

GLOUCESTER

  Good day, my lord. What, at your book so hard?   1

KING HENRY

  Ay, my good lord—"my lord," I should say rather.

  'Tis sin to flatter. "Good" was little better.   3

---

75 thou usest you are accustomed **78 Hard-favored** ugly **79 almsdeed**
act of charity **80 Petitioners . . . back** you never turn away men asking
for blood **82 So come** may it happen **84 post** haste **87 common sort**
ordinary soldiers **90 this** this time

5.6. Location: The Tower of London.
1 book i.e., book of devotion **3 little better** i.e., little more than flattery

"Good Gloucester" and "good devil" were alike,   4
And both preposterous; therefore, not "good lord."   5

GLOUCESTER [*To the Lieutenant*]
    Sirrah, leave us to ourselves. We must confer.   6
                                        [*Exit Lieutenant.*]

KING HENRY
    So flies the reckless shepherd from the wolf;   7
    So first the harmless sheep doth yield his fleece
    And next his throat unto the butcher's knife.
    What scene of death hath Roscius now to act?   10

GLOUCESTER
    Suspicion always haunts the guilty mind;
    The thief doth fear each bush an officer.   12

KING HENRY
    The bird that hath been limèd in a bush,   13
    With trembling wings misdoubteth every bush;   14
    And I, the hapless male to one sweet bird,   15
    Have now the fatal object in my eye
    Where my poor young was limed, was caught, and
        killed.

GLOUCESTER
    Why, what a peevish fool was that of Crete,   18
    That taught his son the office of a fowl!
    And yet, for all his wings, the fool was drowned.

KING HENRY
    I, Daedalus; my poor boy, Icarus;
    Thy father, Minos, that denied our course;   22
    The sun that seared the wings of my sweet boy,   23
    Thy brother Edward; and thyself, the sea
    Whose envious gulf did swallow up his life.   25

---

4 were would be   **5 preposterous** unnatural   **6 Sirrah** (Customary form
of address to inferiors.)   **7 reckless** heedless   **10 Roscius** celebrated
Roman actor much admired by Cicero and regarded by the Elizabethans
as a model of tragic acting   **12 an officer** to be an arresting officer
13 limèd snared with birdlime, a sticky substance smeared on branches
14 misdoubteth is mistrustful of   **15 male** father, begetter. **bird** chick,
offspring   **18 peevish** silly. **that of Crete** (Daedalus escaped from
Crete, where he had fashioned for King Minos a labyrinth to contain the
Minotaur, by devising wings for himself and his son Icarus, but Icarus
flew too near the sun, which melted the wax in his wings, thus causing
him to fall into the sea.)   **22 course** i.e., departure   **23 sun** (with reference to the Yorkist heraldic badge, as at 2.1.25)   **25 envious gulf** malicious whirlpool

Ah, kill me with thy weapon, not with words!
My breast can better brook thy dagger's point   27
Than can my ears that tragic history.   28
But wherefore dost thou come? Is 't for my life?

GLOUCESTER
Think'st thou I am an executioner?

KING HENRY
A persecutor I am sure thou art.
If murdering innocents be executing,
Why, then thou art an executioner.

GLOUCESTER
Thy son I killed for his presumption.

KING HENRY
Hadst thou been killed when first thou didst presume,
Thou hadst not lived to kill a son of mine.
And thus I prophesy, that many a thousand,
Which now mistrust no parcel of my fear,   38
And many an old man's sigh and many a widow's,
And many an orphan's water-standing eye—   40
Men for their sons', wives for their husbands',
Orphans for their parents' timeless death—   42
Shall rue the hour that ever thou wast born.
The owl shrieked at thy birth—an evil sign;
The night crow cried, aboding luckless time;   45
Dogs howled, and hideous tempest shook down trees;
The raven rooked her on the chimney's top,   47
And chattering pies in dismal discords sung.   48
Thy mother felt more than a mother's pain,
And yet brought forth less than a mother's hope,
To wit, an indigested and deformèd lump,   51
Not like the fruit of such a goodly tree.
Teeth hadst thou in thy head when thou wast born,
To signify thou cam'st to bite the world;
And if the rest be true which I have heard,
Thou cam'st—

---

27 **brook** endure 28 **history** story 38 **mistrust . . . fear** i.e., feel none
of the suspicion that I feel 40 **water-standing** i.e., filled with tears
42 **timeless** untimely 45 **night crow** nightjar or owl. **aboding** forebod-
ing 47 **rooked her** alighted, roosted 48 **pies** magpies 51 **indigested**
shapeless, chaotic

GLOUCESTER
  I'll hear no more. Die, prophet, in thy speech.
                                        Stabs him.
  For this, amongst the rest, was I ordained.
KING HENRY
  Ay, and for much more slaughter after this.
  O, God forgive my sins, and pardon thee!   *Dies.*
GLOUCESTER
  What, will the aspiring blood of Lancaster
  Sink in the ground? I thought it would have mounted.
  See how my sword weeps for the poor King's death!
  O, may such purple tears be always shed   64
  From those that wish the downfall of our house!
  If any spark of life be yet remaining,
  Down, down to hell, and say I sent thee thither,
                                Stabs him again
  I, that have neither pity, love, nor fear.
  Indeed, 'tis true that Henry told me of;   69
  For I have often heard my mother say
  I came into the world with my legs forward.
  Had I not reason, think ye, to make haste
  And seek their ruin that usurped our right?
  The midwife wondered and the women cried
  "O, Jesus bless us, he is born with teeth!"
  And so I was, which plainly signified
  That I should snarl and bite and play the dog.
  Then, since the heavens have shaped my body so,
  Let hell make crook'd my mind to answer it.   79
  I have no brother, I am like no brother;
  And this word "love," which graybeards call divine,
  Be resident in men like one another
  And not in me. I am myself alone.
  Clarence, beware. Thou keep'st me from the light;
  But I will sort a pitchy day for thee;   85
  For I will buzz abroad such prophecies
  That Edward shall be fearful of his life,   87
  And then, to purge his fear, I'll be thy death.
  King Henry and the Prince his son are gone;

64 purple bloodred   **69 that** what   **79 answer** match   **85 sort** select.
pitchy black   **87 of** for

Clarence, thy turn is next, and then the rest,
Counting myself but bad till I be best.   91
I'll throw thy body in another room
And triumph, Henry, in thy day of doom.
                      Exit [with the body].

❖

5.7   *Flourish. Enter King [Edward], Queen*
          [Elizabeth], Clarence, Richard, [Duke of
          Gloucester,] Hastings, Nurse [with the
          young Prince], and attendants.

KING EDWARD
Once more we sit in England's royal throne,
Repurchased with the blood of enemies.
What valiant foemen, like to autumn's corn,   3
Have we mowed down in tops of all their pride!   4
Three Dukes of Somerset, threefold renowned
For hardy and undoubted champions;   6
Two Cliffords, as the father and the son;   7
And two Northumberlands—two braver men
Ne'er spurred their coursers at the trumpet's sound;   9
With them, the two brave bears, Warwick and
    Montague,   10
That in their chains fettered the kingly lion
And made the forest tremble when they roared.
Thus have we swept suspicion from our seat   13
And made our footstool of security.
Come hither, Bess, and let me kiss my boy.
                      [He kisses his son.]
Young Ned, for thee, thine uncles and myself
Have in our armors watched the winter's night,   17
Went all afoot in summer's scalding heat,

91 bad unfortunate

5.7. Location: London. The royal court. A throne is provided onstage.
3 corn grain   **4 in tops** at the height   **6 undoubted** fearless   **7 as** to wit
9 coursers horses   **10 bears** (Refers to the Neville family emblem.)
13 seat throne   **17 watched** stayed awake throughout

That thou mightst repossess the crown in peace;
And of our labors thou shalt reap the gain.
GLOUCESTER [*Aside*]
    I'll blast his harvest, if your head were laid;   21
    For yet I am not looked on in the world.   22
    This shoulder was ordained so thick to heave,
    And heave it shall some weight, or break my back.
    Work thou the way, and thou shalt execute.   25
KING EDWARD
    Clarence and Gloucester, love my lovely queen,
    And kiss your princely nephew, brothers both.
CLARENCE
    The duty that I owe unto Your Majesty
    I seal upon the lips of this sweet babe.
                            [*He kisses the Prince.*]
QUEEN ELIZABETH
    Thanks, noble Clarence; worthy brother, thanks.   30
GLOUCESTER
    And, that I love the tree from whence thou sprang'st,
    Witness the loving kiss I give the fruit.
                            [*He kisses the Prince.*]
    [*Aside.*] To say the truth, so Judas kissed his master,
    And cried "All hail!" whenas he meant all harm.
KING EDWARD
    Now am I seated as my soul delights,
    Having my country's peace and brothers' loves.
CLARENCE
    What will Your Grace have done with Margaret?
    Reignier, her father, to the King of France
    Hath pawned the Sicils and Jerusalem,   39
    And hither have they sent it for her ransom.   40
KING EDWARD
    Away with her, and waft her hence to France.   41
    And now what rests but that we spend the time   42
    With stately triumphs, mirthful comic shows,   43

21 blast blight. **if . . . laid** i.e., once you are laid out on the bier in
death (with a suggestion also of grain flattened by a storm) **22 looked
on** heeded, respected **25 Work thou** (Addressed to himself, indicating
his head.) **thou shalt** (Addressed to his shoulder and arm.) **30 brother**
i.e., brother-in-law **39 the Sicils** (See note to 1.4.122.) **40 it** i.e., the
money raised by "pawn" **41 waft** convey by water **42 rests** remains
43 triumphs festivities

Such as befits the pleasure of the court?
Sound drums and trumpets! Farewell sour annoy!
For here, I hope, begins our lasting joy.   46
                      [Flourish.] Exeunt omnes.

46 s.d. omnes all

Date and Text

A shortened and memorially reconstructed text of *Henry VI, Part Three* was published in octavo in 1595 with the title, *The True Tragedy of Richard, Duke of York, and the Death of Good King Henry the Sixth, with the Whole Contention Between the Two Houses Lancaster and York*. The play appears to have been written in about 1590–1592. The First Folio text seems to have been based on an authorial manuscript with some consultation of the third quarto, which seems to have been without independent textual authority. For a more extensive discussion of date and textual situation in all three *Henry VI* plays, see "Date and Text" to *Henry VI, Part One* in this volume.

Textual Notes

These textual notes are not a historical collation, either of the early texts or of more recent editions; they are simply a record of departures in this edition from the copy text. The reading adopted in this edition appears in boldface, followed by the rejected reading from the copy text, i.e., the First Folio. Only major alterations in punctuation are noted. Changes in lineation are not indicated, nor are some minor and obvious typographical errors.

Abbreviations used:
F the First Folio
O the octavo of 1595
s.d. stage direction
s.p. speech prefix

Copy text: the First Folio.

1.1. 2 s.p. York Pl [and elsewhere referred to in the s.p. as Plan and Plant as well as Yorke] **19 hap** hope **69 s.p. Exeter** [O] Westm **105 Thy** [O] My **120 s.p. Northumberland** [O] Henry **259 with me** [O] me **261 from** [O] to **273 s.d. Flourish** [at beginning of 1.2 in F] **Exeunt** Exit

1.2. 47 s.d. a Messenger [O] Gabriel **49 s.p. Messenger** [O] Gabriel **75 s.d. Exeunt** Exit

1.4. 180 s.d. Exeunt [O] Exit

2.1. 94 s.d. Montague Mountacute **113 And . . . thought** [O; not in F] **124 spleen,** Spleene **131 an idle** [O] a lazie

2.2. 89 Since Cla. Since **130 puts** put's **133 s.p. Richard** [O] War **163 s.p. [and elsewhere until 3.2] George** [O] Cla

2.5. 54 s.d. [followed in F by "and a Father that hath kill'd his Sonne at another doore"] **78 s.d.** [F reads: "Enter Father, bearing of his Sonne"] **89 stratagems** Stragems **119 E'en** Men **139 Whither** Whether [also at 2.6.9]

2.6. 6 fall, thy fall. Thy **commixture** [O] Commixtures **8 The common . . . flies** [O; not in F] **19 Had** [O] Hed **42–45 Edward. Whose . . . used** [The speech assignments here follow O; F assigns 42–44, "Whose . . . is," to Richard, and the rest to Edward.] **60 his** [O] is

3.1. s.d. two Keepers [O] Sinklo, and Humfrey [and throughout scene, in s.p.] **7 scare** scarre **12 s.p. Second Keeper** Sink **17 wast** was **24 thee, sour adversity** the sower Aduersaries **30 Is** I: **55 thou that** [O] thou

3.2. 1 s.p. [and elsewhere] King Edward King **8 s.p. [and throughout] Gloucester** Rich **18 s.p. [and throughout] Lady Grey** Wid **28 whip me, then** [O] then whip me **123 honorably** [O] honourable **175 rends** rents

3.3. 78 s.p. Prince Edw **124 eternal** [O] externall **161 s.d.** [at l. 160 in F] **228 I'll** [O] I

4.1. 67 s.p. Queen Elizabeth [O: Queen] Lady Grey

4.2. 15 towns Towne

4.3. 27 s.d. Hastings fly Hastings flyes   **64 s.d. Exeunt** exit

4.4. 2 s.p. [and throughout scene] Queen Elizabeth [O: Queen] Gray   **17 wean** waine

4.5. 4 stands stand   **8 Comes** Come

4.6. 55 goods be Goods   **88 s.d. Manent** Manet

4.8. 0 s.d. Exeter Somerset   **50 s.d. A Lancaster! A York!** A Lancaster, A Lancaster

5.1. 78 an in

5.3. 22–23 augmented . . . along. augmented: . . . along,

5.4. 27 ragged raged   **46 Lest** Least

5.5. 38 thou the   **50 The Tower** [O] Tower   **77 butcher** [O] butcher Richard **90 s.d. Exeunt** [O] Exit

5.6. 43 wast was't

5.7. 5 renowned [O] Renowne   **25 thou shalt** [O] that shalt   **30 s.p. Queen Elizabeth** [O] Cla   **Thanks** [O] Thanke   **38 Reignier** Reynard

Shakespeare's Sources

The chief source for Shakespeare's conception of the entire *Henry VI* trilogy is Edward Hall's *The Union of the Two Noble and Illustre Families of Lancaster and York* (1548), a work written to glorify the Tudor monarchs by demonstrating how their lineage reconciled the fatally warring factions of Lancaster and York. Shakespeare may actually have done much of his reading for historical particulars in the second edition of Raphael Holinshed's *The Chronicles of England, Scotland, and Ireland* (1587), which included much of Hall's material. (A selection from Volume 3 of Holinshed's *Chronicles* is presented in the pages that follow.) He may also have used John Foxe's *Acts and Monuments of Martyrs* (1583 edition), and still other sources. Richard Grafton's *Chronicle* (1568) plagiarized so heavily from Hall that one cannot always be sure which of the two Shakespeare may have consulted. In any event, Hall's interpretation provided the guiding spirit.

To intensify Hall's theme of the horrors of civil dissension, Shakespeare takes considerable liberties with the chronicles. He frequently disregards chronology, telescopes events of many years into a single sequence, invents scenes and characters, and transfers details from one historical scene to another. The artistic unity of each play is his overriding consideration, not historical accuracy.

In *1 Henry VI*, for example, Shakespeare shows the English losing Orleans to the French and then retaking the city (1.5–2.1). In fact, Orleans was never retaken once it had fallen. Shakespeare has transferred events from the recapture of Le Mans to his partly invented account of Orleans. Talbot's visit to the Countess of Auvergne (2.3) is fictitious. The scene in the Temple Garden when the leaders of Lancaster and York pluck red and white roses (2.4) is fictitious in a different sense: antagonisms between the two factions certainly did exist, but not in the allegorically schematized fashion here pictured. In Act 3, scene 2, Shakespeare shows us Rouen lost and recaptured in a day, whereas in fact the city was (like Orleans) never recovered. Shakespeare's intention is to suggest that France is lost through England's

political divisions at home, not through any failure on the
part of Lord Talbot. Shakespeare exalts Talbot's might and
chivalry (hence the scene with the Countess of Auvergne),
and contrastingly overstates the cowardice of Falstaff
(called Falstolfe in Holinshed, Fastolfe in some other historical sources). Joan la Pucelle is another exaggeratedly evil
foil to Talbot; Shakespeare combines her worst traits in
Hall and Holinshed. The play covers the events of about
three decades. When Henry V died in 1422, his son was less
than a year old; by the time of Talbot's fall in 1453 the King
was over thirty.

In *2 Henry VI* Shakespeare accentuates the threat of popular unrest in a number of ways. He conflates reports of the
Jack Cade rebellion in 1450 with those of the Peasants' Revolt in 1381, using the most unattractive features of each.
Shakespeare ridicules the peasants' utopian aims and
omits a list of sympathetic demands. Similarly, the dispute
between the Armorer and his apprentice (1.3) is put into a
context of courtly politics that we do not find in the chronicles. Simpcox's name and his lameness (2.1) are added to
stress the farcical nature of this "miracle." (Shakespeare
could have found this account in Thomas More's *Dialogue
. . . of the Veneration and Worship of Images*, 1529, or in
Foxe's *Acts and Monuments*.) Although the indictment of
Suffolk (3.2) was historically an act of the House of Commons, Shakespeare portrays it as a near riot in which the
people hammer at the King's very door with their strident
demands. In every way, *2 Henry VI* stresses the fickleness,
inhumanity, and ignorance of men caught up in a mob. Despite all this, however, the play alters its sources less than
does *1 Henry VI*. And for all its disapproval of mob unrest,
Shakespeare's play is considerably less hostile toward the
populace than an anonymous contemporary play, *The Life
and Death of Jack Straw* (1590–1593).

3 Henry VI similarly alters its sources less than does
1 Henry VI. The alterations are chiefly those of telescoping
and highlighting for emphasis. The ritual killings, which
form an integral part of the spectacle in *3 Henry VI*, are
cleverly adapted or rearranged from chronicle accounts.
Concerning the death of the Duke of York (1.4), for example,
Hall reports merely that York died fighting manfully,
whereas Holinshed tells us that the remorseless Clifford

caused the dead York's head to be struck off, "and set on it a crown of paper, fixed it on a pole, and presented it to the Queen." Shakespeare's version goes still further: Queen Margaret mocks York while he is still alive by putting a paper crown on his head. The ritual killing of the Lancastrian Prince Edward (5.5) is similarly enhanced. Throughout, Shakespeare's purpose is to intensify the scourgelike role of the Yorkist Edward IV and his brethren. Among the three, Richard of Gloucester is the most ominous. Shakespeare introduces crookbacked Richard into the fighting (2.1) when historically this man was abroad.

According to Andrew Cairncross's Arden edition, *3 Henry VI* contains occasional allusions to Edmund Spenser's *The Faerie Queene* (see 2.1.9 ff. and *FQ* 1.5.2), to *A Mirror for Magistrates* (especially in the sections "Richard, Duke of York" and "King Henry the Sixth"), and to Arthur Brooke's *The Tragical History of Romeus and Juliet* (see 5.4.1–33 and *Romeus* 2.1359–1377). David Riggs argues (*Shakespeare's Heroical Histories: "Henry VI" and Its Literary Tradition*, 1971) that Christopher Marlowe's *Tamburlaine* (1587–1588) was an important source for Shakespeare's *Henry VI* plays, and that behind *Tamburlaine* lay a classical rhetorical tradition of praise for heroism. Shakespeare would have thoroughly absorbed this tradition through the Tudor grammar-school curriculum.

[For *Henry VI, Part One*]

The Third Volume of Chronicles (1587 edition)
Compiled by Raphael Holinshed

HENRY THE SIXTH

After that[1] death had bereft the world of that noble prince
King Henry the Fifth, his only son Prince Henry, being of
the age of nine months or thereabouts, with the sound of
trumpets was openly proclaimed King of England and
France the thirtieth day of August, by the name of Henry
the Sixth, in the year of the world 5389, after the birth of
our Savior 1422, about the twelfth year of the Emperor
Frederick the Third,[2] the fortieth and two (and last) of
Charles the Sixth,[3] and the third year of Mordake's regiment[4] after his father Robert, Governor of Scotland. The
custody of this young prince was appointed to Thomas,
Duke of Exeter, and to Henry Beaufort, Bishop of Winchester. The Duke of Bedford was deputed Regent of France, and
the Duke of Gloucester was ordained Protector of England,
who, taking upon him that office, called to him wise and
grave councillors by whose advice he provided and took order as well for the good government of the realm and subjects of the same at home as also for the maintenance of the
wars abroad and further conquest to be made in France.

[Later, in October of that same year, Charles VI of France
dies.]

And surely the death of this King Charles caused alterations in France. For a great many of the nobility, which
before—either for fear of the English puissance or for the
love of this King Charles, whose authority they followed,
held on the English part[5]—did now revolt to the Dauphin
with all endeavor to drive the English nation out of the
French territories. Whereto they were the more earnestly
bent, and thought it a thing of greater facility, because of

---

1 After that after   **2 Frederick the Third** Emperor of Germany
3 Charles the Sixth King of France   **4 regiment** rule   **5 held ... part**
remained loyal to the English side

King Henry's young years; whom, because he was a child, they esteemed not but, with one consent, revolted from their sworn fealty. . . .

The Dauphin, which lay the same time[6] in the city of Poitiers, after his father's decease caused himself to be proclaimed King of France by the name of Charles the Seventh; and, in good hope to recover his patrimony, with an haughty courage preparing war, assembled a great army.

[The fighting in France begins with "light skirmishes" but soon intensifies. Back in England, "Edmund Mortimer, the last Earl of March of that name" (conflated by Holinshed with his cousin, Sir John Mortimer), dies without issue, leaving his inheritance to Richard Plantagenet, son and heir to Richard, Earl of Cambridge, who was beheaded by Henry V at Southampton. Conflict erupts in 1425 around the time of a Parliament called by the King.]

Somewhat before this season fell a great division in the realm of England, which of a sparkle was like to have grown to a great flame. For whether the Bishop of Winchester, called Henry Beaufort (son to John, Duke of Lancaster,[7] by his third wife), envied the authority of Humphrey, Duke of Gloucester, Protector of the realm, or whether the Duke disdained at[8] the riches and pompous estate of the Bishop, sure it is that the whole realm was troubled with them and their partakers;[9] so that the citizens of London were fain[10] to keep daily and nightly watches and to shut up their shops for fear of that which was doubted[11] to have ensued of their assembling of people about them.

[The quarrel is continued in a Parliament held at Leicester in March, 1426.]

In this Parliament the Duke of Gloucester laid certain articles to the Bishop of Winchester his[12] charge, the which with the answers hereafter do ensue as followeth: . . .

---

6 which . . . time who dwelt at that same time   7 John, Duke of Lancaster i.e., John of Gaunt, father of Henry IV   8 disdained at held in disdain   9 partakers supporters, followers   10 fain obliged
11 doubted feared   12 Winchester his Winchester's

"1. First, whereas he,[13] being Protector and defender of this land, desired the Tower[14] to be opened to him and to lodge him therein, Richard Woodville, esquire, having at that time the charge of the keeping of the Tower refused his desire and kept the same Tower against him unduly and against reason, by the commandment of my said lord of Winchester. . . .

"2. Item, my said lord of Winchester, without the advice and assent of my said lord of Gloucester or of the King's Council, purposed and disposed him[15] to set hand on the King's person and to have removed him from Eltham, the place that he was in, to Windsor, to the intent to put him in governance as him list.[16]

"3. Item, that where my said lord of Gloucester (to whom of all persons that should be in the land, by the way of nature and birth, it belongeth to see the governance of the King's person), informed of the said undue purpose of my said lord of Winchester declared in the article next above-said, and, in letting[17] thereof, determining to have gone to Eltham unto the King to have provided as the cause required, my said lord of Winchester, untruly and against the King's peace, to the intent to trouble my said lord of Gloucester going to the King, purposing his death, in case that he had gone that way, set men-of-arms and archers at the end of London Bridge next[18] Southwark; and, in forbarring of the King's highway, let draw the chain of the stoops[19] there, and set up pipes and hurdles in manner and form of bulwarks; and set men in chambers, cellars, and windows, with bows and arrows and other weapons, to the intent to bring final destruction to my said lord of Gloucester's person as well as of those that then should come with him.

"4. Item, my said lord of Gloucester saith and affirmeth that our sovereign lord his brother, that was King Henry the Fifth, told him, on a time when our sovereign lord, being Prince,[20] was lodged in the palace of Westminster in the great chamber, by the noise of a spaniel there was on a night

---

13 **he** i.e., the Duke of Gloucester   14 **Tower** Tower of London
15 **disposed him** made himself ready   16 **as him list** i.e., as it should
please the Bishop of Winchester   17 **letting** hindering, preventing
18 **next** nearest   19 **let draw . . . stoops** caused to be drawn tight the
chain posts.   **stoops** posts   20 **told him . . . Prince** told him (Gloucester)
that once when young Henry, then Prince of Wales

a man spied and taken behind a tapet*²¹ of the said chamber, the which man was delivered to the Earl of Arundel to be examined upon the cause of his being there at that time; the which, so examined, at that time confessed that he was there by the stirring and procuring of my said lord of Winchester, ordained to have slain the said Prince there in his bed. Wherefore the said Earl of Arundel let sack him²² forthwith and drowned him in the Thames.

"5. Item, our sovereign lord that was, King Henry the Fifth, said unto my said lord of Gloucester that, his father King Henry the Fourth living and visited then greatly with sickness by the hand of God, my said lord of Winchester said unto the King (Henry the Fifth, then being Prince) that the King his father so visited with sickness was not personable,²³ and therefore not disposed to come in conversation and governance of the people; and, forsomuch, counseled him to take the governance and crown of this land upon him."

[The Bishop replies, and the matter is put to the "arbitrement" of the King's Council.]

After the which words thus said, as before is declared, it was decreed also by the said lords arbitrators that the said lord of Winchester should have these words that follow unto my said lord of Gloucester: "My lord of Gloucester, I have conceived, to my great heaviness,²⁴ that ye should have received by divers reports that I should have purposed and imagined²⁵ against your person, honor, and estate in divers manners, for the which ye have taken against me great displeasure. Sir, I take God to my witness that what reports soever have been to you of me—peradventure of such as have had no great affection to me, God forgive it them—I never imagined ne purposed anything that might be hindering or prejudice to your person, honor, or estate; and therefore I pray you that ye be unto me good lord from this time forth, for, by my will, I gave never other occasion, nor pur-

21 on a night . . . tapet one night, by night . . . tapestry   22 let sack him caused him to be put in a sack   23 personable having the status of a legal person, legally competent   24 conceived . . . heaviness understood, to my great sorrow   25 imagined meditated, plotted

pose not to do hereafter, by the grace of God." The which
words so by him said, it was decreed by the same arbitrators that my lord of Gloucester should answer and say:
"Fair uncle, sith ye declare you such a man as ye say, I am
right glad that it is so, and for such a man I take you." And
when this was done, it was decreed by the same arbitrators
that every each of my lord[26] of Gloucester and Winchester
should take either other by the hand, in the presence of the
King and all the Parliament, in sign and token of good love
and accord; the which was done, and the Parliament adjourned till after Easter. . . .

But when the great fire of this dissension between these
two noble personages was thus by the arbitrators, to their
knowledge and judgment, utterly quenched out and laid underboard,[27] all other controversies between other lords, taking part with the one party or the other, were appeased and
brought to concord; so that, for joy, the King caused a solemn feast to be kept on Whitsunday, on which day he created Richard Plantagenet, son and heir to the Earl of
Cambridge (whom his father at Southampton had put to
death, as before ye have heard), Duke of York—not foreseeing that this preferment should be his destruction, nor that
his seed should of his generation be the extreme end and
final conclusion.

[In 1427 the Bishop of Winchester is made cardinal. In
France, meanwhile, Lord Talbot is made governor of Anjou
and Maine, and gains a dreaded reputation for fierceness
and courage among the French. Sir John Falstolf is assigned to another place. Under the Duke of Alençon, the
French resolve to recover the city of Le Mans from the English; he is joined at the city's walls by the Dauphin, Lord
Delabreth, and others. The fighting begins.]

The Earl of Suffolk, which was governor of the town, having perfect knowledge by such as scaped from the walls
how the matter went, withdrew without any tarriance into
the castle which standeth at the gate of Saint Vincent,
whereof was Constable Thomas Gower, esquire; whither

26 **every each of my lord** both lords   27 **to . . . laid underboard** to the
best of . . . put under the table, i.e., put to rest

also fled many Englishmen; so as for urging of the enemy, press of the number, and lack of victuals, they could not have endured long. Wherefore they privily sent a messenger to the Lord Talbot, which then lay[28] at Alençon, certifying him in how hard a case they were. The Lord Talbot, hearing these news, like a careful captain[29] in all haste assembled together about seven hundred men, and in the evening departed from Alençon so as in the morning he came to a castle called Guierche, two miles from Mans, and there stayed awhile till he had sent out Matthew Goffe,* as an espial,[30] to understand how the Frenchmen demeaned[31] themselves.

Matthew Goffe so well sped his business that privily in the night he came into the castle, where he learned that the Frenchmen very negligently used themselves, without taking heed to their watch, as though they had been out of all danger. Which well understood, he returned again and within a mile of the city met the Lord Talbot and the Lord Scales, and opened[32] unto them all things according to his credence.[33] The lords then, to make haste in the matter, because the day approached, with all speed possible came to the postern gate, and, alighting from their horses, about six of the clock in the morning they issued out of the castle, crying, "Saint George! Talbot!"

The Frenchmen, being thus suddenly taken,[34] were sore amazed, insomuch that some of them, being not out of their beds, got up in their shirts[35] and leapt over the walls. Other ran naked out of the gates to save their lives, leaving all their apparel, horses, armor, and riches behind them. None was hurt but such as resisted.

[Lord Talbot returns to Alençon. In the next year, 1428, Lord Thomas Montague, Earl of Salisbury, joins the Duke of Bedford at Paris, where they resolve on a plan to win Orleans. The siege begins in September.]

After the siege had continued full three weeks, the Bas-

---

28 lay resided, was headquartered **29 careful captain** attentive and thoughtful general **30 an espial** a spy **31 demeaned** managed, behaved, conducted. (*Used* in the next sentence has the same meaning.) **32 opened** disclosed **33 credence** belief, understanding **34 taken** i.e., surprised **35 shirts** i.e., nightshirts

tard of Orleans issued out of the gate of the bridge and
fought with the Englishmen; but they received him with so
fierce and terrible strokes that he was with all his company
compelled to retire and flee back into the city. But the
Englishmen followed so fast, in killing and taking of their
enemies, that they entered with them. The bulwark of the
bridge, with a great tower standing at the end of the same,
was taken incontinently[36] by the Englishmen, who behaved
themselves right valiantly under the conduct of their courageous captain, as at this assault so in divers skirmishes
against the French; partly to keep possession of that which
Henry the Fifth had by his magnanimity and puissance[37]
achieved, as also to enlarge the same. But all helped not, for
who can hold that which will away? Insomuch that some
cities by fraudulent practices, other some by martial prowess, were recovered by the French. . . .

The Bastard of Orleans and the Hire[38] were appointed to
see the walls and watches kept, and the Bishop saw that the
inhabitants within the city were put in good order and that
victuals were not vainly spent. In the tower that was taken
at the bridge end, as before you have heard, there was an
high chamber having a grate full of bars of iron by the
which a man might look all the length of the bridge into the
city; at which grate many of the chief captains stood many
times, viewing the city and devising in what place it was
best to give the assault. They within the city well perceived
this tooting-hole[39] and laid a piece of ordnance directly
against[40] the window.

It so chanced that, the nine and fiftieth day after the siege
was laid, the Earl of Salisbury, Sir Thomas Gargrave, and
William Glansdale,* with divers other, went into the said
tower and so into the high chamber, and looked out at the
grate; and within a short space the son of the Master Gunner, perceiving men looking out at the window, took his
match (as his father had taught him, who was gone down to
dinner) and fired the gun, the shot whereof brake and shiv-
ered the iron bars of the grate so that one of the same bars

---

36 incontinently immediately   **37 magnanimity and puissance** lofty
courage and might   **38 the Hire** "Steven de Vignoilles, surnamed la
Hire" (Holinshed)   **39 tooting-hole** peephole   **40 against** pointing
toward

strake the Earl so violently on the head that it struck away one of his eyes and the side of his cheek. Sir Thomas Gargrave was likewise stricken and died within two days.

The Earl was conveyed to Meun-on-Loire, where after eight days he likewise departed this world. . . . The damage that the realm of England received by the loss of this nobleman manifestly appeared in that, immediately after his death, the prosperous good luck which had followed the English nation began to decline, and the glory of their victories gotten in the parties[41] beyond the sea fell in decay.

Though all men were sorrowful for his death, yet the Duke of Bedford was most stricken with heaviness, as he that had lost his only right hand and chief aid in time of necessity. But sith that[42] dead men cannot help the chances of men that be living, he like a prudent governor appointed the Earl of Suffolk to be his lieutenant and captain of the siege, and joined with him the Lord Scales, the Lord Talbot, Sir John Falstolf,[43] and divers other right valiant captains.

[The siege of Orleans continues on into 1429.]

In time of this siege at Orleans, French stories say, the first week of March 1428,[44] unto Charles the Dauphin at Chinon, as he was in very great care and study how to wrestle against the English nation, by one Peter Baudricourt, Captain of Vaucouleurs (made after Marshal of France by the Dauphin's creation), was carried a young wench of an eighteen years old, called Joan Arc,* by name of her father, a sorry[45] shepherd, James of Arc, and Isabel her mother; brought up poorly in their trade of keeping cattle; born at Domremy* (therefore reported by Bale, Joan Domremy) upon Meuse in Lorraine, within the diocese of Toul. Of favor[46] was she counted likesome,[47] of person strongly made and manly, of courage great, hardy and stout[48] withal; an understander of councils though she were not at them; great semblance of chastity both of body and behavior; the

---

41 parties parts, regions   **42 sith that** since   **43 Falstolf** (The name, usually spelled Falstolfe in Holinshed, sometimes appears also in the chronicles as Fastolfe and in similar forms.)   **44 stories . . . 1428** histories . . . i.e., 1429   **45 sorry** wretched, poor   **46 favor** appearance, feature   **47 likesome** agreeable, attractive   **48 stout** brave

name of Jesus in her mouth about all her businesses; humble, obedient, and fasting divers days in the week. A person, as their books make her, raised up by power divine only for succor to the French estate[49] then deeply in distress; in whom, for planting a credit the rather,[50] first the company that toward the Dauphin did conduct her, through places all dangerous as holden[51] by the English, where she never was afore, all the way and by nightertale[52] safely did she lead. Then, at the Dauphin's sending by her assignment,[53] from Saint Catherine's Church of Fierbois in Touraine, where she never had been and knew not. in a secret place there among old iron, appointed she her sword to be sought out[54] and brought her that with five fleurs-de-lis was graven on both sides, wherewith she fought and did many slaughters by her own hands. On warfare rode she in armor cap-a-pie*[55] and mustered[56] as a man, before her an ensign[57] all white wherein was Jesus Christ painted with a fleur-de-lis in his hand.

Unto the Dauphin into his gallery when first she was brought, and he, shadowing[58] himself behind, setting other gay lords before him to try her cunning, from all the company, with a salutation that indeed marred all the matter, she picked him out alone; who thereupon had her to the end of the gallery where she held him an hour in secret and private talk, that of his privy chamber was thought very long and therefore would have broken it off, but he made them a sign to let her say on. In which, among other, as likely it was,[59] she set out unto him the singular feats (forsooth) given her to understand by revelation divine that in virtue of that sword she should achieve; which were, how with

---

49 estate kingdom **50 for planting . . . rather** the sooner to establish her credit (as a performer of miracles) **51 holden** held, occupied **52 by nightertale** through the night. (Joan led those who were escorting her straight to the Dauphin, through places occupied by the English and that she had never seen before.) **53 at the . . . assignment** i.e., when the Dauphin sent her off to relieve Orleans **54 appointed . . . sought out** she ordered a sword to be sought out for her **55 On warfare . . . cap-a-pie** she rode into battle armed from head to foot **56 mustered** come forward ready for battle **57 ensign** banner **58 shadowing** hiding **59 as likely it was** as probably was said. (The conversation, being private, cannot be vouched for by the chronicler.)

honor and victory she would raise the siege at Orleans, set
him in state of the crown of France, and drive the English
out of the country, thereby he to enjoy the kingdom alone.
Hereupon he heartened at full,[60] appointed her a sufficient
army with absolute power to lead them, and they obedi-
ently to do as she bade them. Then fell she to work and first
defeated, indeed, the siege at Orleans; by and by[61] encouraged him to crown himself King of France at Rheims, that a
little before from the English she had won. Thus, after, pursued she many bold enterprises, to our great displeasure a
two year together;[62] for the time she kept in state[63] until she
were taken and for heresy and witchery burned, as in particularities hereafter followeth. But in her prime time she
armed at all points like a jolly captain, rode from Poitiers to
Blois, and there found men-of-war, victuals, and munition
ready to be conveyed to Orleans.

Here was it known that the Englishmen kept not so diligent watch as they had been accustomed to do, and therefore this maid, with other French captains coming forward
in the dead time of the night and in a great rain and
thunder, entered into the city with all their victuals, artillery, and other necessary provisions. The next day the
Englishmen boldly assaulted the town, but the Frenchmen
defended the walls so as no great feat worthy of memory
chanced that day betwixt them, though the Frenchmen
were amazed at the valiant attempt of the Englishmen.
Whereupon the Bastard of Orleans gave knowledge to the
Duke of Alençon in what danger the town stood without his
present help; who, coming within two leagues of the city,
gave knowledge to them within that they should be ready
the next day to receive him.

This accordingly was accomplished, for the Englishmen
willingly suffered him and his army also to enter, suppos-
ing that it should be for their advantage to have so great a
multitude to enter the city, whereby their victuals (whereof
they within had great scarcity) might the sooner be consumed.

---

60 heartened at full rallied, cheered up completely **61 by and by** at
once **62 a two year together** for a period of two years **63 for the . . .
state** for that length of time she remained in power

[The English abandon the siege of Orleans, hoping to encounter the French instead in open battle. The French re-
inforce to the number of 20,000 or 23,000 men.]

All which being once joined in one army, shortly after
fought with the Lord Talbot, who had with him not past six
thousand men, near unto a village in Beauce called Patay; at
which battle the charge was given by the French so upon a
sudden that the Englishmen had not leisure to put themselves in array after they had put up their stakes before
their archers; so that there was no remedy but to fight at
adventure.[64] This battle continued by the space of three long
hours, for the Englishmen, though they were overpressed
with multitude of their enemies, yet they never fled back
one foot till their captain, the Lord Talbot, was sore
wounded at the back, and so taken.

Then their hearts began to faint, and they fled, in which
flight were slain above twelve hundred, and forty taken, of
whom the Lord Talbot, the Lord Scales, the Lord Hungerford, and Sir Thomas Rampston were chief. . . . From this
battle departed, without any stroke stricken, Sir John Falstolf, the same year for his valiantness elected into the Order of the Garter. But for doubt[65] of misdealing at this
brunt[66] the Duke of Bedford took from him the image of
Saint George and his garter, though afterward, by means of
friends and apparent causes of good excuse, the same were
to him again delivered, against the mind of the Lord Talbot.

Charles the Dauphin, that called himself French king,
perceiving Fortune to smile thus upon him, assembled a
great power and determined to conquer the city of Rheims,
that he might be there sacred,[67] crowned, and anointed according to the custom of his progenitors, that all men might
judge that he was by all laws and decrees a just and lawful
king. . . . When Rheims was thus become French, the foresaid Charles the Dauphin, in the presence of the Dukes of
Lorraine and Bar and of all the noblemen of his faction,
was sacred there King of France by the name of Charles the
Seventh, with all rites and ceremonies thereto belonging.

---

64 at adventure pell mell, recklessly   **65 doubt** suspicion   **66 brunt**
assault   **67 sacred** consecrated to office. (The passive infinitive of the
verb *sacre*.)

["Joan the Pucelle" is captured in 1430 at Compiègne, and, for the large sum of 10,000 pounds in money and 300 pounds rent, is "sold into the English hands."]

In which, for her pranks so uncouth and suspicious, the Lord Regent, by Peter Cauchon, Bishop of Beauvais (in whose diocese she was taken), caused her life and belief, after order of law, to be inquired upon and examined. Wherein found, though a virgin, yet first, shamefully rejecting her sex abominably in acts and apparel, to have counterfeit mankind,[68] and then, all damnably faithless, to be a pernicious instrument to hostility and bloodshed in devilish witchcraft and sorcery, sentence accordingly was pronounced against her. Howbeit, upon humble confession of her iniquities, with a counterfeit contrition pretending a careful sorrow for the same, execution was spared* and all mollified into this: that from thenceforth she should cast off her unnatural wearing of man's habiliments and keep her to garments of her own kind,[69] abjure her pernicious practices of sorcery and witchery, and have life and leisure in perpetual prison to bewail her misdeeds. Which to perform, according to the manner of abjuration, a solemn oath very gladly she took.

But herein (God help us!) she, fully afore possessed of the fiend, not able to hold her in any towardness of[70] grace, falling straightway into her former abominations, and yet seeking to eke out life as long as she might, stake not,[71] though the shift were shameful, to confess herself a strumpet and, unmarried as she was, to be with child. For trial, the Lord Regent's lenity gave her nine months' stay,[72] at the end whereof she (found herein[73] as false as wicked in the rest), an eight days after, upon a further definitive sentence declared against her to be relapse[74] and a renouncer of her oath and repentance, was she thereupon delivered over to secular power and so executed by consumption of fire in the old marketplace at Rouen, in the selfsame stead[75] where now Saint Michael's Church stands—her ashes afterward

68 **counterfeit mankind** counterfeited the male sex   69 **kind** sex
70 **towardness of** inclination toward, readiness for   71 **stake not** did not stick or scruple   72 **stay** respite   73 **found herein** found in this to be
74 **relapse** a relapsed sinner   75 **stead** place

without[76] the town walls shaken[77] into the wind. Now, recounting altogether her pastoral bringing up, rude, without any virtuous instruction, her campestral[78] conversation with wicked spirits, whom, in her first salutation to Charles the Dauphin, she uttered[79] to be Our Lady, Saint Catherine, and Saint Anne,* that in this behalf came and gave her commandments from God her maker as she kept her father's lambs in the fields . . . [all these outward shows of divine inspiration not to be trusted,] sith Satan (after[80] Saint Paul) can change himself into an angel of light, the deeplier to deceive.

[The English conclude that their cause would be best served by King Henry VI himself coming into France. He sets sail in 1431, going first to Calais and then Rouen.]

But to return to the affairs of King Henry, who in the month of November removed from Rouen to Pontoise, and so to Saint Denis, to the intent to make his entry into Paris and there to be sacred[81] King of France. There were in his company, of his own nation, his uncle the Cardinal of Winchester, the Cardinal and Archbishop of York, the Dukes of Bedford, York, and Norfolk, the Earls of Warwick, Salisbury, Oxenford, Huntington, Ormonde, Mortain, and Suffolk. . . .

To speak with what honor he was received into the city of Paris, what pageants were prepared, and how richly the gates, streets, and bridges on every side were hanged with costly cloths of arras and tapestry, it would be too long a process and therefore I do here pass it over with silence. On the seventeenth day of December he was crowned King of France, in Our Lady Church of Paris, by the Cardinal of Winchester, the Bishop of Paris not being contented that the Cardinal should do such an high ceremony in his church and jurisdiction. After all the ceremonies were finished, the King returned toward the palace, having one crown on his head and another borne before him, and one scepter in his hand and the second borne before him.

---

76 without outside of **77 shaken** scattered. (She was denied burial.)
78 campestral in the fields **79 uttered** declared **80 sith Satan (after** since Satan (in the words of **81 sacred** consecrated to office

[Lord Talbot, captured at the Battle of Patay, is exchanged for the French prisoner Ponton de Santrailles. King Henry returns triumphantly to London in February 1432, a six-years' truce having been signed. Violations of the truce occur not infrequently, and so in 1435 the Emperor Sigismund and other kings of Europe urge a new attempt at mediation. French and English demands are far apart. The Duke of Burgundy, though pretending friendship to England, sends a letter to King Henry alleging that he, Burgundy, has been constrained to enter into league with King Charles of France. The letter, addressed "To the high and mighty Prince Henry, by the grace of God King of England, his well-beloved cousin," distresses the King's Council, who regard Burgundy as a traitor. The Duke of Bedford dies in this same year, 1435, and is buried at Rouen. But the most serious worry in 1435 is the outbreak of dissension between Richard, Duke of York, and Edmund, Duke of Somerset.]

After the death of that noble prince the Duke of Bedford, the bright sun in France toward Englishmen began to be cloudy and daily to darken. The Frenchmen began not only to withdraw their obedience by oath to the King of England but also took sword in hand and openly rebelled. Howbeit, all these mishaps could not anything[82] abash the valiant courages of the English people, for they, having no mistrust in God and good fortune, set up a new sail, began the war afresh, and appointed for Regent in France Richard, Duke of York, son to Richard, Earl of Cambridge.

Although the Duke of York was worthy, both for birth and courage, of this honor and preferment, yet so disdained of Edmund, Duke of Somerset, being cousin to the King, that by all means possible he sought his hindrance,[83] as one glad of his loss and sorry of his well doing; by reason whereof, ere the Duke of York could get his dispatch,[84] Paris and divers other of the chiefest places in France were gotten by the French King. The Duke of York, perceiving his[85] evil

---

82 anything in any way **83 he sought his hindrance** i.e., Somerset sought to hinder York **84 get his dispatch** obtain permission to leave on his assignment **85 his** i.e., Somerset's

will, openly dissembled that which he inwardly minded,[86] either[87] of them working things to the other's displeasure; till, through malice and division between them, at length by mortal war they were both consumed, with almost all their whole lines and offspring.

[York as regent is faced with other losses as a result, including Dieppe, Bois, and Vincennes.]

So that here partly was accomplished the prophecy of Henry the Fifth, given out in the ninth year of his reign when he lay at siege before Meaux, that Henry of Windsor[88] should lose all that Henry of Monmouth[89] had gotten—for so they are named according to the place of their nativity; and this prediction was complete and full by that time the years of his regiment[90] were expired.

But here is one chief point to be noted, that either the disdain amongst the chief peers of the realm of England (as ye have heard), or the negligence of the King's Council, which did not foresee dangers to come, was the loss of the whole dominion of France between the rivers of Somme and Marne and, in especial, of the noble city of Paris. For where before there were sent over thousands for defense of the holds and fortresses, now were sent hundreds, yea, and scores; some rascals, and some not able to draw a bow or carry a bill.[91]

[The war drags on, and the English are faced with new losses. Paris falls to the possession of King Charles. York and Somerset carry the attack to Anjou. In England, Winchester and Gloucester continue to quarrel. John Talbot is created Earl of Shrewsbury in 1442.]

In this year [1443] died in Guînes the Countess of Comminges, to whom the French King and also the Earl of Armagnac pretended[92] to be heir, insomuch that the Earl entered into all the lands of the said lady. And because he

---

86 minded intended   **87 either** both   **88 Henry of Windsor** Henry VI
89 Henry of Monmouth Henry V   **90 his regiment** i.e., Henry VI's rule
91 a bill a long-handled infantry weapon, a halberd   **92 pretended** claimed

knew the French King would not take the matter well to have a Roland for an Oliver,[93] he sent solemn ambassadors to the King of England, offering him his daughter in marriage, with promise to be bound (beside great sums of money which he would give with her) to deliver into the King of England's hands all such castles and towns as he or his ancestors detained from him within any part of the duchy of Aquitaine, either by conquest of his progenitors or by gift and delivery of any French king, and further to aid the same King with money for the recovery of other cities within the same duchy from the French King or from any other person that against King Henry unjustly kept[94] and wrongfully withholden[95] them.

This offer seemed so profitable and also honorable to King Henry and the realm that the ambassadors were well heard, honorably received, and with rewards sent home into their country. After whom were sent for the conclusion of the marriage into Guienne Sir Edward Hull, Sir Robert Ros, and John Grafton,* Dean of Saint Severinus, the which, as all the chronographers agree, both concluded the marriage and by proxy affied[96] the young lady.

[The French King is "not a little offended" at this treaty. William de la Pole, Earl of Suffolk, is sent to represent King Henry at the Diet (i.e., Assembly) of Tours, where peace between England and France is discussed.]

Many meetings were had, and many things moved for a final peace, but in conclusion, by reason of many doubts which rose on both parties, no full concord could be agreed upon; but in hope to come to a peace, a certain truce as well by sea as by land was concluded by the commissioners for eighteen months, which afterward again was prolonged to the year of our Lord 1449.

---

93 not take . . . Oliver i.e., not be well pleased to be thus foiled by an equal match. (Roland, the nephew of Charlemagne and the most famous of his paladins in medieval romance, is said once to have fought for five days with Oliver, or Olivier, son of Regnier, Duke of Genoa (another of Charlemagne's paladins). Hence *to give a Roland for an Oliver* is to match or trade blow for blow.) **94 unjustly kept** had unjustly kept **95 withholden** withheld **96 affied** espoused

In treating of this truce, the Earl of Suffolk, adventuring
somewhat upon his commission,[97] without the assent of his
associates, imagined that the next[98] way to come to a perfect
peace was to contrive a marriage between the French
King's kinswoman the Lady Margaret, daughter to Reiner,[99]
Duke of Anjou, and his sovereign lord King Henry. This
Reiner, Duke of Anjou, named himself King of Sicily, Naples, and Jerusalem, having only the name and style of
those realms, without any penny profit or foot of possession. This marriage was made strange to[100] the Earl at the
first, and one thing seemed to be a great hindrance to it:
which was because the King of England occupied a great
part of the duchy of Anjou and the whole county of Maine,
appertaining,[101] as was alleged, to King Reiner.

The Earl of Suffolk (I cannot say either corrupted with
bribes or too much affectioned to[102] this unprofitable marriage) condescended[103] that the duchy of Anjou and the
county of Maine should be delivered to the King, the bride's
father, demanding for her marriage[104] neither penny nor
farthing, as who would say[105] that this new affinity[106] passed
all riches and excelled both gold and precious stones. And
to the intent that of this truce might ensue a final concord, a
day of interview was appointed between the two Kings in a
place convenient between Chartres and Rouen. When these
things were concluded, the Earl of Suffolk with his company returned into England, where he forgat not to declare
what an honorable truce he had taken, out of the which
there was a great hope that a final peace might grow the
sooner for that honorable marriage which he had concluded, omitting nothing that might extol and set forth the
personage of the lady or the nobility of her kindred.

But, although this marriage pleased the King and divers
of his Council, yet Humphrey, Duke of Gloucester, Protector
of the realm, was much against it, alleging that it should be

---

97 adventuring . . . commission somewhat overstepping his authority
98 next nearest   **99 Reiner** i.e., René   **100 marriage was made strange
to** i.e., marriage proposal was regarded with some coolness by Reiner,
or René, in response to   **101 appertaining** belonging   **102 affectioned
to** committed to, desirous of   **103 condescended** agreed, conceded
104 demanding for her marriage i.e., Suffolk for his part stipulating as
dowry to be brought by her in marriage   **105 who would say** one might
say   **106 affinity** relationship by marriage

both contrary to the laws of God and dishonorable to the
Prince if he should break that promise and contract of
marriage, made by ambassadors sufficiently thereto in-
structed, with the daughter of the Earl of Armagnac, upon
conditions both to him and his realm as much profitable as
honorable. But the Duke's words could not be heard, for the
Earl's doings were only liked and allowed.

[This success of Suffolk's occurs in 1444. Somerset is made
Regent of Normandy in 1446 and York is discharged but
then reappointed. Suffolk becomes marquess. At this point
the story of *2 Henry VI* begins, but Shakespeare borrows
from the events of 1453 an account of Talbot's death at Bordeaux. Talbot, the Earl of Shrewsbury, is joined there by his
son, Sir John Talbot, Lord Lisle.]

In the meantime, the French King, being advertised[107] of
all these doings, raised an army to resist this invasion made
by the Earl of Shrewsbury. And first he appointed his captains to besiege the town of Castillon, to the rescue whereof
the Earl hasted forward. . . .

The Frenchmen that lay at the siege, perceiving by those
good runners-away that the Earl approached, left the siege
and retired in good order into the place which they had
trenched, ditched, and fortified with ordnance. The Earl,
advertised how the siege was removed, hasted forward
towards his enemies, doubting[108] most lest they would have
been quite fled and gone before his coming. But they, fearing the displeasure of the French King (who was not far off)
if they should have fled, abode[109] the Earl's coming and so
received him; who, though he first with manful courage and
sore fighting wan the entry of their camp, yet at length they
compassed him about and, shooting him through the thigh
with an handgun, slew his horse and finally killed him lying
on the ground whom they durst never look in the face while
he stood on his feet.

It was said that after he perceived there was no remedy
but present loss of the battle, he counseled his son the Lord
Lisle to save himself by flight, sith[110] the same could not re-

107 **advertised** informed, warned   108 **doubting** fearing   109 **abode**
awaited   110 **sith** since

dound to any great reproach in him, this being the first journey[111] in which he had been present. Many words he used to persuade him to have saved his life; but nature so wrought in the son that neither desire of life nor fear of death could either cause him to shrink or convey himself out of the danger, and so there manfully ended his life with his said father.

The second edition of Raphael Holinshed's *Chronicles* was published in 1587. This selection is based on that edition, Volume 3, folios 585–640.

In the following, departures from the original text appear in boldface; original readings are in roman.

p. 417 *tapet [Holinshed adds a marginal gloss: "Or hanging."]   **p. 419** *Goffe Gough. [Holinshed adds a marginal note here and elsewhere for this name: "Or rather Goche."]   **p. 420** *Glansdale Glasdale   **p. 421** *Arc Are [and similarly throughout text] **p. 421** *Domremy Domprin [and later again in this sentence]   **p. 422** *cap-a-pie [Holinshed adds a marginal gloss: "From head to foot"]   **p. 425** *was spared spared **p. 426** *Anne Annes   **p. 429** *Grafton Gralton

---

111 journey battle, day's performance in fighting

[For *Henry VI, Part Two*]

The Third Volume of Chronicles (1587 edition)
Compiled by Raphael Holinshed

HENRY THE SIXTH

[The quarreling between King Henry's uncles, the Cardinal of Winchester and the Duke of Gloucester, never long absent during his reign, breaks out anew in 1441.]

When the King had heard the accusations thus laid by the Duke of Gloucester against the Cardinal, he committed the examination thereof to his Council, whereof the more part were spiritual persons; so that, what for fear and what for favor, the matter was winked at and nothing said to it; only fair countenance was made to the Duke, as though no malice had been conceived against him. But venom will break out and inward grudge will soon appear, which was this year to all men apparent, for divers secret attempts were advanced forward this season against this nobleman Humphrey, Duke of Gloucester, afar off, which, in conclusion, came so near that they bereft him both of life and land, as shall hereafter more plainly appear.

For, first, this year Dame Eleanor Cobham, wife to the said Duke, was accused of treason, for that she by sorcery and enchantment intended to destroy the King, to the intent to advance her husband unto the crown. Upon this, she was examined in Saint Stephen's Chapel before the Bishop of Canterbury, and there by examination convict and judged[1] to do open penance in three open places within the city of London (*Polychronicon*[2] saith she was enjoined to go through Cheapside with a taper in her hand), and after that adjudged to perpetual imprisonment in the Isle of Man, under the keeping of Sir John Stanley, knight. At the same season were arrested, arraigned, and adjudged guilty, as aiders to the Duchess, Thomas Southwell, priest and canon of Saint Stephen's at Westminster; John Hume,* priest; Roger

---

1 **convict and judged** convicted and sentenced 2 **Polychronicon** a chronicle of universal history, by Ranulf Higden, written c. 1324 and subsequently continued to the year 1413; one of Holinshed's sources

Bolingbroke, a cunning necromancer, as it was said; and
Margery Jourdain, surnamed the Witch of Eye.

The matter laid against them was for that they, at the request of the said Duchess, had devised an image of wax representing the King, which by their sorcery by little and little
consumed, intending thereby in conclusion to waste and destroy the King's person. Margery Jourdain was burnt in
Smithfield, and Roger Bolingbroke was drawn to Tyburn
and hanged and quartered, taking[3] upon his death that
there was never any such thing by them imagined.[4] John
Hume had his pardon, and Southwell died in the Tower the
night before his execution, for (saith *Polychronicon*) he did
prophesy of himself that he should die in his bed and not by
justice. The Duke of Gloucester bare[5] all these things patiently and said little. Edward, son to the Duke of York, was
born this year, the nine and twentieth of April, at Rouen, his
father being the King's lieutenant in Normandy.

[The Earl of Suffolk enjoys his daring success of having arranged a marriage between King Henry and Margaret of
Anjou. He journeys into France to bring her to England in
1444–1445.]

The Earl of Suffolk was made Marquess of Suffolk;
which Marquess, with his wife and many honorable personages of men and women, richly adorned both with apparel
and jewels, having with them many costly chariots and gorgeous horse litters, sailed into France for the conveyance of
the nominated Queen into the realm of England. For King
Reiner her father, for all his long style,[6] had too short a
purse to send his daughter honorably to the King her
spouse.

This noble company came to the city of Tours in Touraine,
where they were honorably received both of the French
King and of the King of Sicily. The Marquess of Suffolk, as
procurator to King Henry, espoused the said lady in the
church of Saint Martin's. At the which marriage were
present the father and mother of the bride, the French King

3 **taking** swearing, taking an oath   4 **imagined** contrived, plotted
5 **bare** bore   6 **his long style** (Reiner, or René, Duke of Anjou, styled
himself King of Sicily and Jerusalem, though he enjoyed no revenues or
power in those titles.)

himself, which was uncle to the husband, and the French Queen also, which was aunt to the wife. There were also the Dukes of Orleans, of Calabria, of Alençon, and of Brittany, seven earls, twelve barons, twenty bishops, besides knights and gentlemen. When the feast, triumph, banquets, and jousts were ended, the lady was delivered to the Marquess, who in great estate conveyed her through Normandy unto Dieppe and so transported her into England, where she landed at Portsmouth in the month of April. This lady excelled all other as well in beauty and favor[7] as in wit and policy,[8] and was of stomach and courage[9] more like to a man than a woman.

Shortly after her arrival she was conveyed to the town of Southwick in Hampshire, where she with all nuptial ceremonies was coupled in matrimony to King Henry, the sixth of that name. On the eighteenth of May she came to London, all the lords of England in most sumptuous sort meeting and receiving her upon the way, and specially the Duke of Gloucester, with such honor as stood with the dignity of his person. . . . Upon the thirtieth of May next following she was crowned queen of this realm of England at Westminster, with all the solemnity thereto appertaining.

This marriage seemed to many both infortunate and unprofitable to the realm of England, and that for many causes. First, the King had not one penny with her, and for the fetching of her the Marquess of Suffolk demanded a whole fifteenth[10] in open Parliament. And also there was delivered for her the duchy of Anjou, the city of Mans, and the whole county of Maine, which countries were the very stays and backstands to the duchy of Normandy. And furthermore, the Earl of Armagnac took such displeasure with the King of England for this marriage that he became utter enemy to the crown of England and was the chief cause that the Englishmen were expelled out of the whole duchy of Aquitaine.

But most of all it should seem that God was displeased with this marriage, for after the confirmation thereof the King's friends fell from him, both in England and in France,

---

7 **favor** appearance, countenance. (The date is 1445.) 8 **wit and policy** intelligence and cunning 9 **stomach and courage** courage and spirit
10 **fifteenth** a tax of one fifteenth imposed on personal property

the lords of his realm fell at division, and the commons rebelled in such sort that finally, after many fields foughten[11]
and many thousands of men slain, the King at length was
deposed and his son killed and this queen sent home again
with as much misery and sorrow as she was received with
pomp and triumph. Such is the instability of worldly felic-
ity and so wavering is false flattering Fortune.

[The Duke of Somerset is appointed Regent of Normandy in
1446 and the Duke of York is discharged but is then reappointed as Regent of France. The Marquess of Suffolk
gains in favor and influence.]

Whilst the wars between the two nations of England and
France ceased, by occasion of the truce, the minds of men
were not so quiet but that such as were bent to malicious
revenge sought to compass their prepensed[12] purpose, not
against foreign foes and enemies of their country, but
against their own countrymen and those that had deserved
very well of the commonwealth. And this specially for over-
much mildness in the King,[13] who by his authority might
have ruled both parts and ordered all differences betwixt
them, but that, indeed, he was thought too soft for governor
of a kingdom. The Queen, contrariwise, a lady of great wit
and no less courage, desirous of honor and furnished with
the gifts of reason, policy,[14] and wisdom, but yet sometimes,
according to her kind,[15] when she had been fully bent on a
matter, suddenly like a weathercock mutable and turning.
This lady, disdaining that her husband should be ruled
rather than rule, could not abide that the Duke of Gloucester should do all things concerning the order of weighty affairs, lest it might be said that she had neither wit nor
stomach which[16] would permit and suffer her husband, being of most perfect age,[17] like a young pupil to be governed
by the direction of another man. Although this toy[18] entered

11 fell at division . . . fields foughten fell into conflict . . . battles fought
12 compass their prepensed bring about their premeditated   13 And
this . . . King i.e., and this factionalism was especially encouraged by
the overly great mildness of King Henry   14 policy cunning   15 kind
sex   16 stomach which courage who   17 being . . . age having reached
full maturity, no longer a minor   18 toy whim

first into her brain through her own imagination, yet was she pricked[19] forward to the matter both by such of her husband's counsel, as of long time had[20] borne malice to the Duke for his plainness used in declaring their untruth[21] (as partly ye have heard), and also by counsel from King Reiner her father, advising that she and the King should take upon them the rule of the realm and not to be kept under as wards and mastered orphans.

What needeth many words?[22] The Queen, persuaded by these means, first of all excluded the Duke of Gloucester from all rule and governance, not prohibiting such as she knew to be his mortal foes to invent and imagine causes and griefs against him and his, insomuch that by her procurement divers noblemen conspired against him. Of the which, divers writers affirm the Marquess of Suffolk and the Duke of Buckingham to be the chief, not unprocured by the Cardinal of Winchester and the Archbishop of York. Divers articles were laid against him in open Council, and in especial one: That he had caused men adjudged to die to be put to other execution than the law of the land assigned. Surely the Duke, very well learned in the law civil, detesting malefactors and punishing offenses in severity of justice, gat him hatred of such as feared condign reward[23] for their wicked doings. And although the Duke sufficiently answered to all things against him objected, yet because his death was determined, his wisdom and innocency nothing availed.

But to avoid danger of tumult that might be raised if a prince so well beloved of the people should be openly executed, his enemies determined to work their feats in his destruction ere he should have any warning. For effecting whereof, a Parliament was summoned to be kept at Bury, whither resorted all the peers of the realm, and amongst them the Duke of Gloucester, which, on the second day of the session, was by the Lord Beaumont, then High Constable of England, accompanied with the Duke of Buckingham

19 pricked spurred 20 by such . . . long time had by those close advisers of her husband who had long 21 declaring their untruth i.e., denouncing the self-serving perfidies of Winchester and York 22 What needeth many words what more need be said 23 condign reward merited and appropriate punishment

and others, arrested, apprehended, and put in ward,[24] and all his servants sequestered from him; and thirty-two of the chief of his retinue were sent to divers prisons, to the great admiration[25] of the people. The Duke, the night after he was thus committed to prison, being the four and twentieth of February, was found dead in his bed, and his body showed to the lords and commons as though he had died of a palsy or of an impostume.[26]

But all indifferent[27] persons (as saith Hall)[28] might well understand that he died of some violent death. Some judged him to be strangled, some affirm that an hot spit was put in at his fundament,[29] other write that he was smoldered[30] between two featherbeds, and some have affirmed that he died of very grief for that he might not come openly to his answer. His dead corpse was conveyed to Saint Albans and there buried. . . .

Some think that the name and title of Gloucester hath been unlucky to divers which for their honors have been erected by creation of princes to that style and dignity, as Hugh Spenser,[31] Thomas of Woodstock,[32] son to King Edward the Third, and this Duke Humphrey, which three persons by miserable death finished their days; and after them King Richard the Third, also Duke of Gloucester, in civil war slain. So that this name "Duke of Gloucester" is taken for an unhappy style. . . . But surely by the pitiful death of this noble duke and politic[33] governor the public wealth of the realm came to great decay, as by sequel here may more at large appear.

Ofttimes it happeneth that a man, in quenching of smoke, burneth his fingers in the fire. So the Queen, in casting how to keep her husband in honor and herself in authority, in making away of this nobleman brought that to pass which she had most cause to have feared, which was the deposing

---

24 ward prison   **25 admiration** amazement   **26 impostume** abscess. (The date is 1447.)   **27 indifferent** impartial   **28 Hall** Edward Hall, chronicler, author and compiler of *The Union of the Noble and Illustre Families of Lancaster and York* (1548)   **29 fundament** anus
30 smoldered smothered   **31 Hugh Spenser** i.e., Hugh le Despenser, created Earl of Gloucester in 1397, executed for treason in 1400
32 Thomas of Woodstock created Earl of Gloucester in 1385, murdered in 1397 at Calais perhaps at the instigation of his nephew, King Richard II, whom he had opposed   **33 politic** judicious in public affairs

of her husband and the decay of the house of Lancaster, which of likelihood had not chanced if this Duke had lived; for then durst not the Duke of York have attempted to set forth his title to the crown, as he afterwards did, to the great trouble of the realm and destruction of King Henry and of many other noblemen besides. This is the opinion of men, but God's judgments are unsearchable, against whose decree and ordinance prevaileth no human counsel.

But to conclude of this noble duke: he was an upright and politic governor, bending all his endeavors to the advancement of the commonwealth, very loving to the poor commons, and so[34] beloved of them again; learned, wise, full of courtesy, void of pride and ambition (a virtue rare in personages of such high estate but, where it is, most commendable).

[Holinshed refers the reader to John Foxe's *Acts and Monuments* for further praise of Duke Humphrey.]

In this six and twentieth year of the reign of this king, but in the first of the rule of the Queen, I find nothing done worthy of rehearsal within the realm of England but that the Marquess of Suffolk, by great favor of the King and more desire of the Queen, was erected to the title and dignity of Duke of Suffolk, which he a short time enjoyed. For Richard, Duke of York (being greatly allied by his wife to the chief peers and potentates of the realm, besides his own progeny),[35] perceiving the King to be no ruler, but the whole burden of the realm to rest in direction of the Queen and the Duke of Suffolk, began secretly to allure his friends of the nobility, and privily declared unto them his title and right to the crown, and likewise did he to certain wise governors of divers cities and towns. Which attempt was so politicly[36] handled and so secretly kept that provision to his purpose[37] was ready before his purpose was openly published,[38] and his friends opened[39] themselves ere the contrary part could them espy; for in conclusion, all shortly in mischief burst out, as ye may hereafter hear.

34 **so** accordingly 35 **progeny** lineage 36 **politicly** cunningly, artfully
37 **provision to his purpose** furnishings and supply necessary to his purpose 38 **published** revealed 39 **opened** declared

During these doings Henry Beaufort, Bishop of Winchester, and called the Rich Cardinal, departed out of this world and buried at Westminster. He was son to John,[40] Duke of Lancaster.

[Holinshed gives an account of Winchester's "insatiable covetousness," his forgetfulness of God, and some charitable acts. When a rebellion erupts in Ireland in 1447, Richard, Duke of York, is sent to put it down. In France, Normandy is lost to the English. Popular opinion begins to turn against the Duke of Suffolk as the author of many surrenders to the French. The commoners bring formal complaint against him in a Parliament of 1450.]

The Queen, which entirely loved the Duke, doubting[41] some commotion and trouble to arise if he were let go unpunished, caused him for a color[42] to be committed to the Tower, where he remained not past a month but was again delivered and restored to the King's favor, as much as ever he was before. This doing so much displeased the people that, if politic provision had not been, great mischief had immediately ensued.

[The commoners assemble in various places and elect a chief, whom they call Bluebeard, but he and other leaders are apprehended before the situation gets out of hand. Parliament is adjourned to Leicester, where Suffolk appears with the King and Queen as chief counsellor. The commoners once again insist that Suffolk be punished.]

When the King perceived that there was no remedy to appease the people's fury by any colorable ways,[43] shortly to pacify so long an hatred, he first sequestered the Lord Saye (being Treasurer of England) and other the Duke's[44] adherents from their offices and rooms, and after banished the Duke of Suffolk, as the abhorred toad and common noyance of the whole realm, for term of five years, meaning by this

---

40 John i.e., John of Gaunt, father also of Henry IV. (Beaufort was an illegitimate son.)   **41 doubting** fearing   **42 color** pretext   **43 colorable ways** plausible pretexts   **44 other the Duke's** other of the Duke of Suffolk's

exile to appease the malice of the people for the time and after, when the matter should be forgotten, to revoke him home again.

But God's justice would not that so ungracious a person should so escape; for when he shipped[45] in Suffolk, intending to transport himself over into France, he was encountered with a ship-of-war appertaining to[46] the Duke of Exeter, constable of the Tower of London, called *The Nicholas of the Tower*. The captain of that bark with small fight entered into the Duke's ship and, perceiving his person present, brought him to Dover Road and there, on the one side of a cockboat,[47] caused his head to be stricken off and left his body with the head lying there on the sands. Which corpse, being there found by a chaplain of his, was conveyed to Wingfield College in Suffolk and there buried. This end had William de la Pole, Duke of Suffolk, as men judge by God's providence for that he had procured the death of that good Duke of Gloucester, as before is partly touched.[48]

Soon after, another disquiet befell here. Those that favored the Duke of York and wished the crown upon his head for that,[49] as they judged, he had more right thereto than he that ware it, procured[50] a commotion in Kent on this manner. A certain young man, of a goodly stature and right pregnant[51] of wit, was enticed to take upon him the name of John Mortimer, cousin to the Duke of York (although his name was John Cade or, of some, John Mend-all, an Irishman, as *Polychronicon* saith), and not for a small policy,[52] thinking by that surname that those which favored the house of the Earl of March would be assistant to him. . . .

This captain,[53] assembling a great company of tall personages, assured them that the enterprise which he took in hand was both honorable to God and the King and profitable to the whole realm. For if either by force or policy they might get the King and Queen into their hands, he would cause them to be honorably used and take such order for the punishing and reforming of the misdemeanors of their

45 **shipped** took ship   46 **appertaining to** belonging to the right or privilege of   47 **cockboat** small ship's boat   48 **touched** touched upon, discussed   49 **for that** because   50 **ware it, procured** wore it, caused   51 **pregnant** fertile   52 **policy** stratagem   53 **This captain** this leader or general, John Cade. (Said ironically; *tall* or "brave" in the same sentence is also ironic.)

bad counselors that neither fifteens[54] should hereafter be
demanded nor once any impositions or taxes be spoken of.
The Kentish people, moved at these persuasions and other
fair promises of reformation, in good order of battle (though
not in great number) came with their captain unto the plain
of Blackheath, between Eltham and Greenwich, and there
kept the field[55] more than a month, pilling[56] the country
about; to whom the city of London at that time was very
favorable. . . .

And to the intent the cause of this glorious captain's coming thither might be shadowed under a cloak of good meaning (though his intent nothing so), he sent unto the King an
humble supplication affirming that his coming was not
against His Grace but against such of his counselors as
were lovers of themselves and oppressors of the poor com-
monalty, flatterers of the King and enemies to his honor,
suckers of his purse and robbers of his subjects, partial to
their friends and extreme to their enemies, through bribes
corrupted and for indifferency[57] doing nothing.

[Holinshed presents in full the complaint of the commoners
of Kent and the requests of their "captain," John Cade. The
King's Council advises him to refuse these demands and to
"suppress those rebels by force" rather than by "fair promises." But the soldiers sent by the King to conquer the
rebels refuse to fight against those who are laboring "to
amend the commonweal," so that their commanding officers are obliged to leave off the attempt.]

And because the Kentishmen cried out against the Lord
Saye, the King's chamberlain, he was by the King committed to the Tower of London. Then went the King again to
London, and within two days after went against the Kentishmen with fifteen thousand men well prepared for the
war; but the said Kentishmen fled the night before his coming into the wood country near unto Sevenoaks.* Whereupon the King returned again to London.

---

54 fifteens fifteenths, property taxes   **55 kept the field** held the battlefield against opposition, maintained a military posture   **56 pilling**
pillaging   **57 indifferency** apathy

The Queen, that bare rule,[58] being of his retreat advertised,[59] sent Sir Humphrey Stafford, knight, and William, his brother, with many other gentlemen, to follow the Kentishmen, thinking that they had fled; but they were deceived, for at the first skirmish both the Staffords were slain and all their company discomfited. The King's army by this time commen to[60] Blackheath, hearing of this discomfiture, began to murmur amongst themselves, some wishing the Duke of York at home to aid the captain, his cousin,[61] some undutifully coveting the overthrow of the King and his Council, other[62] openly crying out on the Queen and her complices.

This rumor, published abroad,[63] caused the King and certain of his Council, for the appeasing thereof, to commit the Lord Saye, Treasurer of England, to the Tower of London, and if other against whom like displeasure was borne had been present they had been likewise committed. Jack Cade, upon victory against the Staffords, appareled himself in Sir Humphrey's brigandine[64] set full of gilt nails, and so in some glory returned again toward London, divers idle and vagrant persons out of Sussex, Surrey, and other places still increasing his number. Thus this glorious captain, guarded with a multitude of rustical people, came again to the plain of Blackheath and there strongly encamped himself; to whom were sent from the King the Archbishop of Canterbury and Humphrey, Duke of Buckingham, to commune with him of his griefs[65] and requests.

These lords found him sober in talk, wise in reasoning, arrogant in heart, and stiff in opinion, as who that by no means would grant to dissolve his army except the King in person would come to him and assent to the things he would require.[66] The King, upon the presumptuous answers and requests of this villainous rebel, beginning as much to doubt his own menial servants as his unknown subjects

---

58 bare rule held the real power   **59 advertised** informed   **60 discomfited . . . commen to** defeated . . . come to, arrived at   **61 the captain, his cousin** i.e., Cade, masquerading as Mortimer, York's cousin   **62 other** others   **63 published abroad** spread around   **64 brigandine** body armor composed of iron rings or small, thin iron plates sewed on heavy cloth material   **65 commune . . . griefs** confer with him of his grievances   **66 require** request

(which spared not[67] to speak that the captain's cause was profitable for the commonwealth), departed in all haste to the castle of Kenilworth* in Warwickshire, leaving only behind him the Lord Scales to keep the Tower of London. The Kentish captain, being advertised[68] of the King's absence, came first into Southwark and there lodged at the White Hart, prohibiting to all his retinue murder, rape, and robbery, by which color[69] of well meaning he the more allured to him the hearts of the common people.

After that, he entered into London, cut the ropes of the drawbridge, and struck his sword on London stone, saying, "Now is Mortimer lord of this city!" And after a glozing[70] declaration made to the Mayor touching[71] the cause of his thither coming, he departed again into Southwark; and upon the third day of July he caused Sir James Fiennes, Lord Saye and Treasurer of England, to be brought to the Guildhall and there to be arraigned; who, being before the King's justices put to answer, desired to be tried by his peers for the longer delay of his life. The captain, perceiving his dilatory plea, by force took him from the officers and brought him to the standard[72] in Cheap, and there, before his confession ended, caused his head to be stricken off, and pitched it upon an high pole which was openly borne before him through the streets.

And not content herewith, he went to Mile End and there apprehended Sir James Cromer, then Sheriff of Kent and son-in-law to the said Lord Saye, causing him likewise, without confession or excuse heard, to be beheaded and his head to be fixed on a pole; and with these two heads this bloody wretch entered into the city again and, as it were in a spite, caused them in every street to kiss together, to the great detestation of all the beholders. . . . He also put to execution in Southwark divers persons, some for breaking his ordinance and other being of his old acquaintance, lest

---

67 which spared not who did not scruple or hesitate. (The King fears that the humbly-born members of his own household are as sympathetic to Cade as are the anonymous Kentishmen assembled in arms.) **68 The Kentish . . . advertised** i.e., Cade, being informed **69 color** appearance, pretext **70 London stone . . . glozing** a block of stone on the south side of Canwick (now Cannon) Street which was a well-known London landmark . . . cajoling, deceptive **71 touching** concerning **72 standard** conduit. (The date is 1450.)

they should bewray[73] his base lineage, disparaging him for his usurped surname of Mortimer.

The Mayor and other the magistrates of London, perceiving themselves neither to be sure of goods nor of life well warranted, determined to repel and keep out of their city such a mischievous caitiff[74] and his wicked company. And to be the better able so to do, they made the Lord Scales and that renowned captain Matthew Goffe* privy[75] both of their intent and enterprise, beseeching them of their help and furtherance[76] therein. The Lord Scales promised them his aid with shooting off the artillery in the Tower,[77] and Matthew Goffe was by him appointed to assist the Mayor and Londoners in all that he might; and so he and other captains appointed for defense of the city took upon them in the night to keep the bridge,[78] and would not suffer the Kentishmen once to approach. The rebels, who never soundly slept for fear of sudden assaults, hearing that the bridge was thus kept, ran with great haste to open that passage, where between both parties was a fierce and cruel fight.

Matthew Goffe, perceiving the rebels to stand to their tackling[79] more manfully than he thought they would have done, advised his company not to advance any further toward Southwark till the day appeared, that they might see where the place of jeopardy rested,[80] and so to provide for the same; but this little availed. For the rebels with their multitude drave back the citizens from the stoops[81] at the bridge foot to the drawbridge and began to set fire in divers houses. Great ruth[82] it was to behold the miserable state wherein some, desiring to eschew[83] the fire, died upon their enemies' weapon; women with children in their arms leapt for fear into the river; other, in a deadly care[84] how to save themselves between fire, water, and sword, were in their houses choked and smothered. Yet the captains, not sparing, fought on the bridge all the night valiantly; but in con-

---

73 bewray divulge, reveal   **74 caitiff** despicable wretch   **75 privy** aware, in on the secret   **76 furtherance** aid   **77 promised . . . Tower** i.e., promised them use of the artillery stored in the Tower   **78 the bridge** i.e., London Bridge   **79 tackling** arms, weapons   **80 where . . . rested** what area was in jeopardy   **81 stoops** posts, pillars   **82 ruth** pity **83 eschew** avoid   **84 other . . . care** others, frightened to death

clusion, the rebels gat the drawbridge and drowned many,
and slew John Sutton, alderman, and Robert Heisand, a
hardy citizen, with many other, besides Matthew Goffe—a
man of great wit and much experience in feats of chivalry,
the which in continual wars had spent his time in service of
the King and his father.

This sore conflict endured in doubtful wise[85] on the
bridge till nine of the clock in the morning, for sometimes
the Londoners were beaten back to Saint Magnus's corner,
and suddenly again the rebels were repelled to the stoops in
Southwark, so that both parts, being faint and weary,
agreed to leave off from fighting till the next day, upon condition that neither Londoners should pass into Southwark
nor Kentishmen into London. Upon this abstinence, this
rakehell captain, for making him[86] more friends, brake up
the jails of the King's Bench and Marshalsea, and so were
many mates[87] set at liberty very meet[88] for his matters in
hand.

The Archbishop of Canterbury, being Chancellor of England and as then for his surety lying[89] within the Tower,
called to him the Bishop of Winchester, who for some safeguard lay[90] then at Holywell. These two prelates, seeing the
fury of the Kentish people, by their late repulse, to be somewhat assuaged,[91] passed by the river of Thames from the
Tower into Southwark, bringing with them, under the
King's Great Seal, a general pardon unto all the offenders,
and caused the same to be openly published. The poor people were so glad of this pardon and so ready to receive it
that, without bidding farewell to their captain, they withdrew themselves the same night every man towards his
home.

But Jack Cade, despairing of succors[92] and fearing the reward of his lewd[93] dealings, put all his pillage and goods
that he had robbed into a barge and sent it to Rochester by

---

85 in doubtful wise uncertain as to outcome **86 Upon . . . making him**
during this truce, this dissolute leader, i.e., Cade, in order to make him
87 mates fellows. (Used contemptuously.) **88 meet** fit, useful **89 for
his surety lying** for his own safety residing **90 for some safeguard lay**
for reasons of security resided **91 by their late . . . assuaged** to be
somewhat abated by their recently being driven back **92 succors** relief,
assistance **93 lewd** base

water, and himself went by land, and would have entered into the castle of Queenborough with a few men that were left about him, but he was there let[94] of his purpose; wherefore he, disguised in strange attire, privily[95] fled into the wood country beside Lewes in Sussex, hoping so to scape. The captain and his people being thus departed,[96] not long after proclamations were made in divers places of Kent, Sussex, and Surrey,* that whosoever could take the foresaid captain alive or dead should have a thousand marks for his travail.[97]

[Holinshed reprints the proclamation.]

After which proclamation thus published, a gentleman of Kent named Alexander Iden awaited so his time that he took the said Cade in a garden in Sussex, so that there he was slain at Hothfield and brought to London in a cart, where he was quartered, his head set on London Bridge, and his quarters sent to divers places to be set up in the shire of Kent. After this, the King himself came into Kent and there sat in judgment upon the offenders; and if he had not mingled his justice with mercy, more than five hundred by rigor of law had been justly put to execution. Yet he, punishing only the stubborn heads and disordered ringleaders, pardoned the ignorant and simple persons, to the great rejoicing of all his subjects.

[Other uprisings occur in 1450, contributing to the decline of English rule in France. In 1451, Richard, Duke of York, poses anew his threat to the house of Lancaster.]

The Duke of York, pretending,[98] as ye have heard, a right to the crown as heir to Lionel, Duke of Clarence, came this year out of Ireland unto London, in the Parliament time, there to consult with his special friends: as John, Duke of Norfolk, Richard, Earl of Salisbury, and the Lord Richard his son (which after was Earl of Warwick), Thomas Courtenay, Earl of Devonshire, and Edward Brooke, Lord Cobham.

94 let prevented, hindered **95 strange attire, privily** foreign or unusual attire, stealthily **96 departed** separated **97 travail** labor, effort **98 pretending** claiming

After long deliberation and advice taken, it was thought expedient to keep their chief purpose secret; and that the Duke should raise an army of men under a pretext to remove divers counselors about the King and to revenge the manifest injuries done to the commonwealth by the same rulers. Of the which, as principal, the Duke of Somerset was namely[99] accused, both for that he was greatly hated of the commons for the loss of Normandy and for that it was well known that he would be altogether against the Duke of York in his challenge to be made, when time served, to the crown; insomuch that his goods by the commons were foully despoiled and borne away from the Blackfriars. After which riot, on the next morrow, proclamation was made through the city that no man should spoil[100] or rob, on pain of death. But on the same day at the standard[101] in Cheap was a man beheaded for doing contrary to the proclamation.

Therefore, when the Duke of York had thus, by advice of his special friends, framed the foundation of his long-intended enterprise, he assembled a great host, to the number of ten thousand able men, in the marches[102] of Wales, publishing openly that the cause of this his gathering of people was for the public wealth[103] of the realm. The King, much astonied at the matter, by advice of his Council raised a great power and marched forward toward the Duke. But he, being thereof advertised, turned out of that way which by espials[104] he understood that the King held, and made straight toward London; and having knowledge that he might not be suffered to pass through the city, he crossed over the Thames at Kingston Bridge and so kept on towards Kent, where he knew that he had both friends and well-willers. And there, on Burnt Heath, a mile from Dartford and twelve miles from London, he embattled[105] and encamped himself very strongly, environing his field with artillery and trenches. The King, hereof advertised, brought his army with all diligence unto Blackheath and there pight[106] his tents.

Whilst both these armies lay thus embattled, the King

---

99 namely especially   **100 spoil** pillage   **101 standard** conduit, fountain
102 marches border   **103 public wealth** prosperity   **104 espials** scouts,
spies   **105 embattled** prepared for battle   **106 pight** pitched

sent the Bishop of Winchester and Thomas Bourchier, Bishop of Ely, Richard Woodville, Lord Rivers, and Richard Andrew, the Keeper of his Privy Seal, to the Duke, both to know the cause of so great a commotion and also to make a concord[107] if the requests of the Duke and his company seemed consonant to reason. The Duke, hearing the message of the bishops, answered that his coming was neither to damnify[108] the King in honor nor in person, neither yet any good man; but his intent was to remove from him certain evil-disposed persons of his Council, bloodsuckers of the nobility, pollers[109] of the clergy, and oppressors of the poor people.

Amongst these he chiefly named Edmund, Duke of Somerset, whom if the King would commit to ward[110] to answer such articles as against him in open Parliament should be both proponed[111] and proved, he promised not only to dissolve his army but also offered himself like an obedient subject to come to the King's presence and to do him true and faithful service according to his loyal and bounden duty.

[Holinshed here prints certain letters written by the Duke of York to the King, setting forth his claims, and the King's replies. It is agreed that the Duke of Somerset be committed to prison in order to pacify the Duke of York and his people, whereupon York is reconciled to the King and takes a public oath of loyalty.]

Howsoever the matter went, truth it is that the Duke of York, the first of March [1452], dissolved his army, brake up his camp, and came to the King's tent, where, contrary to his expectation and against promise made by the King (as other write), he found the Duke of Somerset going at large and set at liberty, whom the Duke of York boldly accused of treason, bribery, oppression, and many other crimes. The Duke of Somerset not only made answer to the Duke's objections but also accused him of high treason, affirming that he with his fautors[112] and complices had consulted to-

---

107 **concord** treaty of peace   108 **damnify** injure   109 **pollers** plunderers   110 **ward** prison   111 **proponed** proposed, put before a tribunal   112 **his fautors** i.e., York's followers

gether how to come by the scepter and regal crown of this realm. By means of which words the King removed straight[113] to London, and the Duke of York as prisoner rode before him, and so was kept awhile.

The King assembled together a great Council at Westminster to hear the accusations of the two Dukes, the one objecting to the other many heinous and grievous crimes.

[Somerset demands that York be executed, "because he knew perfectly that the Duke of York daily imagined with himself[114] how to get the crown and to depose and destroy both the King and him." But York's rising fortunes cannot be stopped now, and the case is made for York's innocence. Meantime, a rumor arises that Edward, Earl of March, son of the Duke of York, is marching toward London. An expedition to Gascony being urgently called for, the Council decides to free the Duke of York and permit him to go to his castle of Wigmore in the marches, or borders, of Wales after York has once again sworn obedience to King Henry. In York's absence from court, Somerset's influence continues to be very strong. Aquitaine is lost to English authority in 1453. In that same year, in October, the Queen gives birth to a son, Edward, though the event does not put a halt to talk that Henry is incapable of fathering a son and that the Queen is all too ready to present him with some other man's child.]

After the wars foully ended in foreign parties,[115] civil dissension began again at home, divided specially into two factions. As King Henry, descended of the house of Lancaster, possessed the crown from his grandfather, King Henry the Fourth, first author of that title, so Richard, Duke of York, as heir to Lionel, Duke of Clarence, third son to King Edward the Third, enforced.[116] By reason whereof, the nobles as well as the common people were into parts divided, to the utter destruction of many a man and to the great ruin and decay of this region; for while the one party sought to

113 removed straight moved immediately   **114 imagined with himself** contrived in his imagination   **115 parties** parts   **116 enforced** i.e., laid claim

destroy the other, all care of the commonwealth was set aside, and justice and equity clearly exiled.

The Duke of York above all things first sought means how to stir up the malice of the people against the Duke of Somerset, imagining that, he being made away, his purpose should the sooner take effect. He also practiced[117] to bring the King into the hatred of the people, as that he should not be a man apt to[118] the government of a realm, wanting both wit and stomach sufficient to supply such a room.[119] Many of the high estates,[120] not liking the world and disallowing the doings both of the King and his Council, were fain[121] enough of some alteration. Which thing the Duke well understanding, chiefly sought the favor of the two Nevilles, both named Richard, one Earl of Salisbury, the other Earl of Warwick, the first being the father and the second the son.

[Holinshed describes the lineage and family of the Nevilles, who assist York in insisting that Somerset be imprisoned in the Tower, from which incarceration he is, however, released once the King has recovered from an illness. York and his adherents, seeing that they cannot prevail against Somerset, assemble for war in the marches of Wales. King Henry resolves to fight rather than give in to demands for the imprisonment of Somerset. The first battle of the civil wars occurs at Saint Albans in 1455.]

The fight for a time was right sharp and cruel, for the Duke of Somerset, with the other lords, coming to the succors of their companions that were put to the worse, did what they could to beat back the enemies; but the Duke of York sent ever fresh men to succor the weary and to supply the places of them that were hurt, whereby the King's army was finally brought low and all the chieftains of the field slain and beaten down.

For there died, under the sign of the Castle, Edmund,

117 practiced plotted **118 as that . . . apt to** i.e., representing King Henry as being a man unskilled in **119 wanting . . . room** lacking sufficient intelligence and courage to fill such an office **120 estates** noble classes **121 fain** glad

Duke of Somerset, who, as hath been reported, was warned
long before to avoid all castles. And beside him lay Henry,
the second of that name, Earl of Northumberland; Humphrey, Earl of Stafford, son to the Duke of Buckingham;
John, Lord Clifford, [and others].

———————

The second edition of Raphael Holinshed's *Chronicles* was published in
1587. This selection is based on that edition, Volume 3, folios 622–643.

In the following, departures from the original text appear in boldface; original readings are in roman.

p. 433 *Hume Hun [and on p. 434]   **p. 442 *Sevenoaks** Senocke   **p. 444 *Kenilworth**
Killingworth   **p. 445 *Goffe** Gough. (Holinshed marginally corrects to *Goche;* also
elsewhere in the text.)   **p. 447 *Surrey** Southerie

[For *Henry VI, Part Three*]

The Third Volume of Chronicles (1587 edition)
Compiled by Raphael Holinshed

HENRY THE SIXTH

[The Duke of York, victorious at Saint Albans in 1455, courteously refuses to use any violence toward King Henry. York and his son Edward and several allies are convicted of high treason by Henry's Parliament in 1460. At the Battle of Northampton, in 1460, York's allies gain the victory and convey the King under guard to London, while the Duke of Somerset, son of the Duke of Somerset who died at the end of *2 Henry VI*, narrowly escapes with the Queen and her son Edward. York, not present at the battle, returns from Dublin to England at this good news and travels to London.]

From Chester by long journeys[1] he came to the city of London, which he entered the Friday before the feast of Saint Edward the Confessor, with a sword borne naked before him, with trumpets also sounding, and accompanied with a great train of men-of-arms and other of his friends and servants. At his coming to Westminster he entered the palace and, passing forth directly through the great hall, stayed not till he came to the chamber where the King and lords used to sit in the parliament time, commonly called the upper house or chamber of the peers, and, being there entered, stepped up unto the throne royal, and there, laying his hand upon the cloth of estate,[2] seemed as if he meant to take possession of that which was his right.

[York avails himself of the King's own apartments in the palace while Henry occupies the Queen's chambers. The Archbishop of Canterbury, Thomas Bourchier, carries messages between them. York addresses the lords of the Parliament on the subject of his claim, sitting in the regal seat as he does so. The matter of the Yorkist claim is negotiated.]

---

1 journeys daily stints of travel   **2 cloth of estate** cloth spread over a throne, canopy

After long debating of the matter and deliberate consultation amongst the peers, prelates, and commons, upon the vigil of All Saints it was condescended:[3] forsomuch as King Henry had been taken as King by the space of thirty-and-eight years and more, that he should enjoy the name and title of king and have possession of the realm during his natural life. And if he either died or resigned or forfeited the same by breaking or going against any point of this concord, then the said crown and authority royal should immediately be devoluted[4] and come to the Duke of York, if he then lived, or else to the next heir of his lineage. And that the Duke of York from thenceforth should be Protector and Regent of the land. This was the determination of the Parliament to and fro,[5] tending to peace between the King and the Duke, which was ratified accordingly, as by the articles ensuing doth appear.

[Holinshed prints the articles of agreement between King Henry and the Duke of York. The latter is solemnly proclaimed heir apparent to the crown and Protector of the realm in return for his taking an oath of fealty to Henry.]

The Duke of York, well knowing that the Queen would spurn against all this, caused both her and her son to be sent for by the King. But she, as wont rather to rule than to be ruled, and thereto counseled by the Dukes of Exeter and Somerset, not only denied to come but also assembled a great army, intending to take the King by fine force out of the lords' hands. The Protector in London, having knowledge of all these doings, assigned the Duke of Norfolk and Earl of Warwick, his trusty friends, to be about the King, while he, with the Earls of Salisbury and Rutland and a convenient number departed out of London the second day of December northward, and appointed the Earl of March, his eldest son, to follow him with all his power. The Duke came to his castle of Sandal beside Wakefield on Christmas Even and there began to make muster of his tenants and friends. The Queen, thereof ascertained, determined to cope with him ere his succor[6] were come.

3 **condescended** agreed upon   4 **devoluted** devolved, passed on   5 **to and fro** for and against the question, pro and con   6 **succor** reinforcements

Now she, having in her company the Prince her son, the
Dukes of Exeter and Somerset, the Earl of Devonshire, the
Lord Clifford, the Lord Ros, and in effect all the lords of the
north parts, with eighteen thousand men or (as some write)
two-and-twenty thousand, marched from York to
Wakefield, and bade base to[7] the Duke even before his castle
gates. He, having with him not fully five thousand persons,
contrary to the minds of his faithful counselors would
needs issue forth to fight with his enemies. The Duke of
Somerset and the Queen's part, casting upon their most advantage, appointed the Lord Clifford to lie in one stale[9] and
the Earl of Wiltshire in another, and the Duke with other to
keep the main battle.[10] The Duke of York with his people
descended down the hill in good order and array and was
suffered to pass on towards the main battle.

But when he was in the plain field between his castle and
the town of Wakefield, he was environed on every side like
fish in a net, so that though he fought manfully, yet was he
within half an hour slain and dead, and his whole army discomfited.[11] With him died, of his trusty friends, his two bastard uncles, Sir John and Sir Hugh Mortimer,* Sir Davy
Hall, Sir Hugh Hastings, Sir Thomas Neville, William and
Thomas Aparre, both brethren; and two thousand and eight
hundred others, whereof many were young gentlemen and
heirs of great parentage in the south parts, whose kin revenged their deaths within four months next, as after shall
appear.

In this conflict was wounded and taken prisoner Richard,
Earl of Salisbury, Sir Richard Limbrick, Ralph Stanley,
John Harrow, Captain Hanson, and divers others. The Lord
Clifford, perceiving where the Earl of Rutland was conveyed out of the field (by one of his father's chaplains and
schoolmaster to the same Earl) and overtaking him,
stabbed him to the heart with a dagger as he kneeled afore
him. This Earl was but a child at that time of twelve years of
age, whom neither his tender years nor dolorous countenance, with holding up both his hands for mercy (for his

7 **bade base to** challenged. (Literally, challenged to a chase in the game
of prisoner's base.)   8 **casting** calculating   9 **stale** battle position,
sometimes one that is detached for reconnoitring; here a wing, flank
10 **other . . . main battle** others . . . main body of the army
11 **discomfited** routed, defeated

speech was gone for fear), could move the cruel heart of the
Lord Clifford to take pity upon him, so that he[12] was noted
of great infamy for that his unmerciful murder upon that
young gentleman.

But the same Lord Clifford, not satisfied herewith, came
to the place where the dead corpse of the Duke of York lay,
caused his head to be stricken off and set on it a crown of
paper, fixed it on a pole, and presented it to the Queen, not
lying far from the field, in great despite,[13] at which great
rejoicing was showed. But they laughed then that shortly
after lamented, and were glad then of other men's deaths
that knew not their own to be so near at hand. Some write
that the Duke was taken alive and in derision caused to
stand upon a molehill, on whose head they put a garland
instead of a crown, which they had fashioned and made of
sedges or bulrushes; and having so crowned him with that
garland, they kneeled down afore him (as the Jews did unto
Christ) in scorn, saying to him: "Hail, King without rule!
Hail, King without heritage! Hail, Duke and prince without
people or possessions!" And at length, having thus scorned
him with these and divers other the like[14] despiteful words,
they struck off his head, which, as ye have heard, they presented to the Queen.

Many deemed that this miserable end chanced to the
Duke of York as a due punishment for breaking his oath of
allegiance unto his sovereign lord King Henry; but others
held him discharged thereof[15] because he obtained a dispensation from the Pope, by such suggestion as his procurators[16] made unto him, whereby the same oath was adjudged
void, as that which was received unadvisedly,[17] to the prejudice of himself and disheriting of all his posterity. After this
victory by the Queen, the Earl of Salisbury and all the prisoners were sent to Pomfret and there beheaded, whose
heads, together with the Duke of York's head, were conveyed to York and there set on poles over the gate of the city,
in despite[18] of them and their lineage. The Earl of March,

---

12 he i.e., Clifford   13 despite scorn   14 the like similar
15 discharged thereof relieved of his obligation to remain true to his
oath   16 procurators supporters   17 as that . . . unadvisedly as having
been taken without adequate awareness of all the circumstances
18 despite scorn

now after the death of his father very[19] Duke of York, lying[20] at Gloucester, was wonderfully amazed[21] when the sorrowful news of these mishaps came unto him; but after comfort given to him by his faithful lovers[22] and assured allies, he removed[23] to Shrewsbury, declaring to the inhabitants of that town, and to them of the other towns in those parties, the murder of his father, the jeopardy of himself, and the present ruin of the commonwealth.

The people on the marches[24] of Wales, for the favor which they bare to the Mortimers' lineage, more gladly offered him their aid and assistance than he could desire the same, so that he had incontinently[25] a puissant army to the number of three-and-twenty thousand ready to go against the Queen and the murderers of his father. But when he was setting forward, news was brought to him that Jasper, Earl of Pembroke, half brother to King Henry, and James Butler, Earl of Ormonde and Wiltshire, had assembled a great number of Welsh and Irish people to take him. He, herewith quickened,[26] retired back and met with his enemies in a fair plain near to Mortimer's Cross, not far from Hereford East, on Candlemas Day in the morning [1461]. At which time the sun (as some write) appeared to the Earl of March like three suns and suddenly joined all together in one. Upon which sight he took such courage that he, fiercely setting on his enemies, put them to flight; and for this cause men imagined that he gave[27] the sun in his full brightness for his badge or cognizance. Of his enemies were left dead on the ground three thousand and eight hundred.

[The Queen, encouraged by her recent victory at Wakefield, marches with a northern army toward London and approaches Saint Albans where, she has learned, King Henry is under the guard of the Duke of Norfolk and the Earl of Warwick. The Second Battle of Saint Albans is fought on Shrove Tuesday, the seventeenth of February, 1461. The Queen's forces are victorious.]

---

19 very veritably, indeed   **20 lying** residing, headquartered
21 wonderfully amazed thunderstruck, shocked   **22 lovers** friends
23 removed moved, went   **24 marches** borders   **25 incontinently** immediately   **26 quickened** forced to move quickly, animated   **27 gave** displayed on his coat of arms

When the day was closed, those that were about the King (in number a twenty thousand), hearing how evil their fellows had sped,[28] began utterly to despair of the victory and so fell without any long tarriance to running away. By reason whereof the nobles that were about the King, perceiving how the game went, and withal saw no comfort in the King[29] but rather a good will and affection towards the contrary part, they withdrew also, leaving the King accompanied with the Lord Bonneville and Sir Thomas Kiriell of Kent, which,[30] upon assurance of the King's promise, tarried still with him and fled not. But their trust[31] deceived them, for at the Queen's departing from Saint Albans they were both beheaded. . . .

Such was the success[32] of this second battle fought at Saint Albans, upon Shrove Tuesday, the seventeenth of February, in which were slain three-and-twenty hundred men, of whom no nobleman is remembered save Sir John Grey, which the same day was made knight, with twelve other, at the village of Colney. Now after that the noblemen and other were fled, and the King left in manner alone without any power of men to guard his person, he was counseled by an esquire called Thomas Hoo, a man well languaged and well seen[33] in the laws, to send some convenient messenger to the northern lords, advertising[34] them that he would now gladly come unto them, whom he knew to be his very friends and had assembled themselves together for his service, to the end he might remain with them, as before he had remained under the government of the southern lords.

According to the advice and counsel of this esquire, the King thought it good to send unto them, and withal[35] appointed the same esquire to bear the message, who first went and declared the same unto the Earl of Northumberland and, returning back to the King, brought certain lords with him who conveyed the King first unto the Lord Clifford's tent, that stood next to the place where the King's

---

28 how evil . . . sped how disastrously their companions had fared
29 withal . . . King i.e., thereupon saw no advantage in supporting the King 30 which who 31 trust i.e., in those promises 32 success outcome 33 well languaged and well seen well spoken and well versed 34 advertising informing 35 unto them, and withal i.e., to the northern lords, and thereupon

people had encamped. This done, they went and brought
the Queen and her son Prince Edward unto his presence,
whom he joyfully received, embracing and kissing them in
most loving wise and yielding hearty thanks to almighty
God, whom it had pleased thus to strengthen the forces of
the northern men, to restore his dearly beloved and only
son again into his possession. Thus was the Queen fortunate in her two battles,[36] but unfortunate was the King in all
his enterprises, for where his person was present the victory still fled from him to the contrary part. The Queen
caused the King to dub her son Prince Edward knight, with
thirty other persons which the day before fought on her
side against his part.

[The Queen's northern soldiers pillage the town of Saint Albans. Upon hearing that the Earl of March has vanquished
the Earls of Pembroke and Wiltshire at Chipping Norton
and is now approaching London, and not trusting her own
welcome in Essex and Kent, the Queen retreats northward
with King Henry and their son.]

  The Duchess of York, seeing her husband and son[37] slain,
and not knowing what should succeed of her eldest son's
chance,[38] sent her two younger sons, George and Richard,
over the sea to the city of Utrecht in Almaine,[39] where they
were of Philip, Duke of Burgundy, well received, and so remained there till their brother Edward had got the crown
and government of the realm. The Earls of March and
Warwick, having perfect knowledge that the King and
Queen, with their adherents, were departed from Saint
Albans, rode straight to London, entering there with a
great number of men-of-war the first week of Lent. Whose
coming thither was no sooner known but that the people
resorted[40] out of Kent, Essex, and other the counties adjoining in great numbers, to see, aid, and comfort this
lusty[41] prince and flower of chivalry, in whom the hope of
their joy and trust of their quietness only consisted.

---

36 two battles i.e., Wakefield and the Second Battle of Saint Albans
37 son i.e., the young Earl of Rutland   **38 chance** fortune   **39 Almaine**
Germany and the Netherlands; Utrecht is in the latter   **40 resorted**
traveled, went   **41 lusty** vigorous, handsome

This prudent young prince, minding[42] to take time when time served, called a great Council both of the lords spiritual and temporal and to them repeated the title and right that he had to the crown, rehearsing also the articles concluded between King Henry and his father, by their writings signed and sealed and also confirmed by act of Parliament, the breaches whereof he neither forgat nor left undeclared. After the lords had considered of this matter, they determined by authority of the said Council that because King Henry had done contrary to the ordinances in the last Parliament concluded, and was insufficient of himself to rule the realm, he was therefore to be deprived of all kingly estate; and incontinently[43] was Edward, Earl of March, son and heir to Richard, Duke of York, by the lords in the said Council assembled, named, elected, and admitted for king and governor of the realm.

On which day, the people of the Earl's part being in their muster in Saint John's Field, and a great number of the substantial citizens there assembled to behold their order,[44] the Lord Falconbridge, who took the musters, wisely anon declared to the people the offenses and breaches of the late agreement committed by King Henry the Sixth, and demanded of the people whether they would have him to rule and reign any longer over them. To whom they with whole voice answered, "Nay, nay!" Then he asked them if they would serve, love, honor, and obey the Earl of March as their only King and sovereign lord. To which question they answered, "Yea, yea!" crying "King Edward!" with many great shouts and clapping of hands in assent and gladness of the same.

The lords were shortly advertised[45] of the loving consent which the commons frankly[46] and freely had given. Whereupon incontinently they all, with a convenient number of the most substantial commons, repaired[47] to the Earl at Baynard's Castle, making just and true report of their election and admission, and the loving assent of the commons.

[Holinshed briefly reports Edward's graceful acceptance speech.]

42 **minding** of a mind, intending 43 **incontinently** immediately
44 **order** formation, array 45 **advertised** informed 46 **frankly** willingly 47 **repaired** went

Thus far touching[48] the tragical state of this land under the rent regiment[49] of King Henry, who, besides the bare title of royalty and naked name of king, had little appertaining to the port[50] of a prince. For whereas the dignity of princedom standeth in sovereignty,[51] there were of his nobles that imbeciled[52] his prerogative by sundry practices, specially by main force, as seeking either to suppress or to exile or to obscure or to make him away. Otherwise what should be the meaning of all those foughten fields[53] from time to time, most miserably falling out both to prince,[54] peer, and people?

[Holinshed, before going on to Edward IV's reign, pauses to review the names and careers of the learned men that lived in Henry VI's time, such as the antiquary John Leland and the poet monk John Lydgate.]

EDWARD THE FOURTH, EARL OF MARCH, SON AND HEIR TO RICHARD, DUKE OF YORK

After that this prince, Edward, Earl of March, had taken upon him the government of this realm of England, as before ye have heard, the morrow next ensuing, being the fourth of March, he rode to the church of Saint Paul and there offered;[55] and after Te Deum sung,[56] with great solemnity he was conveyed to Westminster and there set in the hall with the scepter royal in his hand, whereto people in great numbers assembled. His claim to the crown was declared to be by two manner of ways: the first, as son and heir to Duke Richard, his father, right inheritor to the same; the second, by authority of Parliament and forfeiture committed by King Henry. Whereupon it was again demanded[57] of the commons if they would admit and take the said Earl

---

48 Thus far touching so much, then, regarding **49 rent regiment** rule torn apart (by factionalism) **50 appertaining to the port** belonging to the bearing and conduct **51 standeth in sovereignty** is based upon supremacy of power **52 there were . . . imbeciled** there were those among his nobles who enfeebled **53 foughten fields** hardfought battles **54 prince** monarch **55 offered** made a devotional offering **56 after Te Deum sung** after the anthem "We praise you, O God" was sung **57 demanded** asked

as their prince and sovereign lord, which all with one voice cried, "Yea, yea!"

This part thus played, he entered into Westminster Church under a canopy with solemn procession, and there as king offered; and herewith taking the homages of all the nobles there present, he returned by water to London and was lodged in the Bishop's palace; and, on the morrow after, he was proclaimed King by the name of Edward the Fourth throughout the city. This was in the year of the world 5427, and after the birth of our Savior 1461 after our account, beginning the year at Christmas, but after the usual account of the Church of England 1460, the twentieth of Emperor Frederick the Third, the nine and thirtieth and last of Charles the Seventh, French King, and first year of the reign of James the Third, King of Scots.

Whilst these things were a-doing in the south parts, King Henry, being in the north country, assembled a great army, trusting for all this to subdue his enemies, namely sith[58] their chief ringleader, the Duke of York, was dispatched out of the way. But he was deceived, for out of the dead stock sprang a branch more mighty than the stem: this Edward the Fourth, a prince so highly favored of the people for his great liberality, clemency, upright dealing, and courage, that above all other he with them stood in grace alone, by reason whereof men of all ages and degrees to him daily repaired,[59] some offering themselves and their men to jeopard[60] their lives with him, and other plenteously gave money to support his charges[61] and to maintain his right.

By which means he gathered together a puissant army, to the intent by battle, sithence[62] none other ways would serve, at once to make an end of all. So, his army and all things prepared, he departed out of London the twelfth day of March, and by easy journeys came to the castle of Pomfret, where he rested, appointing the Lord Fitzwater to keep the passage at Ferrybridge with a good number of tall[63] men. King Henry, on the other part, having his army in readiness, committed the governance thereof to the Duke of Somerset, the Earl of Northumberland, and the Lord Clifford, as men desiring to revenge the death of their parents,

58 namely sith especially since   59 repaired went   60 jeopard risk
61 charges expenses   62 sithence since   63 tall brave

slain at the First Battle at Saint Albans. These captains, leaving King Henry, his wife, and son for the most safeguard within the city of York, passed the river of Wharfe with all their power,[64] intending to stop King Edward of his passage over the river of Aire.

And the better to bring that to pass, the Lord Clifford determined to make a charge upon them that kept the passage of Ferrybridge.

[In the fighting, Lord Fitzwater and the Bastard of Salisbury, brother of the Earl of Warwick, are slain.]

When the Earl of Warwick was informed hereof, like a man desperate he mounted on his hackney[65] and hasted puffing and blowing to King Edward, saying: "Sir, I pray God have mercy of their souls which in the beginning of your enterprise have lost their lives! And because I see no succors of the world but in God, I remit[66] the vengeance to Him, our Creator and Redeemer." With that he alighted down and slew his horse with his sword, saying: "Let him flee that will, for surely I will tarry with him that will tarry with me"; and kissed the cross of his sword as it were for a vow to the promise. King Edward, perceiving the courage of his trusty friend the Earl of Warwick, made proclamation that all men which were afraid to fight should depart; and to all those that tarried the battle he promised great rewards, with addition that any soldier which voluntarily would abide and afterwards, either in or before the fight, should seem to flee or turn his back, then he that could kill him should have a great reward and double wages.

After this proclamation ended, the Lord Falconbridge, Sir Walter Blunt, Robert Horne, with the foreward,[67] passed the river at Castleford, three miles from Ferrybridge, intending to have environed[68] the Lord Clifford and his company. But they, being thereof advertised, departed in great haste toward King Henry's army; yet they met with some

---

64 power army   **65 hackney** horse   **66 remit** resign, give over. (Warwick insists that God is our only hope in the world, and only He can revenge our wrongs. Warwick thereupon resolves to continue fighting those who have slain his brother, presumably in the hope that God will use him as an agent of revenge.)   **67 foreward** vanguard   **68 environed** surrounded

that they looked not for, and were so trapped ere they were
aware. For the Lord Clifford, either for heat or pain putting
off his gorget,[69] suddenly with an arrow (as some say, without an head) was stricken into the throat and immediately
rendered his spirit; and the Earl of Westmorland's brother
and all his company almost were there slain at a place
called Dintingdale, not far from Towton.

[King Edward's army is ordered to take no prisoners alive.
They are victorious in this Battle of Towton, driving the
forces of King Henry into headlong retreat.]

After this great victory, King Edward rode to York, where
he was with all solemnity received. And first he caused the
heads of his father, the Earl of Salisbury, and other his
friends to be taken from the gates and to be buried with
their bodies; and there he caused the Earl of Devonshire
and three other to be beheaded, and set their heads in the
same place. King Henry, after he heard of the irrecoverable
loss of his army, departed incontinently with his wife and
son to the town of Berwick and, leaving the Duke of Somerset there, went into Scotland and, coming to the King of
Scots, required[70] of him and his Council aid and comfort.

[King Henry is hospitably received, in return for which he
delivers the town of Berwick to the King of Scotland.]

When King Henry was somewhat settled in the realm of
Scotland, he sent his wife and his son into France to King
Reiner her father, trusting by his aid and succor to assemble an army and once again to recover his right and dignity;
but he in the meantime made his abode in Scotland, to see
what way his friends in England would study[71] for his restitution.

The Queen, being in France, did obtain of[72] the young
French King, then Lewis the Eleventh, that all her husband's friends and those of the Lancastrial[73] band might
safely and surely have resort into any part of the realm of

69 **gorget** throat armor   70 **required** asked   71 **study** strive, employ
thought and effort   72 **obtain of** obtain assurance from   73 **Lancastrial**
Lancastrian, of the house of Lancaster

France, prohibiting all other of the contrary faction any access or repair into that country. Thus ye have heard how King Henry the Sixth, after he had reigned eight-and-thirty years and odd months, was driven out of this realm. But now, leaving him with the princes of his part[74] consulting together in Scotland, and Queen Margaret his wife gathering of men in France, I will return where I left, to proceed with the doings of King Edward.

This young prince, having with prosperous success obtained so glorious a victory in the mortal[75] battle at Towton, and chased all his adversaries out of the realm or at the leastways put them to silence, returned after the manner and fashion of a triumphant conqueror, with great pomp, unto London; where, according to the old custom of the realm, he called a great assembly of persons of all degrees; and the nine-and-twentieth day of June [1461] was at Westminster with solemnity crowned and anointed King. In which year this King Edward called his high court of Parliament at Westminster, in the which the state of the realm was greatly reformed and all the statutes made in Henry the Sixth his time which touched either his title or profit were revoked.

In the same Parliament the Earl of Oxford, far stricken in age, and his son and heir, the Lord Aubrey Vere, either through malice of their enemies or for that they had offended the King, were both, with divers of their counselors, attainted[76] and put to execution; which caused John, Earl of Oxford, ever after to rebel. There were also beheaded the same time Sir Thomas Tudenham, knight, William Tyrell, and John Montgomery, esquires, and after them divers others. Also, after this, he created his two younger brethren dukes; that is to say, Lord George, Duke of Clarence, Lord Richard, Duke of Gloucester; and the Lord John Neville, brother to Richard, Earl of Warwick, he first made Lord Montague* and afterwards created him Marquess Montague.

[Matters go well for King Edward in 1462 and 1463. The Duke of Somerset and other lords submit to him. When

74 part side, party   **75 mortal** deadly   **76 attainted** convicted

Somerset soon afterward revolts and joins Henry, he is captured by Edward's forces and executed. Queen Margaret attempts a return to England with French assistance, but
without success. In 1464–1465, King Henry returns to England in disguise and is taken and brought to the Tower of
London. Edward wins much popular favor by offering a
pardon to all those who will submit to him.]

When his realm was thus brought into a good and quiet
estate, it was thought meet[77] by him and those of his Council that a marriage were provided for him in some convenient place;[78] and therefore was the Earl of Warwick sent
over into France to demand[79] the Lady Bona, daughter to
Lewis, Duke of Savoy, and sister to the Lady Carlot, then
Queen of France; which Bona was at that time in the French
court.

The Earl of Warwick, coming to the French King then lying[80] at Tours, was of him honorably received and right
courteously entertained. His message was so well liked and
his request thought so honorable for the advancement of the
Lady Bona that her sister Queen Carlot obtained both the
good will of the King her husband and also of her sister
the foresaid lady; so that the matrimony on that side was
clearly assented to, and the Earl of Dammartin appointed
with others to sail into England for the full finishing of the
same. But here consider the old proverb to be true which
saith that marriage goeth by destiny. For during the time
that the Earl of Warwick was thus in France and according
to his instructions brought the effect of his commission to
pass, the King, being on hunting[81] in the Forest of Wich-
wood beside Stony Stratford, came for his recreation to the
manor of Grafton where the Duchess of Bedford then sojourned, wife to Sir Richard Woodville, Lord Rivers, on
whom was then attendant a daughter of hers called the
Lady Elizabeth Grey, widow of Sir John Grey, knight, slain
at the last Battle of Saint Albans, as before ye have heard.

This widow, having a suit to the King for such lands as

---

77 meet fitting   **78 in some convenient place** i.e., in a suitably royal
family, one providing a powerful alliance   **79 demand** ask (in marriage)
80 lying residing   **81 on hunting** a-hunting

her husband had given her in jointure,[82] so kindled the
King's affection towards her that he not only favored her
suit but more her person; for she was a woman of a more
formal countenance than of excellent beauty, and yet both
of such beauty and favor that, with her sober demeanor,
sweet looks, and comely smiling (neither too wanton nor
too bashful), besides her pleasant tongue and trim wit,[83] she
so allured and made subject unto her the heart of that great
prince that, after she had denied him to be his paramour
with so good manner and words so well set as better could
not be devised, he finally resolved with himself to marry
her, not asking counsel of any man till they might perceive
it was no booty[84] to advise him to the contrary of that his
concluded purpose, sith[85] he was so far gone that he was not
revocable,[86] and therefore had fixed his heart upon the last
resolution, namely, to apply an wholesome, honest, and honorable remedy to his affections fired with the flames of
love, and not to permit his heart to the thralldom of unlawful lust; which purpose was both princely and profitable, as
the poet saith:

> Utile propositum est saevas extinguere flammas,
> Nec servum vitii pectus habere sui.*[87]

But yet the Duchess of York his mother letted[88] this match
as much as in her lay;[89] and when all would not serve, she
caused a precontract to be alleged, made by him with the
Lady Elizabeth Lucy.[90] But, all doubts resolved, all things
made clear, and all cavillations avoided, privily[91] in a morning he married the said Lady Elizabeth Grey at Grafton be-
foresaid where he first began to fancy her. And in the next
year after, she was with great solemnity crowned queen at
Westminster. Her father also was created Earl Rivers and
made High Constable of England; her brother, Lord Anthony, was married to the sole heir of Thomas, Lord Scales;

---

82 in jointure i.e., in the event of widowhood **83 trim wit** sharp intelligence **84 no booty** no use **85 sith** since **86 was not revocable** could
not be called back **87 Utile . . . sui** A useful goal it is to extinguish a
cruel flame and free the heart from shameful bondage. (Ovid, *Remedia
Amoris*, ll. 53–54.) **88 letted** hindered **89 as in her lay** as she was able
90 Elizabeth Lucy (One of Edward's mistresses.) **91 all cavillations
avoided, privily** all cavilling or faultfinding refuted or set aside, privately

Sir Thomas Grey, son to Sir John Grey, the Queen's first husband, was created Marquess Dorset and married to Cecily,
heir to the Lord Bonville. The French King was not well
pleased to be thus dallied with, but he shortly, to appease
the grief of his wife and her sister the Lady Bona, married
the said Lady Bona to the Duke of Milan.

Now when the Earl of Warwick had knowledge, by letters
sent to him out of England from his trusty friends, that
King Edward had gotten him a new wife, he was not a little
troubled in his mind, for that he took it his credence[92]
thereby was greatly minished and his honor much stained,
namely[93] in the court of France, for that it might be judged
he came rather like an espial[94] to move a thing never
minded[95] and to treat[96] a marriage determined before not to
take effect. Surely he thought himself evil used that, when
he had brought the matter to his purposed intent and
wished conclusion, then to have it quaill on his part,[97] so as
all men might think at the least wise[98] that his prince made
small account of him to send him on such a sleeveless[99] er-
rand.

All men for the most part agree that this marriage was
the only cause why the Earl of Warwick conceived an hatred against King Edward, whom he so much before favored. Other affirm other causes, and one specially: for that
King Edward did attempt a thing once in the Earl's house
which was much against the Earl's honesty[100]—whether he
would have deflowered his daughter or his niece, the cer-
tainty was not, for both their honors, openly revealed—for
surely such a thing was attempted by King Edward, which
loved well both to behold and also to feel fair damsels.

[Warwick's grudge against Edward deepens in 1467–1468.]

In this meantime the Earl of Warwick, bearing a continual grudge in his heart toward King Edward since his last
return out of France, persuaded so with his two brethren

---

92 credence reputation   **93 namely** especially   **94 espial** spy   **95 move
a thing never minded** set in motion a thing never intended   **96 treat**
negotiate   **97 quail on his part** fail when matters were in his hands
98 at the least wise at the very least   **99 sleeveless** futile   **100 honesty**
honor

the Archbishop and the Marquess[101] that they agreed to join
with him in any attempt which he should take in hand
against the said King. The Archbishop was easily allured to
the Earl's purpose, but the Marquess could by no means be
reduced to take any part against King Edward of a long
time, till the Earl had both promised him great rewards and
promotions[102] and also assured him of the aid and power of
the greatest princes of the realm. And even as the Marquess
was loath to consent to his unhappy conspiracy, so with a
faint heart he showed himself an enemy unto King Edward;
which double dissimulation was both the destruction of
him and his brethren.

[Holinshed prints the persuasions used by the Earl of
Warwick with his two brothers against King Edward.]

Beside all this, the Earl of Warwick, being a far-casting[103]
prince, perceived somewhat[104] in the Duke of Clarence
whereby he judged that he bare no great good will towards
the King his brother; and thereupon, feeling his mind by
such talk as he of purpose ministered,[105] understood how he
was bent[106] and so wan[107] him to his purpose; and, for better
assurance of his faithful friendship, he offered him his eldest daughter in marriage, with the whole half deal[108] of his
wife's inheritance.

[Clarence marries Isabel, Warwick's eldest daughter. A rebellion breaks out in Yorkshire in 1469 on Warwick's behalf, and the rebels move toward London. They are met by
Edward's forces near Warwick.]

The King in this meantime had assembled his power and
was coming toward the Earl, who, being advertised thereof,
sent to the Duke of Clarence, requiring him to come and
join with him. The Duke, being not far off, with all speed
repaired to the Earl, and so they joined their powers[109] to-

101 the Archbishop and the Marquess the Archbishop of York and the
Marquess Montague   **102 promotions** preferments   **103 far-casting**
forward looking, cunning   **104 somewhat** something   **105 feeling . . .
ministered** i.e., feeling out the Duke of Clarence's mind by various
things that Warwick said to that purpose   **106 bent** inclined   **107 wan**
won   **108 deal** share   **109 powers** armies

gether, and upon secret knowledge had that the King (because they were entered into terms by way of communication to have a peace) took small heed to himself, nothing doubting any outward attempt of his enemies.[110]

The Earl of Warwick, intending not to leese[111] such opportunity of advantage, in the dead of the night, with an elect company of men-of-war, as secretly as was possible, set on the King's field,[112] killing them that kept the watch; and, ere the King was ware (for he thought of nothing less than of that which then happened), at a place called Wolney, four miles from Warwick, he was taken prisoner and brought to the castle of Warwick. And to the intent his friends should not know what was become of him, the Earl caused him by secret journeys in the night to be conveyed to Middleham Castle in Yorkshire and there to be kept under the custody of the Archbishop of York and other his friends in those parties.[113]

[King Edward, though captive, is given the freedom to hunt and exercise.]

Now, on a day, upon a plain when he was thus abroad,[114] there met with him Sir William Stanley, Sir Thomas a Borough,[115] and divers other of his friends, with such a great band of men that neither his keepers would, nor once durst, move[116] him to return unto prison again. Some have thought that his keepers were corrupted with money or fair promises and therefore suffered him thus to scape out of danger.

[Edward, thus freed, comes to York. Attempts are made to reconcile the King with his brother and with Warwick. But Warwick travels to France in 1470.]

When Queen Margaret, that sojourned with Duke Reiner her father, heard tell that the Earl of Warwick was come to

---

110 and upon secret knowledge had . . . attempt of his enemies i.e., and joined in the secret information they had obtained that King Edward, trusting in the fact that the two sides were conducting peace talks under terms of a truce, took small heed of his personal safety, not in the least fearing any overt attempt on the part of his enemies   111 leese lose   112 field camp   113 parties parts, regions   114 abroad out of doors   115 Thomas a Borough Thomas Burgh   116 move urge, compel

the French court, with all diligence she came to Amboise to see him with her only son Prince Edward.

With her also came Jasper, Earl of Pembroke, and John, Earl of Oxford, which, after divers imprisonments lately escaped, fled out of England into France and came by fortune to this assembly. These persons, after entreaty[117] had of their affairs, determined by means of the French King to conclude a league and amity between them. And first to begin withal, for the sure foundation of their new entreaty, Edward, Prince of Wales, wedded[118] Anne, second daughter to the Earl of Warwick, which lady came with her mother into France. After which marriage, the Duke[119] and the Earls took a solemn oath that they should never leave the war till either King Henry the Sixth or his son Prince Edward were restored to the crown; and that the Queen and the Prince should depute and appoint the Duke and the Earl[120] to be governors and conservators of the commonwealth, till time the Prince were come to estate. . . .

The French King lent both ships, men, and money unto Queen Margaret and to her partakers,[121] and appointed the Bastard of Bourbon, Admiral of France, with a great navy, to defend them against the navy of the Duke of Burgundy which he laid at the mouth of the river Seine ready to encounter them, being of greater force than both the French navy and the English fleet. And yet King Reiner did also help his daughter with men and munition of war.

[Many Englishmen eagerly await the arrival of Warwick and promise him support.]

When the Earl had taken land, he made proclamation in the name of King Henry the Sixth, upon high pains commanding and charging all men able to bear armor to prepare themselves to fight against Edward, Duke of York, which contrary to right had usurped the crown. It is almost not to be believed how many thousands men-of-war at the first tidings of the Earl's landing resorted unto him.

King Edward, wakened with the news of the Earl's land-

---

117 entreaty investigation, discussion   **118 wedded** i.e., was betrothed to   **119 Duke** i.e., Duke of Clarence   **120 Earl** i.e., Earl of Warwick   **121 partakers** supporters

ing and the great repair[122] of people that came flocking in unto him, sent forth letters into all parts of his realm to raise an army; but of them that were sent for few came, and yet of those few the more part came with no great good wills. Which when he perceived, he began to doubt[123] the matter, and therefore, being accompanied with the Duke of Gloucester, his brother, the Lord Hastings, his Chamberlain (which had married the Earl's sister and yet was ever true to the King his master), and the Lord Scales, brother to the Queen, he departed into Lincolnshire. And because he understood that all the realm was up against him, and some part of the Earl of Warwick's power was within half a day's journey of him, following the advice of his Council, with all haste possible he passed the Washes in great jeopardy and, coming to Lynn, found there an English ship and two hulks of Holland ready (as Fortune would) to make sail.

Whereupon he, with his brother the Duke of Gloucester, the Lord Scales, and divers other his trusty friends, entered into the ship. The Lord Hastings tarried awhile after, exhorting all his acquaintance that of necessity should tarry behind to show themselves openly as friends to King Henry for their own safeguard, but heartily required them in secret to continue faithful to King Edward. This persuasion declared, he entered the ship with the other,[124] and so they departed, being in number, in that one ship and two hulks, about seven or eight hundred persons, having no furniture[125] of apparel or other necessary things with them saving apparel for war.

[King Edward and his party sail for Burgundy, narrowly avoiding being taken by some ships of Hanse citizens enroute. His friends continue to fight in his behalf, and he returns to England briefly in 1470, but, when Henry VI is proclaimed king by the Duke of Clarence and the Earl of Warwick, Edward flees once again to Burgundy. His friends take refuge in various sanctuaries, and his Queen, Elizabeth, at Westminster, gives birth to a son, Edward. Warwick heads for London.]

122 **repair** assemblage   123 **doubt** fear, suspect   124 **other** others
125 **furniture** provisions

When he had settled all things at his pleasure, upon the twelfth day of October he rode to the Tower of London and there delivered King Henry out of the ward[126] where he before was kept, and brought him to the King's lodging, where he was served according to his degree.[127]

On the five-and-twentieth day of the said month, the Duke of Clarence, accompanied with the Earls of Warwick and Shrewsbury, the Lord Strange, and other lords and gentlemen, some for fear and some for love and some only to gaze at the wavering world, went to the Tower; and from thence brought King Henry, apparelled in a long gown of blue velvet, through London to the church of Saint Paul; the people on every side the streets rejoicing and crying "God save the King!" as though each thing had succeeded as they would have had it; and when he had offered,[128] as kings use to do, he was conveyed to the Bishop's palace, where he kept his household like a king. Thus was the principality posted over[129] sometimes to Henry, sometimes to Edward, according to the sway of the party prevailing, ambition and disdain still casting faggots on the fire whereby the heat of hatred gathered the greater force to the consumption of the peers and the destruction of the people. . . .

When King Henry had thus readepted[130] and eftsoons[131] gotten his regal power and authority, he called his high court of Parliament to begin the six-and-twentieth day of November at Westminster; in the which King Edward was adjudged a traitor to the country and an usurper of the realm. His goods were confiscate and forfeited.

[Edward's statutes are revoked and King Henry's heir, Prince Edward, is reinstated, next in succession being the Duke of Clarence and his male heirs. Warwick is appointed governor of the realm in partnership with Clarence.]

When Queen Margaret understood by her husband's letters that the victory was gotten by their friends, she with her son Prince Edward and her train entered their ships to

126 ward prison   127 degree rank, status   128 offered made devotional offering   129 posted over handed over   130 readepted recovered   131 eftsoons again

SHAKESPEARE'S SOURCES

take their voyage into England; but the winter was so sharp, the weather so stormy, and the wind so contrary that she was fain[132] to take land again and to defer her journey till another season.

About the same season, Jasper, Earl of Pembroke, went into Wales to visit his lands in Pembrokeshire, where he found Lord Henry, son to his brother Edmund, Earl of Richmond, having not full ten[133] years of age, he being kept in manner like a captive, but honorably brought up by the Lady Herbert, late wife to William, Earl of Pembroke.

[Holinshed gives the lineage of this young person who is to be King Henry VII.]

The Earl of Pembroke took this child, being his nephew, out of the custody of the Lady Herbert and, at his return, brought the child with him to London to King Henry the Sixth; whom when the King had a good while beheld, he said to such princes as were with him: "Lo, surely this is he to whom both we and our adversaries, leaving[134] the possession of all things, shall hereafter give room and place." So this holy man showed, before the chance that should happen, that this Earl Henry, so ordained by God, should in time to come (as he did indeed) have and enjoy the kingdom and whole rule of this realm of England; so that it might seem probable, by the coherence of holy Henry's predictions with the issue falling out in truth with the same, that for the time he was endued with a prophetical spirit. And surely the epithet or title of "holy" is not for naught attributed unto him, for it is to be read in writers that he was by nature given to peaceableness, abhorring blood and slaughter, detesting civil tumults, addicted to devotion, very frequent in prayer, and not esteeming so highly of courtly gallantness as stood with the dignity of a prince. In consideration whereof he procured against himself an apostasy of his people both native and foreign, who revolted and fell from fealty.

---

132 fain obliged **133 ten** (Actually, fourteen; Henry Tudor was born in 1457, and the event is described in 1471.) **134 leaving** losing (through ill fortune and death)

[Warwick is concerned about the Duke of Burgundy's having offered hospitality to Edward. Burgundy declines to provide open support for the Yorkist cause, but he does give secret aid. Edward sails for England in March 1471, encounters difficulties with storms, but lands at Ravenspurgh on the Humber (where Henry Bolingbroke had earlier landed to challenge Richard II and become King Henry IV). Edward, receiving little support, talks cautiously as though he has come back solely for his dukedom of York. He heads for York.]

When King Edward had thus gotten into the city of York, he made such means[135] among the citizens that he got of them a certain sum of money; and leaving a garrison within the city, contrary to his oath, for fear lest the citizens after his departure might haply move some rebellion against him, he set forward the next day toward Tadcaster, a town ten miles from thence belonging to the Earl of Northumberland. The next day he took his way toward Wakefield and Sandal, a castle and lordship belonging to the inheritance of the Dukes of York, leaving the castle of Pomfret upon his left hand where the Marquess Montague with his army lay and did not once offer to stop him.

[Edward is joined by some supporters, including Sir Thomas Burgh and Sir Thomas Montgomery. Toward the end of March 1471 he appears before the walls of Coventry and dares the Earl of Warwick to come forth and fight. Warwick, hoping to be reinforced by the Duke of Clarence and his forces, begins to suspect that Clarence's loyalty to Warwick is wavering. And indeed Clarence has begun "to weigh with himself the great inconvenience into the which as well his brother King Edward as himself and his younger brother the Duke of Gloucester were fallen through the dissension betwixt them." A reconciliation between Clarence and Edward takes place between their two armies at Warwick, to the great satisfaction of all beholders. Clarence tries unsuccessfully to reconcile the Earl of Warwick to King Edward. In April, the King is warmly received into

135 made such means took such steps

London, is reconciled with the Archbishop of York, and receives custody of King Henry VI from the Archbishop.

Warwick, perceiving Edward's great success in London, resolves to try his fortunes in battle, and, accompanied by the Dukes of Exeter and Somerset, the Earl of Oxford, Marquess Montague, and others, moves toward Barnet, midway between Saint Albans and London. Warwick and his brother Montague are slain in the fighting.

Also in April 1471, Queen Margaret and her son return from France to England with an army, landing in Dorsetshire. She is joined by the Duke of Somerset and other supporters. King Edward marches to do battle, meeting the Queen's forces at Tewkesbury. The Queen's forces are routed, partly by the bravery of Richard, Duke of Gloucester. "This," says Holinshed, "was the last fought field or pight[136] battle tried between the potentates of this land in King Edward the Fourth's days." The date is May 4, 1471.]

In the winning of the camp,[137] such as stood to it were slain out of hand. Prince Edward was taken, as he fled towards the town, by Sir Richard Crofts and kept close.[138] In the field and chase were slain the Lord John of Somerset, called Marquess Dorset; Thomas Courtenay, Earl of Devonshire; Sir John Delves; Sir Edward Hampden; Sir Robert Whittingham; and Sir John Leukener, with three thousand others. After the field[139] was ended, proclamation was made that whosoever could bring forth Prince Edward alive or dead should have an annuity of a hundred pounds during his life, and the Prince's life to be saved if he were brought forth alive. Sir Richard Crofts, nothing mistrusting the King's promise, brought forth his prisoner, Prince Edward, being a fair and well-proportioned young gentleman; whom when King Edward had well advised,[140] he demanded of him how he durst so presumptuously enter into his realm with banner displayed.

Whereunto the Prince boldly answered, saying: "To recover my father's kingdom and heritage, from his father and grandfather to him, and from him after him to me, lin-

---

136 pight pitched   **137 camp** battlefield   **138 close** in confinement
139 field battle   **140 advised** looked at

eally descended." At which words King Edward said nothing, but with his hand thrust him from him or (as some say) struck him with his gauntlet; whom incontinently George, Duke of Clarence, Richard, Duke of Gloucester, Thomas Grey, Marquess Dorset, and William, Lord Hastings, that stood by, suddenly murdered; for the which cruel act the more part of the doers in their latter days drank of the like cup, by the righteous justice and due punishment of God. His body was homely[141] interred with the other simple[142] corpses in the church of the monastery of Black Monks[143] in Tewkesbury.

[Edward gives thanks at the Abbey Church for his victory, and orders the beheading of Somerset and other of his captured enemies.]

The same Tuesday, the King departed from Tewkesbury towards Worcester, and by the way had knowledge that Queen Margaret was found in a poor house of religion not far from thence, into the which she was withdrawn for safeguard of herself on Saturday in the morning, being the day of the battle. She was after brought to London as prisoner, and so kept till her father ransomed her with great sums of money which he borrowed of Lewis the Eleventh, King of France.

[Edward returns triumphantly to London in May 1471. A different fate lies in store for his hapless Lancastrian counterpart.]

Moreover, here is to be remembered that poor King Henry the Sixth, a little before deprived (as ye have heard) of his realm and imperial crown, was now in the Tower spoiled of his life by Richard, Duke of Gloucester (as the constant fame[144] ran), who, to the intent that his brother King Edward might reign in more surety, murdered the said King Henry with a dagger.

---

141 **homely** simply   142 **simple** of ordinary subjects, common
143 **Black Monks** Benedictines   144 **constant fame** consistent rumor

[Holinshed speaks generously of the spiritual qualities of both kings, saying of Henry VI that "of his own natural inclination he abhorred all the vices as well of the body as of the soul," and of Edward IV that he was "religiously affected," wearing a sackcloth next to the skin on holy days and avoiding all oaths stronger than "forsooth and forsooth."]

———————

The second edition of Raphael Holinshed's *Chronicles* was published in 1587. This selection is based on that edition, Volume 3, folios 655–691.

In the following, departures from the original text appear in boldface; original readings are in roman.

p. 455 *Mortimer Mortimers   p. 465 *Montague Montacute [and also later in the same sentence]   p. 467 *vitii . . . sui vitiis . . . suum

———————

Further Reading

Berry, Edward I. *Patterns of Decay: Shakespeare's Early Histories*. Charlottesville, Va.: Univ. Press of Virginia, 1975. Berry's book explores how Shakespeare's earliest history plays dramatize a process of social and political disintegration. Character in the *Henry VI* plays is generally subordinated to larger thematic concerns: *1 Henry VI* depicts the disintegration of chivalric values and of ceremony; *2 Henry VI* the collapse of justice and law; and *3 Henry VI*, looking forward to *Richard III*, the dissolution of family bonds.

Bevington, David. "The Domineering Female in *1 Henry VI*." *Shakespeare Studies* 2 (1966): 51–58. Bevington traces a thematic pattern in *1 Henry VI* in which domineering women, possessing enchanting powers, seek mastery over men. The reversal of sexual roles, he suggests, is both source and symbol of the cosmic and political disorder that threatens England.

Blanpied, John W. "Breaking Ground: The *Henry VI* Plays." *Time and the Artist in Shakespeare's English Histories*. Newark, Del.: Univ. of Delaware Press, 1983. For Blanpied, the disordered, confused world of the plays is not the result of immature craftsmanship but a deliberate effect of Shakespeare's artistic confrontation with history. The unstable rhythms and sympathies of the plays result from his discovery of the underlying chaos of history that ceremony (and art) would attempt to control and contain.

Brockbank, J. Philip. "The Frame of Disorder—*Henry VI*." In *Early Shakespeare*, ed. John Russell Brown and Bernard Harris. Stratford-upon-Avon Studies 3. London: Edward Arnold; New York: St. Martin's Press, 1961. Focusing on the plays' persistent efforts to control the turbulence of history in ceremony and spectacle, Brockbank discovers the plays' center in the conflict between personal responsibility and historical process. The three parts of *Henry VI*, according to Brockbank, expose the optimistic theology of Raphael Holinshed's providential history (in his *Chronicles*) to the brutal political ideology that history reveals, releasing the tragic potential of that history.

Burckhardt, Sigurd. " 'I Am But Shadow of Myself': Ceremony and Design in *1 Henry VI*." *Modern Language Quarterly* 28 (1967): 139–158. Rpt. in *Shakespearean Meanings*. Princeton, N.J.: Princeton Univ. Press, 1968. Burckhardt suggestively moves from a consideration of the formal discontinuities of the play to Shakespeare's awareness of the inadequacy of the idealized Elizabethan world picture. In seeking an artistic design to order the apparent chaos of history, Shakespeare discovers contradictions at the heart of the Tudor orthodoxy.

Clemen, Wolfgang. "Some Aspects of Style in the *Henry VI* Plays." In *Shakespeare's Styles: Essays in Honour of Kenneth Muir*, ed. Philip Edwards, Inga-Stina Ewbank, and G. K. Hunter. Cambridge and New York: Cambridge Univ. Press, 1980. The style of the *Henry VI* plays, Clemen finds, is formal and highly patterned, designed to reveal not subtleties of character but motives and the significance of events. Paradoxically, the effect of this unsettles an audience, for the plays' eloquence and explicitness conflict sharply with the absurd nightmare of the brutal and bloody history that is enacted.

Cox, John D. "*3 Henry VI:* Dramatic Convention and the Shakespearean History Play." *Comparative Drama* 12 (1978): 42–60. Cox discovers the provocatively ambivalent historical vision of *3 Henry VI* in its relation to its literary forebears. The play mediates between the claims of salvation history in the medieval drama and the "radical assault on traditional dramaturgy in Christopher Marlowe's *Tamburlaine*." In its contrasts between sacred and secular ordering, *3 Henry VI* reveals the particular nature of the Shakespearean history play.

Dean, Paul. "Shakespeare's *Henry VI* Trilogy and Elizabethan 'Romance' Histories: The Origins of a Genre." *Shakespeare Quarterly* 33 (1982): 34–48. Dean proposes a new source for Shakespeare's *Henry VI* plays: the popular "romance" histories, such as Robert Greene's *James IV* and his *Friar Bacon and Friar Bungay*. These, more than the few pre-Shakespearean chronicle plays, inform Shakespeare's dramatic practice. Their stylizations of plot, character, and language and their major thematic concerns anticipate the interests and techniques of Shakespeare's earliest histories.

Hibbard, G. R. "Formalization in the Early History Plays." *The Making of Shakespeare's Dramatic Poetry*. Toronto: Univ. of Toronto Press, 1981. Confronted in the *Henry VI* plays with the challenge of imposing structure and logic upon a mass of historical material, Shakespeare, Hibbard argues, not only organizes each play around a dominant political theme but also weaves the three parts together into a complex whole through recurring poetic devices and patterns.

Jones, Emrys. *The Origins of Shakespeare*, pp. 142–192. Oxford: Oxford Univ. Press, 1977. Jones examines the *Henry VI* plays within the context of a broader literary response to the threat of civil war stimulated by the dangerous political climate of the 1580s. The thematic concerns of the three plays—which Jones insists were designed as a self-contained trilogy, not part of a tetralogy—are fame (*1 Henry VI*,) government (*2 Henry VI*), and disorder (*3 Henry VI*).

Kahn, Coppélia. *Man's Estate: Masculine Identity in Shakespeare*, pp. 51–62. Berkeley, Calif.: Univ. of California Press, 1981. The dominant relationship Kahn sees in the *Henry VI* plays is that between fathers and sons. Patriarchy proves a source of both order and chaos, as sons (including King Henry VI, who must follow in his heroic father's footsteps) discover and affirm their manhood through aggression. Kahn traces in the three plays a decline in the strength of the father-son bonds, from sons emulating fathers to sons avenging fathers to the total dissolution of filial bonds in Richard's anarchic villainy.

Manheim, Michael. "The Meek King." *The Weak King Dilemma in the Shakespearean History Play*. Syracuse, N.Y.: Syracuse Univ. Press, 1973. Finding in the *Henry VI* plays evidence of Shakespeare's frustration with political realities, Manheim examines the plays' polarized presentation of the claims of a weak Christian king and a strong Machiavellian aristocracy. In the disturbing world the plays dramatize, Henry's virtue disables him in the face of the ambition and greed of his nobles.

Ornstein, Robert. "The *Henry VI* Plays." *A Kingdom for a Stage: The Achievement of Shakespeare's History Plays*.

Cambridge: Harvard Univ. Press, 1972. Ornstein challenges the notion of the early histories as orthodox expressions of authorized Elizabethan political thought (e.g., Ribner, below). His analysis focuses on the aesthetic experience of the plays as well as on Shakespeare's emerging conceptions of dramatic form and the theatrical possibilities of English history.

Ribner, Irving. *The English History Play in the Age of Shakespeare*, pp. 92–112. 1957. Rev. and enl., New York: Barnes and Noble, 1965. Shakespeare's purpose in the *Henry VI* plays, Ribner argues, was to warn England of the dangers of civil war and to affirm a providential view of history in accord with the "Tudor myth." To this end, he drew upon various literary traditions—the medieval miracle and morality plays, Senecan tragedy, and poetic accounts of the falls of princes—enforcing a sense of England as a morality hero who, having sinned, must suffer before attaining salvation.

Riggs, David. *Shakespeare's Heroical Histories: "Henry VI" and Its Literary Tradition*. Cambridge: Harvard Univ. Press, 1971. Tracing the complex intellectual and literary legacy of the *Henry VI* plays, Riggs examines how Shakespeare's art draws on popular historical drama, humanist training in classical rhetoric, and Elizabethan theories of history and heroic poetry. The plays themselves, he finds, explore the relationship of heroic ideals and political realities, and dramatize the gradual deterioration of heroic idealism under the pressure of history.

Saccio, Peter. "Henry VI: The Loss of Empire." *Shakespeare's English Kings: History, Chronicle, and Drama*. New York: Oxford Univ. Press, 1977. Saccio considers the events of Henry VI's reign as they are understood by modern and Tudor historians, and examines Shakespeare's often radical reshaping of his source material as he transforms history into drama.

Tillyard, E. M. W. "The First Tetralogy." *Shakespeare's History Plays*, 1944. Rpt., New York: Barnes and Noble, 1964. For Tillyard, the *Henry VI* plays celebrate and elaborate the Tudor myth of history: the plays are governed by a providential design in which a sinful England is the tragic protagonist brought to the brink of ruin and chaos before being restored (at the end of *Richard III*, with the ascension of the Tudor line) to grace.

Wilson, F. P. "Marlowe and Shakespeare." *Marlowe and the Early Shakespeare*. Oxford: Clarendon Press, 1953. Wilson finds no certain evidence for the existence of popular plays on English history before 1588. Shakespeare's *Henry VI* plays, Wilson suggests, are not simply an improvement upon an undistinguished popular form, but perhaps the first English history plays to have been written.

Memorable Lines

Henry VI, Part One

Hung be the heavens with black, yield day to night!
(BEDFORD 1.1.1)

Fight till the last gasp.   (PUCELLE 1.2.127)

Expect Saint Martin's summer, halcyon days.
(PUCELLE 1.2.131)

Glory is like a circle in the water,
Which never ceaseth to enlarge itself
Till by broad spreading it disperse to naught.
(PUCELLE 1.2.133–135)

Between two hawks, which flies the higher pitch . . .
I have perhaps some shallow spirit of judgment;
But in these nice sharp quillets of the law,
Good faith, I am no wiser than a daw. (WARWICK 2.4.11–18)

Just Death, kind umpire of men's miseries.
(MORTIMER 2.5.29)

Choked with ambition of the meaner sort.
(PLANTAGENET 2.5.123)

Delays have dangerous ends.   (REIGNIER 3.2.33)

Done like a Frenchman—[*Aside*] turn and turn again!
(PUCELLE 3.3.85)

But howsoe'er, no simple man that sees
This jarring discord of nobility,
This shouldering of each other in the court,
This factious bandying of their favorites,
But that it doth presage some ill event.
(EXETER 4.1.187–191)

'Tis much when scepters are in children's hands,
But more when envy breeds unkind division.
There comes the ruin, there begins confusion.

(EXETER 4.1.192–194)

. . . in that sea of blood my boy did drench
His overmounting spirit; and there died
My Icarus, my blossom, in his pride.   (TALBOT 4.7.14–16)

Thou antic Death, which laugh'st us here to scorn,
Anon, from thy insulting tyranny,
Coupled in bonds of perpetuity,
Two Talbots, wingèd through the lither sky,
In thy despite shall scape mortality.   (TALBOT 4.7.18–22)

Of all base passions, fear is most accurst.   (PUCELLE 5.2.18)

See how the ugly witch doth bend her brows
As if, with Circe, she would change my shape!

(YORK 5.3.34–35)

Memorable Lines

Henry VI, Part Two

       . . . whose large style
Agrees not with the leanness of his purse.
(GLOUCESTER   1.1.109–110)

My Lord of Suffolk, say, is this the guise,
Is this the fashions in the court of England?
(QUEEN MARGARET   1.3.42–43)

Could I come near your beauty with my nails,
I'd set my ten commandments in your face.
(DUCHESS OF GLOUCESTER   1.3.141–142)

Wink at the Duke of Suffolk's insolence,
At Beaufort's pride, at Somerset's ambition,
At Buckingham, and all the crew of them,
Till they have snared the shepherd of the flock,
That virtuous prince, the good Duke Humphrey.
(YORK   2.2.70–74).

Sometimes hath the brightest day a cloud.
(GLOUCESTER   2.4.1)

       In thy face I see
The map of honor, truth, and loyalty.
(KING HENRY   3.1.202–203)

The commons, like an angry hive of bees
That want their leader, scatter up and down
And care not who they sting in his revenge.
(WARWICK   3.2.125–127)

Forbear to judge, for we are sinners all.
Close up his eyes and draw the curtain close,
And let us all to meditation.   (KING HENRY   3.3.31–33)

The gaudy, blabbing, and remorseful day
Is crept into the bosom of the sea.   (LIEUTENANT   4.1.1–2)

Small things make base men proud.   (SUFFOLK   4.1.106)

There shall be in England seven halfpenny loaves sold for a
penny, the three-hooped pot shall have ten hoops, and I will
make it felony to drink small beer.   (CADE   4.2.63–66)

And when I am king, as king I will be . . . there shall be no
money; all shall eat and drink on my score.

(CADE   4.2.67–71)

The first thing we do, let's kill all the lawyers.

(DICK, *the butcher*   4.2.74)

Adam was a gardener.   (CADE   4.2.130)

Memorable Lines

Henry VI, Part Three

O tiger's heart wrapped in a woman's hide!

(YORK   1.4.137)

Didst thou never hear
That things ill got had ever bad success?

(KING HENRY   2.2.45–46)

Thou setter-up and plucker-down of kings . . .

(EDWARD   2.3.37)

Ah, what a life were this, how sweet, how lovely!
Gives not the hawthorn bush a sweeter shade
To shepherds looking on their silly sheep
Than doth a rich embroidered canopy
To kings that fear their subjects' treachery?

(KING HENRY   2.5.41–45)

Who's this? O God! It is my father's face,
Whom in this conflict I unwares have killed.

(SON   2.5.61–62)

But let me see. Is this our foeman's face?
Ah, no, no, no, it is mine only son!   (FATHER   2.5.82–83)

My crown is in my heart, not on my head;
Not decked with diamonds and Indian stones,
Nor to be seen. My crown is called content;
A crown it is that seldom kings enjoy.

(KING HENRY   3.1.62–65)

'Tis a happy thing
To be the father unto many sons.   (EDWARD   3.2.104–105)

Why, love forswore me in my mother's womb;
And, for I should not deal in her soft laws,

She did corrupt frail nature with some bribe
To shrink mine arm up like a withered shrub.

(GLOUCESTER   3.2.153–156)

Then, since this earth affords no joy to me
But to command, to check, to o'erbear such
As are of better person than myself,
I'll make my heaven to dream upon the crown.

(GLOUCESTER   3.2.165–168)

Why, I can smile, and murder whiles I smile,
And cry "Content" to that which grieves my heart.

(GLOUCESTER   3.2.182–183)

I'll drown more sailors than the mermaid shall;
I'll slay more gazers than the basilisk;
I'll play the orator as well as Nestor,
Deceive more slyly than Ulysses could,
And, like a Sinon, take another Troy.
I can add colors to the chameleon,
Change shapes with Proteus for advantages,
And set the murderous Machiavel to school.
Can I do this, and cannot get a crown?
Tut, were it farther off, I'll pluck it down.

(GLOUCESTER   3.2.186–195)

. . . having nothing, nothing can he lose.   (WARWICK   3.3.152)

What fates impose, that men must needs abide.
It boots not to resist both wind and tide.

(KING EDWARD   4.3.58–59)

A little fire is quickly trodden out
Which, being suffered, rivers cannot quench.

(CLARENCE   4.8.7–8)

Why, what is pomp, rule, reign, but earth and dust?
And, live we how we can, yet die we must.

(WARWICK   5.2.27–28)

Teeth hadst thou in thy head when thou wast born,
To signify thou cam'st to bite the world.

(KING HENRY 5.6.53–54)

"O, Jesus bless us, he is born with teeth!"
And so I was, which plainly signified
That I should snarl and bite and play the dog.

(GLOUCESTER 5.6.75–77)

To say the truth, so Judas kissed his master,
And cried "All hail!" whenas he meant all harm.

(GLOUCESTER 5.7.33–34)

Contributors

DAVID BEVINGTON, Phyllis Fay Horton Professor of Humanities at the University of Chicago, is editor of *The Complete Works of Shakespeare* (Scott, Foresman, 1980) and of *Medieval Drama* (Houghton Mifflin, 1975). His latest critical study is *Action Is Eloquence: Shakespeare's Language of Gesture* (Harvard University Press, 1984).

DAVID SCOTT KASTAN, Professor of English and Comparative Literature at Columbia University, is the author of *Shakespeare and the Shapes of Time* (University Press of New England, 1982).

JAMES HAMMERSMITH, Associate Professor of English at Auburn University, has published essays on various facets of Renaissance drama, including literary criticism, textual criticism, and printing history.

ROBERT KEAN TURNER, Professor of English at the University of Wisconsin–Milwaukee, is a general editor of the New Variorum Shakespeare (Modern Language Association of America) and a contributing editor to *The Dramatic Works in the Beaumont and Fletcher Canon* (Cambridge University Press, 1966–).

JAMES SHAPIRO, who coedited the bibliographies with David Scott Kastan, is Assistant Professor of English at Columbia University.

❖

JOSEPH PAPP, one of the most important forces in theater today, is the founder and producer of the New York Shakespeare Festival, America's largest and most prolific theatrical institution. Since 1954 Mr. Papp has produced or directed all but one of Shakespeare's plays—in Central Park, in schools, off and on Broadway, and at the Festival's permanent home, The Public Theater. He has also produced such award-winning plays and musical works as *Hair, A Chorus Line, Plenty,* and *The Mystery of Edwin Drood,* among many others.

THE BANTAM SHAKESPEARE COLLECTION

The Complete Works in 28 Volumes

Edited with Introductions by David Bevington

Forewords by Joseph Papp

Ask for these books at your local bookstore or use this page to order.

Please send me the books I have checked above. I am enclosing $_____ (add $2.50 to cover postage and handling). Send check or money order, no cash or C.O.D.'s, please.

Name _____

Address _____

City/State/Zip _____

Send order to: Bantam Books, Dept. SH 2, 2451 S. Wolf Rd., Des Plaines, IL 60018
Allow four to six weeks for delivery.
Prices and availability subject to change without notice.   SH 2 3/96

the BANTAM Shakespeare

Bantam is proud to announce an important new edition of:

The Complete Works Of William Shakespeare

Featuring:

*The complete texts with modern spelling and punctuation

*Vivid, readable introductions by noted Shakespearean scholar David Bevington

*New forewords by Joseph Papp, renowned producer, director, and founder of the New York Shakespeare Festival

*Stunning, original cover art by Mark English, the most awarded illustrator in the history of the Society of Illustrators

*Photographs from some of the most celebrated performances by the New York Shakespeare Festival

*Complete source materials, notes, and annotated bibliographies based on the latest scholarships

*Stage histories for each play

ACCESSIBLE * AUTHORITATIVE * COMPLETE

SHAKESPEARE
The Complete works in 29 Volumes